To Diane & Alf,

Alf was one of the nicest boys in our "Little Norway" neighborhood in Ketchikan - This is just a continuation of the story I know we had then -

Jeannette

Trilogy

Trilogy

A Family's Voyage Of Faith

Jeannette Saxton Coon

Dead Reckoning Books
MAUI, HAWAII

ISBN 0-9614443-8-X

Layout & Illustrations, R. Kirra Kurvink

To Eldon

Because I followed the man
who followed the dream.

CONTENTS

ACKNOWLEDGMENTS

Brevity in recounting the early struggles of Trilogy Excursions required that I omit the names of some people who were really very important.

It is fitting that this list should begin with the name of Barbara Ross (then Barbara Rodden), who probably saved my life, and certainly my sanity. She worked side-by-side with me for over eight years of rapid expansion, making cinnamon rolls, salads, teriyaki chicken, and all the rest — in addition to fielding phone calls, taking care of correspondence, and doing an unimaginable amount of on-shore chores while Eldon, Jim, and Rand were out on the boat (later, boats). Besides her remarkable competence in so many areas, Barbara's joyful and sincere Christian witness helped me over many difficult times.

In a way, we have Barbara to thank also for Chris Walsh, now our senior captain. Chris came over from the mainland at age sixteen with his best buddy, who happened to be Barbara's nephew. Both boys were on summer vacation from high school, and they took on the humble job of improving our yard (at that time, Trilogy headquarters). The next summer, Chris came by himself. We were impressed by his industriousness as well as his dependability and charm. As soon as he finished his education, he progressed to less humble jobs — although when he got his captain's license at the age of twenty-two, he still looked so young that sometimes people were terrified at the prospect of having him in charge of their ship.

We owe a never-ending debt of gratitude to hundreds of our guests who took armloads of brochures home with them to advertise Trilogy, and who not only came back again and again but also sent their friends, relatives, and travel agents! It is not possible to list the names of all those who have done this. But to represent them, we have chosen Bill Boland and his wife, part-time residents at Puamana, who made the Lanai trip with us when we were first getting started and many times thereafter, strewing brochures far and wide and bringing with them everyone they could convince. (And Bill is very persuasive!)

And then there is warm-hearted, generous Laurie Robello (now known as Auntie Aloha), always good for a laugh and a helping hand. Thank you, Laurie, for all your help.

Last in time but not in importance, I want to thank editor Paul Wood, without whose skilled and generous assistance this work might have remained gathering dust in my office for many more years. I don't know how he persuaded Jim, Rand, Pattie, and Carole to write their postscripts; I had never been able to do so. Thank you, Paul.

JEANNETTE SAXTON COON's

Trilogy

CHAPTER ONE:
MURDER COVE

Juneau

ADMIRALTY ISLAND

Murder Cove

KUPREANU ISLAND

CANADA
UNITED STATES

PACIFIC

OCEAN

PRINCE of WALES ISLAND

Clarence Strait

Ketchikan

DIXON ENTRANCE

Port
Simpson

Southern Alaska

urder Cove. One day I didn't know such a place existed. The next day, I knew, and this knowledge included the bleak certainty that our lives had been changed forever.

Situated on the southwest tip of Admiralty Island in Alaska, this little harbor is a place of long, black shadows and sighing trees — not too different from a hundred other harbors in Alaska. But considering all that followed, Murder Cove was most appropriately named.

As Eldon Coon, skipper of the luxury charter yacht *Mañana II*, wrote "Murder Cove" in the ship's log, he felt a faint rippling of the hairs on the back of his neck. *I don't like this place*, he told himself. He finished his brief entry and put the log back on the chart table.

It was to be the last entry he would ever make in that log.

Eldon slid back the heavy pilothouse door and stepped out on deck. The night was calm and cool with a gentle off-shore breeze. The afterglow of Alaska's late spring sunset, now just a month from the longest day of the year, gave the water of the cove a deep, rosy hue. *Couldn't be a nicer night*, he told himself — *no rain, not enough wind to worry about. It's May.* Why, then, this persistent feeling of foreboding?

Automatically he rechecked the anchor gear. Shipshape; nothing to be concerned about, he told himself.

It was hard not to feel a glow of satisfaction as he

looked over this beautiful boat which showed in exquisite detail that no expense had been spared in the building — "Boat of the Year" in all the yachting magazines thirty years ago when she was launched. For twenty-one of those years, *Mañana* had been his most prized possession.

He had never expected to own a millionaire's boat. He was not a millionaire.

The carpets were deep and soft, light seafoam green — not the most practical color, but no other color would contrast quite as well with the satin-finished teak paneling. Above the Italian-tile fireplace a large mirror reflected the room, making it seem bigger than it was. On both sides of the main salon, now with curtains drawn, were large, beveled plate-glass windows. By day, passengers had a sitting or standing view of Alaska's inimitable scenery. The bathrooms, one for each stateroom, were white marble with delicately colored tile accents. For weight considerations, the tub was porcelain.

Pretty fancy, he told himself. *Pretty fancy for a country boy.*

Soft, shaded lights between the windows gave a warm glow to the main salon. Deftly, he turned off all but one, which he kept for a night light.

A new ship's radio, operating perfectly until this afternoon, had unaccountably gone dead. Maybe that's what was bothering him.

Oh, well, how many times have I ever used the radio to call for help? It was a rhetorical question, and he answered it in his own mind: never. He'd get it fixed in Juneau. On that thought, the master of this sixty-two-foot charter boat, which contained himself, a chef, two guides, and four noblemen from Spain, prepared for bed.

That last, reassuring look at a bay lying quiet and peaceful in the night was deceptive. Yet, what is treachery but the dagger presented with a smiling face?

Like all improbable accidents, this one required

certain coincidences to create the final debacle. First, the non-functioning radio made it impossible to call for help. Second, a steady off-shore wind held the boat's hull against the sharp point of an undetectable old piling — all that remained of a long-abandoned cannery dock that had once extended four hundred feet into the cove but was only visible at extreme low tide. One savagely-toothed piling was, itself, the third actor in this deadly drama as *Mañana* settled slowly down over its brutal point.

Alaskan fjords are noted for their tidal variation — as much as twenty-eight feet in southeastern Alaska — and on that night the tide was one of the lowest of the year. Steadily, stealthily, as the tide fell, the piling worked its way through the hull, impaling the *Mañana*.

Perhaps those who have lost a home by fire will understand best how the loss of the *Mañana* affected our family. Jim, our eldest son, who was born three days after VJ Day, was two years old when we bought that boat.

For twenty-one years *Mañana* had been a second home and the center of practically all our recreation. True, we did have to charter it for three months in the summer; it was too large, too expensive, and too difficult to maintain in that inclement country to keep it solely for our own private use. However, between charters and all the rest of the year our family and friends made good use of the boat. It was transportation for picnics, fishing, and sightseeing. Now and then it was our bus to Seattle for shopping and for fun. We lived on an island; none of us could imagine life without *Mañana*.

⚓

The news reached me late in the afternoon. A student had just left my counseling office at Ketchikan High School, and I was finishing some paperwork as fast as possible. No other students were scheduled, but that usually didn't prevent any number from dropping by late in the day. The phone rang with wake-the-dead stridency. I answered as I had done countless times in the past ten years: "Ketchikan High School. Mrs. Coon speaking."

Eldon's voice, with the radio-transmitted echo, came through faint and far away. "Honey, I've lost the *Mañana*."

It was as though he were talking nonsense — such a beautiful spring day, not at all the sort of day to imagine boats capsizing. "What do you mean, lost it?" I asked. "Don't you know where it is?"

"Oh, I know where it is, all right." Faint as it was, his voice had a definite edge of bitterness. "But I can only see the tip of the aerial. She sank in thirty feet of water. I did all I could, honey, at least all I could think of doing, but it wasn't enough."

I felt as though I had stepped into an open elevator shaft.

Eldon had worked like a slave for twenty years just to keep the boat seaworthy and beautiful in Alaska's most inhospitable climate. This year, 1969, was the first year he'd had a full season booked; if something like this had to happen, why couldn't it have been at the end of the season?

While one part of my mind was protesting, another part was listening to Eldon's account of the accident. He spoke into his brother's ship-to-shore phone. Afton, Eldon's only brother, operated a flying service out of Sitka; he'd flown over as soon as he heard about *Mañana*'s accident. As is usual on that type of equipment, the connection was bad and the static was worse. Eldon was saying, "So I got everyone ashore as quickly as possible. Carl Lane out of Juneau is picking up the party."

There was a long burst of static, then, "Romantini is standing over on the shore with tears running down his face. I said, 'Joe, you cry when a friend dies; you don't cry for a boat,' and he told me, '*Mañana* was my friend, one of the best friends I ever had.' Poor Joe! He doesn't like the looks of the galley on Carl's boat, and that won't endear him to Carl."

Joe Romantini was the talented and hard-working French chef who had been serving fantastic meals to our guests on the *Mañana* for fifteen years.

Eldon broke off the transmission momentarily, then came back with "Are you still there? Can you hear me? Over."

"Over" was his signal that he was no longer holding down the transmission button and that now he could hear me. "Yes I'm still here, and yes I can hear you. When and how are you coming home? Over."

"I'm coming home with the shore boats, outboards, and whatever I could save before the water got too deep. Had to get everyone and their gear off before I started worrying about what I could salvage. Didn't have too much time; you know how fast the tide comes in, and it had a good start before we knew anything about it. Don't feel too bad, honey chile. Awfully sorry about the boat, but don't let it get you down. We've come through some bad times before now, and we'll come through this. Gotta go now. See you some time tomorrow afternoon. Remember, I love you anyway."

(This last remark was one of our private jokes. It was like saying, "If I've done anything I ought to be sorry for, I forgive you." Whenever we had to apologize, we were always magnanimous.)

I started to answer, even though I was in a state of shock, but the marine operator came on, signaling that the transmission was over and did I want to re-establish contact from this end? By this time I had a lot of questions I wanted to ask, but this wasn't the time to ask them.

Then Pattie, our fifteen-year-old daughter, stopped by my office for a minute after her last class. Should I tell her?

No, I decided, not right now. This isn't going to be easy and it isn't going to be fun; I want to think about it awhile. She certainly will have to know about it when Eldon gets home tomorrow.

Fortunately, Pattie was too much occupied with her

own social milieu to spend much energy worrying about her parents' state of mind. To my great relief, she noticed nothing wrong and buzzed off, light-hearted as ever.

Parents want to preserve that light-heartedness as long as possible. We hate to unload our worries, and especially our calamities, on our children. Experience teaches us, of course, that it's better to let them experience some of the big jolts along with us. Parental instinct, however, tells us not yet; don't tell them yet; let them be happy as long as possible.

When the time came to tell her, though, it hadn't gotten any easier.

Pattie was, at this age, my joy and number one frustration. At fifteen she was already remarkably pretty with large blue-gray eyes, long curly eyelashes, and youth's fine, translucent complexion. Her blonde hair, curly also (no one in our family escaped having curly hair), she regarded with extreme disfavor and ironed it every morning. Straight hair, parted in the middle and hanging relentlessly down on either side, was the "in" thing. On this day she was wearing a skirt she had worn in the sixth grade, now much too short, but mini skirts were, at this moment, fashion's darling. Small-boned, slender, and average in height, she hoped fervently and often that she wouldn't get as tall as her mom (five foot eight inches). This wish was granted although she couldn't be sure of it until several more years had passed.

Pattie was also going through a difficult period, one that all adolescents have to go through but especially painful for her — that of distancing herself from her parents and declaring her separate individuality. It was both harder and more necessary for her because she had had to endure a traumatic separation when she was too young to understand anything about it. When she was nine months old, we had to send her down to Seattle to have a skin specialist remove an unsightly, rapidly growing angioma from her face. She was thirteen months old when she returned, and contrary to all expectation, she had not forgotten me. However, she no longer trusted me. She became my little shadow, following me from room to room, hardly letting me out of her sight lest I should unaccountably disappear again. My advisors in counseling psychology had assured me that her over-dependency would not continue for the rest of her life if I made sure it was not mutual. And I was determined not to be a contributor to the problem; still, it wasn't easy for me as she began growing away from me.

As a youngster Pattie was shy, even painfully so, but as she got into adolescence she discovered that shyness produced shyness in other people and made them uncomfortable. One night she told me that she had figured this out and had made her decision never to be shy or bashful again. True to her word, she became amazingly gregarious, always surrounded by a group of friends, using her innate and wickedly funny sense of humor to the hilt. Wherever she went, there was laughter. She loved school — not the glorious and rewarding process of learning; she never wasted an inordinate amount of time on that — her world was a social world. This was going to make for severe problems when she had to be uprooted by the changes the rest of us were going through.

⚓

Late in the afternoon the following day, Eldon arrived at the harbor tired, sun-burned, and determinedly cheerful. "No more boats," he declared emphatically. "I've been a slave to boats since I was eighteen years old, and it's over. I'm done with them!"

I was familiar with his robust optimism; it's usually at its height when he's hurting inside. And I knew he had to be hurting. He loved that boat. Everything he enjoyed doing depended on a boat.

Trilogy

When I first met Eldon, he had the sort of looks that make people stop on the street and do a double-take. He had dark brown, slightly auburn hair and the fair complexion that frequently accompanies it. He was tall, broad-shouldered, slim-hipped, with perfect teeth and a smile to die for. I was the envy of all my college class-mates, but Eldon didn't even want to hear their silly remarks comparing him to various movie stars. From his reaction, one would have thought they were talking about some horrible defect he was trying unsuccessfully to conceal. (Surely people have much worse crosses to bear than that of being extraordinarily handsome!)

One of my roommates asked point-blank one day, "Are you going to marry that guy?"

"I dunno," I answered. Actually, I hadn't been asked.

"Boy! If you're not, I am," she vowed. "Just let me know; I won't stand on ceremony!"

Eldon never did become really comfortable with personal compliments. Sometimes he would say, "Well, at least I'll grow out of it." Or sometimes, gruffly, "Beauty is no advantage to a man."

I thought it was, though, and I was proud of him.

Our insurance company declared *Mañana* a total loss. They'd been offered two thousand dollars for the hull, so they asked Eldon if he wanted to buy it back at that price and rehabilitate it. He was tempted. But when he consid-ered the miles of ruined wiring, the water-logged insula-tion, the thirty badly damaged electrical motors used to operate refrigerators, winches, fans, and two dozen other gadgets, not to mention the two big GM diesels, he began to visualize years of work and far more money than the thirty thousand dollars of our insurance. He had to say no.

Eldon stoutly asserted that he was through with boats. I knew, of course, that he was never going to be really happy until he had a replacement.

He held out for all of three weeks. Then he began to

concede his willingness to think about a successor for the *Mañana*. Given our slender budget, the most feasible plan would be for Eldon to build it himself. But he was sixty-two. He couldn't see himself spending the best part of ten years working single-handed.

If he could get Jim and Randy to help, it might be possible.

"We'll have to sell the house," I said. This seemed so obvious to me that I wasn't even considering it as subject to debate.

"No, we're not going to sell the house." Eldon was equally determined. "If this doesn't work out, I want something to come back to."

Clearly, we had a decision to make, one that would change our lives. We really needed some guidance, preferably divine. For a lot of years we had made it our practice "when in doubt, pray about it." So we prayed, but we still didn't have any clear idea what the Lord had in mind for us.

Now, some people don't believe in posing tests to find out the Lord's will. Sometimes this is called "putting out a fleece," because that is what Gideon did when he wasn't totally sure that he believed everything the Lord had told him. He needed a sign. So he set out a fleece on the ground and wished that the fleece would be dry in the morning even though the ground was wet. He got his sign, and more.

Gideon seemed a worthy model, so I suggested a preposterous test. "It's been almost sixteen years since we built this house," I said. "In that time no one has ever come to our door and asked to buy it. If someone does now, I'll take that as a sign."

Safe enough. Then we realized that such a buyer would have to have cash; we needed cash to build a boat. How many home owners ever once experience that — a stranger coming to the door offering a solid payment that would set them free for their next life adventure? How many would ever accept such an offer? Would Eldon, I wondered?

"I'll agree to it, but it won't happen," Eldon said with a little shrug and an expression that told me all too clearly that he couldn't see plotting his life by such flimsy landmarks.

Ten days later, although we had neither advertised the house nor told anyone we were thinking of selling it, a woman we'd never seen before knocked on the front door. "I'm wondering if by any chance you might be interested in selling this house?" she began.

I was flabbergasted — oh, me of little faith! Rather weakly, I asked, "Why this one particularly?"

"Well, I've asked several people in this area because I want to be near the high school, but nobody up here wants to sell."

Stunned, I invited the woman to come inside. "Strangely enough, we just started thinking about selling our home a few days ago," I told her, "and I guess I'm not used to the idea yet."

"In case it should make any difference," she said, "I happen to have enough dollars available to buy something outright and soon, without the mortgaging and money-borrowing process. We'd like to move right in and get settled before the next school year. I have a daughter who will be starting to high school this fall, and we're both pretty tired of doing correspondence lessons."

"Correspondence lessons?" Somewhere in this conversation I must have missed something.

"Oh," she laughed, "I should have explained. My husband builds roads for logging camps; I've lived in float camps for eight years now, but I think it's time to get a place ashore."

There it was: our answer, as neatly as it ever could have been devised. I told her that my husband had only very recently agreed even to think about selling, and we hadn't gotten far enough along to set a price.

"Could I come back tomorrow?" she asked. "My father-in-law is in town, and I would like for him to look at the house along with me. Then, if he likes it, we can talk prices."

By the time they came the next afternoon, Eldon and I had decided on a price. It seems ridiculously low now, after years of double-digit inflation. At the time, though, it was a fair price. It gave us about thirty percent profit over what we had spent building and furnishing the house. After a thorough tour of the premises, the father-in-law settled back in my best reclining chair and told his daughter-in-law: "I like it. By far the best-looking place we've seen. Just buy it." And that was that.

Henceforth for quite some time we were going to be without a house of our own.

⚓

After that, there was no turning back. I submitted my resignation at the high school and started packing. Not knowing whether we would be building or buying the new boat, we decided on Seattle as a more convenient place than Ketchikan to do either one.

I would try to get a job in the Seattle area, but there aren't many jobs available late in the summer. Schools like to have their teachers for the next year under contract by March or April. An alternative would possibly be going to school at the University of Washington and working on a Ph.D. I'd always wanted to move into college-level counseling, and a doctoral degree would give me that opportunity.

Early in August, Pattie and I went to Bellevue, near Seattle, where I had rented a small apartment. With us we took her best friend, Marla Peters, in the vain hope that this would make it easier for Pattie to accept all the changes we were forcing onto her life. It only made things easier for the two weeks that Marla stayed. Parting from Marla, with no more friends in sight, brought back all the anger and rebellion that Eldon and I had been dealing with from the start. Why did we have to make all this fuss just because we'd lost the *Mañana*? Why couldn't we just keep on living as we had been? Why? And a dozen more whys. She had to start boarding school early in September, and she was determined to hate it.

Randy, who had returned from Europe on the twentieth of June, stayed with his dad for two more weeks, and then came down to Seattle. He had to find a college that would accept his credits from the Goethe Institute in Germany, where he had spent the previous year. He finally settled on the University of Oregon, or they settled on him as the case might be.

We had sold our furniture with the house, but Eldon still had to go through all of the things in our store-room under the garage. In it he'd stashed not only all the gear and paraphernalia he had accumulated in forty years as a commercial photographer but also everything nautical he had managed to pick up since childhood — especially during a brief but ill-fated time when he was dealing in army surplus commodities just after World War II.

For him, this was by far the most difficult part of the move. He confessed afterward that throwing away or giving away most of this long-cherished junk practically gave him a nervous breakdown; day after day of these difficult decisions left him feeling paralyzed, and he just wished most heartily that the whole problem would go away.

What he found hard to believe, after all that anguish, was how well he was able to get along without all his treasured artifacts.

He came down late in September, hauling a trailer with the rest of our household possessions — most of which had to go into storage until we could rent a house.

Pattie was in boarding school by this time, and Randy was in Eugene attending the University of Oregon. I had searched fruitlessly for a counseling job, then settled on Plan B, the Ph.D. That left just one family member at loose ends. Jim, our oldest, had "dropped out" at age twenty-four and was living in a one-room cabin near Juneau.

I don't pretend to know what motivated all the young people in the late 1960s to make vast pilgrimages to "find themselves" or to contemplate the meaning of life. I just know that Jim was one of them. He had been in charge of a fair-sized insurance office in Oakland, California. Perhaps he was unsettled by the loss of the *Mañana*, the selling of our home in Alaska, and the dispersion of his whole family like a bunch of confused nomads. At any rate, he had retired to the boonies to do whatever thinking he felt impelled to do, and it was from this place that his father summoned him to help search for a new boat, complete or incomplete, or a design from which to build.

Jim had been thinking about putting a pack on his back and heading for South America, a prospect that horrified Eldon and gave me bad dreams at night. To counteract that idea, Eldon promised Jim that if he and Randy would help build a boat, we would travel with it for an unspecified amount of time — at least until he got some of the wanderlust out of his system.

"You'll find that a much better reception awaits you, even in South America, if you come as part of a respectable family than as a lone tramp," he assured Jim.

Of course, Jim had been exposed to all of the "blame your parents and their generation for the world's problems" propaganda that was prevalent at that time. Nevertheless, he still had strong family loyalty. Besides, the idea of a family odyssey through the South Pacific — possibly even around the world — appealed to him. He signed on for the duration.

Eldon and Jim made a trip down the West Coast all the way to San Diego, looking at boats for sale, boats under construction, and designs that interested them. They returned filled with enthusiasm for multihulls. They even had a set of plans, designed by Rudy Choy, for a catamaran, and it began to look as though our new boat would be built on this (to me) revolutionary concept.

Later, Choy's plans for a catamaran, which has two hulls, were set aside in favor of three-hull design. The larger central hull would undoubtedly hold more supplies for extended traveling. Not only that, it would make the boat more stable — that is, less likely to overturn in a howling gale.

"This is just what you need, Mom," Jim told me. "You're the one who gets seasick." (As if I needed to be reminded....) "A multihull can only roll seven degrees. You'll really enjoy sea travel on one of these."

No one thought to tell me, or probably even knew at that time, that trimarans have a quick, jerky way of righting themselves at the edge of the seven degrees that can be just as nauseating as rolling the guards under.

Christmas came and went, and still no real decision had been reached about what type of boat to build or where to build it. One thing was very clear, though, after the five of us had spent the holidays in a one-bedroom apartment: we needed more room. My classes at the university were taking most of my time and a lot of my mental energy; although I endorsed the need for more room as fervently as the rest of the family, I wasn't much help in solving the problem. So Eldon stopped shuttling around from one boat-building project to another and devoted himself to the search for better housing.

It really hadn't occurred to us that the problem of where to live was so closely related to the problem of what to build that one could not be solved without the other.

One day Eldon came home in a euphoric state — a condition not at all foreign to his usual temperament, even though none of us had seen much euphoria lately.

"I've found it!" he shouted. "The boat, the place to build — everything!"

"You have?" I asked, a bit warily. Eldon's enthusiasms are often based on snap judgment, and I've been carried along by the sheer force of them, sometimes to my sorrow.

"Perfect," he assured me, "absolutely perfect! Just what we've been looking for: a boat already partly finished AND a wonderful place to build." He turned to Jim, "You remember Al Koban's forty-eight-foot trimaran? He's going to sell it. He doesn't know it yet, but I'm sure he is. If he does, I've found a fabulous place to live, combined with a great building site!"

Jim was puzzled. "I just talked to Al last week, and he was full of plans for his trimaran. What happened?"

"Two things," Eldon responded. "His wife has a deadline on her Ph.D. the first of May, and she says if Al doesn't quit spending all his time on the boat and give her some help with the house and the kids, she isn't going to make it."

"Okay, that sounds reasonable. What else is pushing him? He loves every inch of that boat, I can tell. I really can't imagine him selling it."

"The other thing is that he just moved it from his yard to a rented space because the neighbors were complaining about the noise all hours of the day and night. But if he isn't going to be able to work on it, he doesn't want to pay the rent."

Eldon had been visiting Al Koban, the registrar at the University of Washington, ever since he'd first arrived from Ketchikan. He was sure that Al would sell his two finished hulls — so sure that he'd put a deposit down to secure a house located just about a mile from Al's building site. "If he does decide to keep his boat, we'll still be better off in a three-bedroom house. We can start our own project there. Well, not in the house, of course."

(That was supposed to be funny. We did move into

17

the house, though, and, over time, so did most of the boat-building project. We might as well have considered that house part of the building site — an adjacent warehouse, perhaps.)

Al Koban had asked for the weekend to decide whether or not he would sell. Even though Eldon professed to be ninety percent sure he would, it was still a tense time.

On Saturday we went over to see the house. Situated at the head of Lake Washington, on Bothell Way, the property extended seven hundred feet from the highway all the way to a creek in the back. The house was set back from the road about two hundred feet. The grounds, though neglected, were still very beautiful with a large lawn, trees of all kinds, and many flowering shrubs. (I won't pretend that the condition of the grounds improved much while we lived there; dedicated boat builders are not the best husbandmen for such estates.)

We were ecstatic. After several months in a tiny apartment, we all thought the house was enormous with its three bedrooms, a living room, a dining room, and all the rest. It was an older home, but well built — so much the kind of house we had been hoping for that we could scarcely believe our good fortune.

"And," Eldon added, "being practically across the road from Lake Washington, we shouldn't have any trouble when it's time to launch."

Those words were not exactly prophetic; launching turned out to be more of a problem than anyone could ever have anticipated.

⚓

Monday, according to their previous agreement, Eldon called Al Koban. Al did a certain amount of hemming and hawing. He was not going to part with two thousand hours of loving labor without letting us know how hard it was

for him. I had a ten o'clock class at the university and had
to leave before Eldon got a definite answer, but at least I
could tell that Al hadn't said no.

When I got back, there was a note on the kitchen
table directing me to a wilderness area north of Kenmore,
the small town where we now planned to live.

North Seattle is full of little hills and streams; the
hills, of course, are the far-flung foothills of the majestic
Cascades, and because of the rainfall there are brooks,
creeks, and rivers around and among them. The roads,
designed as much as possible to avoid a plethora of
bridges, wind around in a most bewildering fashion. Eldon
had left a map for me on the kitchen table, knowing how
easy it was going to be to get lost even though Al Koban's
building site (now *our* building site) was only a mile from
our house. Later, without a map, I got lost regularly. So
did the rest of the family — which none of them
confessed until months afterward, leaving me feeling that
I was the only one without a proper sense of direction.

When I arrived at this little meadow among its
wooded hills, I was surprised at how private it looked and
how far from the world in general. I parked my car next to
Eldon's station wagon and squished my way over to the
boat hulls. A light snowfall and nightly freezing temperatures had left the ground full of tiny open puddles with
lacy white perimeters, half ice, half snow.

Eldon came part way to meet me, wearing a halibut
jacket and heavy twill pants, normal outdoor gear for
Alaska and appropriate here on the eighth of January. Jim
was bundled up in a ski jacket he had brought back from
Kitzbuhel, Austria, in '66. Just now he was helping Al
position one of the ribs for the center hull. At six feet, Jim
was an inch or more taller than the others, but on that
uneven ground it didn't show; they were all tall and thin.

Even in work clothes, sweat shirt, and baggy pants, Al
managed to look scholarly. Partly it was the bone structure

in his aristocratic face, partly the glasses, but most of all his headmaster-like demeanor. He was a kind and gentle person and a good friend through the years. Just now he was grieving over having sold his boat and his dream.

Eldon couldn't share that grief; he was positively incandescent, as though lighted from within. His clear blue eyes, never cynical, never unkind, glowed with happiness. The expression on his face, still smooth at sixty-two, could only be interpreted as one of pure bliss. He had recaptured his long-cherished vision. These parts of a boat, scattered over the soggy, half-frozen terrain, he saw assembled, making their way through fabulous South Seas islands.

I looked at the side hulls, long as railroad cars, and the keel, longer still with six lone ribs protruding upward and outward, and I felt total dismay. How could we ever get it all together while we still had some money to work with?

I could understand the frustration Eldon and Jim felt at not being able to start working immediately; what I could not comprehend was why Al, who had severe time constraints, wanted to squander more hours without additional compensation. Such is the illogical dedication of the boat lover.

The intervening time, while Al ever-so-reluctantly let go of his dream, was not entirely wasted. Eldon and Jim made quick work of moving from the little apartment in Bellevue, and then they started filling the garage and what was probably a tool shed with materials for building. One Tuesday morning I left the apartment in Bellevue, went to the university, then came home to the house in Kenmore; no more crossing the Lake Washington toll bridge twice a day for me. In fact, alarmed at the shrinking of our bank account, I decided to go to work when the spring quarter ended.

⚓

Afton, Eldon's brother, older by only eighteen months but still big brother, came down from Alaska on April first — just to see how things were going. Rand had just transferred from the University of Oregon to the University of Washington; Pattie was home for the weekend, and we all went downtown to Tai Tung's, our favorite eating place.

It was a fun-filled evening, with everyone feeling witty — lots of puns, jokes, and adventure stories. Certainly Afton, who can hardly be outdone in the game of repartee, did his part along with Jim and Rand, but after all the kids had settled down for the night, he talked very seriously to Eldon and me.

"I have some grave doubts," he began, "about this whole project."

"You have?" Eldon showed his surprise; he didn't have any doubts.

"Indeed I have. The success of the whole thing depends on how much help you're going to get out of those boys. I just can't see those clowns having the dedication this job requires. They're good kids, no doubt, and fun to be with, but I can't see them staying the course."

Eldon was accustomed to arguing with his brother. They had been in business together for ten years before Eldon married and went his separate way. "All I can say to that is 'just wait and see.' I know them better than you do. They've never let me down yet."

"I hope you're right," Afton replied. "I really hope so. But it's going to be a worry."

RANDY'S COMMENT:
MY FOLKS' JOURNEY OF FAITH

When we started the "boat project," each of us had different expectations where it was leading. As far back as I could remember Dad had talked about sailing to the South Pacific, but I had long ago relegated that dream, along with the Second Coming, to the circular file labeled "not in my lifetime."

Even as this strange creation began to take shape before our eyes, I still had visions of returning to Europe and pursuing the tortured life of the expatriate. The folks, on the other hand, had a more biblical vision of the future. And, as the months went slowly by, I began to see why Dad took so seriously the public comparison to Noah. Both he and Mom saw a flood of change sweeping across our nation. Civil unrest, political activism, free love, and drugs had already touched their lives in one way or another. In their minds, they saw this socio-political deluge carrying away, like so much flotsam and jetsam, much of what they held near and dear — including their own children.

This apocalyptic vision of the future gave compelling reasons for investing in something as fragile and irresponsible as a sailboat. It drove them to invest every penny they had managed to save over a lifetime of industry and frugality. They took quite literally the admonition to "cast your bread upon the water." And — like Abraham, who, "when he was called, set out by faith without knowing where he was going" — the folks began a journey of faith that would take the family on a voyage of discovery to places it had never been, both in the mind and in the heart.

At the time, I certainly didn't know where it was all leading. All I knew was that God, in His infinite wisdom, must have brought us back together for a purpose.

As the days and weeks went by, that purpose remained obscure, but we learned one undeniable lesson: building a boat is bloody hard work!

CHAPTER TWO:

FROM CHRYSALIS TO BUTTERFLY

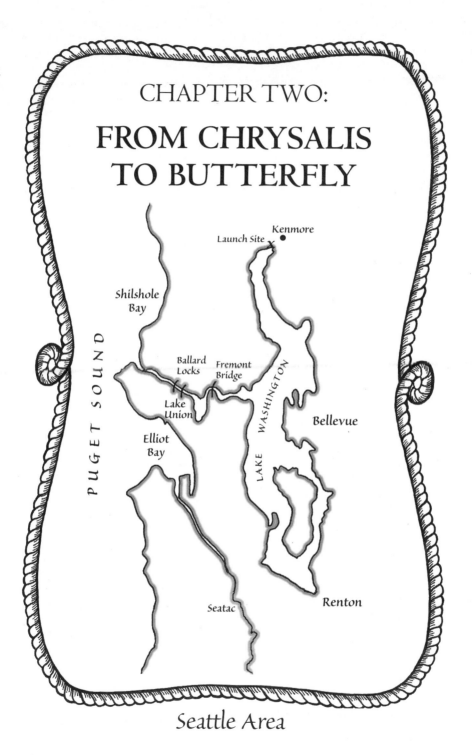

Seattle Area

During the years we'd owned the *Mañana*, the center of many family activities, that boat had never eaten up our lives the way *Trilogy* was threatening to. Eldon's dedication to the project was almost total; Jim's progressed from a tepid semi-commitment to a consuming passion as the months went on. My attitude changed from a very prosaic "let's get the job done" to a total involvement, even though there was little I could do toward the actual building. Randy, as soon as he was able, threw himself into it like a man killing snakes.

Pattie, understandably, resented the fact that our lives revolved around something with which she had little sympathy.

It was now ten months since the *Mañana* had sunk, and the replacement was taking place very slowly. Shortly before spring break, when we would have Randy back as a part-time worker, it became necessary to move our two side hulls from the little forest meadow they had occupied since January. The new building site would be our front yard — between the house and the busy highway, Bothell Way.

The side hulls were each forty feet long. We needed muscle-power infinitely beyond what our family could summon, and Eldon was far from certain that this muscle-power would be provided by the membership of the Northwest Multihull Association. Eldon had been a member since the previous October, but the obligation to help a fellow member was voluntary. Even though Eldon had alerted them at the last meeting, he had grave doubts about how many would actually put aside whatever they had planned for Sunday and come to our aid.

By Saturday night, worry had replaced any lingering confidence Eldon might have had in the altruism of others. He called our pastor's wife; perhaps her influence would be sufficient to shore up the weak spots in our human resources. He explained his problem and added, "If there's some fund that needs replenishing...." After all, church funds always need replenishing.

"I'll contribute a hundred dollars," Eldon offered, "if you'll have a dozen husky young men here at noon tomorrow."

She promised to do what she could.

No matter how many volunteers showed up — there might be three of them or there might be fifty — I would need to feed them lunch. I was up before daylight trying to get it together, not knowing at that time whether we would be eating inside or outside because the weather prediction was for partly cloudy skies. What clouds there were dispersed soon after they did their part in a truly glorious sunrise, and then the sun began its westward march, shining intensely.

OKAY, so we'll eat outside. No one needed to say it.

Hastily, Jim and Eldon assembled sawhorses and planks, making a table of improbable length that was considerably more rugged than handsome. The only table-cloths I owned that would cover this vast expanse were lace, really designed for candlelight and fine crystal; one of them was actually an heirloom, inherited from Eldon's mother. I suppose no one would have cared greatly if we had eaten off unplaned lumber, but at that time I hadn't had nearly as much experience in roughing it as I can now claim.

Bolting a hasty and very minimal breakfast, Eldon and Jim departed in a spray of gravel and unintelligible phrases supposedly telling me when to expect them back.

Trilogy

I began to wish heartily that I had made arrangements for Pattie to come home that weekend. Or it would have been nice if the Multihull Association had some sort of auxiliary organization that would help one lone person feeding such a crowd. Even if I had shared Eldon's apprehensions that no one would show up, I still was obligated to be ready for forty-five or fifty man-sized appetites.

We had decided on fruit punch and iced tea to drink. (No beer, although Jim had argued mightily in its favor.) Saturday night I had made about two hundred sandwiches as well as several fruit salads and desserts; the green vegetables for an enormous salad had been washed and crisped but still had to be reduced to bite-sized pieces. I'd wanted the vegetables to be fresh, and so I'd postponed making the salad until morning. Now I wished I had just forgotten about fresh and had it ready.

Of course the crowd wouldn't arrive precisely at noon, because they first had to assemble at the boat-building site and put the two hulls on a forty-foot flatbed truck. But as the time ticked away, I began to wish them a few little delays —nothing serious, of course. Just enough to ensure that I would be ready when they arrived.

At 12:25 a gargantuan truck rolled into our yard, followed by an entourage of fantastic length.

There must be a word for what occurred immediately thereafter. It was a unique combination of bedlam and pandemonium: bedlamonium, perhaps?

Eldon talks faster than most people can listen even under the most relaxed and favorable conditions. In situations of stress his speech accelerates until he sounds like an LP record being played at 78 instead of 33 1/3. Maybe a tobacco auctioneer could keep up with him and even understand him, but I seriously doubt it. Open-mouthed, his friends stared at him while he yelled things that sounded like "Grabbafrumamidiciousbangdrap-perover-theobob!" gesticulating wildly. "Obfrupt! Spknit!" turning

in mid sentence and whirling off to another equally mysti-
fied helper.

Even Jim, conditioned by long years of listening to this
rapid-fire delivery, could not understand more than an
occasional word. One thing, however, was only too clear:
with forty-six people milling around, nothing was getting
done. Not only that, his father seemed on the verge of
apoplexy. So Jim took over as translator and director.

Instantly, miraculously, order was restored. In a few
minutes the two forty-foot hulls were placed, keel side up,
where our new boat shed was to be built. The massive
center hull, now fifty feet long (the bow extended to give
a more rakish line), would arrive on May eighth, and
when that was finished sometime in June, another
Multihull cooperative effort would put all three hulls
upright, ready to be joined together.

At this point, thirty-six Multihullers and ten young
men from our church turned their attention to the picnic
table like Tatars falling on a defenseless town. The sandwiches disappeared; so did everything edible or drinkable.
So did the Multihullers; having done their duty by a fellow
member, they departed without delay or ceremony to
resume work on their own boats and speed the day when
we would be helping them on a similar occasion.

Jim, Eldon, and two or three friends vanished into the
breakfast room, designated long ago as operation headquarters, to discuss what kind of shelter the boat would
need and what materials would be required. Somewhat
ruefully, I picked up my two bouquets of daffodils and
narcissus that were still behind the front door where I had
placed them, intending to put them on the table at the
last moment. Nobody had missed them; I put one on the
mantle over the fireplace and the other on the windowsill
in the breakfast room.

⚓

Trilogy

In April, Eldon had to make a business trip for a few days, but he was sure that while he was gone Jim and Randy could get started building the boat shed. The dimensions were fifty-six by thirty feet, height sixteen feet. The materials they had decided on were plastic over a sturdy wood frame — sturdy, because the triumvirate had reluctantly conceded that the structure would have to withstand some harsh weather during the next winter. (Up until now, everyone had been sure we could get the boat launched by fall.)

The day before Eldon's return, Jim started cutting the roof angles. Aside from a large stack of materials that looked as though anyone could get them together in a day's time, he didn't have much to show for five days of endless numerical calculations, measuring and re-measuring, buying, and chalking up miles on the station wagon. Before his father returned, he wanted something tangible completed on the structure itself. First he nailed the pre-cut sides together to be set in place, a whole side at a time; then he started on the roof.

Then Randy showed up. In those days, he was attending the University of Washington from seven a.m. until about three p.m. every school day, then spending afternoons, evenings, and weekends working on the boat. He arrived just as Jim was fitting the angle pieces to the two-by-fours that would hold up the roof. It didn't take him long to notice that nothing fit properly.

"Those angles are cut wrong," Randy pointed out. "They're never going to fit."

"In a pig's eye!" Jim retorted ambiguously, but with equal confidence. "Look at the drawings; Dad and I worked it all out very carefully."

"Well, you're going to have to work it out again. Anybody can tell those aren't ever going to fit."

Together, they bent over the sketches. The figures were

in pencil, small and blurred. Jim had followed the numbers as he read them — possibly as they were written, and possibly not. Still, it was no longer important who was to blame; the roof was not going to fit unless new angles were cut. Jim expressed his chagrin in colorful, waterfront language for a few moments and then added, "We're going to get enough of this building up so that it looks like something, even if it takes all night."

It did.

But when Eldon arrived on the morning plane, the building was just about framed up. This, of course, was what Eldon had expected, and no one commented on the two large boxes of angle pieces left beside the fireplace. They made great firewood.

Randy had planned to attend the University during summer quarter in order to graduate as soon as possible, but the boat was demanding more and more of his time. Also, this was the time of the Kent State tragedy. As the University of Washington student body mobilized in protest, Randy became a student leader, needed in many places at once. He spoke to assembled students at colleges and junior colleges in the area, and eventually helped to organize a general strike and march of protest. That he also managed many hours of work on the boat, not to mention acceptable grades for the quarter, amazed me no end.

However, by the end of the quarter Randy had decided that finishing the boat was more important to him than a college degree — at this moment, anyway. I wasn't sure it was more important to me; Randy was studying creative writing, and his major professor, a published writer herself, felt that he had great talent, but Rand was almost twenty-one years old and felt qualified to make his own decisions. Eldon was as strong a believer in education as I, but right now he was an even stronger believer in getting the boat finished. Jim had always told his brother that graduating was fine, but that most of the work was a total waste of time, so he was no help keeping Rand in school.

Little by little, the new boat was becoming everything for us — our work, our school, our home, our future.

⚓

Late in May, I came home from work to find everyone very subdued. Pattie had been crying; Jim looked as though he might at any time. In our usually vociferous family, no one had anything to say.

In quick apprehension, I counted the family members: Eldon looking ill, Jim, Randy, Pattie stricken with some great sorrow. All accounted for.

"What's wrong?" I demanded. "What's happened?"

Jim gently propelled me toward the back yard. There on the lawn, shaded by a big rhododendron bush, lay our little dog Coco. He was curled up on his side, the way he always slept, his light golden cocker fur riffling in the mild spring breeze.

Despite all our warnings he had tried to cross Bothell Way, that busy thoroughfare. He'd almost made it; another foot and he would have been off the pavement. But a speeding car hit him, not even bothering to stop. A kind lady who had seen the accident picked him up and took him to a veterinarian close by. There Jim found him later in the day, when he missed Coco and began looking for him.

A grave had been dug out in the pasture/blackberry tangle where Coco loved to roam, and before we lowered him into it, Jim spoke a few words that reduced us all to tears. "If man stands in the place of God to his dog, then Coco fulfilled all the requirements for reaching Heaven. He loved us with every bit of his fast-beating little heart. That is total commitment. In God's scheme of things, there must be a place for Coco up there somewhere. Good-bye, Coco; we loved you, too, in our bumbling human way. We'll never get over missing you."

From Chrysalis to Butterfly

Sadly, we covered the little grave. There would never be another dog like Coco for us. He'd been part of our lives when the children were young and all at home. Those years will never come again.

Perhaps, though, Coco performed one last service for the family that had already received such boundless devotion: Because Coco left a gap in our family circle, we were suddenly conscious of our importance to each other. We began forming plans for the long trip that we would make when the boat was completed, a family trip where we would share many varied experiences and be interdependent in a way impossible to achieve under usual circumstances in our complex society.

Could we all get along with each other for months or even years confined to a small boat? However much family members love each other, they are seldom as polite to one another as strangers tend to be; past jealousies and fancied or real injuries may have been forgiven after a fashion but not forgotten. No one really knows what "list of grievances" he or she has accumulated until, under stress, the truth comes out and the name-calling begins. Would we find ourselves abandoning the boat, the trip, the dream, and each other in some foreign port? Such things have happened many times, as the annals of small boat cruising will testify; I didn't want it to happen to us.

When I mentioned some of my fears to Eldon, he was shocked. "How can you even think such a thing?" he wanted to know. "The boys have their little disagreements, but they've been pals and best friends all their lives!"

Well, yes and no. Jim was almost four years old by the time Randy was born, and he'd wanted a brother so badly that it was almost an obsession. After hearing the Bible story of Samuel, he decided to pray about it, and every night he prayed that God would send him a little brother. Eventually his prayers were answered. (It never occurred to him that Mom and Dad might have been praying, too.)

He felt that the baby belonged to him, and he took over the care and training of little brother in ways I didn't find out about for years afterward. The course of training was rigorous, designed to make Randy a "tough guy," and it showed just about the amount of good judgment that could be expected of a child Jim's age. Needless to say, Randy didn't always appreciate the solicitude or the domination of his older brother.

Both boys contracted polio when Randy was sixteen months old, and Rand spent several months learning to walk again. In fact, Jim and Rand each had some residual damage, but they'd learned to compensate so well that no one thought about it any more. In addition, Randy wound up with some broken bones (and almost lost his life!) when he was three. He jerked away from Jim, who was holding his hand too tight (according to Randy), and his momentum carried him out into the street directly in the path of a large truck. All these things, and the parental protectiveness that was almost inevitable, conspired to make Jim sure that Eldon and I were going to make a hopeless mollycoddle out of Randy and that it was up to him to save his brother from such a fate.

(Jim was probably the only one who felt that his parents were over-protective. As far as our friends were concerned, letting the boys run skiffs with outboard motors on them from the age of three didn't come under the heading of over-protectiveness.)

Now that both boys were adults and approximately the same size, they seemed to have a good relationship. Would it survive being tested on the world's largest ocean?

Then, since I was anticipating problems, I worried about Eldon's need for privacy. He has always required "alone time" — and so do I, for that matter. "What are you going to do when you can't go down to the boat and work off your frustrations?" I asked. "The boat is going to be right under your feet, and you'll probably have three people looking over your shoulder."

Eldon smiled wryly. "I guess I'll go out on deck," he said slowly, but I could see that he was thinking what it would be like, surrounded constantly by his ever-loving family. These were things that needed pondering, and it seemed to me that it was time he did some of the pondering.

"Then, there's Pattie," I continued. "Maybe the boys don't bicker as much as they used to, and possibly they'll be great pals, but you know they don't find it easy to include Pattie in their activities. Right now she has other friends and other things to do, but when we're traveling she won't."

"True," Eldon conceded, "and I don't know if there's a handy remedy for that one. Jim is nine years older than Pattie, and that's quite a gulf at their age. Rand is nearer Jim's age than Pattie's; besides, she's a girl and they're boys. Their interests are different. Come on, you're supposed to be the expert on teenage problems. What do you think?"

"I am thinking. You know, when she was little, Pattie insisted on being right in the midst of their rough-and-tumble, even to getting her nose broken a couple of times. Now it seems to me that she's given up. She doesn't even try to take part in their music, although she's just as talented and just as well-trained musically. I would be surprised if they've paid any attention to what a good singing voice she has."

Eldon was silent. Pattie occupied a very special place in his heart, and he, having been trained in an almost Victorian mode of social behavior, had always insisted Pattie be treated the way he felt a lady should be. Finally, he said, "This whole idea is new to me, and I don't like it. I always thought the boys treated their sister better than most boys I know."

"Well, they haven't exactly persecuted her — just ignored her is all."

"OKAY, I can see how some of this could happen, but it's probably not too late to do something about it. Pattie's home for the summer now. Let's just see that she gets included more in what the boys do," Eldon suggested.

"It's not quite that easy. I've been trying to do that for a long time, and I can't say that my success has been over-whelming. Sure, do whatever you can to make it better, but don't be surprised if nothing much happens," I said. "This has been going on for years. I think the only way Jim and Rand can overcome a lifelong habit is to realize that the success of this venture may depend on making as good a 'buddy' out of their sister as they have of each other."

"You really think it's a serious problem, don't you? Is it going to jeopardize our whole trip?" Eldon asked with some heat. "Are you getting cold feet about traveling?"

"No; I've burned all my bridges, and it wouldn't be very productive to turn back now. I just think we should antici-pate possible problems and try to see that they don't get too big."

But I knew that, in spite of my protests, Eldon was going to worry from now on that I would abandon both the building project and our plans for future travel.

⚓

Early in June, when the time came to turn the hulls right side up, we again had to call on our friends in the Multihull Association. This time, though, we were not dependent on muscle alone.

Eldon, like his father before him, loved to invent things. Since Dad's inventions had never been profitable, we were conditioned to view all such things with skepti-cism — which was hardly fair, because many of Dad's inventions survived to become very profitable for someone else; he just wasn't a good businessman. Eldon's invention, which he called "wait and see," grew day by day until it looked like two halves of a squirrel cage, only larger. He knew that we regarded it with amused tolerance, and he refused to make any explanations.

From Chrysalis to Butterfly

Up until now, all three hulls had been lying upside down, keels in the air. Before they could be joined together, they had to be turned over and arranged side by side. The center hull, fifty feet long and now fully planked, was going to be beastly heavy. Early in the morning on June eighth, Eldon attached his two half circles, which now looked more like parts of a Ferris wheel, to one side of the center hull.

"I think those things belong on the back if you're going to make a stern-wheeler out of it." Randy observed.

Eldon gave him a withering look and continued with his work. He knew that vindication awaited him. He wasn't going to lessen his triumph by bothering to defend his idea.

When the Multihullers arrived, it was only the work of moments to roll the big center hull into an upright position, with the half-wheels bearing the load. Those who had regarded the strange extrusions on the hull with bewilderment, doubt, and good-natured condescension slapped Eldon on the back and roared their approval.

Life has few enough triumphs. A little well-deserved public acclaim wouldn't really hurt my conscience. But Eldon is almost abnormally modest about anything that could be called an achievement. His modesty requires that he disparage any success as the sheerest accident, a fluke which in no way detracts from his usual bumbling idiocy. With artless surprise, he exclaimed, "Well, whatd'ya know? It actually worked!" And everyone thought he was a very lucky guy and continued to regard him with benevolent superiority.

Strictly in private, though, among those family bystanders who had given him the most flack, he did allow himself a small word of congratulation. "I always knew it would work," he said quietly. "The idea was sound mechanically; I may not have put it together in the best possible way, but it was practical." Above all else, he does consider himself a practical man, even though the adven-

35

ture on which we were embarked must have seemed to many people indiscreet, if not downright senseless.

⚓

As the hulls were joined together with huge I-beams, the boat began to look almost finished. The family, with the exception of Eldon, did not have the foggiest notion of how much work remained. Eldon had built and rebuilt boats in the past and undoubtedly knew that most of our optimism was unwarranted, but it was wiser not to give us the depressing truth. In our touching state of naiveté, we always felt not more than two months away from the launching date. This feeling of near completion helped to give Jim and Rand the energy needed to put in a double shift each day and get up at dawn with renewed zeal — that, and just plain youth, which is a wonderful producer of vigor, effort, and accomplishment.

Eldon didn't have the advantage of youth, but he had a vision. From the time he was a small boy in Port Townsend, Washington, he had dreamed of cruising the South Seas. Listening wide-eyed to the tales of retired sailors on the docks, stories stranger than fiction (and often well-laced with fiction, I imagine), he had vowed that some day he was going to see those far places. Single-minded dedication to such a dream would have been unrealistic if he had not been able to set it aside until he had raised his family to approximately the age of account-ability. Now the vision had returned, front and center. He was unstoppable; neither rain nor snow nor dark of night kept him from his appointed rounds.

Fortunately, Eldon had never required as much sleep as normal people, and twenty-hour working days were old stuff to him.

At this point, work on the boat became more diversi-fied. Problems had a way of coming up faster and requiring more immediate solutions than before. We are, as previously noted, a verbal family, inclined to defend our opinions warmly and volubly. Each decision was subjected to a chaotic but democratic process that we dubbed "Consensus by Combat." Harmony and unanimity reigned only when one idea or merger of ideas came out on top and silenced opposition. Many a luckless bystander who happened to get caught in the crossfire was convinced that physical violence would result and the entire operation would be halted permanently. Not so. Our town-hall method, though cumbersome and time-consuming, turned out surprisingly good results.

Our building plans, purchased from Al along with the hulls, called for flush decks and drooped bows. Neither of these features appealed to our aesthetic taste, honed by many years of boat-watching. Eldon, after thousands of hours spent operating boats up and down the Pacific Coast, was sure he could not be happy inside a boat with no visibility except by periscope. So, purely as a courtesy, he wrote to the designer outlining the changes he intended to make and his reasons for doing so.

The boat designer's answer was so unanticipated that it struck us with quite a shock: he refused to authorize any changes whatever, and he declined to discuss the matter.

Many conversations with boat owners since that time have convinced me that the intransigence of marine architects is endemic to the breed. There is, nevertheless, something to be said in extenuation. In turning his plans over to amateur builders, he has good reason to feel that any departure from the master design would spawn a monstrosity capable of detracting from his reputation both by its appearance and its performance. After all, the plans had been subjected to rigorous theoretical knowledge as well as sea trials; the changes had not.

Knowing all that, and having seen the dismal results of some unauthorized experimentation in boat construction, we forgave our designer. But he did not forgive us, principally because we refused to back down where we strongly believed that changes were necessary, whether authorized or not.

One of the boat's characteristics bothered Eldon considerably, and Jim and Rand agreed with him. The structural strength of the vessel seemed a bit on the puny side for extended ocean travel. However carefully we might plan, the time would come when the boat would have to weather heavy winds and massive seas. To feel secure in the midst of a full-on gale, we had to be able to trust the strength of the boat. After much discussion, the three men decided to beef up the boat's inner strength as much as seemed necessary.

With some trepidation, Eldon sent another letter to the designer. He pointed out that he was not making any changes in hull design or any other factor that would detract from the boat's efficiency in the water, but if he was going to trust this structure with his life, family, and earthly possessions, it was vital that he should be satisfied with its strength and stability. He had already cited his forty years of sea experience in his previous letter, and its impression had been minimal; he didn't refer to it this time.

The response, as expected, was caustic, ending with the statement that we could not use the designer's name in connection with this trimaran.

OKAY, fair enough. We had not expected any approbation, and we certainly were not to have any. Mainly, our reaction was one of relief. Now we could build our boat as experience and good marine principles dictated — or could we? Weight is very important in the construction of trimarans, which are built with shallow draft and much buoyancy so that they surf in a strong wind rather than burrow into oncoming waves as a monohull would do. Too much weight will keep the "tri" from performing as it is designed to do. Eldon had figured all the additional weight carefully, but he wouldn't really know until the boat was launched whether he had overstepped the limits.

From Chrysalis to Butterfly

Several other Multihullers were building with plans from the same designer and had followed the exchange of letters between him and Eldon with great interest. When Eldon was asked to speak at a meeting of the Northwest Multihull Association, he was introduced as Father Noah (because of his white hair and the fact that he was building with the help of his sons). He couldn't resist alluding to this correspondence.

"It is true," he said, "that I have some things in common with Noah, but he had some real advantages: he had more sons, more time, and God for his architect. What I had was an architect who thought he was God."

Eldon's patience had been tried, but afterward he regretted giving way to what he considered a petty display of exasperation. "I shouldn't have said that, even though everyone had a good laugh. Our basic designs are very good, and he's responsible for that. I had no right to make fun of him."

"You weren't making fun of his ability," I retorted. "You were making fun of his inability to tolerate a difference of opinion."

For years afterwards, Multihullers kept sending us pictures showing new designs by this same architect with notes attached: "Isn't it amusing how much these designs are getting to look like *Trilogy?*"

Every day when I came home from work, new sketches had been tacked up on the breakfast room walls. At first, Eldon wanted to build a cabin high enough to give complete wall-to-wall headroom without subtracting anything from the space below the floor. (How many times in our travels he must have wished for this as he stowed and unstowed supplies and hunted for things in the bilge!) The resulting sketch, drawn to scale, showed that this would be out of proportion. A new sketch was made which reduced the height by eight inches. Still overpowering. A compromise was necessary, a combination of lowering the cabin floor and curving the ceiling enough to give headroom (up to six feet one inch) in the center of the cabin. Besides giving lines that were pleasing to the eye, the new plan resulted in additional strength and streamlining.

⚓

Euphoria, wonderful while it lasts, is never a permanent state of mind. It was now a year since we had moved into the house on Bothell Way. The house and land were up for sale, might be sold at any time, and we were by no means ready to move. We were running ahead on expenditures and behind on time. All this combined to dampen the exhilaration we had felt in the early days of the building project.

Our living space had dwindled in a gradual but insidious manner; the dining room table, larger than the built-in breakfast room table, would have been handy once in a while, but it had disappeared under mountains of supplies that would one day be boat. Long before, the living room with its twelve feet of bay window had become a no-man's-land that had no thoroughfares. No one ventured into it except to ferret out needed supplies.

Quite often I found myself looking at this plethora of building materials and wondering how it could all be incorporated into a fifty-foot boat.

Most of the traffic was around the house, not through it. The back door opened into the breakfast room, and guests with any imagination or persistence usually made their way around the house if they found no one in the boat shed and no answerer for the front door. The various obstacles seemed to interfere very little with our hospitality. Breakfast (early breakfast, mind you) was often the only meal served to fewer than ten people. I think our friends and visitors looked on the whole project as some sort of prolonged camp-out that was fun to visit but they wouldn't want to live there.

Some friends did live there, in spite of the hard work and the massive inconveniences. David Payne, Jim's friend from college, came in November, stayed with us until the boat was launched, and traveled with us for several months. Randy's friend Dick Thorpe (now Doctor Thorpe of Paradise, California) came early in January and stayed until the boat was launched, rigged, and ready for travel. Then he departed for medical school.

Randy and Dick enrolled in the local community college, where courses were available covering many skills that we needed for making the boat. The teacher was flexible, letting them choose their projects, convinced that they would learn as much that way as by doing the projects usually assigned to his classes. Boat fittings are expensive; by making them in the shop, they could save up to ninety percent of the retail cost. They were certainly more dedicated than most students, chalking up more shop hours than anyone else in the various classes and turning out numerous boat fittings as well as cupboards, drawers, doors — anything, in fact, that needed making.

As our future navigator (by virtue of the fact that he already had a sextant), Jim started taking a course in celestial navigation at the University of Washington. The professor was a brilliant astronomer but somewhat weak in practical application — the precise science of getting boats from one place to another and ascertaining accurately where a certain boat is on a large body of water. He thought in terms of *Star Trek* and hyperspace rather than one little boat under sail. One night, as he was leaving for class, Jim exclaimed, "I don't know why I keep going back there! So far I haven't learned enough to navigate my way out of a paper bag!" Thinking it over later, though, Jim realized that a good knowledge of the stars could only be an asset to any navigator; so, rather than dropping the course, he also enrolled in Captain Kildahl's class in practical navigation.

Jim and Dave got many of the less glamorous jobs — endless hours of fiberglassing and sanding, wearing masks, sweltering as the weather grew warmer. Once in a while they took off for a day to ski or go mountain climbing. It was therapeutic, they explained; their sanity was at stake.

After so many years of coping with all the machinery on numerous boats, Eldon was hard to stump on most mechanical problems. He had even worked as a plumber's assistant for a few months during his teen years. Of course, he got the stickier mechanical jobs. He marveled at how satisfactory it was to be working with new equipment, and how much he appreciated having knowledgeable marine suppliers close at hand. These words became much more understandable to me later, surrounded by a thousand miles of ocean, when engine parts had to be made by hand.

When I came home from work at 5:45 every day, I always stopped by the boat shed to check on everyone's progress. I was often puzzled that things looked very much the same to me as they had the day before, in spite of the fact that five of them had been working diligently for nearly twelve hours. I learned to make appropriate noises and maintain the polite fiction that I knew what was going on. It was soothing, and kept any frazzled nerves from twanging in my face.

Spring passed and summer moved in capriciously early. The heat inside our plastic-coated shed became almost unendurable. Any job that was portable was carried to the cool depths of the back yard, or to the garage that was shaded by giant evergreen trees.

Jim and Dave received few enough of these benefits because the hulls, alas, were extremely stationary. Sweltering, breathing through masks, they sanded, sanded, sanded, looking at night as though they had been working in a flour mill.

From Chrysalis to Butterfly

Early in June, I submitted my resignation to the State Employment Service; there were jobs for many pairs of hands, and popular opinion among the crew was that, from now on, mine were more valuable working on the boat.

⚓

My first assignment was shopping for carpets, upholstery, wall covering, and the hundreds of little things still needed to complete the interior. The general atmosphere to be achieved was "subdued elegance" (whatever that is).

The first time around, I struck out.

I came home with samples of rose velveteen for headboards in the aft cabin, matching drapery material and bedspreads, varicolored shag carpet in an abstract pattern of rose, wine, black, and white. The carpet alone simply screamed elegance — but I'll have to admit it wasn't subdued.

"I'm afraid," Jim ventured after a long pause, "it's going to look like a French whorehouse."

"Maybe not that bad," Randy offered dubiously. "Maybe stuffy Victorian."

I was crushed. "Didn't you say you wanted elegance?" I protested.

"Well...not quite that much elegance," Jim said. "This is, after all, a boat. What I thought of as elegance is clean lines, and a sort of simplicity that looks expensive."

When Eldon came back from his shopping trip, I made sure the boys didn't have any opportunity to prejudice him before I showed him my samples. He looked them over carefully and listened to my sales pitch. Then he gave his opinion: "Looks like a French whorehouse to me."

The boys shouted with laughter. I replied primly that I had no idea what a French whorehouse looked like, and upon what recollections were they basing their opinions? Privately, though, I began to suspect that the way of the interior designer is fraught with perils.

Trilogy

After trying a color scheme in shades of yellow, green, and white, I got no response from Jim and Rand. Eldon's only comment was, "Don't you think it looks pretty drab?" No, I didn't think so.

I was beginning to realize that the men in the family couldn't visualize the total effect from a few samples of' fabric. Besides that, our time was too valuable to spend it the way I had spent the past two days. The boat was due to take a charter group to Alaska on the twenty-sixth of July, and the interior had to be finished some time before that. So I gave an ultimatum:

"If you want me to do this job, you'll have to trust my judgment. Otherwise, anyone who feels better qualified can have the job with my blessing!"

I would have been relieved if someone else had volunteered to replace me, even if he'd goofed it up, but no one came forward. Besides, I had been chosen for this project because of my years of training and experience in the field of art. What was needed was a show of confidence, so I acted like any expert whose opinion is being questioned by a novice. "Give me a free hand or do it yourself," I decreed loftily.

Eldon looked at me the way he always did when we were trying to agree on names for our children. (I'm surprised so many marriages survive that crisis. He was always sure that my secret intention was to saddle the boys with some wildly improbable name that would be a life-long handicap. But then, any man who has had to suffer through life with "June" for a middle name is entitled to a few misgivings.) Since no one else wanted the job, he agreed to keep me on as decorator, but I could see him thinking, "We can always change it if we don't like it."

Frankly, we couldn't always change it. We had run out of money once and been rescued by Eldon's brother, who loaned us fifteen thousand dollars. (Only a family member would consider making an unsecured loan of that amount to people who planned to bat around on the Pacific Ocean for the next few years.) At this point, we had no margin for errors — a sobering thought, and one that made me take very seriously my responsibility as decorator.

Eldon, always accustomed to long working days, began to lengthen them even more. Dick now had a full-time job near Bellevue, but he continued to work on the boat every night until midnight or later. Dave and Jim denied themselves any days off, even though their work was the most monotonous as well as the most arduous physically. Randy, born chock full of energy and never seeming to run out of it, was charged with vigor and dedication. Not all of his zeal, though, was attributable to the project at hand.

⚓

Most of the people I know attend church with some regularity, but they are distinctly uncomfortable when face to face with anything that could be called miraculous. This is by no means a "God is dead" attitude. They are more than willing to concede that God exists, and that He may have disrupted the orderly patterns of this world somewhat flamboyantly in the past, but they are very sure that He doesn't work that way in the twentieth century.

He *does* work that way in the twentieth century.

I cannot describe Randy's experiences during the building of *Trilogy* without mentioning the miraculous. He is not the same person, in thought or in action, that he was when we began building the boat. There is a word for such a complete transformation of character. It is called conversion, or being "born again," and it takes place through God's direct intervention.

During the summer of Randy's twenty-first birthday he was happily engrossed in many activities, none of them connected in any way with religion. He had never felt less need for divine guidance nor less foreboding about the future. It was two o'clock in the morning; Eldon had

45

crashed, fully dressed, on the living room floor (we still had some floor space at that time) a few minutes earlier, so tired that one place to sleep was just about as good as another.

Randy had worked late, too, but for some reason he didn't feel sleepy. After a few minutes he began to feel rather strange and wondered briefly if he were coming down with some illness. Gradually he began to realize it was not disease but fear gripping him — fear out of nowhere, unexplainable but totally enveloping. As this nameless terror shook him from head to foot, God opened the abyss before him and showed him what it is like to die separated from God and totally aware of the separation. It was an experience of such horror that he doubted he could live through it.

In desperation, Randy awakened his father. "Pray with me, Dad," he begged. "I think I'm dying."

Being awakened from a sound sleep with the news that his son is dying would bring a much less devout father to his knees. Eldon prayed, knowing nothing at first except that his son's life was in danger.

Though he had asked for help, Randy was still full of resistance. There was too much to give up. What would his U. of W. friends think of him? What about the career he had planned for himself? What about money? Would God require him to live in poverty? And ridicule? And discomfort? Finally, all the questions and objections began to seem irrelevant in the presence of God, and he gave in, saying, "Whatever Your will may be, I accept it. I'll do whatever You want me to do."

It was like going from night to dazzling daylight, and he was surrounded and permeated by peace such as he had never felt before. Then God showed him what it means to have a Savior from eternal death. He had graphically illustrated what it was like to die the sinner's death; now Jesus showed him what He meant when He said, "I came that you might have life and have it more abundantly."

From Chrysalis to Butterfly

Eldon told me about it the next morning, face glowing with the good news. "I could hardly keep from waking you up to tell you in the night," he confessed. "Are you sorry I didn't?"

Well, yes, I was. Something very important had happened in our family, and I had missed it — not entirely, of course, because Randy had to tell everyone, me included. He positively radiated the joy he felt, like a prisoner on death row who has been miraculously reprieved. I envied him. Never having descended the depths he had plumbed, I had never risen to those heights, either. His energy was inexhaustible. He became a young people's leader in the church; he composed music, sang, played the guitar and banjo, reached out to other churches, and told his story in prisons and coffee houses.

At the same time, he was working long hours on the boat. Not a skilled cabinetmaker, he was frequently faced with problems beyond his level of expertise. When he didn't know how to do something, he had a very practical approach. "Lord," he would say, "You used to be a carpenter; just show me the best way to do this."

All of us were continually amazed at the things he was able to do and the way he did them — quickly, surely, without hesitation. His explanation was simple: "It says in the Bible, 'If any man lacks wisdom, let him ask of God.' I lacked a lot of wisdom and I did a lot of asking."

⚓

When we arranged to take a charter to Alaska late in July, we thought the boat would be finished by the middle of June. We imagined that we were going to have plenty of time to cruise among the islands of Puget Sound before setting out for Alaska. But it wasn't working out quite that way; we kept postponing our launching date. Now the launch was tentatively set for the tenth of July. Surely we would be ready by that time, wouldn't we?

47

Trilogy

From the time we began building the boat we'd had visitors. Now that it was nearing completion, though, with the cabin top fifteen feet in the air, the stream of visitors became almost constant. Sundays were developing into a total loss as far as work was concerned. The guided tour business was flourishing, but it wasn't getting *Trilogy* finished. Finally we had a council of war, one of the rare times we were in total agreement. It was ridiculous to work to the point of exhaustion day after day and then waste countless hours showing the boat to curious tourists.

Jim made a sign in letters a foot high: NO MORE VISITORS UNTIL AFTER JULY 17. He posted it on the side of the boat shed next to the street. We didn't want to publicize the date of our launching, but we assumed it would be well over before the seventeenth. Like many of our previous assumptions, that date turned out to be a trifle optimistic — but almost prophetic.

Aside from covering a half-dozen dining room chairs once, my experience as an upholsterer was zilch. I'd never even made a slipcover for furniture. Nevertheless, the job of upholsterer had been passed off to me. Not only that, because a friend of Randy's had loaned him a form for making diamond-tufted upholstery, everyone decided that our upholstery was going to be diamond-tufted, by golly, no matter how much ignorance I pleaded.

The corner to be covered was seven feet by nine feet, and the work went so slowly that I wondered if I would be through by Thanksgiving. Foam rubber had to be cut into diamond shapes, then the upholstery fabric fitted into the form with the foam on top and all glued together with a special glue that would remain permanently soft and resilient. Not being overly fond of arithmetic, I never did actually compute how many of the little diamonds there were in the entire thing — thousands, I know it.

On the evening of July third, Jim's girlfriend Kathy was helping me and only four feet remained to be done. I was all for going to bed at midnight and finishing in the morning, but Kathy, being at least twenty-five years younger than I, still had some ambition left.

"Oh no!" she protested. "We don't want to be doing this all day on the Fourth of July. Let's get it done!"

Wearily, I agreed. I didn't want to finish it on the Fourth or any other day, but I was committed. If I didn't do it, Randy would — successfully, of course — and he was needed in many other places.

Before the week was out, I forgot that I had forbidden anyone to mention diamond-tufting to me. The name suddenly became eminently respectable, and I basked in all the compliments I could get. No doubt about it, it did look nice!

By July seventh we had progressed from "Sure, we can get it done by the ninth" to "maybe we'd better postpone launching until the first of the week." On Monday, the twelfth, we had to reach a firm decision. Arrangements had to be made for a truck to transport *Trilogy* to the sea, and for a crane to lower her into the water. No more delays; no more postponements. Ready or not, here we come! Launching date would be July sixteenth, just ten days before we were to depart for Alaska.

We also needed to settle on a name for the boat. Jim wanted the name "*Trilogy*" because the trimaran was an opus in three parts and also because Eldon and his two sons had largely brought it into existence. Now it was imperative, for boat documents and a permanent name on the stern, that we make up our minds once and for all.

We had batted this name around for a long time, and somehow it had outlasted any other ideas. In our present state of exhaustion, we weren't likely to come up with anything more creative. *Trilogy* it would be. We engaged a sign painter to get it on the stern — that is, the stern of the middle hull —before the boat went in the water.

On Tuesday the building that had shielded the boat

from wind, rain, and snow, and that had concentrated the sunshine to broiling temperatures inside, was demolished. Jim, who probably had less reason than any of us to remember the shed with affection, took a fiendish delight in ripping it apart. Strange how much actual pleasure one can take in destroying something, especially if the destruction can be rationalized as progress.

As the walls went down, *Trilogy* emerged — white and beautiful, like a butterfly coming out of the chrysalis. It had been impossible to see all of the boat at once as long as the shed remained. Now we walked around her and admired her from every side, much as Michelangelo might have done with his statue of David. Her sides were smooth and shining, her curves sleek, her decks expansive, her bows proud and buoyant. We viewed our handiwork joyfully, finding it without flaw in our admittedly biased eyes. She had no masts or rigging, and there were countless interior jobs to be done, but to us at this moment she seemed complete and perfect.

It was a proud moment.

Time for gloating was all too short. Wednesday morning came and brought with it the realization that only two days remained before launching. First, the boat had to be raised sufficiently to allow a flatbed truck to run underneath. The jacking-up process began, and little by little the keel came up.

The keel had not been part of our original plans. After conferring with other trimaran owners, though, especially with those who had done deep-sea cruising, we were convinced that *Trilogy* would be easier to handle under sail and less subject to side-slipping with a substantial keel on the main hull. Norman Cross, another trimaran designer who had been putting keels on his boats for some time, helped us to design and build a skeg keel that added a few inches of depth but, because of built-in buoyancy, added no additional weight displacement. The keel also gave our wheel much better protection than it had before. In all our travels we would never have any reason to regret adding the keel.

It was nerve-wracking to me as approximately twenty tons of trimaran were inched aloft and timbers were stacked under the side hulls. The stacks of timbers grew to shoulder height, looking very haphazard to me, but Eldon kept assuring me that they were perfectly strong and stable.

No easy task it was, finding someone to haul *Trilogy* three blocks to the waterfront. The people we ultimately engaged were specialists in house-moving.

On Wednesday some of these men came to inspect the site and to look for difficulties that they might be expected to resolve. One of the most obvious of these was that the flatbed trailer would have to pass between two large fir trees at a sharp angle to get under the keel. What they would do after that puzzled me considerably because the boat was twenty-seven feet wide and the trees were only twenty feet apart. "No problem," the boss told me nonchalantly as he made notations in his little notebook. I only hoped they wouldn't find themselves in the tree-falling business on Friday.

By Thursday the atmosphere around our house was electric with tension. Tomorrow was "the big day," but in its own way this day was big enough. The truckers arrived to position the trailer on which *Trilogy* was to ride. Then, late in the afternoon, the ax fell — the big impediment we had been dreading, not knowing what it would be but hoping it would never happen.

There was no legal way to move the boat from our house along Bothell Way to the Kenmore intersection. Our movers had applied for a permit, and it had been denied.

We were thunderstruck; there was no by-way or alternative route that would accommodate twenty-seven feet of width. Eldon looked pale and more tired than I had ever seen him before. For the moment, he couldn't see any way out of this dilemma. Not so the boss of the trucking firm; he let his bad news sink in for a while, then started making plans, quite undaunted.

"You've got these alternatives," he decreed authoritatively. "One: move along the highway just before daylight when traffic is lightest. At worst, you'll only have to pay a fine. At best, you're home free. The chances are good that way; only three blocks of illegal road. Two: you can hire a helicopter. That will cost at least a thousand dollars, and I don't think you can get one capable of carrying this weight. Three: you can leave the boat here for twenty years while you try to get a legal permit."

None of those choices looked attractive, but certainly number one was the best. We had already checked out the possibility of using a helicopter, and no helicopter company even wanted to try it. Leaving the boat here through a long series of legal hassles was unthinkable. Eldon was uneasy. We were being forced to do something that he felt was indefensible both legally and morally.

"I really think we should pray about this," he told me, "but I can't. I can't ask the Lord to bless me breaking the law."

The movers were going ahead as though no decision was required on our part, and perhaps none was. When we had conceded in our own minds that number one was the only sensible choice, the die was cast. I was as uneasy as a bank robber planning his first big heist. Yet there was a strange element of excitement in knowing that what we were planning was illegal, and knowing we were going to do it anyway. It was more than a little disturbing to find that the cops and robbers game was fun — frightening, but fun.

The movers had enough red and amber lights to decorate a shopping center at Christmas time. Boat and truck were outlined in flashing red lights; the cars, front and rear, that would be used to block off the highway were equipped with amber flashers. Clearly, this was going to be a highly

visible procession whatever time of night we made the
journey. The lights did seem incompatible with our desire
to make the trip unobserved, but we really wanted to be
unobserved by only one group of people: the State Patrol.
Otherwise, we wanted to comply with all safety regulations. We had some friends in the State Patrol, also
trimaran enthusiasts, who had been watching our progress
with much interest. They had offered us an escort to our
launching site earlier, when none of us had any doubts
about the legality of the operation. We even considered,
briefly, telling them our problem and throwing ourselves
on their mercy, so to speak. But we couldn't ask for their
connivance in breaking the law; whatever law-breaking
we did was going to be our own responsibility.

The insurmountable legal problem was not the fact
that our obstruction would cover both lanes of highway,
but that an uncrossable median existed for most of the
three blocks. Theoretically, if a fire truck, ambulance, or
other emergency vehicle needed to pass, we would not be
able to clear a lane for it. In actual fact, there was scarcely
a spot where we could not pull aside enough to let
another vehicle by, but in theory the difficulty existed.

Upon such fine points of law are law-breakers created.

Jim drew up a detailed plan, labeling the cars A, B, C,
and D, and giving each one explicit instructions as to
their duties: guarding the rear of *Trilogy*'s truck/platform;
blocking the access roads; and making sure the truck
could turn left down to the Kenmore Sand and Gravel
Company, where the launching was to take place. Before
we went to bed, some time after midnight, all the lights
were connected and tested. Everything seemed as secure
as we could make it; still, we all retired with butterflies in
our stomachs.

At four a.m. the motorcade began forming. Misty-gray
in the half light, *Trilogy* lumbered out onto the highway at
4:30, miraculously missing the trees I had worried about,

red lights everywhere, and waddling to life like some prehistoric monster.

Traffic was at its lowest ebb — no cars in sight in either direction. Nor did the truck driver let any grass grow under his sixteen wheels. As soon as he reached the highway, he started moving with all possible speed, determined not to be caught in an illegal area. Randy rode on *Trilogy*'s bow and moved the traffic signals aside where they were not high enough to clear the truck-mounted bow and pulpit. By the time the Kenmore intersection was reached, two cars were following car D in the rear, wondering perhaps what strange object was ahead of them. That was the full extent of our traffic problems.

In five minutes — five long minutes I might say — it was all over. The truck, boat, and all cars were back on legal ground. The truck rolled to a stop at the edge of the gravel company's dredged canal, where a few hours later *Trilogy* would be lowered into the water. In my sudden and extreme relief at the successful completion of this tricky maneuver, I felt drained of all energy. I went back home and slept for three hours.

It was a shock when I arrived back at the launching site four hours later to find it a mass of feverish activity. People were everywhere. We had planned in the interest of efficiency to have as few onlookers as possible at this important moment, and not many of our closest friends knew the exact day. So it was a major surprise to find two TV crews on hand as well as numerous newspaper reporters. And not only the media — there were dozens of people everywhere, few that we had ever seen before. From a half-block distance I identified Eldon doing last-minute chores, Jim taking pictures, Rand on top of the boat checking the chain plates.

I tend not to worry much about things outside of my own area of expertise. If I let the experts handle all that stuff, I avoid an enormous amount of potential worries.

From Chrysalis to Butterfly

Unfortunately, just now I wasn't one hundred percent sure how reliable our experts were.

The chain plates are metal strips, secured through the cabin top, from which chains are attached so that the crane can lift the boat and lower it into the water. My inner worrying center told me that only the huge I-beams holding the hulls together could carry such stress. Randy had assured me repeatedly that the plates, chains, metal rings, and cabin top were capable of carrying two or three times the load that would be placed on them. Just the same, the fact that he was up there checking them over so carefully made me wonder if he had a few doubts, too.

Jim had been looking for me, because I was to have the honor of christening *Trilogy*. He was carrying a large, heavy bottle of champagne tied up in a nylon stocking. Sailors are a superstitious lot, reacting no doubt to the unpredictability of life on the sea. Anything but genuine champagne for the christening would be "bad luck." Even worse luck can be brought on by failure to break the bottle with the first whack.

"Hit it hard — really hard," he kept telling me. "You don't realize how difficult it is to break one of these bottles. They're made very thick because of the gas bubbles inside."

"I've dropped a number of bottles," I replied. "They always broke. "

"Not champagne." I could tell Jim felt that he just wasn't getting through to me. "Mom," he began, somewhere between exasperation and apprehension, "this is really important; I've seen several launchings where the bottle didn't break because some lady or child just tapped it on the bow. We're not going to let that happen!"

I used to play a lot of tennis when I was young, and I thought the old tennis arm could still vanquish one champagne bottle. "Don't worry, Jim," I told him, "I'll pretend that it's a tennis racket and I'm serving. Believe me, it will break!"

Trilogy

At last the crane hove into sight, chattering nervously down the gravel road. Well it might be nervous; before it got *Trilogy* into the water, it would come very close to tipping over. That would be my idea of an unlucky launching! The crane operator chose his site carefully, then swung his long boom over *Trilogy's* cabin, and Randy began attaching it to the chain plates.

Just as a ship on the marine ways is christened the moment before it begins its slide into the water, so *Trilogy* was to be officially named just before the crane started lifting her. My platform for the ceremony was to be the cab top of the truck that had delivered *Trilogy* to this site earlier in the day.

No ladders.

It must have been assumed that I was somewhat of an acrobat, but I am not. As I was removing my shoes (I realized immediately that climbing on top of this towering monster would require bare feet), I saw a TV cameraman training his sights on me. I picked up my shoes and walked over to him. "Please, don't take my picture while I'm climbing up on the truck," I begged. "It might add some humor to the proceedings, but I'd rather get along without that."

The cameraman laughed good-naturedly. "OKAY," he countered, "I won't shoot you getting up there if you'll signal me when you're ready to go."

Fair enough, and better than I expected. "Done." I shook his hand to seal the bargain and went back to climbing the dusty, yellow truck. It was really very sporting of him to desist.

Suddenly, standing on top of the truck cab with *Trilogy's* bow just about at eye level, I felt like Balboa as he viewed the Pacific Ocean for the first time. The realization struck me that this was truly a pivotal moment. This was the little isthmus between what we had accomplished so far and all that it portended for the future. Excitement bubbled up in me like the champagne I was holding in my hand. Jim was supposed to give me a signal when the christening was to begin, but right now he was looking everywhere except in my direction.

Time lengthens unaccountably in situations of stress. Eventually, though, he turned, raised his arm, and brought it down in a long sweep like someone signaling the beginning of a race; at the same time he pantomimed: "Hit it hard!"

I did. First I glanced at the cameraman, to be sure he caught the signal. The cameras were already rolling, so I swung the bottle with a good deal of force, saying in what I hoped was good nautical form, "I christen thee *Trilogy*! May you always have fair winds and safe harbors!"

Champagne flowed everywhere as the bottle broke in a most gratifying manner. I heard someone down below me saying, "What a waste! What a waste of good champagne!" There were some cuts in the bow, enough to require repairs, but it was a lucky christening in nautical tradition, and I retired from the field with honor. Fiberglass could be repaired; an unlucky christening, never — not in the age-old superstition regarding such things.

The crane-suspended chains began to tighten, and *Trilogy* rose into the air with Randy and Larry Christianson, commodore of the Northwest Multihull Association, on the front deck of the center hull. As exciting as it was for us to watch, it must have been doubly so for them as they teetered and swung twenty-five feet above the ground.

The crane's boom was extended to its maximum length, and still it hardly seemed there would be enough clearance to get the boat in the water. The crane was as close to the water as good footing would allow, but as the slow descent began, the crane tipped dangerously, at the absolute limit of its scope. Just a foot off the water, the boat seemed to hover for an agonizingly long time. Then, so quickly and skillfully that we could not tell exactly when it touched, it was lowered into the far northern end of Lake Washington.

We had been just a trifle uneasy; the crane operator was really sweating it. He told Rand later that the suspense was far worse for him than for us because he was afraid he would have to drop the boat to keep the crane from tipping over. Just as well we didn't know that at the time.

Pattie, Jim, Eldon, Dave, and Dick swarmed aboard the boat and rode on the front deck over to the other side of the canal, shouting and hugging each other. I had already had my moment of glory, so I was delegated to drive to the shopping center for more movie film.

Jim had run out of film at the crucial instant before *Trilogy* touched the water. So, in our movies of this momentous occasion, *Trilogy* hovers forever one foot above the water.

JIM'S COMMENT:
BUILDING THE *Trilogy*

When we were building the boat, I one day realized that the people I was working with — my dad and my brother — represented the closest male relationships that I was going to have in my life. Someday I might have a son, and he would join the group. But for now, these were the ones.

In fact, I notice that I still tend to describe my best friend-ships in these terms. He's like a brother to me. He's like a dad to me. At this point, I admit, he's like a son to me.

I got a hunger to get deeper into those relationships.

I had left home at fourteen. When I came back at twenty-four, I was quite a different person from the one my dad remembered. I was concerned that, if he got to know who I was, he might not even like me. Before I committed to building the boat with him, I had to settle that concern.

So we took a trip together, looking for boat designs and boat plans. While we traveled, we did quite a bit of sharing.

I remember at one point comparing bars with churches — that going to a bar was, for me, like going to church for him. I said, "You know, Dad, isn't it too bad though that we can't have that kind of fellowship? After all, I'm not going to church with you, and you're not going into a bar with me...."

He said, "Son, I'll go into a bar with you. I don't have any problem with that."

Now, that stopped me.

He said, "Look. You're a man living life the way that you think you ought to live it. I'm the same way. I'm not going to tell you how to live your life. You just have to live it the best you know how."

Coming back as adult, I was a lot more open to his wisdom. At that point, I knew that he generally loved me and that the things he was telling me were valid. I knew that, to the best of his ability, he was giving me good advice.

He told me, for example, that I wasn't a rich kid, that I was going to have to work my whole life. So it was really important for me to get happiness out of my work. Work is a blessing if you love what you do. He gave me lots of basic little homilies like that.

As time went on, I realized I had a lot more common ground with him than I had perceived. In fact, many years later he told me that he related to me more as his brother than as his son. (I must have been his older brother — because I took care of most of the business stuff.)

Trilogy

When we were building the boat, we'd start work at eight o'clock in the morning, take an hour off for lunch, an hour for supper, and work till midnight. We put in fourteen-hour days six days a week. The real dedication came the last four hours, after dinner on a cold night going out and putting in that last four hours. It was cold in the boat shed.

But every Friday night there was a pay-off. My folks were Seventh Day Adventists, so they stopped work from sundown Friday night to sundown Saturday night. On Friday night, then, we'd sit there on a little crossbeam above the boat. We'd look at that boat and see that it had grown. We'd tell ourselves it was the most beautiful boat that had ever been built. It was the same every week. The sun would be setting and we'd be sitting up there congratulating ourselves — what lucky guys we were to be doing this.

All of us wish we could get close to our fathers — to tap into that wisdom and not feel threatened by it. My dad let me realize that I totally was in control. He wasn't going to be offended if I didn't buy in.

Here I thought I was helping him out. But I was the one who was getting helped the most.

CHAPTER THREE:
NORTH TO ALASKA

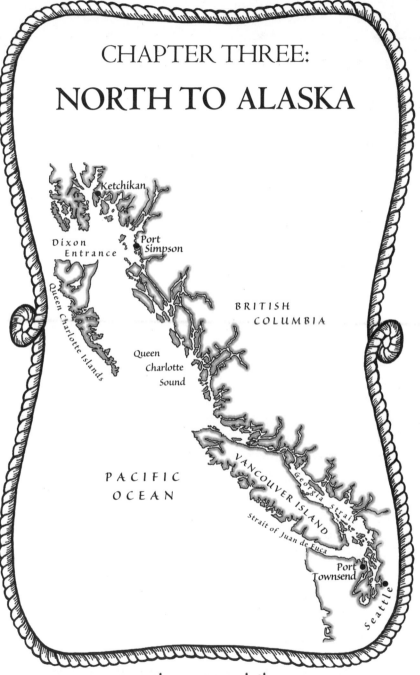

Seattle to Ketchikan

ur boat was tied up to an old barge, about seventy-five feet long and just waist high as one stood on *Trilogy's* deck. Last-minute jobs proliferated in inverse proportion to the amount of time that remained before we headed north, and sometimes various operations were spread out the full length of the barge.

It was dangerous to visit us at this time, especially for anyone with known and usable skills. Bill Kepner, a friend and kibitzer since we had begun building, came to check on our progress; he left some forty-eight hours later, dazed and spent, wondering how it had all happened. It was Bill's misfortune to be quite a jack-of-all-trades, and all his skills were needed.

Early in the week after launching, the masts were stepped — with a lucky penny underneath, of course — and the rigging attached. (It isn't that we're such a wildly superstitious bunch, really, but these are nautical traditions; that's just the way it's done.)

A professional carpet-layer created in one night the greatest transformation up to this time. It was all steps and angles—no job for an amateur. Although I was trying to finish putting up the padded headboards and wall covering in the bathrooms (nautically known as "heads"), most of my time seemed to be taken up going back to the house for tools or materials.

"Why can't you make out a list, at night, of all the stuff you're going to need the next day. Then, in the morning, you can check the list and bring what you need down to the boat?" I asked. It seemed reasonable to me. In reply, though, I got a collective look that questioned my basic intelligence. I kept on commuting.

Eldon was spending his time on plumbing, electrical systems, and endless machinery. Jim and Rand were installing bathroom fixtures, stove, refrigerator. We now had a galley that was functional to all appearances, but we had no time to try it out. Pattie was helping by serving meals at all hours to people who were too tired to know what they were eating.

On Sunday July twenty-fifth, the day before our first charter cruise was scheduled to begin, I began buying groceries. The list was lengthy, and when I was about halfway through it, the store closed. The manager apologized but said he had an emergency on his hands that would make it impossible for him to stay and let me finish my shopping. I had several shopping carts filled with staples, but so far nothing imminently perishable. So I left the carts in his keeping and went down to the boat wondering how everyone would react to no groceries.

I needn't have worried; with communication at its most disorganized, no one had thought to tell me that departure had been postponed another day.

Some members of our charter group had already arrived and were getting nervous about the unready state of the boat — and well they might be, considering the general look of chaos aboard *Trilogy*. Tuesday, already one day past our deadline, we moved the boat over to Lake Union and filled the tanks with water and oil. The guests moved most of their suitcases aboard the boat, but wisely decided to sleep ashore one more night.

At eleven o'clock I talked Randy and Eldon into going back to the house and getting something to eat. The house was now several miles distant, but it was still where we lived, theoretically. While I was heating up some soup, the two of them threw themselves down on the floor to rest for five minutes. When I came to call them, they were in such deep sleep that they couldn't even hear me. I threw a light quilt over them, turned off the stove and the light.

No doubt they would be angry with me in the morning, but right now they were getting some much-needed sleep.

They woke up at six o'clock, appalled at having slept so long, but they both looked so much better that I couldn't be sorry. We were meeting Mr. and Mrs. Harrison and the rest of their charter party at Fisherman's Wharf, and as we passed under the Fremont Bridge, the bridge-keeper leaned down from his lofty height and shouted, "She looks beautiful!" Of course we knew he meant *Trilogy* — who else? — and it gave us an unexpected lift.

Never had we started a trip of any kind with so much untested equipment. The galley stove had never been turned on; not a sail had been unfurled; the boat motor had only run from Kenmore to the oil dock and on to Fisherman's Wharf. Eldon and I had owned a ketch-rigged sailboat, the *Beverly B.*, for seven years, but the rest of the crew had had no experience sailing.

On the plus side, Eldon had made the trip from Seattle to Ketchikan and back at least fifty times in boats of all kinds, from a twenty-foot power boat to a freighter well over four hundred feet in length. In addition, he had dozens of charts, logs, and other paraphernalia of coast-wise navigation, including the famous *Hanson's Handbook*, which is to navigating the Inside Passage what *Bowditch* is to celestial navigation.

Randy was to be the chef on this trip. The all-male crew could bunk in one stateroom, leaving three state-rooms for the charter party.

While the boat and the boys were in Alaska, Pattie and I were going to drive over to Idaho. My parents had been insisting that I come over to see them for what I'm sure they thought would be the last time. They are not seagoing people, and the whole idea of building a three-hulled boat and then sailing the Pacific with rather nebulous plans for the future must have seemed the sheerest insanity to them.

Three days after the boat left, some of Pattie's friends who were driving to Ketchikan invited her to go along. Her grandparents didn't have a chance; Pattie hadn't seen her friends in Alaska since we'd moved to Seattle almost two years before. Besides, Pattie thought it would be a great joke on everyone if she met them on the dock when *Trilogy* came into Ketchikan Harbor.

Trilogy's maiden voyage started auspiciously. Randy lighted the galley stove for the first time at eleven thirty a.m. and served lunch soon after twelve. Everything worked perfectly. A euphoric and entirely false sense of security settled over everyone. Truly, this maiden voyage was going to be a genuine shake-down cruise, but at the moment it seemed as though nothing could go wrong. Even Eldon relaxed and began to enjoy the beautiful summer day on Puget Sound.

Just past Port Townsend a little breeze came up, and Jim, Dave, and Rand all had a chance to show how inexperienced they were at handling sails. At one point, Dave was almost carried overboard hanging onto the Genoa sheet, and in the process lost one of our expensive winch handles. Then, scarcely had they gotten the sails aloft and trimmed when the breeze totally vanished.

On the second day out, while they were navigating the Strait of Georgia, Jim decided to do some diving, mostly for fun but partly to check out the submerged portion of the hulls. It was a memorable decision, of the sort that leaves you mopping your brow, suddenly wet, and thinking, "What if I hadn't?"

As he lightly touched the hull, coming up from his initial plunge, he felt a strange electrical shock. More curious than worried, he dove down again and checked the zinc plates that had been put on only six days before. They were practically eaten away! This was startling enough, but further scrutiny revealed that the rudder shaft was already eaten halfway through by an incredible amount of electrolysis.

As soon as Jim could get his father alone for a moment, he told him what he'd found below the surface. "I can't imagine what's causing this," he said. "There must be a direct short somewhere; we've got to find it."

"Not easy," Eldon replied. "It doesn't matter if the zinc plates get eaten up; that's what they're there for. But the shaft is another matter. If only half of its diameter is left, that means it has a lot less then half its strength. Any strain could break it now."

If you are far out to sea and the rudder shaft breaks, you can probably jury-rig something until you get back into port — but in the narrow Inside Passage, the rocks are too close. You must be able to steer your boat.

Without alarming his passengers, Eldon tossed off a nonchalant remark about having a little electrolysis and perhaps they'd better run in to Campbell River and take a look — no big deal. The charter party was delighted with the prospect of going ashore and getting some exercise.

Only those who knew the extent of the problem, but hadn't a clue to the answer, were not so happy.

Cautiously, Eldon motored into Campbell River, where Jim removed the rudder and, with fortune smiling on him, found a machine shop that was able to repair it early the next day. Meanwhile a very careful check was made of all electrical systems and their grounding. This was no casual or routine check; they hunted for the culprit as if they had an ax murderer hiding aboard. Still, there was no guarantee that they had found the trouble and corrected it. There comes a time, however, when you have to put everything back together and hope for the best. When you have a charter party aboard, that time comes soon.

As soon as the rudder was back in place, the trip resumed with beautiful weather and a general feeling among the passengers that a stop for a few hours exploring this little Canadian town had been exactly what they needed. For the crew, the proof of whether they had done their work well would be the amount of electrolysis that showed up in the future.

When the new zinc plates remained relatively intact, they all breathed a sigh of relief.

⚓

The following day brought good sailing weather on Queen Charlotte Sound, the longest stretch of open water on the Inside Passage, and the deck hands began to seem a little less awkward. The time would come before many months when they would change sails, tack, trim, or reef with professional smoothness, but it had not quite arrived yet.

There were stops at several picturesque coastal towns, especially Bella Bella, where there is a spectacular waterfall, beautiful in spite of the ever-present rain and also because of it. In general the weather was fair; there was just one thing wrong with it — no wind, consequently not much sailing. The motor and the galley stove had been using unmeasured quantities of oil. Just south of Port Simpson they both stopped — a clear case of miscalculation and negligence on the part of a red-faced captain, who had never run out of fuel before on any kind of boat. It was just another of those things for which a shake-down cruise is noted, something that will never happen again after all the unknowns have been tested.

The winds were light, but sufficient for headway under sail; so the situation was more embarrassing than dangerous. The boat ghosted along at two or three knots until Eldon was able to hail a passing seine boat and get enough fuel to run on into Ketchikan. In a town where one hundred fifty inches of rain annually is average and a wet year easily goes over two hundred, not many days are as beautiful as this one was, with brilliant sunshine splashing down through skies of clear, cloudless blue. Foliage still wet from the last shower reflected and refracted the light like a hundred thousand diamonds.

Pattie, many old friends, and a warm welcome were waiting as *Trilogy* eased up to the dock in Ketchikan Harbor. To Eldon, Jim, and Randy it was coming home, yet with a pang of nostalgia because it was home no longer.

⚓

My trip over to see my parents was enjoyable, but sad. They were a little like the famous story of the hen who raised ducks. My brother was in Montana supervising a building project for the engineering firm he owned jointly with his partner; my younger sister lives in California, and I was planning to cruise the uncharted wastes of the Pacific in what might as well have been a rowboat as far as their concept of its safety was concerned.

"Why did my children have to scatter all over the Earth?" my mother wailed. "I have any number of friends whose children live right around here. Why do mine have to go so far away?"

I knew this was mostly directed at me because she had managed Montana as well as most of the Northwest on Walter's schedule, and California was old stuff. Marilyn had lived there for twenty years. Besides, though I didn't need to point it out, my older sister lived in practically the next town. The thing that made it sad was that I could see they were getting older. Mama was seventy-five and Dad seventy-nine — no longer as young or as healthy as they had always been.

⚓

68

North to Alaska

I was back in Kenmore by the first of September, but *Trilogy* still delayed coming south. Eldon had some work for the boat out of Ketchikan. Jim had signed as skiff man on a seine boat, work that he had done before off and on. Rand was doing some building projects out at Gildersleeve's logging camp. They all felt the need to make some money because, at best, we would be starting our long voyage on a shoestring.

It had been our plan to be traveling toward California by the middle of September. After the autumn equinox, the weather is likely to produce southeast winds and storms.

Early in September, Jim called. Of course, I asked why they weren't already headed south. Jim hesitated, "Well... Dad and Rand have kinda decided not to go on with our trip this fall. You know, make some money this winter, wait until spring. How do you feel about it?"

I was so shocked that I didn't answer immediately. I had a firm conviction deep in my soul that if we didn't do it now, we never would.

"Mom, are you still there?" Jim asked anxiously.

"I'm still here. Jim, I don't know what brought on this attack of cold feet or whatever it is, but my vote is 'do it now.' If we don't, I'm afraid we'll never do it, and we'll spend the rest of our lives with a lot of vain regrets."

"Whoopee!" Jim was suddenly shouting in my ear, "Hallelujah! I was hoping you'd say that! I'm all for going ahead right now while there's nothing stopping us. If you're for it, I can convince Dad and Rand. It's up to you to work on Pattie."

"Well, all I can say is get yourselves down here pronto, and I'll take care of Pattie."

I sounded much more confident than I really was. Pattie had never had much enthusiasm for prolonged travel, and she really wanted to go right on to college with her high school friends. But just now I had to sound confident and get the rest of the family at least this far south before the winter storms made boat travel hazardous.

Jim was just about to ring off, sounding euphoric; however, I knew that ultimately whether or not the boat left Ketchikan soon would be up to Eldon.

"Jim, just a cotton-picking minute! Tell Dad to call me. You're all supposed to be in Dick's wedding party, and I hope you haven't forgotten that he and Pat are getting married on the twelfth."

"I know; I know," Jim answered. "We'll be down there on the twelfth, come hell or high water." And truly they had some of each, leaving Ketchikan in a howling gale and arriving less than two hours before the wedding. Dick had gotten his acceptance from medical school and would be starting classes just about the time *Trilogy* would be heading for Mexico and beyond, but we hoped he and his wife Pat would be able to catch up with us somewhere in the world.

⚓

Convincing Pattie that she should travel with the rest of the family proved to be a very unwieldy task. Just when I thought she was yielding to the sweet voice of reason, she would say something like "OKAY If I have to, I have to. But as soon as I'm eighteen, I'm going to fly back and go to college."

Although Pattie is very bright, with a rather formidable IQ, I knew her primary interest in higher education was not in studying per se. It never had been, to the frustration of many teachers who tried to make her do a better job of living up to her potential. But I felt that if she would give the cruising life a fair trial, she would find it just as exciting as college.

At last, in desperation, I made a bargain with her: "If you sail with us for three months and at the end of that time you're still irrevocably decided against it, you can go back to school. Whatever you decide, I'm going to sail with the rest of the family. Your father and your brothers have worked very hard to make this happen, and I'm not going to let one person defeat all their plans."

This relieved Eldon and the boys of a secret worry; they had been afraid that if Pattie refused to go, I wouldn't go either. All our plans had been made with the idea we would be traveling as a family. If even one of us wasn't there, it wouldn't really be a family cruise.

Life proceeded to get even more hectic as we worked frantically to get everything packed and into storage, clean up all evidences of boat-building on the premises, and leave the property in its original condition. I don't know now that it would have made that much difference. Soon after we left, the property was sold and the house, trees, beautiful shrubbery, and all were bulldozed over and carted away; more than half of that lovely wilderness area was covered with concrete — sad story of our civilization.

⚓

On October first we moved onto the boat at Shilshole, still going back to the house every day to finish up our work there. It seemed as though we were never going to finish.

One more thing needed to be done before we left for balmier climates. After all the kindness we had been shown by the Northwest Multihull Association, collectively and individually, we needed to give the club an opportunity to see the finished *Trilogy*. On October fifth they were meeting at Shilshole, so we issued a general invitation to include a visit as part of the meeting agenda.

Neatness and order reigned as they would not ever again, probably, in the foreseeable future. Everything that could be polished shone brightly, and the mahogany paneling of the cabin glowed under the soft lights. Shamelessly, we accepted all the praise heaped upon us by the Multihull members.

Trilogy

It is so hard not to believe the most extravagant compliments about your beloved; they seem the merest statements of fact.

Just when it seemed that we were at last ready to go, fog settled down, thick, impenetrable and apparently immovable. Cautiously, we made our way over to the oil dock and took water and oil aboard. One day passed with frustrating slowness, then two. Still the radio reported thick fog as far as Port Townsend. Eldon had traveled in Alaska many times in fog as dense as this, never slackening speed and making completely blind turns into new channels, but he'd always known the exact speed of his boat and of the current. He was by no means as familiar with this boat, and he refused, in spite of any amount of grumbling from the crew, to venture out.

On the evening of the third day, Commodore Larry Christianson came back from a trip north of town and informed us that the fog was noticeably thinner farther up the channel.

"C'mon! Let's go for it!" Dave shouted, all his pent-up frustration coming out in italics. We couldn't actually prove that visibility was much better than before, but we so fervently wanted it to be that we convinced ourselves it was. Eldon started the motor.

Then a quick head count revealed that Jim wasn't aboard.

"When that guy comes," Eldon promised grimly, "he's just going to have time to jump on board. It might even be a pretty good-sized jump!"

Fifteen minutes later, Jim came strolling nonchalantly down the dock. True to his word, Eldon had the lines cast off and made Jim take a good, flying leap to the deck.

Jim was so totally "stoked" to find us actually on our way that he was not at all discomfited. Probably he would have taken a flying leap at that moment just out of exuberance. We were off on the greatest adventure of our lives.

North to Alaska

PATTIE'S COMMENT:
NOT EXACTLY MY DREAM

The frenzy of getting ready for the Alaska charter was over. I couldn't believe that I'd gotten used to strangers coming and going in our house at all hours, day or night. Speaking as someone who guarded her privacy fiercely, it was disconcerting to come face-to-face with yet another bearded, bedraggled, and blurry-eyed guy coming out of our bathroom or kitchen. Fortunately, no one was ever there who wasn't supposed to be. Then again, if he had been, Dad would have put him immediately to work, thanking God for another pair of hands!

Suddenly there was no more yelling, hammering, door-slamming, or Moody Blues music blaring at multi-decibels. It felt eerie and lonely. All they left was the enormous sound of silence and an even more enormous mess.

Mom wanted to sleep for about two months and then go visit my grandparents in Idaho. I wanted to visit all my friends before I took off on this trip, from which I wasn't sure I would ever return.

I'd turned seventeen in April and had graduated from high school in May. Except for spending the first part of the summer helping to get the boat launched and ready to charter, I hadn't been basing my life on *Trilogy*. I'd been in school.

The family had gone back and forth about cruising, but no plans were definite and no one knew exactly when we would do this. I viewed the whole thing as Jim and Randy's project to get Dad back on his feet again. Because I was in boarding school, I was not only physically removed from the boat-building operation but emotionally removed as well.

Trilogy

The move from Ketchikan to Seattle two years previous had been extremely difficult for me. Because of my past abandonment issues, home was very important. I still vividly remember being five years old, when Randy and Mom and I were about to move to Washington for a year so Mom could go back to school. When everyone was finishing packing, I quietly slipped outside and went around to the corner of the house where no one could see me. I pressed myself against the corner and stretched my little arms out as far as they would reach. I can still feel the scratch of the shingles against my face as I hugged our house good-by. As the tears rolled down my cheeks, I could feel our big, safe house hugging me back.

Twelve years later, making a move felt just as difficult. After two years in Seattle, I finally felt accepted, part of a group. Sailing off to the South Pacific for an indefinite period of time was not at the top of my list of personal priorities. When Jim sat me down and explained that the success of the trip depended on every family member going, he placed an awesome responsibility on my shoulders; I didn't feel as though I had much choice. This was Jim, Rand, and Dad's dream — they'd toyed with it during the almost two years of boat construction — but it wasn't mine. Now I had to make it mine, and quickly, too. My head said that this was a once-in-a-lifetime experience; my heart wanted just to stay in the place that now felt like home.

It took me some time to decide that I would be a willing participant in this adventure. Once I did, once I'd put my college plans aside, I began to realize that there might be other, even better, plans than the ones I'd made for myself.

CHAPTER FOUR:
THE FIRST LEG

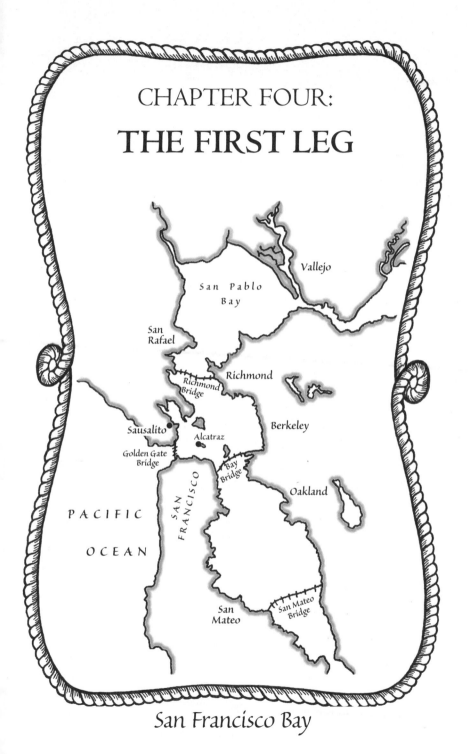

San Francisco Bay

og was still lying in thick and thin layers as we left Shilshole and pointed *Trilogy's* bow toward Port Townsend. Even when we found ourselves momentarily in a clear patch, there wasn't much visibility because fog banks were ahead and behind us. Prudence seemed to dictate that it would be wise to go into the harbor there for the night. Before we got there, however, two things happened. First, the fog began to thin out perceptibly, and second, we met the trimaran *Born Free* heading back into Seattle.

Art Erickson and his all-girl crew were supposed to be well on their way to Hawaii. Less than a week ago, they had left Shilshole in a blizzard of publicity and high spirits; here they were back again.

We pulled up alongside. Boatmen are merciless with one another, and we demanded all the details concerning his defection. Art was weary and defeated, and his answer to our questions was laconic: "Storms, unfavorable winds, and..." (with a shamefaced grimace) "I was seasick the whole time."

We swept on, showering him with good wishes for a better trip next time, but at the same time feeling more adventurous than ever. I might indeed be seasick, at some future date — I had been many times in the past — but I knew our trip would continue whether I kept to my bunk or not. Jim, Randy, and Pattie had all been introduced to ocean travel before they were a month old. Whether or not that makes a difference, I don't know, but not one of them has ever been seasick.

Neither has Eldon; maybe it's just heredity. If so, they certainly knew which parent to pick!

By the time we reached Port Townsend, the stars were out. There was no sign of fog, and the lights of the town glittered like diamonds on black velvet. This was no time to stop; we swept around the point and headed mostly west on the Strait of Juan de Fuca.

The following evening we spent with Keene and Helen Gau, just back from twenty-seven months of travel down the coasts of Mexico, Panama, French Polynesia, New Zealand, and Pitcairn Island. In their Port Angeles home on a cliff eighty feet above the water, we watched their movies, listened to the pounding surf below, and felt as though we were in Bounty Bay or Bora Bora.

Helen and Keene knew about the return of *Born Free* and felt it almost as a personal affront. "If you do that," Helen warned fiercely, "don't stop here on your way back. I won't want to see you!"

⚓

The weather was calm, clear, and totally windless as we motored toward Neah Bay and then out around Cape Flattery. While we had reason to feel lucky that the autumn southeasters hadn't hit in early October, there was a greasy stillness over the water; no stray breeze stirred. A palpable uneasiness breathed in the atmosphere, as though Nature were holding her breath, pulling back for some gigantic change. I've felt the same thing on the periphery of a hurricane.

Dave was not accustomed to ocean travel and was definitely not in tune with the weather. He felt swindled, chugging along on a glassy sea with nothing happening.

"I thought life on the bounding deep would be more exciting," he complained. "I could do more bounding than this in my back yard."

I was getting some strange vibrations from the eerie stillness, though. Looking around at the rest of the family, I knew they were, too.

"It's right in the process of changing," I said. "I think you'll have all the bounding you want before we get to San Francisco."

By morning we had a good sailing breeze, and it gradually increased to forty-knot winds. Soon we were getting gusts up to sixty knots. Fortunately, the Genoa had been replaced with a working jib early in the afternoon, but by the time darkness came down it was apparent that we also needed to reef the mainsail. This proved to be difficult and dangerous for our inexperienced crew, although they finally managed it.

All night we were surfing on mountainous seas, averaging fifteen knots but probably doing twenty on the more spectacular runs. The cacophony of wind-filled rigging combined with the roar of our free-spinning propeller made me feel as though we were shut up in a wind tunnel with a couple of belligerent locomotives.

I had taken the precaution of getting marezine suppositories before we started the trip; I didn't really think I would need them on a trimaran but brought them along anyway. They did keep me from tossing my cookies, but they also made me feel as though I were just coming out of an anesthetic. Nor was my peace of mind improved by Jim, Rand, Dave, and Eldon running around over the deck above me, sounding like some weird dance of elephants. Each time I heard a big thud, I was sure someone had hit the deck and fallen overboard.

Eldon was enjoying himself hugely. To one who had weathered eighty knot winds at Cape Chacon or in Lynn Canal, these were not dangerous wind or sea conditions. When I occasionally poked my head outside, he said, "C'mon out here, honey; it's just like riding a roller-coaster!"

I did worry about someone falling overboard. It seemed

to me that the rope railing around the outside of the boat was decidedly flimsy. In the morning I cornered Jim for a minute and suggested that some precautions be taken.

"Such as?" Jim asked, both wary and defensive, knowing that his experience with boats in storm conditions far exceeded mine.

"Such as, we could shorten sail while we still have some daylight, so if someone falls overboard, we'd have some chance of finding him"

"Sometimes we could," Jim conceded. "Not all the time. Yesterday we should have, without a doubt. Most of the time we just have to be careful. You know the old sailor's maxim: One hand for the boat; one hand for yourself."

"That means that you're either hanging onto something or have a safety line attached. I didn't see any of that last night."

"That's true, and it was foolhardy," Jim agreed.

"OKAY, so we're pretty lucky nothing happened. If someone had fallen overboard last night, do you think we could have rescued him?"

"Not a chance," Jim replied with a frown. "On a night like last night — no way."

It seemed to me that only by the grace of God had we come through the night with our little company intact. In the future, I wanted to be sure that we didn't presume on the tradition that He looks after children and fools.

"Just think of this ship as though it were a thousand feet up in the air," I cautioned, knowing it was probably futile but unable to help myself. "Think how carefully you'd walk with only that little rope between you and a thousand-foot drop. Your chances at night in a storm aren't any better. All of you have to be more careful."

Like all parents of teenage and post-teenage children, I was accustomed to being tuned out most of the time when I was trying to give advice; I only hoped some of it had been heard. Jim walked away looking thoughtful, and later in the day I heard him giving Dave the same lecture, almost word for word. Good, I thought. Next to Jim, Dave was probably the most careless on deck. Dave would take this kind of advice much better from Jim than from me. And as for Jim — the life he saved may have been his own.

⚓

As evening approached, the wind decreased noticeably, although we still had a brisk sailing breeze. Somewhere about two hundred miles to our left should be the coast of northern California. Eldon is a coastwise rather than celestial navigator, and he decided he would rather be closer to recognizable headlands. Turning south by southeast, we sailed through the night on a course that would take us to the Golden Gate.

In the morning, we had to find out where we were and how far and how fast we had come during the thirty hours of storm. By this time, Randy was studying *Bowditch* assiduously; he wasn't going to be in a position where Jim always had the last word. Using charts, compass, and all pertinent gear, our navigators (plural) determined that we had made an arc of about four hundred fifty miles during the storm, which meant that our speed had averaged fifteen knots.

I was quite sure that I would prefer to travel at not more than half that speed. Jim and Eldon, however, had found the storm, and the way the boat handled the storm, both reassuring and exhilarating.

"The most exciting ride I've ever had," Jim said. "The only other ride I can think of that could compare with it was on a friend's Honda when I was thirteen. It took off, and I didn't know how to stop it; all I could do was hang on."

Anyone who had heard Eldon whooping and hollering while he steered the boat knew how he felt about it.

Dave had wanted adventure, but now he wasn't sure that he liked this particular kind of adventure. "It was scary," he admitted, "especially if you're not into boats too much."

While Eldon insisted that we had been in no danger, it wasn't perhaps the best initiation for someone who hadn't been on the water before. Actually, Dave had learned a very important lesson about high adventure: it's great in anticipation or retrospect, but it's something to be grimly endured at the time.

In the evening, we idled along the coast of California, waiting to go under the Golden Gate Bridge at slack water. The bridge was exquisitely beautiful at night, outlined with twinkling lights. Still, we had one bad moment when it looked as though our mast was going to touch. It was an optical illusion, but it's hard to deny the evidence of your senses. Everyone breathed a small sigh of relief when we were safely in the clear.

Our anchor went down close to the Sausalito Yacht Club. Eldon always has a yacht club membership from someplace, and such things are reciprocal. Hot showers and other amenities were beginning to look very attractive.

For the first time in years, I found myself afflicted with "sea legs." At first I attributed it to the constant passage of boats not far away, some of them kicking up quite a wake. But when I went up to my sister's house the following morning, the swaying motion didn't stop.

Every day my sister and I spent some time shopping; there were so many little things we might need some time during our trip. The *Seven Seas Bulletins* and also Helen Gau had warned us to have a good supply of elastic aboard — good, live rubber to hold up against the intensity of tropical weather, not any synthetic stuff. We'd all brought clothing that depended on elastic to stay in place. If it didn't do its job, we might find ourselves surrounded by falling objects at the most inconvenient — and embarrassing — times.

Good elastic wasn't easy to find, but Marilyn knows a lot about shopping in San Francisco. Eventually we found what we wanted. We rounded up bungee cord, too, at a marine supply store. We used bungee cord everywhere to fasten in books and many other small objects that might make a quick trip to the floor in heavy weather.

After a few months of travel, I decided that tough use, not the tropical climate, was really responsible for the short life of elastic on cruising boats. The bungee cord kept its spring forever. The elastic, though, which was exposed to harsh soap and sunshine as well as sweaty bodies, had to be replaced fairly often.

Also, we all needed some lightweight cotton clothing. After so many years in Alaska and then in Puget Sound, we had forgotten how warm it gets in southern climates. Marilyn gave me some shorts and sun tops that she was sure I would need when we got into still warmer latitudes. I accepted them, although I was sure I wasn't likely to wear them.

Soon enough, I was wearing them most of the time — either that or a bathing suit.

⚓

Sunday we took our friends and relatives in the San Francisco area for a ride on *Trilogy*. I think Eldon had more nightmares and cold chills over that Sunday than almost any experience of his life. Most of our guests were quite unaware of any crisis, and even Eldon, modest as he is, hated to disparage his seamanship before our assorted passengers; at the time, he passed it off very casually.

Dave summed it up quite well when he said, "It wasn't really anyone's fault — or else it was everyone's, because we all should have seen it coming. But after this, in a crisis, we should have just one boss, not three!"

We had been sailing for two hours, past Alcatraz, up toward Richmond Bridge, over to the Golden Gate, and back toward the skyscrapers of San Francisco. A little monohull challenged us to a race that we won easily. It was while we were resting on our laurels, a bit overconfident, that it happened.

There were enough people around to create some distractions, and enough boats in the area to create a lot more. Suddenly, out of nowhere, a big gray-green tanker with a rusty, bulbous nose was bearing down on our starboard side — coming fast. Our present course would carry us directly across their bow.

Eldon wanted to fall off toward port, which would presumably get us out of their way. But Jim, at the helm, was afraid we would be stranded in the steamer's path if we lost our wind; there was no time to start the motor.

Jim chose to continue on our course straight across the tanker's bow.

"Relax, Dad," he said. "We're in no danger."

That was definitely debatable; the ship disagreed sharply, and gave us a series of staccato whistles. Thirty seconds after we crossed the center point of that bulbous bow, the tanker swept by, much too close for comfort, and with no charitable thoughts toward a spunky little trimaran.

Jim may well have been right. He insists that he did the only safe and sensible thing, though it was a highly illegal maneuver. We did escape with our lives, but that doesn't necessarily prove him right. Since that time the merits of the case have been discussed over many a dinner table, deck, and campfire. Like armchair generals who never lose a battle, Jim, Rand, and Eldon have second-guessed the whole scenario many times without proving anything except possibly, as Jim says:

"You just need a cool man at the helm." .

Although Jim came through our near clash with the tanker showing great aplomb, he had an experience a few days later that left him considerably shaken. He had been over in the business district shopping for boat supplies, and because public transportation was both circuitous and expensive, he decided to hitch-hike back to Sausalito.

Trilogy

At his first unobtrusive indication that he would like a ride, a sports car screeched to a stop and the driver said, "Get in." It was the last really intelligible thing he would say during the entire trip.

The driver was a huge man, huge both in length and width, and he drove hunched over the wheel of the little sports car, practically enveloping it. Not so much as glancing at his passenger, he began as though he were already in the middle of a conversation: "They're teaching me medicine; I never knew I was going to be a doctor... I've got it in my fingers..." Here he lifted his hands off the wheel for a long moment while he inspected them thoroughly; the gesture was a bit disconcerting because they were moving in heavy traffic.

"I have to have these injections in my fingers... there was gas in the car; they must have known I'd be leaving today... I never knew I was going to be a doctor... why would they leave gas in the car? You have to follow the pattern," he continued, weaving from lane to lane. "It's all in the pattern. I get it all through my fingers." Again, the fingers, six inches above the steering wheel, were inspected for a heart-stopping length of time.

This disjointed monologue continued all the way to Sausalito. Jim was beginning to wonder how he was going to get the driver's attention, or if he was going to have to make a jump for it. Suddenly, and quite rationally, the driver asked, "Where do you want to get out?"

"Right here," Jim replied weakly. To his tremendous relief, the car pulled to a stop. Jim wasted no time getting out; he could never decide for certain whether he had been entertained by an escapee from a mental institution or whether the whole thing was an elaborate put-on, intended to cure hitch-hiking.

Either way, it was undeniably effective.

⚓

The First Leg

On Wednesday, October twenty-seventh, we tried to get some good sailing pictures of *Trilogy* with the Golden Gate Bridge in the background.

Eldon and Randy positioned themselves on the Sausalito breakwater, and the rest of us sailed back and forth, trying to keep wind in the sails because they don't look very impressive when they're luffing. Eldon had taken his four-by-five camera, long his stand-by for commercial photography, but it had no telephoto lens. He kept motioning us to come closer; we could see rocks plainly under the hulls and were uneasy enough without getting closer to shore. It was a complete stand-off — Eldon refusing to take pictures unless we approached nearer than appeared safe; we staying where we were.

Eldon came back on board, frustrated and huffy. "Next time I'll sail the boat and you can take the pictures," he told Jim. "I can't get anything if you won't bring the boat within a half mile!"

"Tell you what," Jim offered. "I'll get you a telephoto for that thing; it'd be a lot cheaper than wrecking the boat."

With a look of pure exasperation, muttering something about "a bunch of panty-waists on this boat," Eldon went below decks.

By the time we got the pictures developed in San Diego, both of them had forgotten that Eldon swore he had no pictures worth developing. In fact, the pictures were much admired, and we decided to use one of them for our Christmas card.

⚓

Shortly before noon, we swept under the Golden Gate Bridge outward bound, and no one worried about having enough clearance for our sixty-foot mast. We soon found, though, that the water was behaving very differently from the way it had on our arrival. They call this stretch of water "The

85

Potato Patch," and it's notorious for being rough. The water seemed to be standing up in white triangles.

Oops! I thought. All this time in harbor had made my tummy forget its training. I headed for the marezine.

Lou Flagg, a Baptist youth minister, and his wife Sue were hitching a ride down to Santa Cruz with us. It wasn't long before Sue began looking pale, so I got her some marezine, hoping it wasn't too late to be effective.

Lou, who had at one time been a sailing instructor, was reluctant to confess that he had any queasy feelings, but his general appearance left no doubts in my mind. He finally allowed himself to be persuaded and accepted a suppository —but it was too late. He contributed generously to the deep. Then the well-known soporific effect of the medicine made itself felt. He stretched out on top of the after cabin, and had to put up with such witticisms as, "Who lowered the Flagg? We've just begun to fight!" or "Why is the Flagg at half-mast? Are we in mourning?"

Randy asked, "Don't you know that Flagg is improperly displayed? It's draped over the cabin."

People who don't get seasick have a strange habit of gloating in this way over those who do. Lou took it with groggy good nature for a while; then he clumped unsteadily off to bed, followed by one parting shot, "Is that Flagg waving again, or just wavering?"

Sue and I slept peacefully while *Trilogy*, with a brisk thirty-five knot wind, averaged ten knots all the way to Santa Cruz. Before the day was over, Lou, either by an unusually industrious metabolism or great effort of will — possibly both — overcame the effects of marezine and sea and was able to help with the sailing.

The wind seemed to be increasing as we neared Santa Cruz, and I was more grateful to the Flaggs than they ever knew. If it had not been necessary for them to stay aboard the boat until their friends arrived to take them home, we would have been slogging down the coast in the ever-escalating storm.

The absolute bliss of coming into a quiet harbor after a storm can only be appreciated properly by someone who has had that experience. In a small way, such a harbor is comparable to a hot shower and a freshly-made bed when one is very tired, or shade and a thirst-quenching drink after hiking through the desert. But these are incomplete analogies.

There is something more total about coming in out of a storm.

Your appetite returns; all the uncomfortable things turn magically into comfort again: the warm cabin, good food, fellowship and conversation, the security of a harbor, relief from stress. The change is so abrupt and so satisfying. Everyone glows a little, and they ask one another, "Wasn't that a great ride? Wasn't it fun?" And no matter what you were thinking during the storm, now, suddenly, you agree that it was a great ride, and fun.

For the past three hours a roast, put in the oven by one of my weather-resistant children, had been sending out a delicious and tantalizing odor. I roused myself from lethargy and, with Pattie's help, whipped up some mashed potatoes, a green salad, and green beans almondine. After dinner, everyone sat around in a pleasant haze of subdued euphoria, giving way bit by bit to genuine fatigue.

Early the next morning Jim went out and bought a local newspaper. Winds up to seventy-five knots were reported for the previous night, with considerable damage around the Bay area. Eldon still insisted that we would have made good weather of it, had we continued down the coast, and he was probably right to the extent that our lives would not have been in danger. But I don't like going through that kind of battering unnecessarily, and I secretly nursed a firm conviction that we were wise to stay in port.

It isn't that I worry about capsizing in a storm; I worry about the kind of human error that results in a man overboard. Violent weather is unforgiving, and who can say that he will never make that one misstep at a time when wind and sea may make him disappear forever?

Gradually diminishing winds still made plenty of noise all day in our rigging, but there was no ocean swell in the harbor. Here, the storm was a chained dog growling through the fence, not the wild beast it would be out beyond the breakwater.

Next day, we started out again with a wind still boisterous enough to give us a good push, but the real fury of the storm was over.

⚓

After three weeks at sea, and in and out of ports, we were all learning to conserve water. Jim was horrified when he discovered early one morning that someone, never identified, had left the fresh water tap slightly open in the galley and run out at least half of our fresh water.

"Just as soon as we get to San Diego, I'm going to make that impossible for the rest of the trip," he promised grimly.

Such an error a hundred miles offshore could be easily remedied; on a long sea passage, though, it could be fatal. Even without the terse lecture to which Jim subjected all of us, the implications were both obvious and ominous. I don't think I ever left a water faucet without double checking thereafter, nor did anyone else.

Lights, too, were an endangered resource. Eldon had fought a losing battle through the years to keep lights turned off when not in use, but now it was not a matter of a few extra dollars on the light bill. Overuse of our electricity might mean that the diesel engine wouldn't start in an emergency or that the water pump wouldn't run. Not having all the light we wanted might be a nuisance, but it didn't weigh heavily against survival. Everyone watched for lapses and were almost too quick about turning out the lights for one another.

"Are you through with this light?" Bang! Out goes the light without waiting for an answer.

"No, I'm not through with it; I just stuck my head out for a second. I'm going right back."

"OKAY, turn it on when you go back then." No apology or explanation was necessary. It had become a rule of life now, and no one felt hassled by it.

To this day, it really bothers me to see water wasted. In Alaska, the enormous rainfall made us unconcerned about it; quantities of the stuff were falling constantly, and rolling off the land into the ocean in countless rivers and creeks. But whatever prodigality I had developed there left me at this point, never to return.

⚓

As we sailed down the coast well offshore, we could see a huge cloud, yellow-brown and very dense, covering the entire coast from Ventura to San Diego and beyond. We watched it in disbelief. Finally Dave enunciated what we all were thinking:

"Did you know that there are millions of people breathing that stuff? Can you believe it?"

"I'm not sure I want to try breathing it," Pattie said apprehensively. "Maybe we could miss it entirely if we just go farther south instead of stopping in San Diego."

Jim and Rand gave her pitying, big-brother looks. "We have to stop in San Diego," Rand said. "We don't have passports or visas or any forms for clearing and entering foreign ports."

"Well, we didn't have any of those things when we went to Mexico before," Pattie argued. "We just drove across the border and they confiscated all our fresh fruit." Only ten at the time, she never had forgiven them for that, feeling that it was poorly disguised highway robbery.

Jim and Rand launched into a lengthy explanation of the difference between going into Mexico on a day trip and going from port to port for several months in a boat. She listened with admirable patience, although I suspected that she was receiving quite a bit more information than she wanted to acquire. In all this interchange, I heard something that no one else noticed: in spite of dire threats about jumping ship and going back to college, it sounded as though she was at least planning to go into Mexico with us.

Great, I thought. If she'll just stay with us long enough to give it a fair trial, we'll be okay

San Diego, however, nearly proved to be our nemesis as far as enrolling Pattie's support for future traveling. Instead of doing our final outfitting in a couple of weeks, as we intended, we spent nearly two months. This used up the largest part of the time I had offered Pattie as a trial period, and she found San Diego frustrating in the extreme. Because going uptown from our anchorage led through some of the worst sections of the city, Eldon and the boys agreed that she could not go unaccompanied. And because everyone else had less free time than she had, and no one was eager to interrupt work to escort her downtown, Pattie considered herself a prisoner of middle-class respectability. She was approaching the point of mutiny before we finally were able to move on.

Walt Wood, who had built a trimaran similar to *Trilogy* and sailed it down to San Diego several months earlier, loaned us a car to use during our stay. It was close to twenty-five years old and had apparently led an undisciplined if not totally abandoned life in recent years. A collection of bad habits held together loosely by tattered and rusty metal, she was given the name Hecuba; she looked as though she had been through the fall of Troy. We did appreciate the transportation, precarious as it was, but we seldom let ourselves get out of sight of a service station.

The doors wouldn't stay closed, water leaked out of the radiator almost as fast as we could fill it, and, worst of all, Hecuba had a pronounced aversion to shifting from neutral to low gear except at full throttle. Our take-offs from various runways were awesome, leaving spectators goggle-eyed (and leaving us rather limp). Even the most souped-up sports car seemed tame after Hecuba's roaring, door-flapping excursions. She had real personality, but constant association with her raffish ways tended to be wearing.

In addition to transportation problems, there was also the breakwater to be negotiated every day before going anywhere with or without an automobile. It was designed to be used by gymnasts or possibly chimpanzees. The metal ladders, always slippery from being submerged most of the time, slope outward at the top; so getting out on street level is like climbing out from under an overhanging cliff. I always required assistance from above as well as the hopes and prayers of anyone below me.

Then, one day when we all planned to go downtown and get our passport pictures taken, Hecuba disappeared. It happened between the time when Eldon finished coaxing her into running and the ten minutes it took to get us all from the boat to the breakwall. No doubt about it, the car was gone.

Because the police had towed it away without giving us any warning, they eventually decided we could have it back without paying any towing or storage charges, but this was a hollow victory. Hecuba steadfastly refused ever to start again, and Walt couldn't even drive it out of the storage garage.

Carless, we trudged uptown and got our passport pictures, and we began the plethora of paperwork required for leaving our homeland. We learned that Uncle Sam doesn't give a hoot about immunizations when you are outward bound, but he can be very picky when you try to get back into the country again. At the public health office, we began bringing our immunizations up to date, and learned to our amazement that Eldon had never had any — not even smallpox. Nor was that all.

Trilogy

He had no desire to start in now.

For a while, it was the irresistible force versus the immovable object. The public health office was well-filled that day, and most of the waiting public, having nothing more interesting to do, got involved in the argument. The overwhelming consensus of opinion was that one had better conform to governmental idiosyncrasies, both here and abroad, or give up any idea of extensive travel. Eldon finally capitulated, although he had many dark forebodings about all the dangerous and repulsive bugs being introduced into his bloodstream.

Even so, he couldn't help noticing that he felt better than the rest of us, who had been getting various immunizations all of our lives.

After Hecuba's demise, another ex-Alaskan, Clay Bliss, who was currently living in Van Nuys, loaned us one of his cars for a week. The next week, we rented a car from a place called Budget Rentals. It was surely not our budget they had in mind when they named that place, and we were soon on foot again. We were saved from total frustration and possible bankruptcy by Chet Novak, from Connecticut, who spent the best part of three weeks chauffeuring us from place to place in his Volkswagen bus, mostly out of the goodness of his heart, but possibly encouraged by three meals a day on *Trilogy*.

We spent forty-eight hours in a shipyard on Coronado Island undoing the damage done to the rudder shaft during our wild ride off the coast of Oregon and Northern California. And although we had been in the water less than six months, it seemed like a good idea to copperpaint the bottom again.

Our passports arrived — not by the twentieth of November as originally planned, but still in plenty of time. Our stay in San Diego seemed to be lengthening interminably; every week we thought would see us in Mexico, and still we found things that needed to be done first.

The First Leg

⚓

When we'd been in Sausalito, Greg and Fiona Dufus and their four children, ranging in age from four to fifteen, had anchored their boat close to ours. They'd come from Canada, with high hopes, some time before we ourselves had left Seattle. Along the way they'd run into a storm similar to the one we'd encountered, but with more serious consequences: Fiona had to be flown back to Canada for treatment of back injuries, and Greg, with four children to care for, was losing some of his impetus for extended cruising. By the time we left San Francisco, Fiona had returned with a back brace and many restrictions on her daily activities — restrictions that would be hard to obey in rough waters. Still, they had spent several years building *Ara Moana* and were not ready to give up their dream without giving it a fair trial.

They were made of sturdy stuff, those Dufuses.

One morning shortly before our departure from San Diego, I awoke with a strong feeling that the Dufus family was nearby. Certainly there was nothing in the immediate landscape to give that impression.

At breakfast, out of the blue, Jim said, "I wonder what happened to the Dufuses; they should have been here by now." This startled me. I hadn't mentioned to anyone my strange feeling that they were just over the horizon.

"I was just going to say the same thing!" Eldon exclaimed. "I dreamed about them last night. Not a good dream; they were having trouble."

"Well, I didn't dream about them," I chimed in, "but I woke up with a strong hunch that they were nearby. I even went out on deck to see if they had come into the harbor." It was indeed odd that they were hovering there in all our minds when we hadn't mentioned them for weeks.

A few minutes after three o'clock in the afternoon it became clear why we had been having this back-of-the neck feeling; the *Ara Moana* came limping into harbor, having had a troubled passage down the coast. Elspeth, fifteen years old and the only one of the children who was really old enough to help with the sailing, had broken her leg. Eldon's troubled dream was not far from the truth. Greg was exhausted and discouraged; Fiona, still unable to carry most of the responsibilities she would normally have had.

The prognosis was poor for extended sailing. However, they were determined to get down into Mexico where they could live cheaply while the invalids recovered. They sailed for Ensenada twenty-four hours before we did.

⚓

Day by day, I was buying and checking off my list all the things I could think of that we would need in a year or more of travel. The list was impressive, but I still had an uneasy feeling that I must be forgetting something important.

Fresh produce we would get in the countries we visited, also probably flour and other grains when the present supply was exhausted. On long ocean passages we would depend on fish and rice, even though some travelers had told us there were no fish to be found a thousand miles from shore. We had enough dehydrated foods to take care of any such emergencies.

Afton, Eldon's brother, and his wife Vera arrived on the departure date we had given them, December fifteenth. They'd come to see us off, and after another eight days of frantic effort, we really did seem to be ready to go.

To celebrate our long-awaited departure, Afton took us to a Swedish restaurant where the proprietor's small daughters, heads wreathed in flowers and candles in their hands, sang Christmas carols as they went from table to table. It was beautiful and touching; more than anything up to this time, it reminded us that Christmas was really upon us. For us, Christmas had always been accompanied by snow and cold weather, so warm days in San Diego didn't seem very Christmasy.

The First Leg

It was past midnight when we pulled away from the dock, already the day before Christmas. We did feel mildly sorry for Afton and Vera, left on the shore. They would be touring the continental United States in VW and motor home, but that seemed quite prosaic to us — compared with South Sea Islands and totally new countries.

Surely there was a feeling of accomplishment when we got *Trilogy* launched, and again when we finally left Seattle on the first leg of our journey. But this was different. Now we were headed for foreign ports. We had finally made it! Our voyage stretched before us full of glamour and mystery – no longer impossible, although countless times it had seemed nearly so.

We stood on deck, arms intertwined; Dave too, in spite of the fact that he was never able to feel quite like a member of the family. The process of assimilation takes a long time if one hasn't been born into it.

JIM'S COMMENT:
GETTING IN THE WATER

Every Sunday was visitor day. We didn't want to stop work, but we had all these friends and neighbors, people in the community who wanted to see how we were doing on the project. So Sunday there was a steady stream of people coming through that we would show around the boat.

Among this stream, there were a couple of state patrolmen. This was their beat. Real nice guys. Like everybody else, they were interested in how the project was going.

We had a charter that was committed to start at a certain

95

moment. We thought that we could very easily get the boat finished within that framework. As it turned out, we were really scrambling to get done.

Then we applied for a permit to move the boat, and the state said that we couldn't. We had an arterial highway right in front of us; it was illegal to move the boat.

That was quite a dilemma

I mean, it wasn't really a dilemma for me, just an exciting passage. I had no doubt where I was going with it. We pulled that off really nice.

Then the launching. We got the biggest portable crane in Seattle. I remember it stretching to the furthest extent of its ability. Its back wheels were just starting to lift off the ground. It was dicey, the launching.

All of this happened in one day. It was a relatively short event, but it was a culmination.

But there was still so much work to do. We didn't have a mast, no rigging, systems that weren't done. And we had a charter that started in six days! We literally worked around the clock. It's just a blur in my mind, that last stretch.

And suddenly we had people on a charter — and we had never run a thing on that boat! We were still tightening up the water system and making sure the fuel was getting to the engine. We'd never hoisted a sail.

We got up about as far as Campbell River, and I jumped over the side just to check things out. I had a cut, a pretty bad cut, on my thumb. When I jumped into the water, I felt electricity pumping right into that cut. I used it just like a direction finder. I realized I could follow that buzzing sensation right to its source.

The First Leg

And here, at the rudder, we had a direct short in our electrical system shooting electricity out into the water. We'd installed a two-inch stainless steel pipe with a wall thickness of probably three-quarters of an inch, and electrolysis had eaten more than half of it, just in two and a half days.

It was a miracle we spotted that.

We went ashore and found a sharp welder who laid a bead in there and ground it down. He improvised a patch as strong as he could. Later, sailing down the coast, we had problems with the rudder and finally had to rebuild the whole thing.

The next thing we realized, our fuel consumption on the engine was more than we had calculated. We found out the hard way — when we ran out of fuel.

And we didn't have wind. We were sitting there in Dixon entrance.

I saw a fishing boat, so I flashed it with the mirror. Turned out it was a guy that I had commercially fished with in Alaska for several years. He came over and dropped off fifty gallons of fuel, whatever, and we kept rolling.

He said, "Jim, as soon as you get to Alaska, come on out." I ended up fishing with him that same summer. That's what can happen sometimes when you get into trouble.

By the time we got to Alaska, we were pooped. Our clients, however, were having a great time; they wanted to extend the charter another week. But we just said, "This is it. We're here."

I think we slept for a week.

Then we all took jobs. At that point we were definitely planning on cruising. It was a decision that had evolved during the building process. We'd talked about it a lot. We just said,

Trilogy

"Yeah, we're going to do this. We want to do this."

At first, we threw it out as an idea.

"Well, maybe we can go just for a few months."

"Maybe we can go down to Mexico."

"Or maybe we...."

I don't think there was an exact day that we said yes. We just got the bug that we wanted to cruise.

In Alaska, Dad told me that he didn't know if Mom was going to join us. I called Mom and said, "Mom! I've got to know — are you committed to this or not?"

That was the only moment of hesitation. I knew if she didn't do it, we weren't going to go. She had a job, and I assumed she was committed to it. I'd heard that Pattie didn't want to go, that maybe Mom and Pattie weren't going to go. That was when Mom said, "Hey, absolutely. I'm in there. I'm going for it."

That's when Dad and I ran the boat back down from Alaska, just the two of us. Rand had a job that kept him working for another two or three weeks. Dad and I brought it down in tough weather — gales most of the way south.

We had some more work just to get ready for cruising, about a month, and then we took off.

CHAPTER FIVE:
DREAMERS ALL

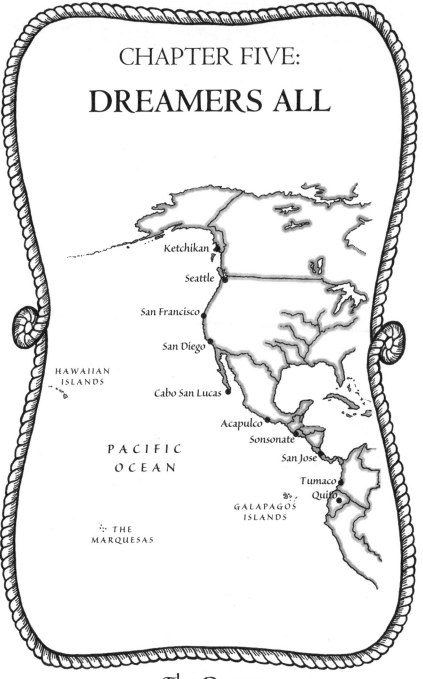

Ketchikan

Seattle

San Francisco

San Diego

HAWAIIAN
ISLANDS

Cabo San Lucas

Acapulco
Sonsonate
San Jose

PACIFIC
OCEAN

Tumaco
Quito

GALAPAGOS
ISLANDS

THE
MARQUESAS

The Dream

ven before we started cruising, and more often as we traveled, people asked us, "How did you happen to do this anyway?" The question came as much from chance acquaintances as from good friends; it was triggered more by innate curiosity than by degree of intimacy. And it was always asked with a sweeping gesture that included the boat and, presumably, our entire way of life.

Sometimes I answered flippantly, depending on the questioner and the circumstances: "Well, it wasn't easy, but it helps if you're a little bit crazy to start with."

But if the question was truly thoughtful, even though inspired by a total lack of comprehension, I always tried — and still do try — to give a thoughtful and honest answer.

Even among our family members the reasons are not all the same from individual to individual. For Eldon this was the last and best hope of living out his boyhood dream of sailing to fabled lands where the culture is exotic, where the climate is milder than in Alaska or the Pacific Northwest, and where one can get away from the treacherous daily routine that robs people of life before they have really lived it (his words, often expressed).

For myself, while I didn't grow up with any unconventional ambition to spend my adult years going native on a tropical island, I owed him one, so to speak. When our children were younger, I insisted on being in one place long enough to ensure uninterrupted schooling and a stable environment with friendships that could be built through the years. My own family had moved a lot when I was a child; it was almost like having a death in the family every time I left my cherished friends behind. My children might have had a wonderful time if we'd headed for the tropics when they were little tots. So, no one can say at this date who was right and who was wrong. In Eldon's submission to my ideas on child-raising, however, it was understood that sometime we were going to do what he wanted to do with his life.

The time was now.

Pattie, as previously stated, was not at all in favor of the gypsy life. She made it very clear that it would only last until she was old enough to go her own way. This was a profound worry because her eighteenth birthday was coming up in April. While her parents didn't feel that one is capable of making that kind of decision at eighteen, she certainly did.

Unlike Pattie, her brothers were old enough to be enamored of the romantic possibilities within our travel plans and self-assured enough to know that, if this lifestyle proved unrewarding, they could do something else. They, like me, felt some obligation to their father's vision of the fabulous tropical life, the retirement life lived in the sunny climes.

(Of course, they understood their father well enough to know that he would never be able to take life easy, no matter how propitious his circumstances. Whenever one of us chided Eldon about being a workaholic, his answer was always "No, I'm actually very lazy. But I'm ashamed of myself for being lazy, so I have to work hard to prove to myself that I'm not!")

Surely all three of the men had worked hard to bring about what we were currently doing, and their commitment equaled their investment. Pattie had been in school most of the time during the boat-building; she felt controlled, helpless, and unhappy.

As with our little group, so with the main. You find

tremendous variety in the motivations of those who sail small craft around the edges and across the vast reaches of the Pacific Ocean, where a single run from one island to another may be as far as the width of the entire United States. There are timid souls who dart from harbor to harbor, uneasy until they are again in a safe anchorage — or, better yet, tied up to a dock. There are the brave and sometimes foolhardy ones who multiply the odds against themselves by a lack of respect for the power and the unpredictability of the sea. There are the seasoned experts, the bright novices, and countless sailors who fall some-where between.

You find youngsters barely out of high school, sailing boats of their own building. Parents with young children. Retired people, frail for the rigors of sea life. All of them have given up conventional comforts to pit themselves against challenges and frustrations that range from stimu-lating to overwhelming. There is no logic in it at all, but they have one thing in common:

They are all dreamers.

The dreamers of this world traditionally get short shrift from their more practical contemporaries. Yet there is more than a little evidence that they are needed in the cosmic scheme of things. Consider how much of the world's progress has been the result of romantic dreaming, coupled with the toughness required to pit oneself against the untried, as well as the ingenuity to manage the seemingly unworkable. The great voyagers, the explorers, the covered-wagon pioneers all were dreamers, willing to endure danger and hardship because of this overmastering vision.

My grandmother, youngest of thirteen children, walked most of the way "out west" behind an ox team. Life wasn't easy for them. Nor were they looking for an easy life, sensing perhaps that ease and plenty seldom call forth the best of the human spirit's capabilities.

The cruising family has chosen its own style of freedom

in place of commonly accepted security, and it can hardly escape being misunderstood by people who have chosen otherwise. To barter the normal trappings of permanence and stability for the sheer enjoyment of experience — to possess, instead of personal real estate, the untrammeled sea and the Earth's constantly changing landscapes — this is sheer madness except to the few who see it as this:

The poverty that enjoys true wealth.

Indeed, if true wealth consists of time — that is, of the ability to spend one's time enjoying life — then this poverty is a fair exchange, even a tremendous bargain, because many encumbrances have been exchanged for infinite riches in enjoyment.

In every generation there are some individuals to whom a regimented existence seems totally meaningless, and the frustrations of "getting ahead," normal to the majority of mankind, are nearly unbearable. For such persons, the cruising life has great appeal.

In addition to the adventurers and the romantics, we also encountered a small number of malcontents from various countries, people dissatisfied with opportunities or governments at home and hoping to find Utopia in some other part of the world. They, too, had a vision. But its fulfillment, which depended on other efforts than their own, was less probable, and their adaptability seemed to me less than that of the adventurers or romantics.

Some people have chosen the cruising life simply out of boredom with a more regimented existence. As an antidote to boredom, cruising might be considered a bit of overkill. But whatever its difficulties — with a family, cruising is anything but boring.

Ernest Gann, writer and sailor of long standing whom we met through our friend Ed Kennell, calls cruising the world's most expensive way to travel third class. He knew whereof he spoke.

Besides the physical discomfort and occasional actual

danger, there are many inconveniences: shortage of fresh water as well as fruits and vegetables; primitive laundry facilities (outside of the cruising population, I wonder how many American families do their washing on an old-fashioned washboard or a flat rock in a stream?); lack of privacy; the recurrence of watch duty faster and oftener than seems possible; disrupted sleep; monotony of diet on long passages....

The list is extensive.

Sometimes, when one or another of these difficulties becomes acute, it's hard to remember all those lyrical descriptions of life at sea as it was going to be. But every seafarer has a dream. We all do. Not every dream is as full-blown and well articulated as Eldon's. But the dream sustains us through the non-lethal deprivations we encounter.

This dream has as many facets as human hope does, as optimism. If the land or seascape has been bleak and depressing, the dream calls up a vision of lush coral islands and vivid flowers. If all the fruit and vegetables have perished before a landfall is made, the dream conjures up enormous amounts of them at the next port, more beautiful than a page from a seed catalogue and at least as lacking in verisimilitude.

I had my own version of the dream while *Trilogy* was in the planning and building stage. In my dream it was usually evening, with a blue-black sky and a full moon highlighting our wind-filled sails. I always visualized the sea as smooth, even though brisk winds and smooth seas are conditions that seldom co-exist. But that was my dream, and everyone knows that dreams don't have to be logical.

My mental image showed the family scattered artistically over the deck, singing and playing musical instruments, while our trim ship plowed its triple-jeweled furrow through phosphorescent waters.

This vision wasn't totally false. There were actually times when it happened just like that. More often, though, when we had enough wind to get from one place to another rapidly, the sea was rough, and members of the family were running around adjusting sails, making sure everything was lashed down or stowed below decks, and generally making themselves useful.

⚓

Having started soon after midnight, we entered Ensenada Harbor at eight o'clock in the morning and found the *Ara Moana* anchored there, expecting us momentarily.

The trip had been uneventful for both parties, but Greg had found nine uninterrupted hours at the wheel grueling. The thought of much more of the same with no one to relieve him even for a few minutes had him in a state close to despair.

"I just don't see how I can manage on longer passages," he said sadly, in his musical Scottish brogue.

"We can do it," Elspeth encouraged. "In three more weeks I can stand a wheel watch. You won't have to do it all alone." She glanced down at her cast impatiently.

"I tan hewp," Jamie, the littlest Dufus, offered with great seriousness. "I tan; I tan hewp you."

His father picked him up and tousled his curly brown hair. "Couldn't make it without you," Greg assured him. The other small Dufuses crowded around him, presenting their offers of assistance, worried about their implied lack of value.

"Elspeth is right," Eldon told Greg. "Don't be discouraged; these are passing misfortunes, and time will take care of them. You just need to hole up here until Elspeth's leg is healed. Fiona is getting better, and by that time she'll be able to help."

Greg brightened up temporarily. Beyond the encouraging words, though, we all knew that the Dufus cruise would always have to contend with a shortage of able-bodied crew — not to mention the fact that half the people aboard were so young that they would have to be watched constantly.

After all the years of planning, saving, and hard work

that had gone into building the *Ara Moana*, we hated to see them give it up and go back to an existence they had described as humdrum and pointless. When a family like this, who began with such hope and enthusiasm, deserts the cruising fraternity, it strikes at all of our cherished dreams.

Now I understood much better what Helen Gau was feeling when she said if we gave up on our cruise she didn't even want to see us coming back.

No one knew at this point whether the Dufus family would find the strength, both physical and mental, to carry on. But I did know that when you're tired and discouraged, just a dinner away from home can be a real lift. Tomorrow was Christmas, and though the weather was drizzly and dreary, it wouldn't affect our spirits, nor the great dinner that we had planned.

"Why don't all of you come over to *Trilogy* tomorrow for dinner?" I asked Fiona.

For a moment her face lighted up; then she began to look dubious. "Oh, I'd love to, but there are rather a lot of us. We'll crowd you too much."

"Not at all. We can seat nine at the big table, and some of the children can eat at the chart table." For me, twelve people for Christmas dinner would be a smaller group than usual.

"If you're sure, then we'll be awfully happy to come." Fiona looked as though the happiness had already started.

As the gray day slowly darkened into Christmas Eve, Pattie and I made stuffing for the turkey that would go into the oven before daybreak, pumpkin pies, and all the traditional things that make Christmas dinner special. In the evening the Dufuses joined us for a sing-along with Christmas carols and other songs. The air was full of delicious, spicy odors; a feeling of pure contentment settled over us like a warm blanket.

Long ago, we had agreed not to have a tree or exchange gifts in the traditional manner, knowing that we had overrun our budget dangerously while in San Diego.

Dreamers All

However, on Christmas morning we had a mock-formal ceremony of presenting to each other what we felt the coming year would bring: a year of travel in jolly good company; a trip to the few island paradises left in this world; a year of adventure and learning experiences.

We even had gift wrapping.

Eldon, feeling a certain vindication at this moment for all the struggle that had preceded it, said, "Wrapped in well worn but still shining dreams, tied with the love that binds us all together." Jim presented his as being "wrapped in days and weeks and months, each one a new gift." Randy, who is always going to have fun as he goes along, added, "Wrapped in love and laughter and the joy of living."

A bit overwhelmed by all these lofty sentiments, Pattie and I decided on "beautifully wrapped by God Himself, Who gave us our reason for Christmas." That was lofty enough for anyone.

After a bountiful Christmas dinner we played games, sang carols (After all, you only get to do this once a year; nothing is so over as Christmas, once it's done.) and laughed over the adventures and misadventures of the past year until the little Dufuses started falling asleep. Visiting between boats is somewhat different from visiting neighbors ashore. First, Greg got into their skiff; then Jim and Rand started handing down the sleeping and sleepy children. Elspeth with a cast on her leg was as helpless as the smaller ones, and more unwieldy. Last, Fiona got in, and they rowed away silently in the ghostly mist.

The following day was that very British holiday, Boxer Day, and Fiona invited us over to *Ara Moana* for Yorkshire pudding, roast beef, and all that goes to make up a traditional English dinner, followed by that elegant dessert misnamed the trifle. Pattie talked about that trifle for months, but even though I found a recipe for it in one of my cookbooks, we could never really duplicate the one Fiona made.

Trilogy

RANDY'S COMMENT:
My Dream

For the first few months of our voyage, *Trilogy* was still a "work in progress." Although she had proven seaworthy off the Washington and Oregon coasts, there still remained an endless list of projects to complete before some of us felt that our vessel was truly shipshape. Dad and I shared this view more strongly than the rest of the family. Perhaps this was our way of dealing with the uncertainty that lay ahead. For me, this uncertainty included sudden storms, hidden shoals — and the fervent hope that all my glue joints would hold together! Dad, on the other hand, maintained supreme confidence in his workmanship and his seamanship, for he had already met successfully the challenges of one of the most hostile environments in the world. Staying busy was his way of dealing with the discomfort he felt over abandoning all visible means of support.

So we sewed awnings, built self-steering vanes, fabricated spinnaker poles, and little by little *Trilogy* was starting to look like something out of an Eric Hiscock *Cruising Guide*.

I don't know what images had kept Dad's cruising dreams alive for all those tough years in Alaska. Descriptive passages by Melville, Conrad, London, Joshua Slocum, Harry Pidgeon, and others no doubt played a part. And there was personal correspondence with circumnavigators like David and Nancy Griffith, and Keene and Helen Gau, providing powerful testimonial to the mesmerizing magic of the South Pacific.

For me it probably started with *National Geographic*

magazine and the voyages of the *Yankee*. Under the command of Captain Irving Johnson and his wife, the *Yankee* became home to fifteen or twenty teenage boys and girls who sailed as her crew on eighteen-month voyages around the world. Still, as much as I may have envied these privileged vagabonds, I never really imagined myself as one of them. The images from those pages, images of crystal clear lagoons and white sand beaches, deep blue ocean waves reflecting an even bluer sky, these stood in sharp contrast to the dark green waters, rocky coastline, and gray skies that defined my home.

That all changed the summer I turned fifteen and a thirty-some-foot yawl sailed into Ketchikan from Hawaii. The two brothers aboard, one my age and one slightly older, were everything a kid who'd grown up with the sounds of the Beach Boys wanted to be — bleached blonde, sun-tanned, self-confident, and completely independent and self-reliant.

I watched with envy as they gave daily tours of their tidy ship to anyone who asked, especially any pretty girls who came along. As unattainable as it seemed at that time, this was the lifestyle I knew I wanted, if only in my dreams.

(Years later, after we were firmly established on Maui, I was recounting this seminal event to a couple of friends at the Blue Max, a bar in Lahaina. Halfway through my narrative they both started laughing hysterically. After a few minutes, during which I was struggling to see the humor, they admitted that they were the two brothers on that Bristol little yawl those endless summers ago, and that I had every reason to be jealous!)

As we sailed farther and farther south, and as waters warmed, trade winds softened, and palm trees whispered to

Trilogy

us from one deserted beach after another, each of us was coming to terms with his or her role in this magnificent obsession. Perhaps most importantly, some of us were finally beginning to accept what most others had already discovered: it's all right to live in the moment, embracing life one day at a time. Sometimes dreams really do come true.

CHAPTER SIX:
FOREIGN SOIL
AT LAST

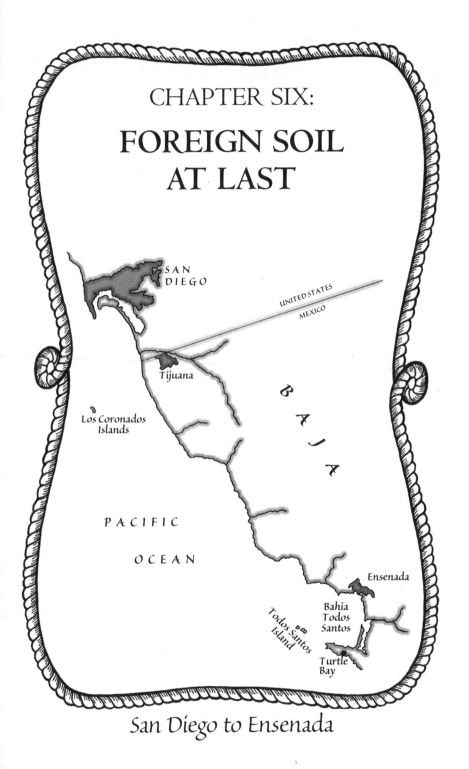

San Diego to Ensenada

onday, Jim began the routine of clearing customs.

When Eldon designated Jim as first officer on our ship's papers, he couldn't possibly have known how much he was escaping — how much frustration, how many hours wasted on trivialities. Rather, he thought of it as an honor he was conferring on his eldest son. (He would have made him captain if Jim had had the proper certification at that time.) Eldon had run his boats within the coastal waters of the United States and Canada. In Eldon's experience, customs offices were brisk, business-like, and, above all, efficient.

In Mexico and other countries to the south, the customs offices and officers wasted the time of those who had to deal with them as though there was eternal merit to be gained through trials of patience and they, certainly, were not going to stint its application and rewards. Jim is willing to grant that he learned, if not how to be patient, at least how to act it, and how to practice the rudiments of diplomacy.

Diplomacy is a worthwhile lesson, ultimately, and there were others in our group who could have profited from it. Even so, no one really wanted to trade places with Jim. All of us stopped briefly at the port captain's office in Ensenada, and then scattered out — all of us except Jim, who was going to be there for some time.

Pattie and I hunted for a bank where we could exchange some US currency for pesos. It's amazing how wealthy and spendthriftish a person feels after exchanging

a few dollars for a whole fistful of foreign currency.
Knowing it is an illusion makes little difference. I
reminded myself that twelve and a half pesos would not
buy twelve and a half dollars worth of anything, that
those things like five dollar bills are only worth forty cents
— but I didn't really believe it.

I was happily browsing through various shops and had
found a piece of pottery for my aunt. Knowing that her
youngest sister was fond of Mexican pottery, my mother
had given me twenty dollars — now translated into two
hundred fifty pesos — to spend on just the perfect gift.
Pattie hadn't found this proxy shopping exactly riveting,
so she'd wandered off on her own. All in all, our group
had ungrouped and spread out over quite a bit of
Ensenada when Jim caught up with me.

"C'mon, Mom," he urged, almost propelling me out
the door, ignoring the disappointed saleslady; "we all have
to go back to the immigration office." He cast a couple of
hurried Spanish phrases over his shoulder, apologizing and
saying I would be back.

Jim had been rounding up family members one by one.
When he and I got back to the port captain's office,
everyone was there except Eldon; he had gone back to the
boat to get some other documents. Irrelevant they were,
but the port captain's curiosity was extensive. We sat
down on the hard, wooden, backless bench in that drab
and dingy office, looking like blackbirds on a fence, and
waited... and waited... while I pondered the fact that this
same bench was the only thing in the whole office that
seemed to be well polished.

While the captain of the Port of Ensenada was indu-
bitably enjoying his usual siesta from noon until three
o'clock, we sat fidgeting and making wry jokes. Randy has
never been known for his patience; he came near to being
born without a doctor's assistance because he was in a
hurry, and he hasn't changed much. After we had waited

far beyond a reasonable length of time, he jumped up and announced:

"Dad has had time to make a dozen trips out to the boat. I'm going out there and see what the trouble is."

"Sit down. You can't get out there; he has the skiff," Jim pointed out.

"I can get someone to row me out for a couple of pesos." Randy made a quick exit. The rest of us wished we'd thought of it first. But no sooner had Randy vanished in one direction than Eldon came hurrying in from the other way. It was like a Marx Brothers comedy.

"Hey, Randy's looking for you," I told Eldon. "Didn't you meet him coming up from the waterfront?"

Eldon looked embarrassed. "Well, I got lost, sort of, and wound up coming here from the other direction." He sat down and began arranging papers on the bench beside him. "Don't worry about Rand; when he sees the skiff, he'll know he missed me."

It remained a mystery why we had all been required to report back to the immigration office. When the port captain finally came out of his inner sanctum, he gave the whole pile of papers a most cursory glance and dismissed all of us except Eldon and Jim, who only lasted two more minutes. He had said that our papers were incomplete, but if they were improved by the new additions, there was no way he could have known in the brief moment he spent looking at them.

⚓

We spent two more days in Ensenada, but no one especially wanted to stay. The city was in no way at fault. The rain had stopped; the air was clear, and we were enjoying the winter sunshine. But we had already made a trip down here by automobile in November, and it seemed as though there was nothing left to explore.

I spent some time painting watercolor pictures of the

harbor, decided that they were never likely to be auctioned off for six million dollars a hundred years from now, and consigned them to the wastebasket.

It was time to go.

Enthusiastically the boys hoisted anchor, and we swept out to sea, wondering if the Dufuses would somehow find the stamina to continue their journey. Neither we nor they had any hard and fast rules for an itinerary, and it was difficult for cruising boats to keep track of each other.

Months later, before leaving Costa Rica, we met another cruising boat whose captain had met Greg Dufus in Mexico. He was quite sure they had gone back to Canada.

⚓

After our water leakage scare between Ventura and San Diego, Jim changed all the water faucets to salt water except the one in the galley — and there, you can't simply turn on the water. First you open the faucet and then you press with your knee against a lever under the sink. Then fresh water comes trickling out, shrieking all the time like some animal under torture.

The salt water presented other problems. All of our hand soap was as useless as so many pieces of plastic.

I assured everyone (having done my homework) that along the coast of Baja all fresh water has to be shipped in. It's so precious that it's only used for drinking. So of course we'd find salt-water soap in the stores.

Not so. The first time I saw any salt-water soap was in the Galapagos Islands, and by that time we had discovered that liquid Joy lathers very well in salt water.

⚓

In spite of all our preparatory reading (Steinbeck, Cannon, and the Sierra Club books), we found Turtle Bay so dry, so barren that it almost defied belief. That three thousand people could exist — or would want to — where there isn't a single blade of grass, or a tree, or any flowers, baffled us. The houses are small, square or rectangular, and without eaves, randomly scattered over the barest hills anyone could imagine.

The lack of eaves on the houses is just one more indication of life at its most basic level. Even though there is no rain, eaves would be useful in warding off some of the intense sunshine and making the houses a bit cooler inside. But architectural refinements aren't a high priority where there are so many other deprivations. In fact, in this land of rock, earth, and unrelenting, brilliant sunshine, all the signs of human habitation seem strangely misplaced.

It was New Year's Eve when we arrived, almost dark, but not the sudden and total darkness that closes in after sunset when you're twenty-five degrees farther south. Nor was it the lingering twilight we were accustomed to in Alaska. The sky gave us fair warning that night was approaching, and then got on with it. There were few lights to be seen in any of the houses, and it seemed prudent to wait until morning for any exploring or visiting.

In the morning we made our way up a small hill to the cathedral, the most impressive building on that austere coast. It was surprisingly beautiful, and it was filled with people. (We had to keep reminding ourselves that three thousand people live here and so we shouldn't be exactly amazed that two or three hundred happened to be in church.) Some of those sitting near the doorway motioned to us to come in, but we felt, somehow, that it would be an intrusion. Even though no service was in progress at the moment, everyone was very quiet and reverent.

It seemed to be the only church in town.

Pattie and I went down the little hill toward town; Eldon climbed to a higher elevation in order to take pictures. Dave, Randy, and Jim went in search of a post office.

The hard-packed streets boiled with children, ricocheting and bouncing off each other like marbles in a pinball machine. Dressed in their New Year's best, they were a kaleidoscope of color, flowered dresses, and dazzling white shirts. How on earth do they keep these white clothes so white where there is no water for washing except the sea, I asked myself. At first I thought, Well, today is a big holiday; let's see what they look like tomorrow back in their grubbies. But the next time I saw them, they looked just as sparkling clean.

We managed to get dirtier than that even though we were completely surrounded by water.

The children were shy but very polite. Glowing dark eyes and teeth whiter than any toothpaste ad flashed smiles at us as they wished us happy New Year. One little girl, a touching combination of timidity and boldness, like a kitten that wants to play but jumps back as you come nearer, advanced toward us with many hesitations. Her glossy, dark hair curled around her face and hung nearly to her waist. "Novo Anno," she breathed almost inaudibly. "You are from Estados Unitas?"

"Yes — I mean si," Pattie answered. "Do you speak English?"

"Un pocito," the child held up her hand, measuring a tiny amount between her thumb and index finger. "Do you speak Espanol?"

"Un pocito," Pattie laughed, imitating the child's gesture — "un pocitito," which means very, very tiny. Both girls were laughing by now as Pattie asked, "What is your name — uh, I mean nombre?"

"Maria," she paused, then added a long string of names in rapid-fire Spanish.

We decided to stick with "Maria"; certainly we would never remember half of her other names. Two boys had sidled up close to her and announced that their names were Raphael and George (sounding like Grrraphael and Horhay).

Turning to Maria, Pattie said enthusiastically, "You can

be our interpreter; I'm sure we're going to need one." Pattie had taken three years of conversational Spanish in high school, but she was still reluctant to depend on it.

"I am not so good interpreter," Maria disparaged her skills with a rueful little smile. " I have not so much Anglais."

Compared with my none-at-all Spanish, she sounded like a real linguist. "How old are you?" I asked.

"I have ten years," she replied, holding up both hands so we could count all ten fingers. Small and slight as she was, I wouldn't have guessed her age to be more than eight. But before long we realized she was very mature for ten years old.

For some time we had been unconsciously following the tantalizingly delicious odor of fresh bread. "Maria," I asked, do you know where the bakery is?"

Maria looked blank. "Baker-ree?" she asked in a puzzled tone. "This word I do not know."

Suddenly, Pattie's high school Spanish came to her aid. "Panaderia," she prompted. "Where is the panaderia?"

"Oh! Panaderia, this way."

Quickly Maria led us to a large brick mound shaped very much like an igloo. Baking was undeniably in progress, but no baker was in sight. Surely someone would have to take it out of the oven before too long. We waited for fifteen or twenty minutes but gave up in frustration eventually. Nor was the mystery of the missing baker ever solved. We deliberately retraced our steps a half hour later and found the bread still baking and no one around.

Maria took her responsibility as interpreter and guide very seriously and gave us a walking tour of all the places she thought might be interesting for tourists from the Estados Unitas. First we visited a pre-school or kinder-garten that Maria said was for niños and niñas. Of course, this was a holiday and no one was present to show us the classrooms, but we could see them quite well through the windows. Everything was colorful and very orderly.

Then we progressed to an elementary school that could

have been transplanted directly from the United States. With the exception of the cathedral, the elementary school was the largest and best-maintained building in town. The people in Turtle Bay, and indeed in all of Mexico, are proud of their educational system, and more than one person pointed out to us that half the national income is spent on education.

With Maria in front and thirty-five or forty children in our wake we moved on through the town like some majestic procession.

Our old stereotype of a lazy Mexican resting under a cactus, sombrero pulled over his eyes, underwent some revisions that day. Evidences of industry, neatness, and local pride were everywhere. The yards and streets were hard-packed earth, carefully swept and free of litter. Stark and simple it might be, but it was not neglected.

There wasn't much of a business section to the town — a cantina or two and a store with a few wilted vegetables displayed in front; that was it. Though it appeared to us that we had seen everything, we had yet to find a post office. Speaking of a post office drew a very puzzled look from Maria, but when Pattie remembered the word "correa," she sprang to attention. Turning down a little side street, she showed us the building, but it was closed on New Year's Day. (What post office wouldn't be?) There was a slot for mailing letters, but we hadn't brought any with us, and obviously our boys were long gone.

We stood around irresolutely, not really wanting to go back to the boat so soon. Maria, as though she understood our dilemma, offered a diversion.

"I show you my house. You like? Very new house; only one year." We liked. I had been wondering how we were going to get acquainted with anyone enough to get a glimpse of how they lived. Later in our voyage, Jim and Rand solved that problem with music, but at this time we hadn't yet discovered that wonderful open sesame.

Trilogy

⚓

Maria's father worked for the oil company that provided gas and oil for fishing and cruising boats and also fuel for the kerosene stoves and lamps in the little houses. So Maria's house was fairly luxurious by Turtle Bay standards. It was larger than most, not just one room but three — a kitchen on one side of a living room that was also the master bedroom, and a smaller bedroom on the other side. The small bedroom was completely covered with either mats and quilts or possibly sleeping bags with quilted covers. Maria has eight brothers and sisters, and it looked as though the living room/bedroom was reserved for the parents alone. Bright turquoise on the outside, the house had one more comfort that many others did not have: a concrete floor, not hard, polished earth like the poorer houses.

Without piped-in water or electricity, most of the appliances we take for granted were of no use in Turtle Bay. The kitchen contained two tables: one, where the family ate and another, a sturdy work table used for kneading bread, making tortillas, chopping vegetables or whatever. There were six very plain wooden chairs; they must have to eat in two shifts, I surmised.

Chairs were brought from the kitchen, and we sat stiffly, trying to make conversation with Maria's mother and older sister, neither of whom spoke English. This sixteen-year-old sister was the only one of the nine children besides Maria who was at home today, and she was leaving for a dance later in the afternoon. She was already wearing her dancing dress, a bright pink taffeta in which she looked very pretty.

Both Maria and her mother urged us to stay for lunch, but we felt it would be an imposition. We refused as politely as possible. This was probably a mistake; Maria looked truly disappointed. "It would be an honor," she told us sadly, with downcast eyes.

Foreign Soil At Last

We explained that we really did have to get back to the boat because the rest of the family would be waiting, but nothing we said changed her look of distress or our feeling that we had failed to meet her expectations. Thinking that she might have been paid in the past for acting as interpreter and tour guide, I gave her some pesos and tried to make it important by calling it "professional fee for interpreters." She took the money reluctantly, but obviously that was not the problem.

By the time we arrived at the dock, the tide had dropped. It was awkward getting into the dinghy — not for my agile children so much as for me. I went around grumbling that floats should be attached to the dock, the way they are in Alaska (where they probably wouldn't have bothered if their tidal drop were, like this one, a mere four feet). My grumbling only proved that I was a novice at cruising; many times as we moved ahead, I would have been very happy for a good, solid dock in a quiet bay.

⚓

Our dependable little six-horse outboard buzzed us quietly back to the ship while I contemplated the fact that I was developing quite an affection for this little fellow. I had christened him JJ because of the Johnson symbols all over the casing. He deserved a name, and probably a better name than that, because of his unusual trustworthiness.

Never failing to start, usually at the first pull — that alone put JJ in some elite outboard category. Even I was able to start JJ. Most machines instantly recognize my antipathy toward their ilk and respond by being as maddeningly contrary and uncooperative as possible. Of all the outboards we had had through the years, JJ was the least temperamental.

A succession of monsters from ten to sixty horsepower had introduced us to almost every difficulty that could be invented by quirky and endlessly versatile machines. Even with shops handy that specialized in outboard repairs, they were a constant source of trouble. If they started with reasonable ease, they developed hiccups halfway to our destination. Or they would whisk us out to some distant cove and refuse utterly to start for the return voyage. The only thing one could depend on was that, somewhere along the way, strong shoulder muscles and a good pair of oars would get you home.

What a joy it was to have an outboard motor that seemed to take no delight in trying to determine the limits of human frustration! True, JJ wasn't all that powerful. But of all the machines I've had to deal with, he had the best disposition.

⚓

Across the bay, a bright orange skiff was being launched from the sleek little sloop *Gitaña* and, rowing powerfully, Duncan MacGregor soon came alongside.

"Hi, *Trilogy!*" he called, tying up next to our skiff. "I saw you coming down from Cedros; never caught up with you, though."

We assumed what we hoped was a proper demeanor of modesty. Multihulls are designed to be faster in the water than most monohulls, and you pay for it by having a much more limited storage space below decks. So it's a trade-off. We had already found that *Trilogy*, with three hulls, was not as speedy as a catamaran with only two, and we accepted that, knowing that the catamaran couldn't possibly carry all the stuff that we found essential for extended cruising.

"Yeah," Duncan continued as he climbed aboard, "I saw your sails and I couldn't figure out why you weren't tipped over like me."

There was a faint Highland lilt both to his speech and his laughter. A true MacGregor, no doubt. His reddish-blonde hair was stacked into wind-tossed sheaves, and his perpetually sunburned face was creased in a warm smile.

Soon another boatman asked permission to board, a

young physics professor from UCLA, thirtyish, dark, and rather handsome. He said his name was John, and while he told us his occupation, from which he was currently playing truant, he didn't ever bother with a last name. He and Dave were soon engaged in a hard-fought chess game.

The game was never to be finished, unfortunately. As row after row of dark clouds came rolling in, John stood up. "Sorry to leave you, Dave, without at least beating you, but I think we're in for one of Turtle Bay's famous dust storms."

"Huh!" Dave snorted, "you haven't proved yet that you can beat me."

"No, but I will," John promised confidently. He turned to Eldon, "If you haven't been through one of these dust storms, I'd better tell you a few things. You'll have to close everything up, even if you think you're going to suffocate. And when the wind finally stops, you'll have enough dirt on your deck to start a farming operation."

He hurried off, and Duncan followed quickly, each one in some haste to prepare for the storm.

We weren't unduly concerned. We had a protected harbor and a good anchorage; what did we have to worry about? The clouds looked a bit ominous. But we had lived with clouds, sometimes very black clouds, constantly in Alaska.

When the first big gust of wind hit our rigging, we began to find out what we had to worry about. It was going to be one of those shrieking-in-the-rigging, anchor-watch-around-the-clock nights. John's boat dragged anchor three times during the night, and with an off-shore wind, he was in danger of drifting out of the bay. We finally added one of our extra anchors to the lightweight one he was using. After that his boat managed to stay in one place.

There were no visitors the next day. Instead, the wind, unabated, picked up all that hard-packed earth around Turtle Bay as well as quantities of sand off the beach and deposited it all on our decks. *Trilogy's* decks were so covered that the dirt rippled like sand dunes in miniature. Through the windows we watched this accumulation with sinking spirits, knowing how difficult the clean-up was going to be. Just ahead of the storm a glossy black ketch, the Aegean, had slipped into the harbor. There were no signs of life aboard; they seemed to be waiting it out with battened hatches.

By the second day of wind and dust, everyone was getting bored. The ventilators had been turned away from the wind; otherwise they would have simply scooped the dirt-laden wind right into the cabin. But with their backs to the wind, they didn't seem to be supplying much fresh air. We felt stifled, but it was more from being shut up in the cabin than from lack of oxygen.

Ordinarily I had to make bread every two or three days, and this was one of the days. It also seemed like a good time to make some cinnamon rolls, and, while the oven was still hot, I made a cake from an old family recipe. We were still close enough to San Diego to have all the more exotic ingredients: applesauce, seeded muscat raisins, walnuts, genuine butter, powdered sugar, grated orange rind. (First you grate the rind off and then use the juice in a delicious butter-orange icing.) This is an old-fashioned recipe from the days before there were cake mixes — skimpy little things — and it makes a very big cake. It was just as well, because we were about to be invaded.

By late afternoon the wind had died down enough to make travel between boats possible, if not really pleasant. The wind still carried enough sand and other grit to make it hazardous for the eyes of anyone who ventured out, but we weren't the only ones with cabin fever. From Gitaña came Duncan; from the Aegean a young dentist and his wife; from Molokai Girl, Fred and Elsie Mach; and John, the physics professor, whose boat had found its final mooring very close to Trilogy. I don't believe all these boats were moored downwind from us, but they all insisted they could smell the fresh bread, cinnamon rolls, and cake and couldn't stay away.

Jim and Rand got out their musical instruments: banjo, guitars, recorder, and mouth harp. Rand plays all of these but not simultaneously. Jim says he's been working on the guitar for ten years and his present virtuosity doesn't warrant branching out into other instruments. The cake, still warm, was received with enough lavish praise to satisfy the most megalomaniacal cook. The time, the mood, was just right for a party. We all joined in singing folk songs and exchanging sailing experiences on into the night — a fitting celebration for the end of vociferous winds and wearying anchor watches.

Dr. John's predictions were all too accurate. In the quiet moonlight after our guests left, we all went out on deck to assess the damage. The ground cover would have delighted a whole colony of gophers; it did not delight us.

Our original hope, that the next good dunking in salt spray would easily remove this accumulation, was obviously wishful thinking. It was going to take hard, thorough brushing; what seemed to lift off the land too easily was amazingly tenacious on our deck. Our sun-powered water distiller seemed all but ruined, with dust in every crevice. But Randy assured us that it could be salvaged. Therefore, automatically, Randy was awarded the job of rehabilitating it.

Lightheartedly we brushed these details aside. The moon was shining across water as smooth as a lake. The whole world awaited us out there. Tomorrow we were moving on.

Trilogy

JIM'S COMMENT:
Playing The Game

I had already learned how to navigate my way around a bureaucracy because I'd gone to several religious boarding schools. I was one of those kids with a bad attitude, so I got in trouble a lot — but I learned a lot in the process.

So when we first started going through customs, I took it on myself as the one who would do those things.

I realized it was just a game, and I started figuring the game out. Here it is: they make life difficult for you, and they look for some money or something so they can make your life easier again. But you can't ask what they're looking for; they can only make life difficult for you.

I was bound and determined never to pay a nickel for the mordita, for the bite. Not only was I broke, but I felt that it was really unrighteous to do that.

When you sail into a new port, you have to visit two separate offices, immigration and customs. Sometimes they're in the same building, and sometimes they're in two different sections of town. Nobody can get off the boat until you've cleared these two entities.

So I'd take the ship's papers and our passports. Most important of all, I'd take our sheet of good conduct from the last port, which said that we were the people on this boat and that they had experienced no problems with us.

When I presented the sheet of good conduct at the first port, they said, "Oh, you have to have three sheets of good conduct." So the next time I brought three, and they wanted five.

Whatever you had, they always wanted two more. That

was the first thing I learned about the game.

Pretty soon, I started typing out five copies of the good conduct sheet. Then I would present the port authorities with three. They would look them over and say, "Lo ciento mucho, capitan. Es muy importante, dos mas papiers."

I'd say, "Gee, my boat is ten miles away. It's taken me half a day to get in here. That's going to be very difficult for me."

"Si señor, lo ciento mucho."

So I'd say, "Look. If I'm able to get those two copies, will things be okay?"

"Oh yeah, that would be okay, but we must have these next two copies."

So I would open my briefcase and rummage through and rummage through. Then I'd pull out the two copies. Everybody would laugh. "Hey, he knows the game!"

They'd invite me in the back, and we'd have a toast. It was a party. They honored the fact that — well, let's put it this way: your need pays part of the bill.

In fact, one of the customs agents in the Galapagos even helped me play the game. On our first visit, I had really protested paying him a dime. So the next time we came through, he came out to the boat to do the paperwork. He said, "Listen, you come in my office, I've got to charge you. But I don't have to charge you if I come out to the boat." Instead of getting the mordita, he ate cookies and popcorn, whatever we had.

The game was hardly ever hostile. I kept a good attitude, friendly but firm.

In Manta, though, the port captain was a very powerful man — the highest ranking political officer in the whole state. This was a military government. When I came to clear customs, he said he wanted, effectively, fifty dollars.

Trilogy

To put this in perspective, the whole family — six of us — was living on about a hundred and fifty dollars a month. Fifty bucks was big, big money. At that point in my life, I'd walk a mile to save a nickel.

I said absolutely not. I won't do it.

So we tussled back and forth. But he had two men standing beside him with sub-machine guns. This was real hard-negotiation time. Real unbalanced, at least.

I said, "Listen, I'm a yacht, and you have no right to do this. If you don't give me my papers, I'll be forced to leave this port without them."

He said, "If you leave this port without my papers, I'll be forced to shoot you."

So I said, "Okay, what do we do?"

He said, "I'm tired of talking to you. You go to my bank and make this deposit of fifty dollars, and then come back."

I said, "I want a receipt that I've done this, and I'm going to make a protest to the consulate in Guayaquil."

He knocked the price down to a tenth of what he was originally charging. It was fifty sucres, about five dollars. Then he said, "Okay, fine. This is my bank account. They'll give you a receipt. I don't care what you do with it."

The next day I asked to speak to the president of the bank. I told him the port captain was extorting fifty sucres from me. He said, "You mean fifty dollars, don't you?"

"No," I said. "Fifty sucres."

He said, "Big deal."

When I went up to give the port captain my receipt, he wouldn't see me. An English ship broker met me at the door. He said that the port captain had looked into the rules, and in fact I was right. He'd never had yachts in his port. Yachts get to clear duty-free; there was no charge. My papers were in order, and I was free to go.

I said, "You know, I just put fifty sucres in this guy's bank account. Do you think you could go in and ask him if he could give that back to me?"

The English broker looked at me with sort of a sad look in his eyes. He said, "I'd forget that if I were you."

In Guayaquil, we totally ran out of money. They had to wire us more from Seattle. I had to go up there and wait several days for the money to come in. I was just flat-out broke.

I was buying some Honda parts or something and I met a guy who took pity on me. I said, "I have some money coming, and I can pay you when it comes in." So I was sleeping on this guy's floor in his little place out of town.

My mom had made a money-belt tee-shirt for me. It was stitched with pockets on the inside, so I could spread the dollar bills around.

It wasn't a lot of money — maybe a thousand bucks. But life is tough in Guayaquil. There, a thousand dollars was a ton of money.

I wanted it all bills. Mostly ones and fives. So they gave me a bag of money. All I had was this bag and me.

So I said, "Where's your bathroom?"

In the bathroom, I took off my shirt and stuffed all the money in the tee-shirt pockets, put it on, and strapped myself in. I didn't even save myself a nickel.

I walked out, and everybody looked at me.

I went out in the street. Suddenly I realized — I was wearing a fortune, but I was still broke! My life was worth nothing.

That was always the message when I was clearing customs.

CHAPTER SEVEN:
FIESTAS AND FRUSTRATIONS

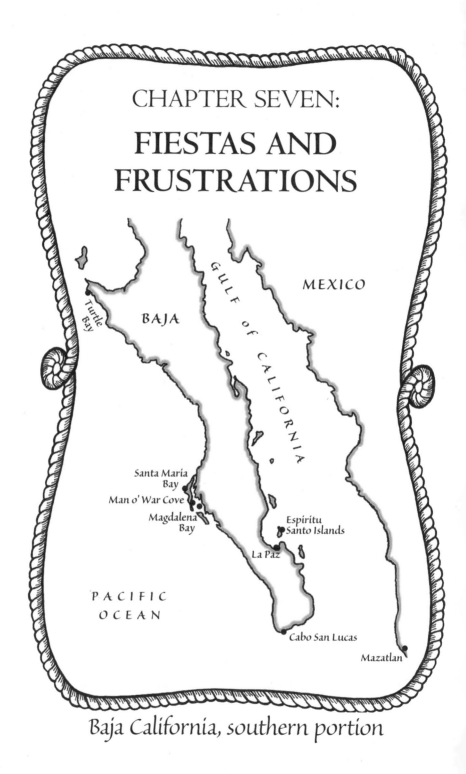

Baja California, southern portion

n reading sea stories, one is often led to conclude that nothing ever happens to sailors except storms and misadventures. Unfortunately, the lazy, delightful days of perfect weather and no mishaps — the most rewarding and addictive part of cruising — make remarkably dull reading.

When an amateur sailor is carried aloft kicking and screaming, hanging for dear life onto a jib sheet he should have released moments before, such a mishap holds the attention much more in the telling than do dozens of perfectly executed sailing maneuvers. Our crew had passed the bungling stage and now could hoist or drop sails, tack or reef with speed and finesse.

That morning as we cruised out of Turtle Bay, waving to the boats still at anchor, the weather was ideal, light breezes moving us along at three or four knots and barely rippling the vast sea before us.

Eldon, more sensitive to weather, I think, than any of the rest of us, was reveling in the perfect day and the broad expanse of freedom before him. Countless times when he was working around the clock in our portrait studio, or when he was preparing the *Mañana* for charter, which required many hours of overtime, he had dreamed of a day like this. He put an arm around me and one around Pattie as he stood at the wheel. "How are my girls this morning?" he asked, sure that we couldn't feel less than wonderful on such a day. "I'm glad I've had to work hard all my life; otherwise I couldn't really appreciate all of this."

Trilogy

And that was, no doubt, absolutely true. The Protestant work ethic is so strong in Eldon that if he hadn't put so much effort into getting here, he would have thought this good sailing undeserved.

Pattie laughed, "Well, don't think I can't appreciate it just because I haven't worked as hard as you have."

Over Pattie's head, Eldon gave me a significant glance that I translated to mean: *See, she's getting to like the cruising life; she's going to be okay.*

And I gave him a quick hug that meant: *I think you may be right, and I do fervently hope so!*

Indolently, we drifted along the beige and purple coast of Baja. From the water it looked like an endlessly prolonged Grand Canyon or the Dakota Badlands stretched to infinity.

Thirty hours after leaving Turtle Bay, we sailed into Bahia Magdalena. Most cruising boats anchor in Man O' War Cove, but to get there it is necessary to make a dog-leg around a long point of land, at least twenty-five miles, and then you are just a narrow isthmus removed from Santa Maria Bay. We decided to spend the weekend in Santa Maria.

⚓

A halcyon weekend it was, too, riding in the dinghy through mangrove swamps (I think whoever invented the first labyrinth or garden maze must have gotten his idea from a mangrove swamp), sunbathing, fishing, reading. I found myself exhaling a sigh of deep contentment. Truly this is the life we had all dreamed about — and it wasn't disappointing. Realization almost always seems to fall short of anticipation, but not in Santa Maria.

I began in a desultory fashion to collect sea shells. They were lying everywhere. At this point I didn't know the difference between sand-scoured beach shells and those with their original finish intact. Unhampered by any technical knowledge, I picked up quantities of fragile bubble shells, turbans, augers, and iridescent oyster shells. Most of them had to be thrown away as I grew more discriminating, but it was a beginning.

Eldon started a collection, too — one that would never become as extensive as mine, though it was at least as aromatic. He collected oddly-shaped bones. Some of them are quite beautiful in an abstract way, if you can forget their origins.

Now, there's no good reason that Eldon's hobby should seem stranger than mine, but it did. For all I knew, the whole thing was an elaborate put-on. If he didn't really approve of my dragging quantities of uninhabited mollusk shells back to the boat, this might have been his subtle way of telling me so.

⚓

We hadn't been contemplating the chore of getting into Magdalena Bay with much joy. If we had a favorable wind leaving Santa Maria, it would mean a headwind going back toward Magdalena. On Sunday morning, though, all our batteries seemed to be recharged with that extra bit of energy required by unpleasant jobs. The wind was still directly out of Man O' War Cove, but suddenly the prospect of tacking our way in seemed challenging and interesting.

("Challenging" and "interesting" lasted for about a half hour after we hit that headwind. After that, we exchanged them for "tedious" and "possibly pointless." Tacking is much less exciting after you find you're losing headway.)

"Let's start the motor," Eldon urged. "We've wasted enough time going back and forth."

Randy, at the wheel, gave his father a glance that would have seared his edges, except that his father wasn't watching. "Where's your sporting blood?" he asked loftily.

Eldon turned around and gave Randy his full attention.

Trilogy

"I have tired blood, and it isn't improving as I see us being pushed out of the bay while we're tacking back and forth. What is a motor for if we can't use it when we need it?"

Randy, still viewing the situation from his lofty stance as the purist, the sportsman, delivered his own dictum: "Motors are for emergencies; this is not an emergency. This is an exhilarating experience."

"There's a good exhilarator down in the motor room if I can just turn it on without causing a family squabble," Eldon continued. He has spent too many years on power boats to be impractical about traveling only under canvas.

Up until now Jim had remained neutral, but he was ready to admit that our progress left something to be desired. Besides, we were taking an unnecessary pounding in these waves. "Let's get over there in the lee a bit and motor in," he suggested.

Outnumbered, Randy shrugged. "OKAY, but I hate to arrive so ignominiously in a good sailing breeze."

"It would be a better sailing breeze," Dave offered mildly, "if it were blowing from the other direction." Right on, Dave.

We dropped our sails and motored to the spot where the other boats were moored, many of them the ones we'd seen in Turtle Bay. After we had the anchor down, Duncan MacGregor stuck his head out of *Gitana's* cabin.

"Oh, hi there," he greeted us, looking at the same time as though he doubted the evidence of his senses. "When did you get here? I didn't even see you coming."

We looked at each other and then at Randy with just a touch of I-told-you-so. Tacking for another three hours wouldn't have been worth the work, not even if the whole fleet had been watching. But if no one had paid any attention, it would have been a terribly wasted gesture.

⚓

Until now, knowing no language except English (western USA variety), Eldon had felt greatly handicapped

Fiestas and Frustrations

in a Spanish-speaking country. In Magdalena Bay he was lucky enough to find just the person he'd been looking for: a Mexican who spoke English and had enough time on his hands to make visiting possible.

Juan Garcia, one of the port officials from La Paz, was spending two weeks with his parents here in Magdalena. His English was fluent, and, best of all, he seemed to have no trouble with Eldon's double-speed verbal delivery. They were buddies from the start. They visited on the boat and on the shore, Eldon constantly plying him with the multitude of questions that had occurred to him all those frustrating times when he'd had no one to talk to.

Before the day was over, they had arranged for us to show our Alaskan slides in the schoolhouse that night. And so began our first real adventure in a foreign culture.

Swift tropical darkness had already descended as we made our way up to the schoolhouse over a landscape as dry and bare as Turtle Bay's had been. Not a shrub, not a flower or blade of grass adorned this bleak landscape. True, there was one lonely palm tree up a small slope, which the residents called with irony "el parque" or just "la palma." That it had survived for enough years to grow ten or twelve feet high showed real dedication on the part of some public-spirited persons.

We brought our little AC generator to provide power for our slide projector; we hadn't given a thought to the fact that the generator only produced four hundred watts and the light on our projector required five hundred watts. So, predictably, the projector refused to function.

Not to worry; Mr. Garcia produced a huge generator from someplace nearby that he said was good for fifteen hundred watts. It certainly sounded brawny enough for the task. The racket was ear-splitting, something like an enormous electric mixer beating up ball bearings. Realizing that no lecture could accompany the picture show in the middle of all this noise, Juan and a few helpers took it into another building and ran extension cords to the school room.

All was hushed; we were ready to begin. In the flickering light of an occasional flashlight we could see that
the room was crowded. But no sound escaped from the
crowd. I think they were all holding their breath. Finally,
the projector was plugged in, and a beautiful Alaskan
glacier appeared on the screen for somewhat less then five
seconds. Then, total blackness. Our only projector bulb
had burned out!

All the pent-up air escaped from our audience in a
huge sigh.

At Eldon's suggestion, Jim and Rand had brought
along their guitars and Rand's banjo, and they apologized
for the fiasco and began making some music. Even in
Magdalena Bay, almost all the kids had transistor radios,
so a lot of the folk songs popular north of the border were
well-known here. It wasn't long before some brave souls
began to join in the singing; then the boys began to get
requests from the audience.

But the best was yet to come.

A small, middle-aged man came over to Jim and asked
timidly if they would like to have some more musicians.
Jim was enthusiastic. "Si! Si! The more the merrier!" (or
whatever its equivalent is in Spanish), and an orchestra
was formed with the addition of an accordion, a bass
fiddle, and another guitar. These new musicians were
great, better than you might expect to find in a tiny place
like Magdalena Bay. And suddenly it was party time!
Several cases of soft drinks were brought out, and the
party went into high gear; whatever song my kids couldn't
think of, the other fellows remembered.

Before the evening was over, Reuben, the principal of
the local elementary school who seemed to be the
spokesman for the community, informed us that the residents of Magdalena Bay were inviting all the people from
the visiting yachts to a fiesta the following night. Also,

Fiestas and Frustrations

because Pattie had mentioned that she had studied conversational Spanish but wasn't very sure about the correct
grammar, Reuben offered to come out to the boat every
day during siesta and give her Spanish lessons.

Oh, those Spanish lessons! Pattie originally accepted
Reuben's offer because time was hanging heavily on her
hands. With the advent of an young man named Ramon,
however, along with other friends in Magdalena Bay, she
would have no problem filling her time. But the lessons
wouldn't go away. Every day at twelve o'clock, Reuben was
waiting on the shore to be shuttled out to the *Trilogy*. She
could never say, "I just don't feel like studying today,"
because Reuben was giving up his lunch hour (two hours,
actually) in order to help her. So she kept grimly on with
it, even doing the assigned homework, and she learned —
reluctantly perhaps, but true progress was made.

If you were asked to pick out the most teacher-like
person in a group of Mexicans, Reuben would be an
unerring choice: eyes dark and serious, shiny and round as
a young seal's; face long and bony; teeth big and smily. He
was accustomed to teaching reluctant learners, slow
learners, and those who could scarcely learn at all. His
manner balanced both authority and patience. Other
young men in the village might have been flipping their
wigs over Pattie, whose blonde beauty was too obviously
appreciated, but Reuben showed plainly that she was just
another pupil to him — and not necessarily the brightest
one he'd ever had. He was an excellent antidote for too
much hot-eyed Latin admiration.

In the best pedagogical tradition, he took absolutely
nothing for granted. So, she had studied Spanish; obviously
it hadn't done her much good; let us begin with the
primers. She began with the Mexican equivalent of LOOK,
JANE, LOOK. Just listening to these sessions helped me
develop a little vocabulary and some basic grammar. My
long-ago Latin was some help in reading Spanish, but not

much when listening to it spoken rapidly.

Every day I prepared a lunch for Reuben, which he ate abstractedly, probably not even tasting it much. Nothing deterred him from his primary concern — teaching. Such single-minded devotion could not fail to produce results. Day by day, Pattie's fluency and self-confidence improved. Reuben wasn't one to volunteer many compliments. Even so, by the time we left Magdalena Bay, he had to concede that his effort hadn't been entirely wasted.

⚓

No one in our yachting fraternity knew what to expect of a Mexican fiesta, nor what to wear. Would they wear wide skirts and peasant blouses, flat black hats with ball-fringed brims?

We needn't have worried; those assembled looked much like any group in the US casually dressed in warm weather. (Sometimes now we thought about what the weather must be like in Alaska or Puget Sound in mid-January, and that made us feel very lucky.) Men and boys wore the usual white shirts and dark trousers; the ladies and girls, print dresses — very short ones on the teenage girls. Obviously, the mini skirt had crossed the border.

Last night's accordionist and four other musicians began playing Latin, Spanish, and Mexican songs. Rand had chosen to be part of the orchestra. If he didn't know a song already, he could usually follow along anyway. Several cases of soda pop had been provided for refreshments.

As soon as the fiesta was well under way, Jim came and sat down beside me. I knew he wouldn't choose to spend his evening there when there were a number of pretty girls circulating around, so I asked, "What's the trouble?"

"No trouble," he said uneasily. "It's just that I think this fiesta thing is going to be a dance."

I nodded; it seemed extremely likely.

Jim knew that my parents — and Eldon's — had

viewed dancing as a snare of the devil's invention. We had never been allowed to dance, nor had our children been encouraged to do so, although from subsequent observation I realized that they were not as unfamiliar with dancing as I had supposed.

Jim still hadn't gotten to the crux of the matter, and he was uncomfortable with this whole scenario. "Well," he went on, "I thought I'd better warn you and Pattie. Probably you can get out of it if you want to. Lots of the older people don't dance, I'm told. But if anyone asks Pattie to dance, you'd better tell her to accept and do what she can with it."

"I don't even need to think about it, Jim," I replied, "to tell you this much: if Pattie doesn't want to dance, no one is going to get her out on that floor. You know how bashful she can be, and also how stubborn."

"I may be wrong; it may never come up." Jim stopped and drew a deep breath. He understood the clash of cultures here and didn't want our hosts to be offended. "But I'm sure if someone asks Pattie to dance, it would be a real breach of etiquette to refuse. I'm not a great dancer, but I'm going to get out there and show these folks that their hospitality is appreciated."

Several couples were dancing by this time; Pattie, who had heard part of my conversation with Jim, took the seat he had so recently vacated. Next to her were Grimjaws and Cement Head, off the motor-sailor *Island Queen*, two ladies of mature years and delightful wit.

"I hope they don't ask me to dance," Pattie confided to all and sundry; "I've never seen this kind of dance before."

"Come on, now!" Grimjaws scolded. "You should be out there having fun. I certainly intend to." She stood up to dance with Duncan MacGregor.

When Duncan came back, no doubt well briefed by Grimjaws, he grabbed Pattie's hands and pulled her to her feet.

"C'mon," he urged in what was supposed to be a whisper, but was clearly audible at twenty paces. "Y're supposed to be the guest of honor. D'ya wantum to think y're not enjoyin' it?"

They weren't a notable success as dancing partners; Duncan's dancing style showed more enthusiasm than grace. But he had accomplished his purpose. Before Pattie could sit down, a dark young man was bowing in front of her. Hesitantly, she stood up, and suddenly a stag line was forming about fifteen men deep between her chair and the open door.

Soon Pattie was having a perfectly wonderful time.

At this moment, Eldon arrived. He was less than pleased to see his daughter being whisked around the dance floor by a strange Mexican youth. His recurring nightmare was that Pattie would marry someone in one of our ports of call and spend her life deprived and unhappy in some far corner of the earth.

He leaned toward me. "What" (he whispered furiously) "did you let her do that for?"

"I don't recall being asked for permission," I replied truthfully. I explained what Jim had told me and added, "She had to use her own judgment."

Eldon snorted, "God invented parents because kids don't have any judgment!"

He sat glowering at the well-filled dance floor, but his glowering didn't seem to blight anyone else's pleasure — least of all, Pattie's. Jim, I noticed, was dancing with the best-looking Mexican girl in the room.

Pattie was getting more light-footed and sparkle-eyed as the evening progressed; she looked as though she could hold out until morning. As a spectator sport, though, dancing tends toward monotony after the first two or three hours. By midnight I was having no end of trouble trying to stifle my yawns.

However, there was no question about the success of

Fiestas and Frustrations

the fiesta, the first one this community had had, Reuben told us, since he'd arrived early in the fall. And so much good will had been generated that the yachting people issued an invitation for the people of Magdalena Bay to attend a beach party the following night, with the yachters providing refreshments. This had never happened before in living memory, even though yachts had been coming and going for years. Reuben made the announcement at half past twelve, signaling the end of the fiesta. Everyone applauded vigorously — some like me, no doubt because they were a bit weary of watching other people dance, but most of them because a party with the yachting people was unprecedented and exciting.

However dull the evenings had been previously, they were not to be so in the near future. This little community had suddenly sprung to life.

⚓

I volunteered to make a hundred tarts, some cherry and some lemon meringue, enough to insure that each person in the community would be able to get one. (I'm sure they were not that evenly distributed. In the semi-darkness the next evening, I saw some of the young men making off with two or three.) Depending on their cooking facilities, others baked what their ovens would accommodate, made sandwiches, and we all contributed to a ten-gallon container of fruit punch.

While Pattie was helping me in the galley as we made our part of the refreshments, she asked, a little too nonchalantly, if I had noticed a certain young man at the fiesta. He'd sat across the room from us. I could only remember a mass of dark-eyed, dark-skinned young fellows in white, white shirts. (Oh, those white shirts! After I saw how the Baja women slaved over their washboards, those ubiquitous sparkling white shirts almost made me feel angry.)

I should have been paying more attention, that day in

the galley. Pattie's comment was the beginning of trouble with a capital T, but I was busy making tarts. I only vaguely remember her saying that he didn't dance with her because he was bashful.

He didn't remain bashful very long. It became quite apparent at the beach party that this young man, Ramon, and his friend Ricardo were monopolizing most of Pattie's time. They spoke some English, but Pattie wanted to practice Spanish. She wanted me to believe that her primary motive in spending that evening and subsequent days with Ramon and Ricardo was linguistic. It seemed harmless enough, but still, not knowing the customs in this remote community, I thought I would talk to her about it. Frankly, it looked like a plain old flirtation to me.

"Pattie," I began, feeling awkward but determined, "you don't know what the dating customs are like in this country. You are giving Ramon a lot of flattering, undivided attention. He may mistake that for a serious attachment. He could feel very hurt and possibly lose face in his community. I'm sure you don't want to embarrass him or really hurt his feelings."

Genuinely surprised, Pattie responded. "Oh, no! I told him we're only going to be here for a few days. He knows it's no big, romantic thing."

I knew Pattie had no intention of settling down over a Baja washboard, but I had no way of knowing whether Ramon knew it. My uneasiness remained, but I didn't mention it to Pattie again. She would only respond, "Oh, mother, honestly!" in total exasperation.

⚓

Thursday night, guess what? Another fiesta.

Eldon slapped his forehead with the palm of his hand. "Not another one! I've got work to do. I can't spend all my time partying."

"We're going to have to leave pretty soon so we can

get some sleep," I said wearily. "It was at least two o'clock this morning when we got back to the boat."

"I'll go," Eldon offered generously. "You get some sleep. All this hospitality is wonderful, and I don't want to hurt anybody's feelings."

I immediately felt guilty. Eldon put in more genuine work time than anyone else in our group, and he probably enjoyed the dancing least — unless it should happen that he could visit with Juan Garcia at the same time.

"Don't you think Jim and Randy's presence there will be enough?" They were both past twenty-one and quite responsible.

"Who knows?" Eldon retorted, his mind made up. "I've seen lots of fathers chaperoning their daughters — not many big brothers, though. I'll go and uphold the family honor. If they have one of these..." (he never could bring himself to say 'fiestas') "tomorrow night, it's your turn."

By Saturday night, having consulted the folk wisdom and local knowledge of Mr. Garcia, Eldon decided that Jim and Randy could take care of Pattie, and both of us had a night off.

⚓

Sunday all of us except Eldon, who never felt he had anything to prove by trying to ride a surfboard, caught a ride on a large and rickety truck across the isthmus to Santa Maria Bay. Here the waves were reportedly ideal for beginning surfers — long rollers, a gradually sloping beach, waves about chest height. My children were soon standing on their boards, waving to all and sundry like royalty acknowledging the applause of their subjects, and indeed showing considerable aptitude for this sport.

Not me.

What I showed was unbelievable ineptitude. The surfboard was totally uncooperative, slippery as a fish, darting off in every direction including straight up. As soon as it got away from me, my board showed that it had always intended to head for the beach, but not necessarily with me on it. I gave it a good try, I really did, but eventually I had to concede that even if I managed to stand up on the board, which seemed unlikely, I was not going to excel at this sport.

It was another three hours before the successful surfers showed any inclination to come ashore, and that was only because of my urging. The truckdriver had been sitting in the cab, too polite to hurry the surfers but obviously ready to go at any time. I waded out through the surf until I got within hailing distance of Jim and Rand.

"C'mon, kids, let's go. That poor truckdriver has been waiting more than four hours."

"He has?"

Rand sounded more surprised than that piece of information warranted. But then time goes by faster, they tell me, when you're "catching waves."

Jim came over and joined in, "He hasn't tooted the horn; he said he'd toot when it was time to go back."

"He doesn't want to interrupt your fun," I said, "but I can tell he's getting restless. When I went over to the truck, he brightened up and asked if we were through with our 'exercicio.'"

Several kids from Magdalena Bay had come over with us. They now joined the group along with Cindy Smith, whose parents owned a big tuna boat anchored in Magdalena Bay. They had brought Cindy over in a car, but she wasn't sure when they'd be back for her and preferred to catch a ride with us. Opinion seemed to be divided about whether it was I or the truckdriver who wanted to go back. Granted that my sympathy for the truckdriver was mixed with some for myself, I still thought we had been there long enough.

I turned to Jim. "You're the best at speaking Spanish. Ask him if he wants to go back. It's long past lunch time, and, as far as I can see, he didn't bring anything to eat."

The Magdalena Mexicans had gone back to surfing, and it looked as though we might be here for a long day. Jim went over to talk to the truckdriver, who was a volunteer and was not being paid for his time. Belatedly, Jim asked if he wouldn't like to try surfing before we went back.

"Not me," he replied, shivering delicately. "Too much like diving for lobster and abalone." He laughed at the idea. "All week I do that."

Although it took some time to get everyone assembled, the driver definitely seemed more relaxed after we began to show signs that he wasn't going to be stuck there for the entire day.

Many months later I learned that the shore at Santa Maria is one of the best shell-collecting beaches in the world, and I hadn't made much of my opportunity. Vain regrets; I tell myself that some day I'll go back there.

⚓

When we got back to the village, Eldon was taking care of the never-ending clothes washing. In doing so, he was giving up one of the traditional privileges of the men, who somehow, back in the dim ages of the past, had managed to worm their way out of that tedious chore. Little boys do help carry water, but the actual scrubbing routine seems to be for ladies only.

Pattie was especially struck by the cruel discrepancy between the flowery romanticism with which young ladies are courted and the near slavery of the married state. Nevertheless, disillusioning as this might be to a North American girl accustomed to comforts these girls had never heard of, the young women of Baja seemed surprisingly contented with their concrete washboards and succession of babies. Some of the women were old, tired, and overworked, and they showed it, but even they didn't seem unhappy with their lot.

Trilogy

To be perfectly fair, the men don't have such an easy life, either. Lobster fishing and diving for abalone are physically very demanding and, by our standards, poorly paid.

Nevertheless, we all discovered a warmth and serenity about all of these people that would be hard to find in most big cities. They are very trusting, hospitable, and quick to offer friendship. Later in our travels we would see the gray, pinched faces of real poverty, the silent endurance of burdens too heavy to be borne, and we would re-evaluate the simple austerity of Magdalena Bay. Here, no one had much, but everyone had enough.

⚓

Two more days passed, and Eldon was finishing chores that spelled departure. I felt vaguely relieved to be moving on; it was time. Ramon and Pattie seemed to be having more and more lengthy conversations on the boat and on the shore. I knew I was going to feel more comfortable when they were separated by several miles of ocean.

It wasn't until they were separated that I learned that we hadn't really solved the problem that way.

One by one, the boats that had participated in the yachter's beach party left Magdalena Bay until only four remained besides *Trilogy*. Reuben came out to the boat for one last teaching session and to bid us good-by. He was far too polite to show that he was at all relieved with our departure, which meant that he would have his lunch and siesta hours back, but he would have been less than human if the thought hadn't occurred to him. He would have liked very much to buy our solar still, which would manufacture six quarts of fresh water every twenty-four hours. However, we had to refuse; this was an important part of our survival equipment. It might be handy for a family on Baja, but their lives wouldn't depend on it. Ours could. We gave him the address of the manufacturer in San Diego, not an impossible distance away.

Fiestas and Frustrations

It was with mixed feelings that we pulled away from Magdalena Bay, a unique community of hardy people, affectionate and trustworthy, with the strong independence of those who wrest their living from an inhospitable land and ask no concessions of anyone. They might joke about "el parque" and "la palma," the lone inhabitant of that park, but the humor was gentle and good-natured with an underlying feeling that life on Baja was good, even with its deprivations.

I can't even imagine how many rations of precious fresh water had been sacrificed to bring that lonely palm tree to its present height.

⚓

Magdalena Bay, like Scammon's Lagoon farther south, is a basking ground for mating whales. This was right in the middle of the mating season, and the whales seemed almost as close together as sardines in a can — although much, much larger.

Fortunately, most whales are surprisingly good-natured, and some even have a sense of humor. Once in Alaska a big gray whale, substantially longer than the sixty-two foot *Mañana*, swam around the boat for some time itching his barnacles on the sides and keel. Then, just as a parting joke, he lifted a cubic yard or so of water with his enormous tail and deftly tossed it into the pilot house. Instant waterfalls cascaded in all directions, and he swam away, no doubt smugly pleased with himself and the panic he had caused.

We knew that most whales are not looking for trouble, but we weren't sure how the mating season might affect their dispositions. Records of whales gone berserk and reducing boats larger than ours to kindling made us proceed very cautiously. Slowly, carefully, we worked our way through the seemingly inert bodies until we had a clear passage out to sea. With the aid of a half moon, we avoided any real collisions with these gentle monsters — but often at the last heart-stopping moment.

Under star-filled skies we set sail for Cabo San Lucas, southernmost point of the Baja peninsula. Here, the water is deep almost purplish blue and clear to unbelievable depths. Three towering rocks known as The Friars mark the point where the Sea of Cortez merges with the Pacific Ocean. The scenery is indeed spectacular. At least half of this scenery lies below the water's surface, and many people enthusiastically assert that this submarine half is the better one.

We all donned masks and snorkels, I for the first time. My amphibious children showed remarkable patience dealing with my ineptitude. I did have trouble learning to breathe through my mouth. When the "can't breathe" feeling became overpowering, I would jerk off my mask and gulp some air. I always hoped the kids weren't watching, but they often were. They shook their heads in patient exasperation, just as I had so often done toward them from my adult position of natural or fancied superiority.

Eldon put on mask, flippers, and wetsuit one time and thereafter claimed he could see everything he needed with a pair of goggles. It is true that there is good visibility that way, but having to get one's face out of the water for every breath is a nuisance. At first the kids and I tried to change his mind, but we abandoned the effort quite soon for the simple reason that we were all so fascinated with the underwater world.

Dave spent every waking moment in the water, and so did the rest of us as much as our simple and abbreviated household duties permitted. With monumental unconcern, the fish swam all around us, never quite touching but coming within a fraction of an inch. Every color of the rainbow was represented in this passing parade: needle fish, striped blue-and-gold snappers, amethyst wrasses with turquoise spots that looked like sequins; the variety was endless. The rocks, covered by stationary sea creatures, resembled a submerged flower garden.

I don't really know what the incidence of sharks is in this area, but they were always on my mind to some extent. So whenever Jim tapped my arm to get my attention, I just about went into levitation. After several of these sudden terror incidents, Jim pantomimed taking off masks and snorkels, and I removed mine.

"Sorry, Mom," he apologized. "I didn't want to scare you, but you can't hear me under water."

Jim had majored in biology in college, especially marine biology, and he wanted to explain to me some of the things we were seeing. "Maybe you could think of some way I could signal you without getting the startle reflex."

I laughed. "Don't worry about it, Jim; the extra adrenaline will probably improve my swimming!"

"OKAY, I hope so. Just then, I wanted to tell you not to get your face so close to those rocks. There's a moray eel in a hole there, and they have a nasty habit of coming out suddenly and biting people."

One of the local residents who hadn't taken up snorkeling, but who certainly interfered with ours, was a large, black Labrador retriever. Possibly he thought we were distant relatives in our black wetsuits. We weren't distant enough; however quietly we slipped off the far side of the boat, he was there in a few moments, happily galloping through the surf and swimming out to meet us. He splashed a lot and scared the fish, but worse, he wanted to put his big feet on our shoulders when he got tired. Wet suits are fragile and his claws were sharp. No amount of remonstrance made any impression on him; the only solution was to get in the skiff and find a snorkeling place farther away.

⚓

Cabo was the first of many ports where we had to jump out of the skiff and bring it through the surf. Though the water was only a little over knee-deep, I managed to get myself fairly well dampened all over on this first try. It seemed a rigorous method of getting letters to the post office, and I attached a postscript to each envelope to be sure my efforts were appreciated. I felt heroic enough about getting all these letters written without having to wade ashore carrying them in my teeth.

Little did I know that Cabo was one of the better places; the surge in many future harbors would reach shoulder height, and letters would have to be held high overhead while we struggled to keep solid footing and balance.

Almost everyone in our party wanted to stay for another week or two at the Cape — in fact, had subconsciously planned on doing so. The swimming was wonderful, the snorkeling even better. We even had a tennis court at our disposal, thanks to the manager of the Hacienda Cabo San Lucas. Then why did we have to leave so precipitously?

Pattie got the blame for it, but she could hardly have out-voted all the rest of us without some solid backing from her dad, who seemed to suffer from a compulsion to keep moving. Dave almost jumped ship then and there, and he did so a month later, still unhappy about having to leave this place so soon.

It all started, it seems, when we were leaving Magdalena Bay and Ramon asked Pattie if he could come see her while we were in La Paz. Her Spanish at that time was only a little better than his English, leaving a sizable communication gap. She thought he said that Villa Constitution, where his family lived, was a mere six miles from La Paz. Only after we were out at sea did she think of consulting a map, and she learned that the two cities are at least one hundred and fifty miles apart.

Laboriously (it took her twelve hours), she wrote to Ramon in Spanish, telling him that we would not be in La Paz as soon as she had thought.

One copy went to Villa Constitution and one to La Paz.

Fiestas and Frustrations

Still, mail service was uncertain, and she worried that he'd make the long trip to La Paz and not find *Trilogy* there.

Eldon sided with Pattie; although he granted that she shouldn't have made any such arrangements without consulting the rest of the crew, he still felt we were duty-bound to show up in La Paz as soon as Ramon did. In reply to her brothers' innuendoes, Pattie protested that she had no romantic attachment to Ramon, that she hardly knew him, in fact. But they, frustrated at leaving Cabo when they were having so much fun, wouldn't let her off lightly. Flouncing off to her stateroom whenever the subject surfaced, she repeated, "I just don't want to talk about it."

She spent a lot of time in her room, door closed, as we slogged our way to La Paz with contrary winds and a disgruntled crew.

⚓

After the sparsely settled coast of Baja, La Paz seemed like a real metropolis, with supermarkets and a genuine laundromat. The laundromat lost most of its charm, and all our patronage, after the first big day of laundering. Devoted as it was almost entirely to the tourist trade, and having a virtual monopoly, its prices were roughly four times what they had been in San Diego.

It was back to wash-it-by-hand, dry-it-in-the-rigging for *Trilogy*.

Still, it did feel wonderful for the moment to have all those clean sheets, jeans, big fuzzy towels — all the things that were sheer murder to wash by hand.

Since San Diego we'd been carrying an old bicycle on our back deck. Jim had paid eight dollars for it, and no one felt he had gotten a bargain. It didn't improve the appearance of the deck, and a month of salt-spray had turned it from merely old to old and ugly.

The bike, however, had a large basket in front of the handlebars that would carry many pounds of produce. Here in La Paz it was a three-mile round trip to the nearest market. When I was walking, I always found I had accumulated more weight in my packages than I realized and that the weight doubled every half mile. All the things we craved — oranges, lemons, limes, pineapple, papayas — turned out to be very heavy in transit. We suddenly began to realize that for the price of a half-dozen hamburgers Jim had picked up a priceless two-wheeled convenience. I grabbed it whenever I could.

Even before we started on our travels, we had heard many horror stories about the difficulty of getting money sent south of the border. Strangely enough, we had given it very little thought until it happened to us.

When we first arrived in La Paz, Eldon went to a bank — probably not the only one in town, but it looked as though it would suit our purpose. This institution's preferred method of transferring funds was by mail. We were to write to our home bank and have a bank draft sent in their care. "Not more than a week," the bank manager assured us.

OKAY, we could wait a week

Promptly, after one week, Eldon went back. The bank manager was puzzled. "Give it a few more days," he said. "Nothing to worry about."

Well, not for him, probably. For us, it definitely was a worry. We were traveling on the proverbial shoestring, and we knew it — but we hadn't even considered the possibility that we might not be able to get hold of a piece of that string when it was needed.

After three weeks, during which time the transfer and dearth of funds was the main topic aboard *Trilogy*, Eldon sent a wire to the bank in Kenmore. They replied that the money had been mailed sixteen days previously.

They sent a tracer (whatever that is) after the missing money, and we prepared to wait it out. If we moved on, we'd just complicate things and make delivery more uncertain.

I had six hundred fifty dollars in traveler's checks saved

from my last paycheck, and I finally offered it as a stop-gap measure so that we could keep on eating regularly. My original purpose for it was to buy mementos of our travels, curios and artifacts, whatever I saw along the way that I couldn't live without. But what we really couldn't live without was food. So, my ace-in-the-hole disappeared into the common fund.

Meanwhile, most of us agreed, much to Pattie's discomfiture, that we would have enjoyed the time a lot more if we could have spent it in Cabo San Lucas. We couldn't even swim in the harbor because La Paz was having an epidemic of hepatitis and we had been warned that the harbor water was polluted.

One morning, out of the blue, Dave announced that he was going up the Sea of Cortez with John, the physicist we had met in Turtle Bay. They planned to go fishing, diving, snorkeling, and photographing sea life — all things Dave loved to do. We had to grant that he wasn't getting to do much of them in La Paz.

Dave had always been a congenial member of our group, always polite, always helpful, and, now that he was developing into a good sailor, an even more valuable member of the crew. We hated to see him go. But his mind was made up, and he was gathering up his gear even while he was telling us his plans.

The day after Dave left, Ramon arrived.

⚓

Ramon had received Pattie's letter and postponed his trip until there was a good possibility we had gotten to La Paz. His welcome might have been more enthusiastic if most of us hadn't been thinking that, after all, we might just as well have stayed in Cabo for another two weeks.

Ramon's fishing buddies in Magdalena Bay had evidently thought it a good joke to recommend a hotel for his stay that was largely inhabited by prostitutes. A kind

passer-by, seeing Ramon looking the place over in a somewhat bewildered fashion, suitcase in hand, noting his youth
and obvious lack of worldly wisdom, told him that it wasn't
a suitable place for him to stay, and why. He walked on
down to the boat harbor, thinking that Jim and Rand
might be able to help him find a better place.

Pattie was hesitant about asking him to stay on the
boat, but I felt sorry for him; his so-called friends had
played a dirty trick on him. After all, he was barely twenty
years old and had hardly ever been away from home except
for his time fishing, staying with relatives in Magdalena
Bay and going home weekends. I invited him to use the
stateroom Dave had just vacated. I wasn't sure it was wise; it
might have encouraged him to imagine that we were
considering him as a prospective son-in-law. But I will never
know. With a Spanish vocabulary of fifty words or less, I was
not competent to discuss situations of such delicacy.

Ramon had heard about La Paz night clubs and was
sure he didn't want to take Pattie to any of them. So, he
and Pattie spent a lot of time walking around the town,
usually eating lunch in some little cantina and coming
back to the boat by mid-afternoon. Ramon had exception-
ally good manners, an unstudied courtesy that is the result
of natural kindness more than training. I liked him. So did
Pattie, to about the same degree.

Unfortunately, "like" was not what Ramon had in
mind. On the morning of his departure he tried to tell me
about his plans for the future. He wanted to go to the
United States, make a lot of money, and marry Pattie.
Many have had similar dreams. Some have dreamed with a
girl in mind; some have even made it come true, but the
odds are overwhelmingly against it.

I knew he had relatives in California, and with Pattie
translating I advised caution.

"You can probably get a visa to visit your relatives. Do
it. Look the situation over. Not everyone in the US makes

lots of money. If the opportunities look good, your relatives can probably sponsor you on a more permanent
basis. But before you commit yourself, be sure it's better
than what you're doing here."

I knew that Pattie had no intention of marrying him,
rich or otherwise, and that message probably came
through in this speech. He thought it over for a long time.
Finally he nodded. "That is a good plan," he agreed. "I
will do as you say."

He left, showering me with a profusion of flowery
Spanish that left me completely unenlightened, except
that I was sure it was intended to be complimentary.

Pattie and Randy accompanied Ramon to the bus
depot. Eldon was vastly and visibly relieved. He was
inclined to see a prospective husband for his daughter in
every rural swain. When Pattie and Randy did not return
immediately, he began worrying again. "She probably
decided to go with him," he surmised gloomily.

It was no use arguing. By some sort of women's intu-
ition I knew that Pattie was tired of the whole thing and
overjoyed to see Ramon depart, but the men in our family
didn't believe me.

⚓

PATTIE'S COMMENT:
Latin Men And My Dad

I'll never forget sailing into Magdalena Bay. Ensenada was
fun, but we all felt that it wasn't "really" Mexico just because
so many tourists visited there. Magdalena was the real thing. It
was a heady feeling to be surrounded by such beauty,
simplicity, and friendliness.

Trilogy

That night was my first experience really mingling with the local people, and was I ever ready! There weren't any other kids my age cruising with their families, so my social life felt very barren at that point. I was ready to do something fun with other young people. A party sounded great!

I felt kind of embarrassed to dance in front of my parents — especially my dad. Neither Mom nor Dad approved of dancing, and the fact that I knew how was going to be a certain giveaway that I'd learned somewhere! However, at that point, my desire to have some fun far outweighed any apprehensions I had about dancing in front of my parents.

It wasn't long before I was having a great time — though it was a little distracting whenever I glanced over at my folks. Mom was smiling and laughing (living it up vicariously through me, I felt). But Dad was scowlingly watching my every move. I knew he didn't like it. But I decided I'd deal with the consequences of his wrath later. Most of the evening I tried to ignore his stares.

This wasn't the first time that Dad's over-protectiveness (at least, that's what I called it) had reared its ugly head. He was always that way — not only with boyfriends but even with my girlfriends. He didn't like to share his kids with anyone very much, but his eye seemed to be directed much more at me than at Jim or Randy. Oh, the joys of being an only daughter!

Most of the time I didn't let it bother me too much. Our dad was always very loving, though he communicated his love much more through action than word. He was always there for a hug or a squeeze. I had come into puberty, though. Like many fathers of young women, he didn't know quite what to do with me. He did feel that he needed to protect me from all those guys, with their raging hormones, who were lurking around every corner waiting to pounce on his little girl. Eventually, this obsession with protecting me was going to feel so suffocating that it would almost drive me away.

I'm sure I didn't help matters any. I didn't understand the complete cultural differences between Latin America and the United States. I'd just started to taste independence back in Seattle, and I didn't want to let it go. I thought Mom, Dad, Jim, and Rand were all being dramatic and unnecessarily sheltering when they said I couldn't walk somewhere by myself. I know now that they didn't want to scare me with the horror stories they'd heard.

In fact, if I'd heard them, caution might have sunk in sooner.

That night at the dance, when I met Ramon, I didn't have any idea that he might get different signals from the ones I intended. I definitely liked him and enjoyed spending time with him, but I certainly wasn't planning to marry him! I didn't understand his culture. I may have been young and naive, but I was always careful not to hurt anyone's feelings, just as I didn't want mine hurt.

When Ramon showed up in La Paz, I realized that I'd made a big mistake — a mistake involving someone else's heart. It was one thing to flirt and romance in his small village, where he was well-respected, where he could show me around and show me off. As we sailed away from Magdalena, though, I knew I didn't want it to go any further. Then, in La Paz, there he stood — a simple fisherman, uneducated and out of place, with love-lights shining in his eyes. I knew I'd trifled unintentionally with his emotions, and I felt terrible.

It's hard enough to break up in a language you both understand, but imagine doing it when neither is fluent in the other's language. Somehow, though, just as love can be communicated without all the right words, so can breaking up (even though I never intended to be a "couple"). I found enough words to let Ramon know that I cared about him, but that we were from very different worlds. Unfortunately, I knew he completely understood my deeper meaning. It was a lesson I've never forgotten.

I felt fairly safe striking up a friendship with Miguel, whose family owned a restaurant in La Paz. He wanted to learn better English and asked if we could talk together for an hour or so every day so he could practice. I, on the other hand, wanted to learn better Spanish. We made a deal: I'd converse with him in English for a half hour if he'd then speak Spanish with me for the same length of time. He seemed satisfied with our arrangement.

Every day during siesta I would go to the restaurant where Miguel worked. After finishing whatever work he had, he would sit down at the table and we'd talk. Miguel was a typical Latin flirt. Even though I thought he was really handsome, I wasn't interested in him for a couple of reasons. He was about a foot shorter than I, which didn't exactly turn my crank. Besides, after my experience with Ramon, I'd decided that I wouldn't date, flirt with, or give the wrong impression to any of these Latin guys.

I knew that Dad was very uneasy with my tutoring lessons. I assured both my folks that this was very innocent and completely safe. There were always other people in the restaurant when we were there; we were well chaperoned.

One day while I was there I realized that it was getting late and that I should head for the boat. Just as I was getting up, I felt an excruciating pain in my abdomen. I doubled over onto the chair next to mine, writhing in agony. The ladies in the restaurant ran over to me, fussing and trying to help. I broke out in a cold sweat, then started to vomit. I didn't know if this was food poisoning or something else; I only knew that the room was swirling around me. I kept blacking out.

I do remember Miguel asking me if I wanted to lie down on his bed in the back room. (He lived at the restaurant.) Fortunately I had enough presence of mind left to decline his offer, realizing that it would put us both in a very compromising position. Instead, Miguel pushed some chairs together from me to lie on. I remember asking for someone to go to the boat, to get my brothers or my dad, but I don't think anyone understood what I was asking. I was burning up with fever, and I probably wasn't very coherent.

During the night the ladies washed my head with a cool cloth. I came in and out of semi-consciousness, hearing a bustle of concern around me, yet I had no concept of time.

The next thing I clearly remember was waking up and realizing that it was either nighttime or early morning and that my family must be absolutely frantic. I still felt quite ill, but the worst was past and I needed to get to the boat. Miguel helped me up. The Mexican ladies were still there, clucking over me to make sure I was well enough to be walking. They didn't think I should go anywhere, but they finally let me go.

With Miguel's help I slowly made my way down to the boat. All I could think of was how scared everyone must be. I'd only been about four blocks away the whole time, yet no one from the restaurant had gone to find my family. I never could figure that one out.

As Miguel and I walked out on the pier, we could see Trilogy anchored out in the bay. As soon as we came into view, I saw my dad jump into the skiff. With one yank he started the engine and stood in the skiff, white hair and beard blowing in the wind, as the little rubber boat bounced over the waves toward us. I knew Dad was beside himself, but I was sure he'd want to thank Miguel for helping me safely back to the boat.

The next incident is a blur in my memory. All I remember is my dad jumping out of the skiff yelling at Miguel and starting to chase him. Miguel was backing up with a completely astonished expression on his face, frantically explaining the situation in a volley of Spanish words. Dad was so upset that he wouldn't have listened even if Miguel had spoken in English. All my dad knew was that his little girl had been missing all night; now this Mexican Romeo was bringing her home after probably having his way with her. I was crying and shouting at my dad not to hurt Miguel, that he hadn't done anything wrong, but there was no reasoning with my father. I thought he was going to strike Miguel. Miguel threw me a look that said, "I don't know what to do," and he turned around and ran — with my dad in hot pursuit. Dad didn't chase him for long. Next he turned to me and, grabbing me by the arm, plunked me down in the skiff. We headed out to the boat. I was crying and trying to explain what had happened, but my pleas fell on deaf, and very angry, ears.

To make matters worse, Jim and Lila Hanley had flown into La Paz the day before to join us for a couple of weeks of cruising. Not only had my family been in great distress about me, but it had also happened right in front of these very dear friends.

Dad wasted no time in pulling up anchor and sailing away from La Paz. He couldn't get me out of there fast enough.

Fiestas and Frustrations

While we sailed out to the San Blas Islands, I endured endless questioning from everyone. No one believed my story except Mom. My story sounded so implausible that I actually considered making up a better one, but I quickly decided against it. What had happened was the truth. I had nothing to hide.

What we didn't know at the time was that I'd contracted a cyclical form of infection that would recur every week, almost to the hour. Each successive time the symptoms were a little less severe. During the next two or three weeks, though, I ran a fever of over 104 degrees.

The hardest part of the ordeal was my family's mistrust. (Now, as I look at the story from a mother's perspective, I can see why they found it difficult to believe.) I hated feeling that I'd worried and disgraced them when, in fact, I'd done nothing wrong.

Harder yet was the forgiveness I received from Jim and Lila. These lovely people, who were like grandparents to me, put their arms around me, telling me how much they loved me and that they forgave me for the wrong I'd done. It made me so frustrated I could hardly stand it! I knew they didn't believe me, either.

I decided at that point I had to go back to the States. This was too oppressive.

CHAPTER EIGHT:
HARBORS AND HAZARDS

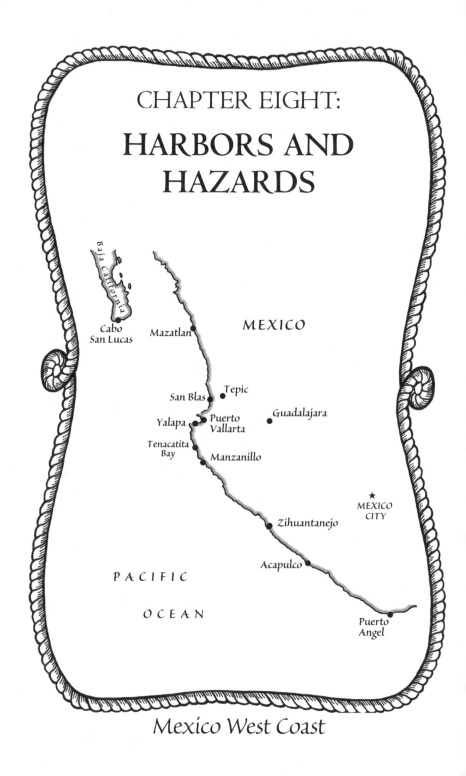

Mexico West Coast

The saddest thing we saw in Mexico was the disproportionately large number of little ladies in black. Custom there decrees that all members of a deceased person's family wear mourning and refrain from all frivolity for three years. This, presumably, shows proper respect for the dead. It also places an intolerable burden on the living.

We met a young man, George, whose father had died eight months previously. His sisters were wearing black and would continue to do so for at least another year, after which they could begin, very discreetly, to wear more colorful things and engage in some social activities. His mother (actually a stepmother thirty-two years old, just a few years older than George himself), would have to wear black for the rest of her life unless she should remarry.

Considering the restrictions that widowhood placed on her social life, her prospects for a new marriage looked very dim.

With his father's death George had become head of the household, and he invited all of us there for dinner one evening. He requested Jim and Rand to bring their musical instruments. After a very good meal of tortillas, refried beans, and a fried pastry for dessert, George asked the boys to play some folk songs.

On the patio outside, a few friends of George's deceased father were playing cards. They did this several nights a week, paying the widow a small fee for the card-playing area; they would also buy beer and soft drinks from her at tavern prices. This was their way of providing their friend's widow with a little financial assistance.

As the first bars of music came crashing through, the men leaped from their chairs and came running into the kitchen. "Dispassio! Dispassio! Por favor," they begged most urgently. The music stopped instantly, and the men, singly and in unison, began trying to explain — if other people heard such music coming from the widow's home, her reputation would be badly damaged! Quiet, soft music, especially of a religious nature, would be acceptable, they assured us.

George glowered in the background. Maybe he'd known this would happen; more likely, he'd hoped it wouldn't. He was not in mourning and thought the whole idea was ridiculous. He seemed fond of his stepmother and probably wanted her to have some entertainment, so totally denied her by the rules of mourning. At the same time, he obviously didn't want to embarrass his father's friends by disagreeing with them.

After the men returned to their cards, George apologized to Jim and Rand and asked them to continue, which they did in a most subdued manner. But the sparkle had gone out of the evening, and we didn't stay long.

George's wife, a chic young secretary named Anita (shortened to Nita), had even less patience than he with the death-in-life situation of widows.

We invited the family to eat on the boat, and we especially wanted his mother to come. For this reason, we invited them for lunch; in the evenings, widows could only go to church. But it was no use. When George showed up with only his wife and sisters, he explained that his stepmother was afraid to chance it for fear it would be construed as lack of respect for her dead husband.

Nita was seething and didn't waste any time telling us how she felt about it all.

"George's father was a nice man," she conceded, "but he was an old man and shouldn't have married someone young enough to be his daughter. That's one thing that is wrong with our society. These old men with one foot in the grave marry young wives and then leave them to this awful thing called widowhood."

Nita's English was excellent, and she was making sure that we understood how she felt. "Really," she went on, "it was more humane the way they used to do it in India when they just burned them up."

George didn't disagree. "Women outnumber men here in La Paz, so the chances of my stepmother getting married again are small."

"The men there," he added ruefully, "are looking for a cute teenager instead of a steady, industrious person like her."

"Steady and industrious she may be," Jim interposed, "but she also is darned good-looking. I don't see why she can't get a job, go somewhere else where she can stop playing widow for the rest of her life."

"In your country she could," George said sadly. "Here, all our customs are against it. She could even have a pretty good life here if she weren't hemmed in by a bunch of stupid regulations." He paused, brow furrowed, looking around as though he thought some solution could be found within the boat. "The worst part of it is that she agrees with what she's been taught. She'll never look for a way out."

"Couldn't she just ignore public opinion," Rand asked, "and have some social life?"

"Most of the younger people wouldn't care," Nita replied. "Most of my friends feel the same way I do about these weird, outdated customs. But her friends are something else again. They would think she was at least as bad as a prostitute if she flouted their cherished little social laws."

Lunch, meant to be a happy occasion, lost much of its festivity when it lost its guest of honor. After we thought we had changed the subject, George burst out, "What kind of life can she have, locked up for fifteen or twenty years?" Then, noticing our surprised glances, he added, "Well, as good as locked up. When she's an old lady she can have a little freedom. I'm wondering if that's something to look forward to."

"Not me!" Nita exclaimed airily. "If anything ever happens to George, I'll get my company to transfer me to the US. They need Spanish/English secretaries there as much as here, I've heard."

⚓

Our trips to the bank had netted nothing so far, and the bank officer had suggested with exquisite politeness that we might do just as well waiting until next week rather than coming in every day. I'm sure his patience had been sorely tried by our disappointment as well as our perseverance.

We decided to spend the intervening time in the Espiritu Santo Islands, whose praises we had heard from sailors who had gone before us: golden, curving, unoccupied beaches; fishing so good that you either have to stop after an hour or keep throwing the fish back in the water; great snorkeling and shell-collecting.

These tales proved true. Even so, the Espiritu Santo Islands weren't my favorite place. They're totally barren — just rocks, sand, blue water, and sky. I'm not picky, but I do enjoy having some grass and trees around.

For hundreds of years these were habitual loitering places for pirates, and for that purpose they must have been ideal. There are numerous caves on the various islands. Halfway up a mountainside we found a perfect cave for a pirate, with room after room of soaring, cathedral-like proportions and incredible visibility in every direction. No one could have approached by land or sea without being seen long before he could have done any damage. We think of pirates as being totally outside the law, but most of them in the beginning had the blessing of their respective governments. Only later did piracy degenerate into freebooting, claimed by no nation and regulated only by greed.

The air was surprisingly cool in these huge caves, and the thought of their unscrupulous former occupants brought on a few extra shivers.

I said, "I wonder how it would feel to be sitting on top of a few million dollars worth of gold and jewels. Suppose you're a pirate. You can't take this stash with you unless you have a boat that will outrun all the other pirates. On the other hand, you can't leave it here because there isn't anyone you can trust."

"Yeah," Randy agreed, "when does it get to be more of a burden than an asset? You don't want to stay here the rest of your natural life, and all this treasure is worth nothing here —no place to spend it."

With more than a flicker of interest, Pattie joined in. "Do you suppose there's still any of that treasure hidden in these caves?"

"Probably," Jim said, looking around at the hard rock floors and steep walls that surrounded us, "but if it weren't extremely well hidden, it would have been found long ago. Not much chance of a casual tourist stumbling onto it."

That brought our thoughts back to our wandering bank draft — never very far from mind, really. It, too, seemed to be very well hidden.

We left our nice cool cave and braved the hot sun down to the shore where the skiff was secured to a big boulder. Eldon had chosen to stay on the boat for two reasons: he was getting ready to run back to La Paz, and he had been told not to leave the boat unattended in these waters. Whoever told him that, however, did the Mexicans a disservice; no one ever stole so much as a thumbtack off the boat while we were cruising the coast of Mexico.

⚓

Trilogy

A half-dozen miles out of La Paz we were hailed by the boat *Discovery*, out of Port Townsend. Eldon went out on deck in order to hear better because the boats were fifty or sixty feet apart.

"Did you know," the captain shouted, "that there's a Coast Guard search under way for you from Baja to Panama?"

"Negative," Eldon shouted back. "I had no idea. Do you know who started the search?"

"Haven't heard," *Discovery*'s captain replied, starting to move away. "Suggest you call the Coast Guard."

"Thank you; I'll do that," Eldon yelled after him, having now equipped himself with a megaphone. Of course, calling the Coast Guard was the first thing he had intended to do as soon as he heard this disquieting news.

I thought of my parents and all their foreboding about this trip; I hoped they hadn't heard about the search for us. News that such a vast search was under way for us would have justified their worst fears. We would have to send telegrams to our close friends and relatives.

Eldon went into the pilot house to call the Coast Guard. So far we hadn't had much use for our radio and weren't really sure of its range — so he was startled as well as pleased when the Coast Guard station in Long Beach, California, answered instantly.

"I just heard that you've been looking for us," Eldon said after giving our call letters and identifying *Trilogy*. "We checked in with the port captain in La Paz on January twenty-sixth, and we've been right in this area since that time."

"Well," the Coast Guard officer returned dryly, "you were reported missing; glad you're okay. No harm done."

"Oh, we appreciate what you've done," Eldon hastened to reassure him. "If we'd really been in trouble, we would have been most happy for it. Too bad you were bothered to no purpose, though."

"Always happy to find the objects of our search well and happy. Shall I tell Mr. Woods you're all right?"

"Please do."

Eldon signed off, and we looked at each other. Walt Wood. We hadn't done a proper job of keeping him informed of our whereabouts. Naturally, he had expected us to; naturally, he was worried.

"I'll send Walt a telegram and apologize," Eldon said, "just as soon as we get to La Paz."

And so it was that friends and relatives up and down the coast as far as Alaska heard that we were lost at sea; many of them were quite startled to hear from us later on.

⚓

Even before we sent any telegrams, we first checked with the bank. Success at last! Our draft had been missent to Mexicali. We were in funds again; I never did get my six hundred fifty dollars back, though. Once it got into the general fund, I seemed to have lost ownership somehow.

Jay, Eldon's nephew in Alaska, had forwarded a large box of Christmas cards and letters, even some presents. Never were the annual greetings more appreciated!

It was about this time that we began to feel less vulnerable than our friends and relatives ashore. Without radio (we had to save the batteries for navigation), without sensational journalism, television and all to inspire fear of various knowns and unknowns, life ceased to be fraught with much apprehension. Without six newscasts a day to describe how, and possibly when, the world is going to hell in a hand basket, this planet came to look very beautiful and remarkably untroubled.

Such peace may have been a total illusion. Life on the ocean has its cause for fear, too. No matter what the situation, a truly dedicated worrier can always find dozens of "what if's" to fret about. In actual practice, though, the boating life gave our days a certain unaccustomed serenity.

Ironically, it was the Christmas cards that made us think this way. Halfway through our box of cards, I came across one signed by Jean Kennell. I showed it to Eldon. "Isn't this strange?" I asked. "Ed always signs his Christmas cards. In twenty years I've never gotten one that didn't have a personal note attached — just to let us know how things are going. You said he was planning to fly down here while we're in La Paz."

Eldon looked at the card for a long time. At last he said, "I'm afraid something has happened to Ed."

"Maybe he and his wife have separated. Maybe there's another card from him somewhere in this pile." Ed was on his third marriage, so we didn't always know how stable his matrimonial status might be.

We looked through the whole pile; nothing there from Ed. Eldon immediately dispatched a letter to Jean asking what was wrong. He was so sure that Ed had met with some mishap that Jean's reply only confirmed what he already knew at a deeper level. She sent newspaper clippings that told of Ed's fatal accident, which had happened on the very day that we were heading up the Strait of Juan de Fuca toward Port Angeles. Ed had been flying in his Beechcraft, alone, and no one will ever know exactly what went wrong.

Eldon truly grieved for Ed; they'd been friends for a long time — both photographers, both lovers of boating, both spending as much time on the water as possible. "Ed," he said, "you should have stuck with boats." Eldon's brother, in the twenty-five years he had been flying, had survived two near-fatal crashes.

After that, we never opened a package of mail without having to nerve ourselves. We felt quite safe out on the water, but our loved ones on the land began to seem terribly unprotected in their cars and planes, besides being exposed to heaven-knows-what poisons and diseases. The longer the time between mail pick-ups, the worse the news seemed to be, until we hit the ultimate low in the Galapagos Islands.

But that was far in the future.

⚓

When we first arrived in La Paz, Eldon had dispatched invitations to a very few of our close friends to vacation with us for a while in La Paz and the adjacent islands. So far, we hadn't gotten a single answer, and we almost decided to head out to the Espiritu Santo Islands again. We were all ready to go, but we kept putting it off due to an uneasy feeling that we shouldn't leave just yet. Then one day, at four o'clock in the afternoon, a taxi pulled up to the boat harbor and Jim and Lila Hanley got out.

Jim is as near to a godfather as my children ever had. He supplied Jim's name (James Eldon Coon) before he was born, when Eldon and I were in hopeless disagreement, and looked after both Jim and Rand when they were in college. He and Lila had cruised with us on the *Mañana* in the summer of 1968 all through the glacier country of Southeast Alaska. They'd been our friends practically forever.

They beat their telegram to La Paz by three days.

Over the weekend Lila and I went shell-collecting. A big sand bar in the harbor had a new supply of conch shells almost every day. I picked up quite a supply to use for trading stock later in our travels. On the way out to the Islands, Lila caught so many fish that we started putting all the bonito and skip-jacks back in the water, telling them, "Let that be a lesson to you." Who knows? It may have made them so wary that they lived to extreme old age.

We stopped for a while at Pichilinque to unearth a cache of creamy-white olive shells that had too much of their former inhabitants still inside them. Pattie and I had buried them a week before, following instructions from one

of the *Seven Seas Bulletins*. According to them, the little
beasties that live just above high tide level will eat all the
offending stuff and leave them as polished inside as out.

Sorry, but 'tain't true. They were a little cleaner than
when we buried them, but not much. We transferred them
to a very busy anthill.

"Okay, now," I told the scurrying little scavengers, "I'll
give you one more week; if you can't get the job done by
then, you're all fired!" I even threatened to write to the
publications that were giving them free advertising.
However, I didn't have to make good on that threat
because the ants did a much better job than the other
insects had done.

Jim and Lila had to make a difficult decision after
three days in the Espiritu Santo Islands — whether to sail
across to the mainland now or spend four more days here
and fly to the mainland of Mexico. Either way, Lila wanted
to spend two or three days in Guadalajara before they flew
back home. Jim really wanted to sail across, but Lila was
just recovering from major surgery and the trip across in a
small boat might not be best for her or her incision. They
decided to spend four more days out in the Islands just
being lazy. As soon as they caught their plane to
Guadalajara, we started across the Sea of Cortez to the
mainland of Mexico.

One reason we were determined to get under way as soon
as possible was that Pattie was again making dark threats
about what she was going to do as soon as her eighteenth
birthday arrived, only a little over a month away now. She
wanted to work so she could fly back to college when the
new quarter began, but I assured her that the original bargain
was still in force. If she really didn't want to continue traveling with us, we would pay her way back there.

One of the yachtsmen in the harbor suggested that if
time was heavy on her hands, she might start a boat-
cleaning business. There were a number of very handsome

yachts in the harbor, and most of the owners would
welcome some help and pay well for it, he said. She was
quite excited about the prospect and asked me what I
thought about it. While I was thinking, he blew the whole
thing by trying to date Pattie. She immediately became
very skeptical about the prospect of being alone on his
boat with him. So did I. He was twice her age, a complete
stranger to all of us.

Most of these minor skirmishes I didn't report to Eldon.
He was very happy with the way our children were getting
along, and I didn't want him to worry unduly; it was just
hard to tell which was unduly and which might be duly. The
boys still seldom thought about inviting Pattie to go with
them, and much of her restlessness was sheer boredom. We
had spent more time in La Paz than the place warranted,
and truly there wasn't a lot for her to do — not even swimming unless we got out of the polluted harbor. I breathed a
big sigh of relief when we started traveling again.

⚓

On the way to San Blas, the sleepy little town that
Eldon had decided to make our port of entry to Mexico
proper, we stopped for a few hours at Isobellita, a small,
uninhabited island off the coast. What you do on any
uninhabited island is explore. First Eldon and the boys
went exploring while Pattie and I finished up the breakfast
dishes and a minimal amount of straightening up here and
there. After a couple of hours Eldon came back and took
Pattie and me ashore. Jim and Randy were taking pictures
not too far from where we landed on the beach.

Jim came over to talk to us when he noted our arrival.
"This won't make you happy," he told me, "but here is a
small tragedy in the making." Two fuzzy little white
boobies — a type of gull — were sitting in a nest not too
far off the ground. Their heads were together and their
eyes were shut.

"They must be orphans," Jim said. "No bird willingly deserts its babies. Trouble is, they have very strict rules about taking care of any family but their own."

Rand came over. "Just the same, we're going to see if we can get them adopted," he said, cheerfully. "Unless you try, you'll never know if it might happen."

Carefully, covering their hands so no human smell would be on the baby birds, they put each of the birds in separate nests where there were already young boobies. "Now, let's get out of here so our presence doesn't ruin their chances for adoption," Rand suggested. We agreed and started on around the island. It was a fairly small island, and we were back at our starting point by mid-afternoon. Both of the birds had been thrown out of their nests; the weaker one was already dead.

Sometimes the ways of nature seem unnecessarily cruel.

"Jim," I asked as he picked up the live bird, "can't we do something to keep this one alive until it gets a little older? It looks about half grown."

He shook his head. "Even if he were totally healthy, he'd have less than a fifty-fifty chance. As it is, really none at all. He's dying." He put the little bird back in the nest where he and Rand had found it. We all felt sad as we made our way back to the boat to round up some lunch.

All day I had been collecting shells. The perimeter of the island was nothing but sandy beaches, and the beaches were covered with shells. I was becoming more discriminating these days and didn't pick up every shell I saw. But I found one tangerine red-orange one that I felt was a real prize.

At first, though, I had trouble holding onto this special shell. It kept disappearing from my shell collection. I thought others in the family were failing to put it back where it belonged. One night, however, I had all the recently collected shells on the table when this shell began moving away from the rest, all by itself.

Obviously, it had a tenant, a hermit crab who also

prized it highly. Eldon began eviction proceedings at once. He tossed the shell into a container of water on the deck, and in a few moments the crab started cautiously easing himself out of his borrowed home. When he was a little more than halfway out, Eldon caught him and flipped him overboard.

"Go find yourself another house," he ordered.

⚓

Walt Wood, who had spent several vacations in San Blas, had advised us to find a Mexican girl to do our laundry. "They'll only charge a few pesos and do a better job than you can."

I thought this was good advice because my prowess at the washboard was probably even less than he suspected. And for some reason that defies explanation, we seemed to get just as dirty in the middle of the ocean as we had at home. So Jim and Rand set out to find a laundress for us by interviewing the resident Americans. A young woman named Lucia was well recommended. The bags of laundry were delivered to her house and promised back in three days — the length of time we expected to spend in San Blas.

But that was before we found out about the surfing.

At first, I was less than lukewarm about the prospect of trying to surf again, after my disappointing trial at Santa Maria Bay. Pattie, Jim, and Rand went surfing the first morning after we got to San Blas and came back so enthusiastic that nothing less than new converts to surfing would satisfy them. "You've got to try it, Mom," Jim urged. "You can catch a wave on the point, just like catching a trolley car, and ride it for a half mile or more."

To clinch the argument Rand added, "You don't even have to get up on your board, Mom. Here you can ride it on your tummy, boogie-board style." That sounded good; most of my problems at Santa Maria could have been elim-inated if I hadn't had to keep the board under me while I stood up. To show me how it was done, and convince me that no superhuman athleticism was required, Jim drew a diagram of the surf pattern with a point of land coming out at right angles to it. "Look, you catch the wave right on the point, no walking out through six blocks of shallow water."

So I was won to surfing. We stood chest-deep in the water just off the point until a good set was sighted. I could tell better by watching the other surfers than by estimating the height of the waves. When they started getting on their boards, I started getting on mine.

At this instant, a good surfer paddles like mad in order to be going the same speed as the wave. Instead of trusting me to work up sufficient speed, my stalwart sons gave the board a twenty-knot shove, and the wave carried me a half mile to the other side of the bay. When the board grounded, I caught a ride back with one of the cars that were always going back and forth along the beach. All afternoon I rode the waves, and the next day, and the next.

Pattie got up on her board the first time she caught a wave, but I was able to watch without envy. While it must be a fine, triumphant feeling to stand up and twirl your board around on the face of a rolling wall of water — casually waving to your friends and scanning the horizon in all directions — I was perfectly content on my tummy, traveling with what felt like the speed of a bullet train.

Eldon didn't really take to surfing, but he was right out there with us, playing his own variation with the outboard and dinghy. He stayed just outside the surf break, where the waves frequently tilted the boat up to a forty-five degree angle. It wasn't really dangerous. But if he had a mishap and ruined the outboard, we would have had a lot of rowing to do. Before we left Mexico, he did get flipped over in the surf, with some serious consequences.

One of the dangers of surfing, even here where it wasn't overcrowded, is that some surfer zigzagging his board up and down to increase speed may bump into someone else. This danger is increased when the someone else isn't standing up within easy range of vision. So, a surfer came shooting along on my wave and clipped me on the shoulder. It wasn't enough to make him lose his balance, but it gave me a very sore shoulder.

For three days Randy, Jim, Pattie, and I slathered our faces with zinc oxide and rode the waves, taking time out for only the sketchiest meals. As the kids got bolder, they began surfing off another point farther away. This gave them some spectacular rides, and Eldon thought it was a good time to get some movies.

There is one little-publicized problem at San Blas, a problem as unpleasant as it is impossible to ignore. Quite promptly at four o'clock in the afternoon, clouds of little gnats seem to come out of nowhere. Few of them go out over the water far enough to bother surfers, but anyone on shore is covered with them. Besides itching almost unbearably, our bites were inclined to get infected. Months afterward, I still had scars on my legs from the attacks of these nasty gnats.

It was exactly at this hour that Eldon decided to take movies of his surfing family. He ignored the gnats, locally known as no-nos, but they didn't ignore him! He got some good movies; one sequence shows Rand and Pattie on the same wave with Jim close behind on the next one. Eldon stayed there, shirtless as usual, for almost two hours taking photographs. When he got back to the boat, he looked as though he had a bad case of measles.

I was really worried about a severe allergic reaction. If the half-dozen bites I had were causing me endless trouble, what were a few thousand likely to do to him? I made him swallow an antihistamine pill even though he was sure it was unnecessary. The next day the bites were all gone except for a very few reddish spots, and these disappeared within the next twenty-four hours. I could hardly believe it; I don't know anyone else who survived such a massive onslaught of these insects with so little to show for it.

Trilogy

⚓

As we headed down the coast of Mexico, we thought of ourselves as going south; in fact, our course was more east than south most of the time. Every day someone in the family would look at the big map that covered one whole wall in the pilot house and say, "Now we're as far east as the Mississippi River," or "Look, we're farther east than Chicago!" In time, we were farther east than Florida. This was confusing, and it never seemed quite real because we were always on the western shore of Mexico, Central America, or South America.

Occasionally, there were rumors of Chabascos, those vicious winds of near-hurricane force that sometimes batter the shores of Mexico. While we did a reasonable amount of worrying when one was forecast, we didn't encounter any storms until we were much farther south.

Our next port after San Blas was to be Puerto Vallarta, made famous by the Burtons, Richard and Elizabeth, who owned a villa there. I'm sure their intention was not to form a colony of all those who wanted to establish residence close to VIPs, but that is what happened.

As we pulled into port in the early, gray dawn, we were surprised to see the *Macquinna* anchored about fifty feet away. This is a very large yacht, well over a hundred feet long, owned by John and Surri Van Golen from Vancouver, Canada. The last time we'd seen them was when we were all collecting shells at Isobellita Island. John and Surri, just back from Guadalajara, convinced us that we ought also to visit that city. The harbor at Puerto Vallarta was muddy; the surf was nonexistent. It seemed like a wonderful time to make a trip into the interior.

Jim and Rand were disappointed when Eldon said he wasn't coming on this trip. They each offered to do part of the boat-sitting so that we all would have some time in Guadalajara. Later, we were able to work this out so Eldon could go on trips with the rest of us, but this time he flatly refused.

Harbors and Hazards

⚓

Although the distance from Puerto Vallarta to Guadalajara looked insignificant on the map, it turned out to be two hundred seventy miles — an eight-hour bus ride. Jim surprised us, since he is an inveterate bargain hunter, by getting tickets on the first class, deluxe bus. But his reasons were sound; the difference in fares was negligible and the difference between the two types of busses looked important in terms of comfort and safety. "And," he added to clinch the argument, "an eight or nine hour ride on even the most comfortable bus is going to get tiresome."

What he didn't know, and we all found out, is that Mexican busses have a built-in safeguard against boredom. It doesn't matter much how your seat is sloped or padded because you're going to be on the edge of it most of the time.

It is a little over three miles from the harbor to the bus station. We planned to catch the city bus at 6:30 in order to connect with the Guadalajara bus at 7:00. A half hour seemed adequate for such a short distance, but it wasn't. The city bus was late and stopped frequently to pick up passengers. When it got to be 6:55 and we were still some distance from the bus depot, we began to be alarmed. Our tickets were paid in advance, and Jim had been warned that the money would be forfeited if we failed to arrive on time. Under terms like those, obviously, the Guadalajara bus wasn't going to wait around for us. For that last five minutes, the city bus moved with agonizing slowness. However, just on the stroke of seven it pulled up in front of the Guadalajara bus, whose engine was already running. We leaped like trained fleas from one bus to the other. Before we could get seated, the bus was on its way.

The first ride in a Mexican bus — if you live to be ninety-five, you will never forget it.

For the first few miles there was no traffic, and we relaxed, enjoying the cool morning and the green country-side. Then a village came into view, speckled with people like ants around an anthill. Everyone in the town seemed to be right out in the street. Collision with the outermost group of people became imminent, but this didn't worry the bus driver. He bore down on the horn. Like the Red Sea parting, the crowd drew apart hardly more than the width of the bus, then surged back together in our wake. The impassive faces that we glimpsed as we whizzed by bore no expressions of alarm, no sign of relief at danger narrowly averted. There were some sighs of relief from our group on the bus, but also an ongoing tension and worry.

What was this Hairbreadth Harry going to do when we got to Tepic — a larger town where there would be other cars and busses? Would he barrel right through, the way he did here? What does he do if he hits someone, or hits another vehicle? These were our topics of conversa-tion as we approached the town, but we needn't have worried about Tepic. It was one of our scheduled stops, and H.H. (as we dubbed him) obeyed all the rules of the road. We were surprised that he even knew them!

We hadn't been introduced to Mexican vendors before, and it was an interesting experience — more so because we were all hungry, having eaten little or no breakfast. Just the smell of all the available concoctions made us realize how hungry we were. I attempted to ask the price of a tray full of fried food outside my window, and before I had the "quanta questo" fully pronounced, I was the owner of three doughnut-like pastries for which the vendor collected a peso and a few centavos. I was glad I hadn't asked about the fried fish with heads on being hawked at the same window. Fried fish eyes are very unap-pealing to me. My next inquiry netted me six tacos with meat or bean filling. Jim and Rand were acquiring several varieties of fruit. Phil Peterson, who worked on the *Maquinna*, and his friend Rick were also dealing in burritos, bananas, and oranges. It looked as though by trading among ourselves we could all have a good lunch.

Harbors and Hazards

While I was having trouble adjusting to the toot-and-zoom method of going through small villages, not to mention the villagers' utter indifference to death on wheels, I felt secure in the belief that H.H., though he was remarkably unconcerned about people on the ground, doubtless placed some value on his own life and that of his passengers.

This proved to be a misconception.

Cars were scarce as we proceeded up into the mountains, but there were many busses. The public, having few automobiles, really makes good use of the bus system, and the rates are unbelievably low — less than one cent per mile for each of us on this trip. When one begins to worry about actual survival, however, economy becomes a secondary consideration.

Many of the busses were operated by rival companies, and attempting to pass was like a challenge to a duel. It was different from a duel, though, because the seconds and onlookers all had their lives at stake, too.

The first time we passed another bus, luck was with us. The other driver speeded up, as the rules of this game seemed to indicate he should, but we had a long, straight stretch of road and a faster bus. We were back in our own lane before any other traffic showed up. Certainly H.H. was not at fault, and we mentally cheered him as he waved good-naturedly to his rival.

Then the road grew winding, the curves tighter and closer together. We began to feel, uneasily, that H.H. was pushing his luck. We came upon another bus laboring on an uphill curve. Absolutely no visibility ahead. Any sane person would have slowed down until it was safe to pass. Blithely, H.H. passed just as though he had perfect vision around such curves, nor was he prompt about getting back into his own lane. He was still straddling the center line when, head-on, we met an open bus with little, black-haired children hanging out of every aperture. The other driver thundered past, swerving out onto the shoulder just enough to avoid a head-on collision, but dangerously close to a drop of several hundred feet.

Jim turned to Phil, who was sitting right behind him, and said in an awed whisper, "Did you see that?"

"Yes," Phil replied, "but I don't really believe it."

"That guy is crazy!" Jim exclaimed. "Straight from the loony bin!" Usually unflappable, Jim is a rather aggressive driver himself, but this was beyond anything in his experience. "Wow! I've seen some hell-for-leather drivers in Europe, and some that took a lot of chances, but nothing like this. The stuff they did might cause a real fender-bender, but it wouldn't wipe out fifty people!"

Phil replied philosophically, "Well, they say God looks after children and fools — children in that bus and fools in this one."

We were going to need all the looking-after we could get. Short of getting out and walking here in the wilds of nowhere, we didn't seem to have any choice but to trust the maniac at the wheel. Every time another bus attempted to pass, H.H. treated it as a personal affront — but the stakes were high when we were running neck and neck around tortuous mountain curves. Jim kept his eyes on the road, tense and unblinking; Pattie and I felt more like putting our hands over our eyes until we had a fatal accident or arrived at our destination. Still, we continued to watch the road in horrid fascination.

Randy and Rick were engaged in animated conversation and really didn't seem to notice. As for me, I can still see the mountain roads full of curves, the little houses with their banana groves and jacaranda trees, now in full bloom. The thought that every moment may be your last tends to etch your surroundings deeper on the consciousness.

Later, when we attempted to tell some of our friends about this wild ride, they waved it all away with, "But didn't you know, all the bus drivers in Mexico drive like that?" Well, not quite. The driver we had on our return trip would have won no prizes in a safe driving contest, but after Hairbreadth Harry, his style seemed staid and positively ordinary.

⚓

Finally, after, we had reconciled ourselves a dozen times to death, maiming, or disfigurement, not to mention the responsibility for inflicting all of these on some other busload of people, we came through a high mountain pass. Lovely Guadalajara lay before us in the late afternoon sun, pink, white, and dark green, with clouds of lavender jacarandas everywhere. None of our advance information had prepared us for a city of two million people, nor for one so beautiful.

As soon as the bus stopped, Jim and Rand went to look for a pension while the rest of us stayed with the luggage in the bus station. Baggage, though indispensable, is particularly uninteresting to watch. Rick and Phil were eyeing the coffee shop, and I could tell that it wouldn't be long before they decided that it didn't require four people to watch our bags. But I did them an injustice; what they suggested was that all of us just pick up the bags and move over to the coffee shop.

Through the glass doors it wouldn't be too easy to identify specific persons, especially within the booths. "Maybe I could get something and bring it out here," I suggested.

"Now, let's think about this a minute," Phil interposed. "Where would you find Randy if you left him in a spot like this for an indefinite length of time?"

"In the coffee shop," I conceded.

"Okay, then he's sure as thunder going to know where to look for us; let's go." Phil picked up two suitcases and headed for the coffee shop.

In a half hour Jim and Rand were back, having located a pension only three blocks away. They were pleased with the results of their house-hunting.

Trilogy

"Wait till you see this, Mom," Jim said enthusiastically as he picked up a good-sized stack of luggage. "It's all marble and tile, and I'll bet it was built before the *Mayflower* landed at Plymouth!"

The pension was old, no doubt, but in excellent condition, and probably had been some important person's mansion in earlier days. In the center, a courtyard surrounded by white marble pillars brimmed over with flowering plants. Central to the courtyard was a pool made of blue tiles; all the rest of the floor was white tile trimmed with the same blue. The old place still wore an air of opulence and, more than that, of beauty.

Our very tiny rooms were on the second floor, probably not part of the original structure. We wondered if they had been servants' quarters. But all the rooms fronted a large deck, where tables and chairs had been provided. Evenings were especially lovely there with the soft, winking lights of Guadalajara all around and the mountains hunching their dark shoulders in the distance. There were no flies or mosquitoes; the air was clean and fresh and just warm enough for absolute comfort. No wonder people say this city has a perfect climate.

It was almost evening, and we suddenly all realized that we were very tired — probably a reaction to more than eight hours of H.H.'s magnificent disregard for human life, our own included.

"Let's just take short nap," Rand suggested, "and then see some of the city later this evening." Some of us were half asleep already, so no one argued with this.

⚓

One nice thing about the siesta custom — everything in town stays open at night. By the time we woke, it was dark, but in siesta country that isn't a problem. Rick advocated going to a movie, preferably one in English. Jim could hardly believe he was serious.

"That's a waste," Jim argued. "Movies you can see anyplace; Guadalajara you can only see here!"

"I got a pretty good look coming into town," Rick replied. "That'll probably do me." Rick, it seemed, wanted his adventures by proxy. All of the rest of us wanted to see something of the city.

"I'd like to see one of the big markets," Pattie said, hesitantly. She was afraid her suggestion would get jumped on the way Rick's had. But no — shopping apparently came under the general heading of seeing the city. When she saw that she wasn't going to have to deal with scorn and rejection, she added, "Do you suppose they're open evenings?"

"If there's a buck to be made, they'll be open," Phil said confidently. He had traveled extensively for someone in his mid-twenties, and he had a profound respect for the Mexican mercantile instinct.

I was well aware that Pattie's interest in shopping didn't necessarily mean she intended to buy anything. The hundred-plus dollars of baby-sitting money that she had brought with her from Alaska had remained intact through all the boat-building operation as well as the stays in San Francisco and San Diego, both reputed to be excellent shopping places.

"First, we have to find a place to eat," Randy stated flatly. He and Jim hadn't eaten at the bus terminal.

"Why don't we walk up to the market and eat there?" Phil asked. "They're bound to have all kinds of eating places in a big market. Then, if Rick and I aren't into shopping too much, we can go to a movie." He had neatly combined most of the stated preferences, diplomatic and efficient. We all agreed.

So we set out at a pace that was beyond brisk. I was having a hard time keeping up, even though I've always had the reputation of being a fast walker. "Just a minute," I called, and the boys came to a stop. "How do you know where you're going? We may be hurrying off in the wrong direction entirely!"

"Celestial navigation," Jim said, and he started off again as though we were all in training to run the four-minute mile. I knew from Jim's answer that he knew where he was going — probably a secret conference with our flashy, purple-clad Spanish landlady.

All the busses seemed to be going in the same direction we were, and that was a good sign. I had a better idea than trying to keep up with this bunch of joggers. "Why don't we take a bus?" I asked. "Bus travel is ridiculously cheap; we don't have to punish ourselves this way."

Jim gave me a look that included all the experiences of the day. "After today," he said solemnly, "I may never ride another bus!" He gestured toward a gray building that seemed to stretch out an infinite distance in all directions. "That is the market for the Juarez section of town." Aha! I thought, proof positive that he had somehow acquired definite information about its location. He would never have said it that way if he'd been guessing.

The first floor of this enormous market, four blocks in each direction, had so many different kinds of food stalls that it was mind-boggling. I contented myself with fried chicken and enchiladas, but the hit of the evening was the fresh orange juice. Pattie and I each drank two very large glasses. We looked at those Mexican orange-squeezers and decided we must own one. They were simple, efficient, and strong enough that they would probably never wear out. From the time we arrived in orange country, Eldon had been using our little plastic orange-squeezer every morning.

We did get one of these squeezers before we left, but its purchase led to undreamed-of complications.

Pattie and I headed upstairs to the clothing section, and the boys all went in a different direction with vague promises about meeting at one of the restaurants in an hour. I had other things than shopping on my mind. After paying our hotel bill in advance and buying most of the food on our trip, I could see that I hadn't brought enough money with me. All but one of the credit cards I was carrying were in Eldon's name; I doubted that I could get any money out of them. The card in my name was a Hilton Hotel educator's card, and I had used it in Seattle several times. I had to find a Hilton Hotel. Surely there would be one in a city as big as Guadalajara.

After an hour and a quarter Pattie and I went back down to the food section, and of course the boys weren't around yet. Pattie hadn't bought anything although she said she was planning to.

"It wasn't all a waste of time," she said defensively. "We wanted to see the market anyway. I'll decide what I really want and go back to buy it tomorrow." It wasn't hard to see why she still had her baby-sitting money after all this time.

Actually, she did go back before we left and bought a leather skirt, shoes, and matching purse.

By ten o'clock most of the little stores were putting away their merchandise, and as soon as the rest of the family showed up, we trudged wearily back to the pension. All night I was speeding around curves on the wrong side of the road as countless busses full of smiling Mexican children hurtled at me from the opposite direction.

⚓

In the morning I announced my urgent need for a Hilton Hotel, and Jim produced a city map showing the location of hotels, parks, cathedrals, and public buildings. It was only about ten blocks away. I'd rather have had it closer because I was going to wear a dress and shoes with heels in the fervent hope that I would look respectable, maybe even mildly prosperous, to a hotel manager.

In the lobby of our pension a happy little Mexican boy

was mopping the white tile floor. We hated to walk over the newly mopped tiles. But he bowed with a sweeping gesture and with a thousand-watt smile said, "Andale, amigos. Ees ho kay!" He brought out the English words triumphantly.

We tiptoed across the floor as carefully as possible and set out to do battle with the Hilton. As soon as we reached the hotel, Pattie vanished into one of their very plush powder rooms. The boys stayed outside because, they said, their boat-casual attire would not help my cause much. Too true; they were clean and combed, but the hotel guests scattered around the lobby had a crispness added to their cleanness, an indefinable look of expensive price tags recently removed.

I couldn't help remembering a time up in Alaska when one of our super-wealthy clients, someone who was chartering the *Mañana* for a couple of weeks, wanted to cash a check for several thousand dollars — more than the bank wanted to risk without some local person to identify him. They called me, and I went downtown. Mr. Borg had three days' growth of beard and was wearing jeans and canvas shoes — very appropriate for boating, but it hadn't yet become a national costume. When I got there, the banker was reminiscing about Major Fleischmann, owner of the Fleischmann Yeast Company, who frequently came up to Ketchikan on his fabulous yacht *Haida*. The yacht was a dream of spit-and-polish perfection, but the major himself went around looking like a wharf rat, and he got a tremendous charge out of it when some kind-hearted person gave him a dime for a cup of coffee. (Yes, this dates back to a time when you could get a cup of coffee for a dime.) Hearing this story, Mr. Borg glanced down at his own clothes, rubbed his triple five o'clock shadow, and added, "Yes, and those dimes really do come in handy!"

The manager of the Hilton, a frosty but mannerly

type, regarded me silently for what seemed like a long time. Not even bankers have more experience than managers of top-level hotels, I imagine, in making instant assessments of people at their desks. I had greeted him in Spanish, and he had answered in Spanish, but I was hoping, nervously, that the whole conversation wouldn't have to be in that language.

"Do you speak English?" I asked.

"A little," he replied. "Not with great fluency."

He could tell I had a favor to ask and helped me out by asking, "May I assist you in some way?" There was a faint glint of understanding, possibly even humor, in his eyes, and I suddenly realized that he was going to help me, at least as far as the rules would permit.

I pulled out my Hilton card. "I would like to cash a personal check, if I may."

Naturally he asked, "Are you a guest of this hotel?" It was inevitable, but I was hoping he wouldn't.

"No, I have a boat in Puerto Vallarta; we're traveling down the coast." Maybe he would think I had just flown in for the day.

"How large a check did you wish to write?" He was still courteous, still seemed to see some humor in the situation.

I hesitated. The papers that came with the credit card said very specifically that guests of the Hilton could write personal checks up to two hundred dollars. But I wasn't a guest; maybe I'd better be more modest in my request.

"Would one hundred dollars be okay?"

He nodded, "That will be all right. Do you want it in Mexican currency?"

I did, and he counted out twelve hundred fifty pesos. Then, as though he had read my mind about scaling down the size of my request, he added. "You can do this again tomorrow if you like; the hundred dollar limit only applies one day at a time." Now there was no doubt about the smile in his eyes.

Trilogy

I thanked him profusely and left, solvent and happy. I began counting up the coastal cities that might have Hilton hotels; this was so much easier than having funds missent to Mexicali.

⚓

There are many beautiful cathedrals in Guadalajara, some built in the early 1500s, and we tried to see them all. By mid-afternoon, though, our culture absorbers were overloaded. I was wishing I had been thoughtful enough to bring a pair of walking shoes. There weren't many places to sit down except in the hot sun. When we saw a side entrance standing open in one of the public buildings, we warily stepped through into the dim and remarkably cool interior. A string ensemble was rehearsing for a concert and didn't seem to object to our presence. Wonderful! We sat there enjoying the music for a long time, until they packed up their instruments and left the stage.

No one can make more scathing remarks than Randy about American tourists who, rather then enjoying the gastronomic delights of the country they are visiting, look for McDonald's or Dairy Queen wherever they go. But when we saw a Dairy Queen on that hot afternoon, Randy was the first inside. Phil, Pattie, and I didn't exactly hang back. We kidded ourselves a bit, but nothing ever tasted better than those thick, frosty Dairy Queen milk shakes!

By this time our group had dwindled; Jim had last been seen presenting an attractive señorita with one perfect red rose. She let him walk on with her. Rick had a Spanish-speaking blonde in tow and had decided he was in love. Phil was observing the foibles of mankind, especially those of his close associates, and waxing philosophical. He said if we were going to tramp through any more ancient build-ings, no thank you, he was going to stay here in the city square. Rand, Pattie, and I went on alone.

We spent less time on our patio the next two evenings

because someone with a dead-white mask and very black eyes kept watching us from a small, high window across the alley. Day or night, that face was in the window, staring at us. It was definitely alive; sometimes it moved away from the window for a while, but it always came back. I thought we should mention to the landlady that a face, apparently encased in plaster of Paris, was watching us around the clock. But she spoke little English. If the landlady found out about this strange apparition, it must have been from other guests because our bunch didn't want to bother — themselves or her.

Suddenly it was the last day of our visit, and our bus to Puerto Vallarta was leaving at two in the afternoon. We did want to visit the arts and crafts center at Tlaquepaque and also get an orange-juicer from one of the appliance stores. This little (but heavy) juicer turned out to be one of our best purchases ever. In the beginning, though, it caused an unbelievable amount of trouble.

We found a juicer, about fourteen inches high and similar to the ones used by all the juice stands. The one we chose was durable all right; Randy still has it. But it was made out of some kind of metal at least as heavy as lead. No one wanted to pack it around all day until we got on the bus.

"I'll come back and get it while the rest of you pick up the luggage," Rand offered.

Jim wasn't going to Tlaquepaque with us; he had a date to meet the señorita of the rose. We were back to riding busses again, having found the city drivers to be a safe and courteous lot. Jim should have come with us; his date stood him up. I can see why she might not have felt there was much future in the relationship, with him going back to Puerto Vallarta that same day.

Our time in Tlaquepaque was all too short; Randy, Pattie, Phil, and I were greatly impressed with the skill of the pottery makers, one on loan from the University at Mexico City. It nearly broke my heart to see him destroy each of his creations after he showed us how it was made.

Then there were the glass-blowers, a trade learned by apprenticeship from the age of eight or ten. Very matter-of-factly, our guide mentioned that frequently these young-sters forget they cannot, must not, inhale the superheated air after it has been blown into the molten glass. Such inhalation is almost always fatal. This fact didn't rate any italics in his telling it — as though these little folks were infinitely expendable.

Pattie and Rand simply couldn't tear themselves away from the glass-blowing. I wandered away to some of the shops. Among all the beautiful art objects, I found a pottery lamp with interesting cut-out places all over for the light to shine through. The shop girl lighted it for me, and I loved it! Dragging Rand away from the glass-blowers, I made him come and look at it.

"It's only fifty-five pesos; can you believe it?" That's about four and a half dollars. I wanted it.

"Too fragile; that thing would break if you looked at it cross-eyed." Rand was thinking about the long ride back to the boat, although you couldn't have told that from what he actually said.

"I really like it, Rand. Don't you think I could just hold it on my lap?"

"No."

"You really think it wouldn't survive the bus trip?"

Randy looked at me as though he couldn't believe I had already forgotten H.H. and our wild ride. "We'll be lucky if *we* survive, and our edges are more chip-proof." Seeing that I was really disappointed, he added, "Sorry, Mom, but it's big and it's fragile. After the first rough weather we'd be shoveling it out of the closet in pieces."

The salesgirl suggested that we have it mailed to our home address, but that was no solution; we didn't have a home address. Jay was taking care of our mail in Alaska, but it would have been foolish to ship it up there.

Harbors and Hazards

I went back to the glass-blowing with Rand, but somehow my buying impulse had been thwarted. I couldn't decide among the flying fish, sailboats, birds, and the incredibly fragile four-footed animals that the glass blowers so casually pulled into shape. Pattie got a half dozen, and she spent the next few months gluing legs and other parts back on them.

Noon, our absolute deadline, came before I had bought anything. As we hurried to catch the bus, we almost fell over an ancient beggar — a widow, as her black garments identified her, but holding a tiny, newborn baby in her arms. The sight was so incongruous that it shocked us. Maybe the family thought that she might as well baby-sit while she was doing her begging. Possibly she was the only support of this tiny child. Randy gave her some money, then, afraid it might not be enough, ran back and gave her some more.

"Tears came to her eyes," Randy told us. "She said I was a good boy and God will repay me. I hope it's enough so she can take the rest of the day off." Tears came to his eyes, too.

"Randy wants to save the whole world," Phil said as we got ourselves settled on the bus, "and you can't do that." But the way he said it was more compliment than criticism.

Rand left the bus in the vicinity of the appliance store, where the juice gadget, already paid for, would be wrapped and waiting. The rest of us got off the bus near the pension. It was one o'clock by the time we got back, and Jim had the luggage assembled, except for Rick's. Rick had been unable to part with his señorita and was staying two more days.

Jim hurried us along as we changed our clothes and rushed. We steamed into the bus station fifteen minutes before the bus for Puerto Vallarta was due to depart. One fifty-five came, and still no Randy was in sight. We boarded the bus, still looking in all directions for Randy. Promptly at two, the driver started the bus. Jim got off, telling the rest of us, "If Randy's going to be stuck here for another day, I'm going to stay, too; I've got all his luggage and most of his money."

Just as the bus started easing gently ahead, we heard Jim's whistle and another one answering. Both boys have whistles that can be heard easily for three or four blocks. Jim grabbed the doors of the bus as though he would bodily keep it from moving; perhaps he did. Randy came on a dead run. He had run for ten blocks.

When we were all settled in our seats, and after Randy had caught his breath enough to be able to talk, he started explaining what had happened.

"I got the juicer," he began, "and then caught a bus going in this direction —"

"Didn't you ask where it was going?" Jim interrupted.

"Let me tell this," Randy demanded. "It's my story."

"Well, it just about was my story, too, because if you hadn't caught this bus, I wouldn't be on it, either."

"Okay, as I was saying, I caught this bus and asked the driver if he was going close to the bus depot. He kept saying 'si, si,' and then we made a big turn at the circle in the center of town and started going out in the country."

"You should have gotten off and caught a bus back," Jim said, still feeling with some justification that the whole contretemps could have been avoided.

"Probably; hindsight is always so much better, y'know. But the driver kept telling me he'd get me back where I wanted to go. Finally, when we got back into familiar territory, I jumped off and started running. I was still as far away from the bus station as I was when I got the juicer."

Such are the problems of getting around in a strange city and a strange language.

Harbors and Hazards

⚓

With great ceremony, we presented Eldon with our new juicer; it seemed appropriate to give it to him because he almost always squeezed the oranges with my palm-sized plastic squeezer.

He wasn't much impressed.

"Where on earth are we going to keep a big contraption like that?" he asked. "I was getting along fine with the little one."

We all felt hurt that our most important purchase in Guadalajara, and one that had caused so many difficulties, was getting such a poor reception. The little squeezer we had been using required strong wrists and a lot of patience.

"It works, though," Eldon insisted stubbornly. "And it doesn't take up much room."

The time would come when Eldon thought our juicer was the greatest invention since the wheel. Oranges were cheap in Mexico, and we were using quantities of them. It didn't take long.

⚓

Seventeen miles by water from Puerto Vallarta is the little port of Yalapa where, the local inhabitants told us, the motion picture *Night of the Iguana* was filmed. This place looked the most tropical of any place we had seen so far, with palm trees, pale yellow beach, and little woven houses with thatched roofs. I spent most of one day painting a picture of it. Somehow it gave us a sense of achievement, as though we had arrived, almost, in the South Seas.

It would be a long time before we found ourselves in another place of such tropical appearance.

Women complain that their work is never done because so much of it has to be done again the next meal or the next day. On the boat, it was Eldon whose work was never done. Whenever Eldon wasn't hiking around the hillsides taking pictures, he could be found working on some of the little maintenance chores that never seemed to diminish.

In Yalapa, Rand and Jim rented horses to ride over the mountain and into the interior, and they tried hard to get their dad to go along.

"Come on, Dad," Jim urged. "You're the one more than any of the rest of us that wanted this trip. Wouldn't you like to see a part of the country that isn't accessible by any road? It's the real, primitive, practically unexplored Mexico. This is adventure; isn't that what you wanted?"

Eldon didn't find the offer even tempting. "First, it's five hours in the saddle each way. I don't know if you've done enough riding to know what that means, but I have. I'd rather not have to eat standing up for the next week. Also, I wouldn't leave Mom and Pattie alone on the boat overnight in case we didn't make it back in one day."

His argument must have been convincing, because the boys said no more about it and rented only two horses. At nine the next morning they started up a mountain trail that was scarcely visible. They soon learned to trust the horses, who were totally familiar with the way, visible or not. After the predicted five hours they arrived in the village of Chacalla, only accessible by horse or mule. If there was going to be any place in their travels where one would expect the people to be suspicious of strangers, it was this isolated community.

Surprisingly, the people were very friendly, and one middle-aged man with a house full of children and grand-children invited the boys to have lunch. It was a good bet that there wouldn't be any restaurants handy catering to the tourist trade, so they gladly accepted. After that, it was siesta time; they felt as though they could spare an hour before they started back, and stretched out on the verandah, politely refusing the offer of the master bedroom.

Harbors and Hazards

When they awoke, it was after five o'clock, and the trip back down the mountain began to look formidable. Their host urged them to stay overnight and make the trip down the mountain in daylight, pointing out that going downhill is more dangerous than going up. Knowing they would have to pay another day's rent on the horses if they stayed, they decided to chance it.

After sunset the night grew black very fast, the way it does in the tropics, and they had no choice but to trust their horses to stay on the trail and get back safely. They were saddle-sore and weary of riding, but they couldn't have found their way down on foot.

I began to worry when it got dark, but Eldon refused to be at all alarmed. "They had ten or maybe eleven hours of riding, plus time out for eating and seeing the village," he said. "They couldn't possibly get back this early."

"But you can hardly see that trail," I worried. "And it's so rocky. How can they come down there in the dark?"

"Well, they probably can't. If I were in their shoes, I'd stay overnight and come down in the morning."

Sometime between eleven o'clock and midnight the boys stumbled in. They had had enough riding to last for the indefinite future. Rand was asleep in less than five minutes.

Jim always sees things no one else notices. This time it was ticks — tiny little things, some wandering aimlessly around on his body and clothing, some already partially embedded and not nearly so tiny. He woke Randy. Since their staterooms were separated by the full length of the boat, he woke me, too, although I was planning to go right back to sleep.

For some reason, the sight of all those bugs with their heads buried in his brother's hide sent Rand into gales of laughter. Jim stuck his head into my stateroom. "Mom," he asked, "what do you do to get ticks out when they've got their heads buried under the skin?"

Ticks! Instantly, I was totally awake. Spotted fever! I jumped out of bed and groped for the turpentine can in my painting supplies. "Here," I said as I saturated a piece of cotton, "put some of this on them."

"Does it work?" Jim asked, dousing two ticks that were close together.

"I hope so; I just remember my mother doing this when I was a little kid down in southern Idaho. I was only three or four years old; the sheepherders were always driving sheep past our door, and we kids used to get ticks on us — not this many, though."

"I'll do it," Rand said, thoroughly awake now but still quite amused. He started putting turpentine on Jim's ticks.

"How about you, Rand?" I asked. "If Jim is covered with these things you must have some, too."

"Not me," Rand said. "At least I didn't see any."

He peeled off his shirt, and sure enough — he had as large a colony as Jim. Jim started laughing, and this set Randy off again. Soon the two of them were rolling on the floor, laughing helplessly, tears running down their faces.

I was not amused; it was the middle of the night, and I hadn't slept well knowing they were out on the mountainside somewhere. I wanted to get back to bed.

"If you two can be serious for a minute," I said with some asperity, "you'd better look at each other's heads. That's a favorite spot for ticks."

They picked themselves up off the floor and started peering at each other's heads, but they soon were overcome with laughter again.

"Doctor, I have this tick in my head —" Randy began.

"Maybe you think you're a clock," Jim interrupted. "What you need is a psychiatrist." More laughter.

"Well, if I'm a clock, I'm going to strike. No more tick-talk." They kept thinking of more puns, and the hilarity continued.

I tried once more for a rational response. "Listen, now.

Harbors and Hazards

Before you go back to sleep, Randy, you'd better inspect your bed and your clothing for more ticks. Jim, look over your clothes thoroughly; your bed should be okay because you haven't been in it yet." Seated side by side on Randy's bunk, they looked at me owlishly and nodded like a couple of drunks trying to act sober.

⚓

Except for its lush, tropical covering, Yalapa is a rock pile. I have never seen so many rocks of all sizes and shapes on one hillside. Many houses had no yard except for the huge, flat rock which also served as a foundation. The rock yard was used for drying coffee beans, legumes, and whatever needed drying.

Yalapa was not nearly as tidy as Turtle Bay. More than once we remarked that some Turtle Bay wind would be very useful here.

Garbage patrol had apparently been assigned to a large contingent of pigs, and they were shirking their duties badly. Like a bunch of Keystone Kops, they rushed around with an appearance of great industry, mostly just bumping into each other and upsetting things. They might have done better at cleaning up the garbage if there had not been so many coconuts available. These were cracked open and left drying in many spots, and it looked as though the pigs were too well fed on coconuts to bother about most of the garbage. They merely poked through it from time to time and scattered it around.

In this part of Mexico, the first thing a land owner does is build a rock wall around the perimeter of his property. The house may or may not get built, but one thing is certain: the wall will take ten times as much rock and mortar as the house that will eventually be built.

Eldon and I hiked up on a hill above the harbor and found a swarthy little Mexican man finishing the last few feet of such a wall that enclosed about an acre of ground.

"Ask him if he's building this all by himself," Eldon suggested. He thought that after my years of studying Latin, I should be at home in any related language. He was wrong, but I tried.

"Fabricar, solo?" I asked, hoping he could understand the basic words, sort of pidgin Spanish.

"Si," he replied with an inclusive gesture toward the wall, "todo."

Here was a good person to ask why the property was walled off so carefully before anything else was built, but my Spanish was not up to it. I did know the word for house, so I pointed to the center of the enclosure and asked if he was going to build a house there. To my surprise, he understood me, and replied in simple words so that I could understand, that he was going to build the house next.

"For you?" I asked.

"No," he said, it was to be a very big house, "muy grande," but he was building it for someone else.

Eldon and I went on up the hill, reflecting that while in rural Mexico the walls may outshine the houses, in the cities it is just the opposite. A very plain, high wall and well-locked door may lead to a house of great splendor.

The trail we were following was supposed to lead to a waterfall of unusual beauty. The trail was difficult and obscure, but eventually we found ourselves facing, across a reflecting pool, a waterfall that was indeed beautiful. It descended, white and sparkling, between huge, creamy-white boulders. Ferns, palms, and plumeria surrounded the pool and the trail going up to the top of the waterfall. Eldon wanted to go up to the top of the falls. I was wearing thong-sandals, and it didn't look like a thong-sandal trail. I stayed below to make sketches and take some slides with my little point-and-shoot Instamatic.

After making some quick sketches, I looked around for something else to draw. Downstream, a group of teenage girls were doing their laundry. Because of the large rocks and dense foliage, we hadn't seen them from the trail. They were very scantily clad, but not as scantily as they became when they decided to wash the underwear they had been wearing. They washed it quickly and put it back on, dripping wet. One of the girls spied me just as she was dressing and turned away with a careless toss of her heavy, dark hair. The other girls, through dressing, just laughed and gathered up their laundry. As they were leaving, Eldon came back, sorry to have missed the best part of the show.

⚓

Between Yalapa and Manzanillo we stopped for the weekend in a little bay called Tenacatita, a tricky place to get ashore by small boat. Heavy surge meeting the river delta breaks abruptly, and we saw more than one shore boat upended in that surf. By watching carefully, Jim and Rand got our skiff through the break without mishap. Of course, we had to jump out of the boat in waist-deep water and quickly pull the boat up on the beach. But I was used to it now and didn't feel as heroic as I had at first.

Our charts showed the river navigable for about two miles, so we decided to have our own jungle ride. Mistake number one for me on this memorable day was leaving my sandals on *Trilogy*. The second mistake was to keep on going after I realized my feet were getting burned. At the end of our jungle ride upstream, we were only about ten feet above sea level. Down a little embankment and across some sand laced with coarse grass was a singularly lovely beach. Jim, Rand, and Pattie weren't wearing shoes, either, but they were accustomed to going barefoot. Their feet were tougher than mine.

The sand was roughly the same temperature as the Sahara at high noon. I tried to be careful, using every scrap of grass, palm fronds, even paper to keep from being in constant contact with that hot sand. When I caught up with Pattie, she was examining some pieces of coral just brought in by some fishermen, and a Mexican lady was telling her that she shouldn't buy any of this because better pieces were available on the next little beach.

Jim was drinking ceviche at one of the roof-only shacks to be found on most of the beaches in Mexico. I should have spent my time there with him, but instead I went across with Pattie over an area of black lava, each rock a veritable frying pan. By the time I got to the coral, my feet were badly burned on the bottoms. Blisters were forming, and I felt as though I were walking on peeled grapes. I was three-quarters of a mile from the place where we had tied up the skiff. There seemed to be no way to get back without making the burns worse.

No doubt there was a way if we had thought of it. This beach was on the ocean, and the kids could have run down the river and around the little point while I stood in the nice, cool surf. Anyway, that isn't what we did; I walked back across the frying pans.

When we got to the beach shack, Jim was horrified at the big, sagging blisters on the bottoms of my feet. "I'd better carry you piggyback, Mom," he said. "Rand can spell me off if it's necessary."

"I don't think the piggyback ride would be much fun for either one of us," I replied, glancing back toward the river several blocks away.

"Well, you can't walk in that condition. You know this country's reputation for getting things infected. If those blisters break, you'd have a better than average chance of infection as well as burns."

"Just get me something to walk on that won't be one hundred seventy-five degrees, and I'll manage," I said. "Maybe some of those palm fronds that are lying around, especially the green ones; they look pretty cool."

Jim and Rand each found a nice, green palm frond about twelve feet long and took turns putting them in front of me. I began to feel like Queen Elizabeth I with a succession of Raleighs. It was cumbersome, but I did get back to the dinghy without breaking any blisters.

"Hey," Randy shouted as soon as he started to move the dinghy, "what happened to the oars?" We didn't always take oars with us for short outboard trips, but this time we needed them for maneuvering among the mangroves.

"Did we have them when —" Jim began, then started over. "Sure, we had them on the way up here. Well, somebody ripped them off."

Whoever had stolen them was long gone by now. Glumly, we made our way back to *Trilogy*, fending off mangrove roots with our hands instead of the oars. I dangled my feet in the cool water.

⚓

For the next three days, both in port and while traveling to Manzanillo, I stayed close to my bunk. The blisters were nearly an inch deep, one continuous blister on each foot from heel almost to my toes, and nearly impossible to walk on. Besides, I was hoping to keep them from breaking. And I succeeded, although all of us were amazed that it really happened. By the third day the blisters were quite flat and feeling much better.

In Manzanillo, it became necessary to go grocery shopping. We were out of several things, and, of course, port to port we always ran out of fresh fruit and vegetables. The store was about four miles out of town, but had been highly recommended by the *Seven Seas Bulletins*. I remembered my excursions to town in La Paz, and asked for volunteers. Randy designated himself as my helper.

The clerk spoke excellent English, having lived in the United States until about eight months prior. He explained to us why some things such as flour, sugar, rice, and beans are so very cheap, and other things like canned fruit or butter are so expensive.

"Staples," he said, "things that are considered necessities, are all price-regulated by the government."

"Butter isn't considered a necessity?" I asked.

"For me it is," he said with a little laugh, "but that's because I grew up in the US. Most Mexican families don't use butter. Did you ever get a buttered tortilla in Mexico?"

"No, I don't think so," I agreed, "but it sounds good. How does the government keep track of all the little stores selling price-regulated things?"

"Ah, that's the thing we always have to worry about," he said with a little grimace. "They have inspectors, shoppers sent out by the government. Usually you can pick them out quite easily, but not always. We had one here last week, and I didn't know until after I had rung up her groceries. I felt good, though, when I found out because I knew our prices were right."

"What would have happened if your prices hadn't been right?"

He was silent for a moment, his expression indicating that this was too awful to contemplate. "They fine you," he began, "and they can take away your right to run a store — ever."

"Wow!" Randy exclaimed. "That sounds pretty serious!"

"Believe me," he said with great earnestness, "it wouldn't be worth it to cheat. The biggest problem is something turning up that you didn't know about — price changes, something being put on the restricted list that wasn't there before. I worry about things like that."

So would I, I thought. It is all too easy for a little fellow to get caught in the unwieldy cogs of Big Brother government.

⚓

One thing we had vowed to do in Manzanillo was to visit a restaurant recommended by some of our cruising friends. We had very specific directions, but there were so many little restaurants all in a row that we had a hard time deciding which one was the right one. The "right one" was supposed to have a tenderloin steak dinner for one dollar and fifteen cents.

"You could go in and read the menu," I suggested to Jim, who continued to be our best conversationalist in Spanish although Randy and Pattie were certainly catching up.

"I don't have to," Jim responded with just a touch of exasperation. "I know this is the place. C'mon; they've already seen us."

Rand was still dubious. "What difference does that make? They see a lot of people out here on any given day."

"Well, they're going to see me inside!"

Jim walked in and sat down at a table. After glancing at the menu, he beckoned furiously for the rest of us to join him. "See, it says bifstek fourteen pesos."

"It doesn't say 'tenderloin,'" I pointed out. But we went ahead and ordered.

The steaks were T-bone rather than tenderloin, but we didn't mind. They were cooked to perfection, and we were all happy with them, even Eldon, who having been raised a vegetarian doesn't claim steak as his favorite food.

I should say we were all happy except Jim, who likes his steak rare. "Rare" and "raw" are the same word in Spanish, at least in Mexican Spanish, so Jim's steak arrived cold. Totally raw. He tried to take a bite but couldn't manage it.

"I hope it won't hurt their feelings if I ask them to cook this," he mumbled to his father.

"Well, I would," Eldon said positively. "They're probably wondering why you ordered it that way."

The waitress was not at all offended. "I knew you wouldn't like it. No good raw; we never do it that way."

She returned in about fifteen minutes with a steak cooked properly, according to their standards — it wasn't rare, but it wasn't overcooked, either. Jim had to concede that it was better that way than raw.

"Still, I'd like to show them what a good, rare steak is like," Jim said after we left the restaurant.

⚓

Manzanillo has one of the most outstanding public squares that we saw in Mexico, surfaced with glazed tile of beautiful design and surrounded by lofty trees and many flowering plants. On Saturday nights clusters of teenage girls, three or four in a group, walk up and down in the square. They pretend not to notice, though they're always very conscious of, their admirers. The boys outnumber the girls three or four to one, which probably has a lot to do with keeping the custom alive and well.

Saturday night Jim and Rand, invited by some of the local young men who had visited *Trilogy* during the week, played and sang for a while in the public square. A large crowd gathered to listen, and before long some of the young people began dancing. Everywhere we went in Mexico and Central America, the young people had tiny, portable radios and knew all the songs that were currently popular in the USA. Before very long the concert developed into a sing-along. Even the dancing couples sang as they danced.

Eldon was so full of satisfaction at this moment that it positively emanated from him visibly. He always loved to hear the children practice; whatever instrument and whatever their command of it was immaterial. He just enjoyed knowing that someday they were going to be competent musicians. And now they were. He was enjoying it as only a proud parent can.

I found it a bit heady myself.

By the next morning, though, he was getting impatient to move on. He might hope to be in a public square come next Saturday night, but it wouldn't be this one.

Harbors and Hazards

We had a family conference. Eldon wanted to set up a schedule that would get us to the Galapagos Islands by the first of June. Most of us hated such arbitrary deadlines. We felt that they gave us a false sense of urgency and tended to cloud our enjoyment of the present with some sort of guilt for not being somewhere else.

Jim, especially, hated to feel pushed. We had skirted this subject in family caucus before, Eldon's dissatisfaction with the progress we were making, the rest of us reveling in our sense of freedom taking life on a day-to-day basis. But this time Eldon tackled the subject directly, making three strong points: first, we had already taken longer getting to Manzanillo than he had originally allotted to all of Mexico; second, while the trip was to be of undetermined duration, the state of our finances would bring it to an end, probably sooner than later; and third, when that happened, he didn't want to have missed things that were really important to him.

It was a good argument, quite convincing I thought. But Jim was not so easily swayed. "Those are all things to consider," he said, trying not to offend his father but knowing also that Eldon didn't like to be disagreed with. "Just the same, the thing that makes this trip the kind I always hoped it would be is that we don't have to be any place at any given time. I want to see the Galapagos Islands; they may well be the most interesting place of all, but at the same time I want to enjoy right where we are."

In spite of Jim's best intentions, his father was a little bit huffy. "We can't spend the rest of our lives in Mexico," he retorted. "I've got other places I want to see." Still, having gotten it all off his chest, Eldon seemed somewhat more relaxed, although he made little remarks occasionally that showed he didn't quite approve of his family's insouciance.

⚓

Trilogy

We had been warned about three kinds of storms off the coast of Mexico and Central America: the Chabasco, which we avoided by traveling here when it wasn't in season; the Tehuantepecker, which we luckily avoided although we'd been given quite a pyrotechnic display of its powers; and the Papagayo, which whistled at us pretty convincingly once or twice. So far, we'd had good sailing winds and not very often more than that.

Our trip from Manzanillo to Zihuatanejo, just over two hundred miles, was uneventful. But it got eventful fast after we got there. The beach at Zihuatanejo is steep, and the surf breaks very close to the shore. When Rand and Jim saw that Eldon was going to do his usual skiff surfing, they both said almost the same thing: "You'd better not, Dad. You'll get rolled over in the shore break and wreck the outboard."

Parents, men especially, aren't used to taking that kind of advice from their kids. Eldon ignored it; he'd heard it all many times before, and he and the skiff were both still intact. He had been running the skiff on the steep wave front for about half an hour when it happened. He got rolled in the surf as predicted.

While he did rescue the outboard, he lost his glasses. Without them he was nearly blind. He couldn't read or work on the motors (including JJ, now full of salt water) or even write in the ship's log, and it would take weeks to get another pair from his ophthalmologist in Washington.

Jim cleaned and oiled the outboard, but he couldn't do anything about the other things for which Eldon needed glasses.

It was almost dark when the accident happened, too late to look for them that night although the boys gave it a shot. They tried to cheer Eldon up by saying, "Just as soon as it's light in the morning, we'll get a bunch of the local kids together and look for your glasses."

Harbors and Hazards

Early in the morning about fifteen of the local boys, from twelve to about twenty years old, came down to the beach to help Jim and Rand look for the glasses. Some had masks and snorkels; some had goggles. The rest said they could see under the water anyway. They spread out along the shore break several feet apart and started looking and diving.

I went over to the beach; the boat was so far out in the bay that I couldn't tell from there what was going on. After about an hour a boy named Raphael came over to talk to me. He spoke English quite well. "Too bad," he said, "because they never find those glass. Not possible."

"Why isn't it possible?" I asked.

He pointed to a wave breaking on the steep beach. "See that wave, how it break? Anything you drop there, it never stay there. Either it go up the beach or out to the ocean. Big undertow; nothing stay where you drop it."

This kid knew his beach, and what he said sounded reasonable. I started wondering how Eldon might get to a larger city where he could have glasses made. But Raphael wasn't through yet. "Even they find them, those glass be no good."

Raphael was a most cheerful prophet of doom. "Why not?" I asked. "Why wouldn't they be any good?"

"See how that water carry many, many small rock every time? Whoosh! rock go up the beach. Whoosh! roll back down thousand time all night. Glass be all broken, scratch everywhere. He never can wear again."

I couldn't help saying, "Raphael, if you think all this diving is a waste of time, why are you helping?"

He seemed surprised that I would ask. " 'Cause I wanta be good guy. These my friends; I wanta help!"

Soon after this, Randy decided they needed more help than he could get from the local teenagers. He gathered all his helpers in a big circle, arms around each other's shoulders. They bowed their heads. "Dear Lord," Randy prayed,

"You are the only One who knows exactly where Dad's glasses are, and You know, too, how much he needs them. Please help us find them."

On the next dive, Jim came up with the glasses in his hand.

The boys all formed a circle and said a quick "Thank You." Then they passed the glasses around the circle, and each one shook his head in wonderment. There were no scratches on the lenses!

While Jim and Rand, along with as many helpers as the skiff would hold, ran out to the boat to deliver the glasses to Eldon, Raphael came over to talk to me. He was very serious. "That was a miracle, no?" he asked.

"It was a miracle, yes!" I answered.

Raphael turned to go, then came back. "No," he said, holding up two fingers. "It was two miracles! One miracle: they even find them. Another miracle, no scratches. God put His hand over those glass so the rocks don't scratch them all night."

There were no atheists in our foxhole that night.

⚓

April tenth was Pattie's birthday, the day presumably she would declare her independence and fly back to Washington — but we ignored all that she had said and planned to set out for Acapulco as soon as the birthday dinner was over. We did know that the friend with whom she had been planning to share an apartment had left college and gone back to Alaska. No one brought up the subject of Pattie's imminent departure and her dad, her brothers, and I all hoped it wasn't imminent after all.

Jim had bought Pattie a beaded necklace in Guadalajara; Rand had made her a macramé belt; I had been saving a bottle of perfume for her, and her dad gave her some US dollars. Then Pattie opened the sack of things Linda had given her when she and her husband left

the *Macquinna*. It was enough to start a drugstore: skin
creams, hair care products, perfume and cologne, dusting
powder. It was a real windfall, and Pattie was sure she had
enough supplies to last for the next five years.

None of us had the slightest idea that Pattie wouldn't
be the only one using them. The only one who could have
made such a prediction was my brother Walter, and he was
writing us a letter in the utmost secrecy.

⚓

It took some scurrying around and some fast dish-
washing, but everything was shipshape by four o'clock. We
weighed anchor, bound for Acapulco.

Paradoxically, Rand and Jim chafed at the poor speed
we were making, ghosting along at three knots, even
though they professed to be profoundly bored with their
contemplation of Acapulco. "Three hundred high-rise
hotels, and the beach jammed with tourists," Randy
predicted. However, Acapulco was one of our mail stops,
also one of the few places left where I could expect to find
a Hilton Hotel. We couldn't just bypass it.

When the city with its white, curving beach came in
sight, we were undeniably impressed, although the boys
sounded as though they were grieving over the degenerate
appearance of a fallen woman.

"Think what she must have been like before they built
all that garbage along the waterfront!" Jim said.

"I can imagine," Rand answered. "This had to be one of
the real beauty spots of the world! It's a shame."

I didn't think the city looked all that bad in its present
condition; neither did Eldon. It wasn't exactly wilderness,
but it had a certain charm. As for Eldon, he always said he
didn't mind roughing it as long as he had all the comforts
of home. For both of us the beautiful buildings, the look of
elegant sophistication, was very appealing, but we didn't
argue with the kids.

Trilogy

We had never been a camping-out family, sleeping on the ground and all that. My own father, mother, brother, and sisters were very gung-ho campers, and I learned at an early age that sleeping on rocks or pine boughs was for hardier souls than I. Eldon and I had managed our forays into the wilderness with the *Mañana* in great comfort. Maybe our kids had missed an elemental contact with nature, or maybe they just thought they had.

As we threaded our way through the yachts at anchor, headed in the general direction of the Acapulco Yacht Club, we found several old friends. *Molokai Girl* was there with Fred, Elsie, and Phil aboard, and *Rolling Hills* with Mary, Ray, and the kids. It was old home week. Since they all seemed to be stopped quite some distance from the yacht club, we threw the anchor over, wanting to find out why.

"Hah! I thought you were going to go right on by and tie up at the Acapulco Waldorf," Mary accused.

"We were headed in that direction till we saw you," Eldon agreed tentatively.

"Looking for a place to take showers and wash some clothes," I said.

"Listen, kids." (We're all kids to Mary, even Eldon with his halo of white hair.) "We've got such a good deal going here that you absolutely won't believe it! Far better than you'll get over at the yacht club."

"You have?" we chorused incredulously. Just showers and clean clothes had sounded pretty good to us — not that we didn't have showers, but they were cold and salty.

"Sure have," Mary continued. "It's the off-season after Easter, you know. Well, before I go into that, see that hotel over there?" She pointed to the Club de Pesca over on the beach, shining like alabaster above dark green lawns and shapely shrubs. It had a slightly curved central portion with wings in a shallow V shape. It looked ridiculously out of our budget.

"How does that pile of elegance fit in with the humble

cruising fraternity?" I asked.

"As I started to tell you — the Easter rush is over, and the hotel isn't very busy. They're letting the boats use their pool and showers, and in return most of the yachtsmen patronize their restaurant and bar."

It sounded good to us, almost too good to be true!

"Oh, one more thing," Mary added. "There's a place on the dock where you can wash clothes." She waved airily toward the *Rolling Hills*. On rails and rigging a colorful assortment of garments flapped idly in the light breeze. "Please note the sparkling cleanliness of the Hills' clothing, as of now."

I noted. I also thought about all the Coon's laundry bags cowering in dark corners all over the boat. But, first things first. Before we got bogged down with laundry and other mundane business, we all wanted a nice, leisurely dip in the pool.

Mary took us over in their skiff; the Hill girls were already in the water. I'm not sure but what they slept in the pool, too. Champion swimmers, both girls were more at home in the water than out of it. Even Eldon went there occasionally — not, he said, from love of swimming, but to get some of the salt off his skin. For one who loves the water so much, it seems strange that he doesn't care much about swimming in it. But the rest of us made up for it. From that time until we left Acapulco, we lost Pattie to the swimming pool. I would have been afraid she would be sunburned if she hadn't already gotten such a deep tan.

At one time in my life, I remember wondering why big resort hotels on magnificent swimming beaches also have freshwater pools. Now I know. Freshwater pools don't fill your suits and hair with sand and salt, and they are frequently warmer than the ocean.

When I got back from the pool and reality set in, I started working on some strategy that would get at least fifty percent of the laundry off my hands. Eldon always did his own laundry; he knew how difficult jeans and denim jackets are to wash on a board, and he didn't want me to be stuck with more of it than necessary. I didn't want to be, either.

In mid-afternoon, when all the family were together for five minutes, I started assigning duties. "Each of you wash your own shirts, jeans, underwear, sheets, pillowcases, and whatever else belongs to you personally. I'll take care of my own stuff plus towels, tea towels, and things like that. Dad always does his own stuff, so he doesn't need any instruction."

The kids vanished to pick up their laundry. Pattie came out presently with a stack of laundry that would have fit easily inside a shower cap.

"Surely you must have more than that," I told her. "Where are your sheets? They haven't been washed since we were in San Blas."

"They don't need it," she called as she jumped in the skiff. "I always sleep on top of the bed."

I stopped her departure with, "Just a cotton-picking minute! If that's the case, why aren't you taking your bedspread? It must need washing."

"It's clean; just go take a look," and she sped merrily off with a couple of tee-shirts and some bikini panties like postage stamps folded diagonally.

Rand had a big bagful for himself and Jim. Drying space was going to be a problem; I didn't mind postponing the rest until the next morning. No task is so formidable that it doesn't look better viewed from at least twelve hours' distance.

⚓

Due to the hospitality of the Club de Pesca, our Acapulco interlude is a bright spot in my memories. The pathway to the pool was flanked with ixora, large orange clusters of flowers that bloom almost all year around. A half dozen flamingoes stood one-legged on the lawn, their

*Al Koban and his three
girls with one of Trilogy's
hulls under construction*

Seattle
USA

*The shipwrights:
Jim, Dave, Rick, Eldon,
Rand and Mr. Bojangles*

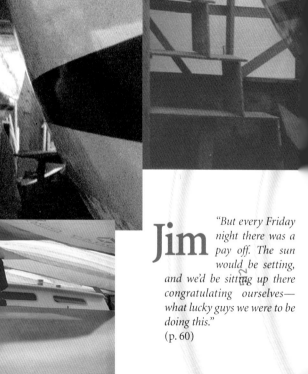

8192

Seattle
USA

Jim and Randy at the boat-building site.

Jim

"*But every Friday night there was a pay off. The sun would be setting, and we'd be sitting up there congratulating ourselves— what lucky guys we were to be doing this.*"
(p. 60)

Trilogy

The starboard cabin, the girls' stateroom. Pattie: "When you live with someone on a boat, you learn either to love 'em or to hate 'em.... We spent many nights lying in our bunks discussing childhood memories and talking about all sorts of things, from guys to our philosophies of life."
(p. 297)

Dreamers

"I had my own version of the Dream while Trilogy was in the planning and building stage. My mental image showed the family scattered artistically over the deck, singing and playing musical instruments, while our trim ship plowed its triple-jeweled furrow through phosphorescent waters. This vision wasn't totally false. There were actually times when it happened just like that."
(p. 104)

Yalapa
MEXICO

"Seventeen miles away from Puerto Vallarta by water is the little port of Yalapa where, the local inhabitants told us, the motion picture Night of the Iguana was filmed. This place looked the most tropical of any place we had seen so far, with palm trees, pale yellow beach, and little woven houses with thatched roofs. Somehow it gave us a sense of achievement, as though we had arrived, almost, in the South Seas." (p. 195)

Randy

"I suspect we also share something else: a little sadness for those idyllic days of sailing, youthful innocence and enthusiasm, trade winds abaft the beam, flying fish on deck in the morning, bananas hanging from the rigging, the Southern Cross off the port bow—days when we were still just brothers enjoying being friends."
(p. 224)

Espiritu Santo Islands
MEXICO

"whose praises we had heard from sailors who had gone before us: golden, curving, unoccupied beaches; fishing so good that you either have to stop after an hour or keep throwing the fish back in the water."
(p. 166)

Puerto Angel
MEXICO

"Just as we turned to enter the harbor at Puerto Angel under full sail, a gust of wind caught us. Suddenly we were zooming toward the anchorage going at least ten knots. This was one of the fanciest maneuvers we had yet attempted—or possibly ever will— and it was unpremeditated."
(p. 220)

Guatemala

Entering Central American waters. Without realizing, we had just sailed across the imaginary political line separating Guatemala from Mexico. A patrol plane buzzed us, then shot across our bow. We got the proper flag up in a hurry — I had to sew it on the spot!

Playa del Cocos
COSTA RICA

Carole and Rand, with Trilogy below.

Culebra
COSTA RICA

"Almost as soon as Carole was aboard, we headed Trilogy out to Culebra and beached her at high tide. Randy's new whisker poles were pressed into service to keep the side hulls from tipping as Trilogy rested solidly on her keel. Rand, Jim, and Eldon worked fast and efficiently, first scrubbing the hulls as the tide ebbed, and then applying new copper paint. Even the boot top got a new coat of paint. Amazingly, for the two days the boat was beached, there was no rain."
(p. 250)

San Jose
COSTA RICA

Picking up Carole. Pattie is sitting on Carole's suitcase.

THE ROLLING HILLS

The Hills paid for their boat with money they raised with their family orchestra. We hooked up with them in L[a] Mexico, and we traveled together to Costa Rica. went through the Panama Canal; we headed acro[ss] Gulf of Tehuantepec to Tumaco, Colombia.

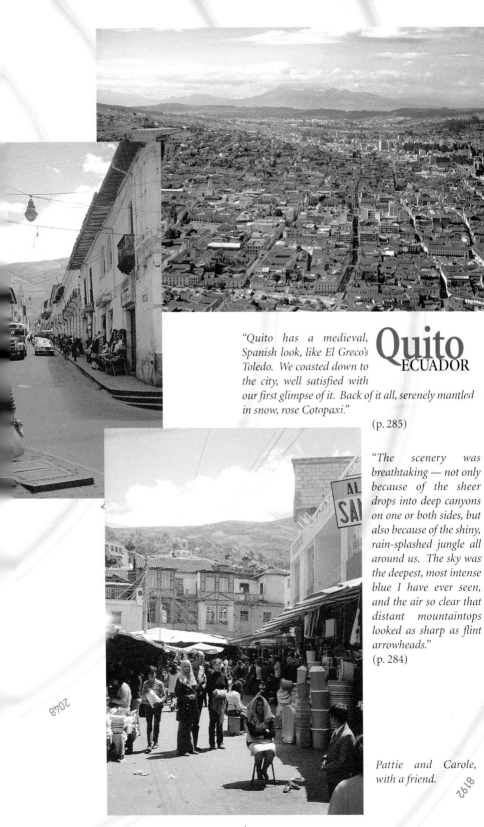

Quito
ECUADOR

"Quito has a medieval, Spanish look, like El Greco's Toledo. We coasted down to the city, well satisfied with our first glimpse of it. Back of it all, serenely mantled in snow, rose Cotopaxi."

(p. 285)

"The scenery was breathtaking — not only because of the sheer drops into deep canyons on one or both sides, but also because of the shiny, rain-splashed jungle all around us. The sky was the deepest, most intense blue I have ever seen, and the air so clear that distant mountaintops looked as sharp as flint arrowheads."
(p. 284)

Pattie and Carole, with a friend.

Eldon

The skipper stands on Trilogy's pulpit, a platform at the bowsprit end of the ship.

The elusive Vermilion Flycatche Rand: "It took me forever. I ke waiting and waiting until final one landed right in front of me.'

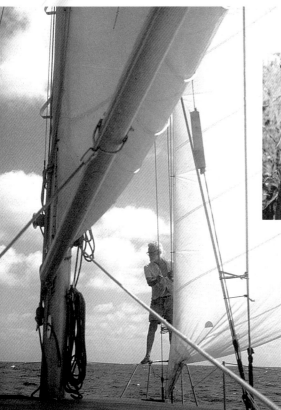

Plaza Island
GALÁPAGOS

"On the far side of the island found huge cliffs of black la That was a surprise, but o astonishment was far grea when the whole cliff under feet started moving."
(p. 315)

Barrington Island
GALAPAGOS

"We found ourselves surrounded by little iguanas. They were the same color as the dust and rocks and resembled nothing so much as small dragons, even to the armor plates down the back. They scarfed down the peelings readily enough, but when Eldon threw them some orange sections, they went totally crazy. Such a troop of them gathered around him that he could hardly keep from tripping over them." (p. 310)

"Later, when Jim and Rand swam with two friendly seals called Lou-seal and Sea-seal through beautiful lava caves and undersea castles, we always kept a sharp watch for the big males that we called Big Daddies. Once I helped Jim out of the water just ahead of those lethal jaws!" (p. 309)

Plaza Islands
GALAPAGOS

"Here on the weather side of the island, waves that surge all the way from Antarctica, unimpeded along the way by any land mass, crash against the cliffs. The steady beating has sculpted the rock into fantastic shapes. I wanted to sketch them."
(p. 315)

"With all those sails lugging, she looked as though she should be making about twenty knots. In less than an hour, though, we had passed Romance and left her dwindling in the distance. We did get some good photographs of this authentic hermaphrodite brig, fully rigged and accurate in every detail."
(p. 314)

"Jim, the biologist, was spending his time studying plants, flowers, and butterflies that were new to him."

Wreck Bay
GALAPAGOS

A penguin at the equator! The Humboldt Current is so cold that these Antarctic birds are comfortable even at this latitude.

China Hat Cove
BARTHOLOME ISLAND

The view in the distance includes the southern point of San Salvador and, on the far horizon, Isla Isabela rising to 5,000 feet.

Tower Island
GALAPAGOS

Floreana Island
GALAPAGOS

Mules carried provisions that we bought for our crossing to the Marquesas. We filled a fourteen-foot skiff with supplies, for which we paid $7.50!

Jim

"You get this spark in your brain, and somehow the forces of the universe stack up behind you, moving you—with little course corrections—right to that point. Even if you don't know what's going on."
(p. 444)

Fatu-Hiva Island
MARQUESAS

"While Everyone else went ashore, I stayed on the boat and painted Omoa as it looked from there.

Omoa
MARQUESAS

"Coming into Omoa, we rounded a rugged headland reminiscent of Diamond Head in Honolulu, but many times taller, greener, steeper..."

uku-Hiva
land
ARQUESAS

ourigger rests near the beach.

Jim

Manning the 16mm movie camera.

2048

Ua-Huka Island
MARQUESAS
The little church at Vaipaee.

512

Teuaua Islan·
MARQUESAS
"In some nests the gulls had hatched, looki· fuzzy little chicks; Jim took a picture of holding one of them".
(p. 404)

Jim

On Erika, A friend's boat.

Jim

Lands a mahi-mahi in mid-ocean.

a-Pou Island

MARQUESAS

The whole gang at Hakahetau.
. 404)

Maui
HAWAII

"*For Eldon this was the last and best hope of living out his boyhood dream of sailing to fabled lands where the culture is exotic, where the climate is milder than in Alaska or the Pacific Northwest, and where one can get away from the treacherous daily routine that robs people of life before they have really lived it (his words, often expressed).*" (p.100)

Trilogy

pearly-pink color intensified to jewel-like loveliness by the surrounding green tones. Occasionally they walked around with high-stepping awkwardness, alternately ignoring the hotel guests or gazing at them severely down their exaggerated beaks.

Saturday, the kids went over to watch the famous Acapulco divers; Eldon and I did a tour of the city, having no idea which bus we were taking or where it would go. It was a fantastic ride, eventually circling through large areas of the residential section of town and bringing us back to our starting point two hours later. Fare: one peso each.

I am convinced that every architect in the world possessed of more than average imagination has built his most far-out dream house somewhere on the hillside in Acapulco. Some of them are incredibly beautiful; some are just incredible. But there is no monotony, and in the best of them you see wonderful ingenuity in the use of the huge boulders that abound all around the city.

Our bus tour, however, was not limited to the section of town designed by architects. We traveled up several canyons full of tiny, nondescript little dwellings that had never heard of an architect, eons removed from twentieth-century technology. Here, you realize that the lush prosperity of the waterfront has not penetrated much beyond its own well-groomed landscaping.

One of our homespun American humorists once wrote, "Poverty isn't so bad if you have enough of it." And that may not be as frivolous as it sounds. These homes are no poorer than those at Magdalena Bay; neither had running water or electricity. But poverty looks different on the doorstep of wealth and abundance.

⚓

The day before our departure, picking up our mail for the last time, we found an unexpected letter from my brother asking if we would consider letting his sixteen-year-old daughter travel with us. "Carole is intelligent and talented," he wrote. "But right now we feel that a few months at sea may be the only way to break up some undesirable associations. If you feel you can't do it, we'll understand. If you decide you can, you'll have to issue the invitation as though it came from you spontaneously. If she knew I had asked you, she would never come." He added, wistfully, "She is worth saving."

This was a shocker. I knew from the start that we had no choice; this is the sort of thing families do for each other. Such a cry for help from someone as proud and independent as Walter was especially poignant. Nevertheless, Eldon and I assembled the whole family and spread the letter before them. Randy was the first to recover his power of speech.

"We're not a home for wayward girls," he said flatly. "If she comes and she's a real bitch, it will spoil the trip for all of us."

Jim remembered the Carole of three or four years ago, a warm-hearted, lovable tomboy who doted on Jim and his buddy Kent Dawson. "She can't be all that bad," he protested. "I'm sure she's basically a good kid. No fooling, she's my pick of the litter."

Of Walter's five daughters, Carole is the most like Jim — affectionate and impulsive, high-spirited and frequently in trouble because of it, a boundlessly energetic people-lover, yet easily rebuffed.

I knew what Eldon's response would be without even asking. If Carole needed help, we should give it willingly. He couldn't understand how any of us could feel that there was any alternative. "We can't refuse a request like this without at least giving it a fair trial. What is there to talk about? Just ask her to come."

"So far," I reminded my assembled family, "we don't even know if she would accept our invitation. I think Walter's letter leaves quite a bit of room for doubt."

"At least, let's invite her to come," Jim urged. "The decision is up to her. We can't do any more than invite her, but we can't do any less, either."

"How do you feel about having your cousin travel with us, Pattie?" Eldon asked. "You'll have to share the same stateroom, and the real burden of getting along with her will be on you."

"I know that," Pattie answered thoughtfully. "I think it would be nice to have another girl along. I know Carole; she's a good kid. I haven't seen her for over a year, but she couldn't have turned into a monster."

Rand, a little ashamed of himself for being the only one to voice any negative thoughts, added, "We'll give it a fair trial. There's a pretty good chance that she won't accept anyway."

Underneath all this discussion, we all felt an obligation to Walter and his wife Anne that went beyond the claim of family. When Pattie was a baby, they had taken care of her while she was having the operation that removed an unsightly angioma from her face. (No one in the little town of Ketchikan was a specialist in this kind of work.) Then, when the boys were in boarding school and in college, they had spent frequent weekends with their aunt and uncle.

So naturally, and with much kibitzing from everyone, I wrote a letter to Carole inviting her to travel with us.

It was past the middle of April, and Eldon was still hoping to get to the Galapagos Islands by the first of June. We asked Carole to join us in Costa Rica by the middle of May. It wouldn't be possible to get a reply until our next mail stop, but it seemed best to just assume that she was coming.

⚓

You wouldn't think that a brand new boat with all mechanical gadgets in pristine condition would require constant maintenance, but Eldon thought otherwise. During our stay in Acapulco he had the depth sounder repaired, the oil filters changed, the propane tanks filled, and numerous other improvements made. On the last day he picked up new frames for his glasses, ordered as soon as we got to town. The others were too loose, he said, one reason he had lost them in the surf.

All the time, a nasty infection on his arm that had started from an insect bite was getting worse. Eldon kept expecting it to disappear. I'd asked him several times to see a doctor, but he hadn't done so. Now his whole forearm was swollen and magenta-red. I could imagine us far from any medical help and the arm having to be amputated. So when he came back without having seen a doctor on this, our last day, I issued an ultimatum: we are not going anywhere until that arm looks better.

When Jim announced that he was going downtown to get some things for our first-aid kit, Eldon went along, and he was lucky enough to get an appointment with a doctor. The doctor treated the arm and gave him a shot of powerful antibiotics. By morning his arm had improved dramatically.

Jim's visit was not so successful. He got most of the supplies he needed but no painkiller worthy of the name. The doctor who put our first kit together in San Diego had been sure that Jim wouldn't have any trouble getting enough morphine in Mexico to take care of an emergency.

"I'd like to give it to you," the Mexican doctor told him. "There is certainly a good chance that in a year or more of traveling you may need it badly. But the government restrictions are so stringent that I don't dare."

"How am I supposed to cope with a serious accident out at sea with no anesthetic?" Jim asked.

"If worse comes to worst," the doctor said in parting, "Have a couple of bottles of whiskey aboard. Whiskey was used for a pain reliever long before we had opiates."

Drug-running was rampant up and down the coast, but

the laws prevented us from getting what we needed legitimately — even though it might mean the difference between life and death.

Jim came back from this frustrating excursion looking as though he had most of the cares of the world on his shoulders. He announced to all of us that from now on we were to observe care, prudence, and every known safety regulation because we were not prepared for serious accidents. Coming from an accident-prone kid who'd always been a daredevil, this caution might well have provoked gales of mirth on the part of his audience. But it didn't. We realized how deeply disturbed he was and quelled any tendency to make his lecture less effective by saying, "Look who's talking!"

Our next port was Puerto Angel, our last stop in Mexico. *Rolling Hills* and *Molokai Girl* planned to travel with us at least that far and possibly on to Costa Rica. The night before our departure, the yachts that were staying on gave a party for us at one of the Club de Pesca's private swimming pools.

The setting for this bon voyage party was pure tropical idyll. Against the pale yellow wall that separated the pool from the rest of the grounds were low-growing purple vines. Banana trees shone bright yellow-green under the floodlights; lilies and hibiscus, blooming profusely, splashed color on either side of the walk. Towering high above the pool was a huge old mango tree, surely one of the world's most handsome trees, and from its branches ripe mangoes dropped into the pool every few minutes. Of course they dropped on the ground, too, but these splatted when they fell and weren't much good for eating. The ones that hit the water were still perfect; Elsie, Mary, and I took most of them back to our boats at the urging of all the others assembled.

Trilogy

They would be able to get mangoes as long as the season lasted; we would not.

Having come, as instructed, in bathing suits, we played a sort of aquatic volleyball until dinner was served: steak, salads, hamburgers, and desserts. Then Randy and Jim along with the Hills organized a musical group that kept on until after midnight. The harbor was black and the sky frosty with stars as we made our way back to *Trilogy*. Across the water, a cruise ship outlined with hundreds of twinkling lights looked like a floating carnival.

At first light, *Rolling Hills* and *Molokai Girl* left the harbor. It took us a little longer. There is probably a ratio, precise and predictable, between the number of days spent in harbor and the length of time spent in getting ready to leave port. If we have only stopped overnight, we can pull the anchor and be gone in five minutes. Should our stay be a week or two, it takes a day of frantic effort to get on the high seas again. I hate to contemplate the time and turmoil it would take to get us out of a port in which we had spent several months.

But at three in the afternoon we hoisted our anchor and, with a good sailing breeze, swept smoothly out of the harbor. The breeze held until ten that night, then suddenly left us with luffing sails. Eldon started the motor, and we alternately sailed and motored, trying to make the most of a very fickle wind. Always on our minds were comments of former travelers that the coastal lights are frequently out of commission. If this is so, then we were very lucky because we found most of the lights in good working order, blinking out their messages faithfully.

Just as we turned to enter the harbor at Puerto Angel under full sail, a gust of wind caught us. Suddenly we were zooming toward the anchorage going at least ten knots. This was one of the fanciest maneuvers we had yet attempted — or possibly ever will — and it was unpremeditated. We brushed by *Molokai Girl* two boat-lengths away, turned into the wind and dropped sails and anchor almost in less time than it takes to tell it. Everything worked perfectly even though, because the harbor was crowded, we felt uneasy until we'd secured the anchor.

Then, because this had been such an outstanding (albeit unplanned) demonstration of seamanship, we looked around to see how much of an audience we might have had. Would you believe — not one single, solitary person? Of all those boats in the harbor, none had anyone out on deck! And so what might have been a legendary display of boat-handling dropped into oblivion.

So it goes; whenever the crew blatantly flubbed anything, it was always in a crowded port with far more onlookers than we really required.

Several minutes later, Fred came out on the deck of *Molokai Girl.* "Hey! When did you get here?" he asked in surprise. "I didn't hear you come in."

"We came in under sail," Jim said with just the tiniest bit of smugness. But it was a hollow victory. Some things just need an audience to make them worthwhile. Imagine winning at Wimbledon with no one in the stands!

⚓

Usually, Jim took our ship's papers and our passports ashore as soon as we landed in a new port. Here, evidently, the port captain preferred to board the visiting boats himself. That would have been all right, and a nice courtesy, except for one thing. On the bow of his sixteen-foot skiff was a huge and wicked spike that he seemed determined to ram into our hull. Jim fended it off twice, becoming angrier each time.

When the port captain was swinging around to make another run for it, all the forbearance that Jim carefully cultivated for dealing with officialdom left him. "Look, you stupid bastards," he shouted in English, "keep that thing away from my hull!"

The port captain understood the tone if not the words, and came alongside without pointing the spike directly at our hull. When they left, it was the same thing over again, with the captain maneuvering to get a whack at the hull and Jim trying to prevent any real damage and shouting at him in very salty language. The rest of us were in a state of suspended animation, fearing the officials might under-stand enough English to be insulted. They certainly had been, and all their forebears as well.

"Why didn't you talk Spanish to him?" I asked when the boarding party had left.

"Because if I called him an s.o.b. in Spanish, he'd prob-ably have to shoot me to preserve his honor."

"What if he had understood English?" I knew Jim had pumped a lot of adrenaline during that exchange, and I wondered if he knew the possible disaster he was skirting. Port officials in these places can give you a very bad time if they so desire. Their authority over visiting yachts is extensive.

"Oh, he understood enough," Jim replied. "He knew what I was saying. He's probably been sworn at in Lithuanian, Patagonian, or whatever. I think he likes to make nice, jagged holes in the fancy yachts of rich Americans and other foreigners."

"Even if he does," Rand spoke what all of us were thinking, "he's really stupid for abusing the authority of his office that way."

"One thing he has demonstrated," Jim said, still steaming a little, "he's poorly qualified to be a port captain." No one could argue with that.

"What are you going to do if he comes charging out here again to clear us when we leave?" Eldon asked.

"I think that can be avoided." Jim thought about it a minute, then continued. "I think it absolutely must be avoided."

Before we left, Jim was very careful to take all our papers ashore.

Harbors and Hazards

RANDY'S COMMENT:
JIM AND I

From biblical times the relationship between brothers has been the subject of endless narratives, parables, and, all too often, protracted battles and bloodshed. Certainly the image of the "first born" has been so indelibly stamped on our Judaic/Christian psyche that even thousands of years later we tend to accept this as one of the family's enduring institutions.

Jim and I were no exception. Jim, being four years older, established his role as older brother very early in my childhood. This was not, however, a relationship based totally on power and control. It took on more the characteristics of a mascot and his trainer. At age two I had contracted polio in the terrible epidemics of the early '50s, and for the next three years I was fighting paralysis. It was Jim's job to toughen me up and prepare me for survival in an unsympathetic world where weakness and timidity of any kind was subject to ridicule.

I must have been a keen disappointment. While Jim thought nothing of defending his honor, or paper route, with his fists, and a day without at least one good fight was somehow a day squandered, I recoiled at violence of any kind. This timidity was blamed on the effects of polio, and I was spared the usual humiliation from my peers and my brother's older friends. But lessons in wrestling and boxing were introduced about the time I started school.

Fortunately for me, I was blessed with good reflexes and an upper-body strength disproportionate to my height and size. Although I never developed the zeal for a good brawl that my older brother seemed to relish, eventually I was able to fight my way out of most situations I couldn't talk my way out of first.

As we grew older and Jim began to pursue less barbaric interests, I found myself following willingly in his footsteps — first boarding school, then music, then, as the '60s accelerated into social meltdown, a year in Europe, drugs, free love, and political activism.

We roomed together for my freshman year at college. Jim was a senior finishing up his degree in pre-med. Music became my bridge to full acceptance by his older and, compared to mine, much more interesting group of friends. Along with his childhood buddy Kent, we performed on and off campus and became increasingly more political as the war in Vietnam heated up. Eventually, this activism in a painfully conservative environment resulted in our expulsion from school.

This camaraderie carried on through the building and sailing of Trilogy, and it provided the foundation for a partnership that, in spite of differences and disagreements, continues to this day. And now, as middle-aged men with sons and daughters of our own, I suspect we also share something else: a little sadness for those idyllic days of sailing, youthful innocence and enthusiasm, trade winds abaft the beam, flying fish on deck in the morning, bananas hanging from the rigging, the Southern Cross off the port bow — days when we were still just brothers enjoying being friends.

CHAPTER NINE:

THE IN-BETWEEN COUNTRIES

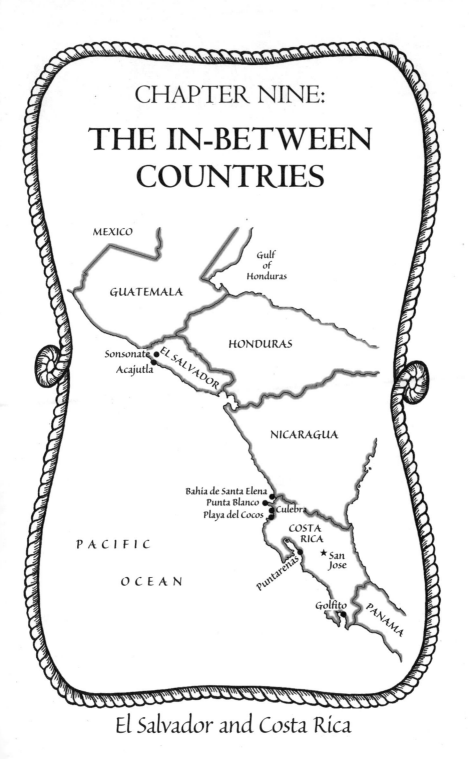

El Salvador and Costa Rica

rossing at this time of year, we weren't expecting any of the fierce winds for which the Gulf of Tehuantepec is famous, nor can I say that we ever experienced the full fury of a "Tehuantepecker." Even so, the gusty squalls we encountered before we got across were exciting enough, especially with lightning added.

All three boats, *Rolling Hills*, *Molokai Girl*, and *Trilogy*, started within ten minutes of each other, but *Trilogy* was faster than the others. Soon we were having trouble keeping our running mates in sight. We did keep in radio contact, and Mary Hill's messages were always good for a laugh.

"Come in Condominium *Trilogy*; that's a nice-looking stern you have." (This was a good-natured admission that we had the edge for speed. When we first talked of traveling together, Ray told us he had a fast boat, and, while he didn't mind traveling with other boats, he would not wait for them.)

"Thank you, *Rolling Hills*," we radioed back with becoming modesty. "Nice of you to say so."

"Hotel *Trilogy*," Mary radioed again, "could I get a room for the night?"

I sent the message back, trying to sound like the stately manager of the Guadalajara Hilton: "Back to *Rolling Hills*. All our rooms seem to be occupied. Did you have a reservation?"

Raucous laughter, then, "I have a lot of reservations about this whole trip!"

While we were kidding each other on the ships' radios,

the wind was picking up — already past nine knots according to our wind indicator. We must have been traveling at precisely the right speed because, simultaneously, we hooked two Sierra mackerel. As Jim was landing one of them, it bit him across the arch of his foot — a nasty gash, deep and ragged. If we had been ashore, it would have required stitches. The best I could do was put some butterfly bandages across. Eldon had gotten several tubes of antibiotic ointment on the prescription of the doctor who'd treated him in Acapulco, and I applied it liberally.

All through the night, we had intermittent gusts of wind up to thirty-five knots, along with some impressive displays of lightning. The thunder was loud and almost constant, but the lightning was fairly high overhead. We were going to have a chance to see it at much closer range before we got across the Gulf of Tehuantepec.

Back in San Diego, Randy had dealt with the necessity of flags for all the little countries whose coastal waters we would be passing through. He'd picked up an illustrated folder of the flags of the world, also a bag full of scraps of parachute cloth in all the colors of the rainbow and a few more besides. We had a sewing machine aboard, so I became a flagmaker in the tradition of Betsy Ross. (Unlike Betsy, though, I didn't get to design them.) Before I realized that we had passed into Guatemalan waters, a Guatemalan Coast Guard plane swooped down over our bow, telling us in no uncertain terms that it was time to start flying a new flag. We had passed some invisible line between Mexico and Guatemala, and we couldn't have been more than five minutes on the other side of it; these countries are very particular.

⚓

A new storm hit the following night, and we knew at once that this one meant business. After the second big gust, *Molokai Girl* called and reported that they had blown out a sail. It looked as though all of us would be wise to shorten sail, and Eldon told Fred that we would get our sewing machine out on deck in the morning, weather permitting, and sew it up.

As darkness came on, thunder boomed at us. The explosions were following the flashes of light immediately, so we knew that lightning was striking very close by. Once, hanging onto our metal steering wheel, Eldon got a real jolt. His hair stood up the way you imagine it would if you stuck your finger in a light socket.

Mary Hill called on the radio, "*Trilogy! Trilogy*, are you hit?"

Eldon grabbed the mike; he'd soaked up a few volts of electricity, but he wanted everyone on the other boats to know that it wasn't serious. "Back to *Rolling Hills*. No, we're fine. Some of those bolts were close, though."

"Close? I should say it is close!" Mary called stridently. "Did you know your whole boat is glowing like a neon sign?"

"Just Elmo's fire," Eldon said calmly and passed the mike back to Jim.

We had been discussing this Elmo, wondering how he got a variety of electricity named after him, so Jim passed the question on to the other boats: "Any of you know who this Elmo was and how he got this stuff named after him?"

For a while there was no answer, then Fred came back with, "I think his name was Saint Elmo, but I don't know what his connection is with electricity."

Whatever the connection, Saint Elmo was giving us a first-class display. Bright flames, blue at the bottom, danced along the crossbars of the masts and over the rigging. Very pretty, but it did tend to make us nervous.

Eldon, knowing the additional hazard of the metal wheel in his hands, refused to turn it over to anyone else. When Jim offered to take it, he said, "I think you and Rand had better see what you can do about rigging up a lightning rod. The masts are probably natural lightning rods, but they need grounding."

Those tall masts did look like prime candidates for a real strike of lightning, with all that electricity careening overhead. The boys disconnected all electrical appliances, including the radio, and jury-rigged a grounding system for the masts.

Rand had the first night watch, but Eldon sent him to bed. "I can keep track of things until this storm passes on," he insisted.

With Eldon courting instant electrocution, I didn't feel much like sleeping, so I stayed up with him. His hair was still standing up, partly from the wind but mostly from static electricity. He seemed to be more excited than worried, and he talked for three hours almost non-stop about his boyhood experiences, some of which would make anyone's hair stand up.

Finally, the storm wore itself out. I went below and woke Randy, and Eldon and I went to bed.

⚓

It was surprising to find serene blue skies and a calm ocean when I woke up.

Trilogy and *Rolling Hills* had both lowered their sails to allow *Molokai Girl* to catch up. Then began the frustrating task of trying to repair *Molokai Girl*'s sail. Every time the machine had to deal with more than one thickness of material, the generator stopped. The only way a torn sail can be repaired is by putting as least two layers of canvas together. We cursed the stupidity that had caused us to get a four-hundred-watt generator. Finally, Fred took the sail back for Elsie to sew by hand.

Under sail again, we soon outdistanced our running mates, arriving in Acajutla, El Salvador, in the late afternoon as another storm seemed to be brewing. The anchorage here is not protected — just an open roadstead with big swells breaking continuously against the cliffs on shore a half mile away. Small boats do not anchor here because of the enormous surge; instead, buoys are provided for securing the boats. We tied up to one of them and settled down to wait for *Rolling Hills* and *Molokai Girl*.

It would soon be dark; already the skies were murky with the approaching storm, and the surf against the cliffs on shore was shooting up like a series of geysers. We could not dispense with night watches here as we could if we'd been in a protected harbor. We kept hoping the other boats would arrive before visibility reached zero.

I was making some soup and sandwiches when some scuffling and yelling on deck brought me out of the galley on the double. *Rolling Hills* was tying up about fifty feet away, and the Hill family lost no time getting over to *Trilogy*. The soup and sandwiches proved to be enough for everyone, *Molokai Girl* having put into another port for sail repairs. There was some speculation that Fred was freaked out by the electrical storm, but no one really knew.

On the following day, Jim took our papers ashore to the port captain's office, and Mary and I, Pattie, and the Hill girls prepared to go ashore. The dock was large and high — built to withstand the ocean swells, and high enough to service the ocean liners that stop there. The iron ladder we had to ascend seemed to tower to infinity. When we reached the top, somewhat breathless, we were challenged by a small, boyish, and very resolute soldier with an extremely realistic looking rifle.

He spoke first in Spanish, asking our intentions, and Pattie answered that we just wished to visit the village of Acajutla over on the shore.

He switched to Inglais, "I must have the papers before you are going."

"I'm sorry," I told him, and I wasn't just being polite; I was truly sorry. He looked like a major impediment to our plans. "My son has taken all our passports to the port captain."

The In-Between Countries

"We can wait until he is returning," the little soldier stated firmly.

Up until now, we had never been greeted by armed guards in any port. Never mind that he looked to be about twelve years old; he held that rifle as though he would certainly use it if the occasion demanded. So we spent our time walking around on the dock while Cathy Hill and her younger sister dove off the dock, swam around, and dove again, ad infinitum. So much energy! Since swimming was the major interest in their lives, they were perfectly happy. The rest of us, even if we had wanted to spend our time diving and swimming, hadn't worn bathing suits under our other clothing. We felt frustrated, but the rifle indicated that the situation wasn't negotiable.

After a little less than two hours, we saw Jim approaching in the distance. (It was a long, long dock.)

"This is your son?" the sentry asked, doubt very plain in his voice.

"Yes," I answered truthfully. "It is my son."

"No, it cannot be your son. It is your father." This puzzled us, but after we had a chance to travel a bit in El Salvador, we decided he had reached this conclusion because young men in El Salvador do not wear beards — only very elderly men do.

But as Jim drew closer, the sentry decided he might be a young man after all. Putting a little more faith in what I had told him, he set his rifle down and prepared to look at the papers Jim brought with him. After giving them the closest scrutiny, he returned them to Jim and told us we could go ashore. It was easy to choose our direction as long as the dock lasted, but when we got to the end of it, we were faced with roads going in all directions.

While we were pondering in which direction Acajutla might lie, a bus came along carrying workmen into town and offered us a ride. They were a rough-looking lot who had evidently been doing some grubby type of work. At other times we might have just walked into town. But we were hot and tired after two hours on the dock, and we gratefully accepted.

The bus was crowded already, and one man scrunched over a few inches to make room for Mary to sit beside him. She refused, but in such a clever way that no one was offended. In a few words of Spanish and a lot of clever pantomime, she explained that if she did, his espousa would slap her face and pull her hair — probably his, too. The men on the bus understood her very well and there was much uproarious laughter. Almost before she finished, the bus arrived at its stop in Acajutla. We disembarked amid loud laughter and many Spanish witticisms that Pattie said she was not going to explain for me.

⚓

We trudged around Acajutla, a hot and dusty town. At the fast-food places we discovered a new kind of lunch made from two tortillas fastened together on the outside and filled with beans, meat, or cheese. Mary bought her girls each an embroidered muslin dress, but when I told Pattie this kind of material was really going to be hard to iron, she decided she didn't want one. We walked home, only a couple of miles plus the long dock.

In our absence, Jim, Rand, and Eldon had made plans for all of us to go to Sonsonate, about twenty miles away, the next day. Eldon was going to get Ray Hill or his son, now seventeen, to stay with the boats, but he soon found that they were all going to Sonsonate, also. Then Eldon determined to stay with the boats. Rand thought the three of them should take turns doing this, and it was his turn, but Eldon wouldn't budge. So there was nothing to do but make another trip the next day. We weren't going to let Eldon miss all the side trips by boat-sitting.

The Hills were gone before Rand, Jim, Pattie, and I got started. For the sake of variety, we thought it would be fun to take the bus into town and the narrow-gauge rail-road on the way back. But before the bus arrived, a shiny red Mustang stopped and the driver asked us if we wanted a ride. He sounded so totally American that he might have been from anyone's hometown USA, but he told us he was born in El Salvador. He'd emigrated to the United States when he was eighteen. Both of his brothers, he said, had done the same thing.

"All the land here is owned by a very few, very wealthy families. Unless you are born into one of these families," he said, "there is no way to get ahead in this country." He had been successful in the land of his adoption, and driving a fancy car down from Los Angeles was one way of demonstrating this.

"It's a terrible drive, but my mother looks at the car and the nice clothes, and she knows I'm doing okay in the States. Every year, if I possibly can, I make this trip" — he grimaced a little — "this very grueling trip to see my mother. It gives her more prestige with her neighbors than if I fly down. They don't even understand airplanes."

"Wouldn't your mother prefer to live where her children are, even if it isn't the land of her birth?" I asked.

"Not really," he said. "She's been up to visit twice, but it's a different world. She doesn't understand the language, and life in the fast lane frightens her." He laughed, "Frightens me sometimes, too. But my wife is a California girl, and my kids have no idea what life is like down here."

"What is life really like down here?" I asked. We were nearing Sonsonate. I knew this conversation would have to end, but there was so much I wanted to know.

For the first time, his face lost its cheerful expression. The one that replaced it was bitter and a little hard. It made him look very different as he answered, "Life is pure hell down here unless you belong to the landed aristocracy. Almost everyone else lives in poverty you can't even imagine. I have a good business in California, and I can do a lot to make things easier for my mom, things I could never have done if I had stayed here. Same with my brothers."

Of one thing I was sure: his mother had a pretty good son.

"One more thing I'd like to ask," I said as the car came to a stop in the middle of town. "How did you learn to speak English without any Spanish accent? Not many people do, you know."

He laughed, pleased at the implied compliment. "It wasn't easy; I worked hard at it. I'm sure you know there are lots of speech tutors around L.A. who will help you drop an accent or develop one." For the first time he sounded just a little self-conscious. "It isn't that I mind letting people know I'm from El Salvador; I just don't want them to know it from the way I talk."

As we left the car, we invited him to come out and visit us on the boat. But he was soon going to start the long drive back to Los Angeles, and most of the remaining time, he told us solemnly, must be spent with his mother. "She doesn't let me out of her sight when I first get here and for the last day or two before I leave. In between, I can visit my old friends, and she can visit hers."

And brag about her successful and dutiful son, I'll bet, I said to myself. Well, who wouldn't?

⚓

Ray and Eric Hill were both very tall, and, being blonde as well, they were not difficult to locate in any crowd. And wherever the blonde ones in our group, Randy and Pattie, went, there always was a crowd. Pattie's hair was long, almost to her waist, putting it within reach for fairly small children, and she frequently felt a sharp little tug on her scalp as another urchin collected a hair or two for a souvenir. They probably didn't think it was real.

The whole town of Sonsonate was a genuine antique,

not too different from some sets for wild west shows. The drugstore was straight out of the 1890s, with apothecary jars and balance scales, old-fashioned, high, glassed-in counters held together with polished wood, even little glass jars full of penny candy.

The railroad, too, was a vision out of the last century. The engine was a smaller replica of the big steam engines that had been replaced eventually by diesel engines. Randy, who had reached his twenty-second birthday before we left Kenmore, was still enough of a kid to want to get in the engineer's cab and fiddle with the controls. I don't know why the yardmaster let him do it.

Children everywhere were carrying brothers and sisters almost as large as themselves. Jim felt sorry for all the little people, hot and tired, carrying such burdens, and treated about fifty of them to a glass of lemonade (about one cent a glass, US funds); he became an instant Pied Piper, followed by hundreds of children hoping to have the treat repeated. He tried it once more with a crowd at least twice as large as the first, but then his following increased even more. He realized it was hopeless.

The lemonade looked as though it had been made with muddy water. Knowing there might be worse germs than those that cause tourista, all of us but Jim drank only soda pop of recognizable brands. He thought that he'd survived enough bouts of tourista to have acquired total immunity. Maybe he had; at least he didn't get sick. In Sonsonate we didn't find any of the tortilla sandwiches we had enjoyed in Acajutla, but we did find some piping hot burritos, spicy enough to bring tears to our eyes.

Too soon, it was late afternoon. We rushed over to the train station, a different place entirely from the roundhouse where Randy had played with that overgrown toy locomotive. It took much longer than it should have to get our tickets, and we hurried onto the train just as it was leaving.

While no train of my acquaintance is quiet, this

Trilogy

Toonerville Trolley was especially noisy. The windows had no glass. The seats were polished wood and just about as adhesive as a gun barrel, so we proceeded to polish them some more as we were flung around on every curve. Where doors should have been, there were only wide open spaces. Having the misfortune to be seated next to the door, I had nothing to grasp for support and expected at any moment to be flung ingloriously across the green Salvadorian farmland.

Next to me were big baskets of laundry, and I decided that if I fell, I'd try to land in one of them. But the little mahogany-faced lady sitting across from me misunderstood my interest in her laundry, and she regarded me with a most malevolent and unblinking stare until she reached her destination. At this point Jim noticed the difficulty I was having on the slick seat and traded places with me.

⚓

Jim and Rand gave Eldon the guided tour of Sonsonate the following day and got back by mid-afternoon. The previous day Eldon had spent getting ready for the next leg of our journey, and that was doubtless the reason we were ready to leave the harbor at four p.m. *Rolling Hills* was next and *Molokai Girl* last.

For a while we had very light winds, but suddenly and very unexpectedly the wind began rising, reaching forty knots in a few minutes. Then came the rain — a downpour like the one we'd witnessed on the way to El Salvador. To refresh our memory, in case we had forgotten anything, lightning began flashing overhead. I was fervently hoping it wasn't going to be a repeat performance of the storm three nights ago.

With the same unnerving abruptness with which it started, the storm ceased. The dark clouds disappeared; the sea changed from murky gray to bright blue again, and all was tranquil once more. Just a trifle too tranquil; we had no wind for sailing. It was as though we were in the hands of some weather god who was trying to carry out our wishes but just didn't know how to make fine distinctions.

Grumbling, Eldon turned on the motor, and we alternately motored and sailed until we had covered about two-thirds of the distance to Costa Rica. Then a strong easterly wind came up, a good sailing breeze — except for the fact that it was right on the nose.

Our course indicated we should go 120 degrees, but we couldn't hold that close into a wind coming at 90 degrees. We could hold it at 125, and knowing that trimarans have the reputation of being unable to sail into the wind, 35 degrees off wasn't too bad. With the working jib and a reef in the main we were making eight knots for several hours. By two in the afternoon Punta Blanco was abeam, and we entered Bahia de Santa Elena heading for Point Parker.

In a way we were sorry to bypass Nicaragua and Honduras, but because of unsettled internal conditions and their reputation for being unfriendly to cruising boats, it seemed best to do so.

We dropped the anchor in the northeast corner of Bahia De Santa Elena, close to Point Parker. Not far away, a large trawler about seventy feet long was beached, applying bottom paint, and suddenly it seemed like a good idea to do that to *Trilogy*. We were in an area of reasonably high tides — quite essential for beaching boats and for getting them off the beach again. Also, the higher the tide, the longer your boat will be dry enough to work on.

Over on the shore frangipani and poinciana or flamboyant trees were blooming riotously, and the fragrance of the frangipani carried out to our boat three blocks away. I cannot remember ever being in a place that smelled so wonderful. Come what may, I was going to have some of those lovely blossoms to carry out to the boat. Jim and Rand had taken the skiff and run ashore as soon as we anchored, but, not to be thwarted, Pattie and I donned our masks and snorkels and swam ashore.

Trilogy

From the boat, the frangipani blossoms looked about two feet above the water. But when we got there, none were within reach. Some of the trees came far out over the water, and I was sure I could reach them from the skiff. The boys obligingly brought it over, but I still couldn't quite reach. I finally climbed out on a limb and picked one big cluster that immediately dripped liquid latex all over my hand and wrist. But never mind; it smelled absolutely heavenly.

Jim, following his usual custom of eating everything that grew wild and looked edible, ate a small, green, apple-like fruit that even the beach scavengers wouldn't touch. The first inkling he had of anything amiss was a strangely paralyzed feeling in his mouth and throat as though it had been swabbed with Novocain. He began feeling slightly unsteady, and he decided he should tell someone in case he collapsed. He found me in the galley (where I spent quite a bit of my time).

"Mom," he began very quietly, "I ate one of these." He held out his hand with one of the green apples on it — only it wasn't really an apple. "I think it's either poison or else it has some weird effect on the nerves."

"What kind of effect?"

I was really alarmed; Jim would never mention it unless he was worried, and he isn't one who is easily worried. For all I knew, it might be fatal.

"Oh, I just have a buzzy feeling in my head, and my mouth and throat feel sort of paralyzed."

That sounded like enough to be going on with, as the British say. Jim was the keeper of the medicine chest, which fortunately we hadn't had much use for so far. "Do we have any ipecac?" I asked.

"Uh... is that the stuff that makes you up-chuck? Yeah, I think we do."

"Well, we don't have a stomach pump; I think that's the next best thing. How long has it been since you ate that thing?"

"Oh, a half hour. Maybe not quite that long, I dunno. Listen, I'm not too fond of the idea of tossing my cookies all night. Let's just wait and see what happens."

It would take a bigger and more determined person than I to give Jim ipecac if he didn't want to take it. We waited. He stayed in the galley for half an hour while I watched him closely. Then he announced he was feeling better; both the dizzy feeling and the paralysis seemed to be wearing off. In good spirits, he went off to bed.

Later, when Jim was telling some of his Costa Rican friends about this experience, Eldon confessed he had eaten the same thing with similar results. Their friends were really surprised they got off so lightly.

"That fruit very bad poison," they said. "No one ever eats it, no animal either. You two ver-rry lucky you not dead! Should ask local people first!"

That was good advice, but it was a lesson they had both already learned.

⚓

After a weekend at Point Parker, we ran over to Playa del Cocos, or Coconut Beach, as we say in English. It isn't a town at all, just a resort community. The closest place where one can actually buy anything except beer, ice cream, and soda pop is twenty-five miles away, a small town called Liberia.

Rand and Jim got quite well acquainted with that place because they did all the grocery shopping while we were in Playa del Cocos and they carried the groceries in backpacks. We always liked to have a good supply of fruit and vegetables. In addition, we got fifty-pound sacks of beans, rice, popcorn, and peanuts. Though they rode the little commuter bus, a truck with benches back of the cab, these shopping trips were still quite a chore. The boys had to walk with their full backpacks at least a quarter of a mile.

Arriving here just at the end of the dry season, we were

able to see the incredible transformation that takes place when the rainy season begins. Overnight practically, the country lost its dry, dusty, twiggy appearance and turned into dozens of shades of living green. Even the fence posts sprouted green leaves. Every day at two o'clock the clouds came rolling in from the sea, followed by a torrential downpour for about two hours. After that, they rolled back again, leaving a dewy, sparkling super-cleanliness everywhere.

After the rains started, we began to hear the monkeys. I always wondered why we hadn't heard them before, but the explanation is probably very simple. During the dry season there might not have been as much for them to eat down by the ocean, and they stayed in the highlands where it is always green.

For a while I thought I was hearing packs of wild dogs out there. But the inhabitants assured me that the deep voices belonged to the local monkeys, who didn't come around human dwellings much and were harmless. I'd always thought of monkey talk as the high-pitched, high-speed chatter I had heard in zoos.

The sunsets in Costa Rica were spectacular. They didn't last long — too close to the equator, just about eight degrees now — but while they did, they out-painted any I'd ever seen. One that I remember particularly was almost lime green close to the horizon, and above that, a riot of vermilion and purple clouds with delicate gold filigree edges. The speed with which darkness followed took some getting used to after living in Alaska most of my adult life, where a good sunset can go on for three or four hours. Here it is gone in ten minutes, and darkness on the equator is really dark.

Some of our cruising friends whom we had last seen in Baja were here in Playa del Cocos: Duncan MacGregor, and Grimjaws and Cement Head — who were neither stern or stupid as their nicknames might suggest, but two wise and wonderful ladies who had decided to spend their retirement years courting adventure. They were not feeble by any means, but they did concede that in stormy weather it sometimes would be handy to have some manly muscles.

Shortly after the rainy season began, we decided to visit San Jose, the capital of Costa Rica. Eldon had grown so accustomed to staying on the boat that he didn't see any good reason for going up to San Jose, even though Phil from *Molokai Girl* had promised to look after *Trilogy*. But we all took turns persuading Eldon until he reluctantly agreed to go with us. After we got under way, I think he enjoyed the trip more than anyone else. This excursion also put a stop to his pattern of being the ship's guardian so that the rest of us could travel; after that, we took for granted that he would go along to whatever interesting places we visited ashore.

We wanted to ride the little railroad but had to go by bus to Puntarenas in order to make connections. And the connection wasn't the best — it was siesta time, so we had a three-hour wait without much to do. In fact, it was almost time for the afternoon shower when the narrow-gauge train finally showed up. Already a few drops of rain were falling, but not the intense deluge to be expected in a few minutes. The boarding platform was just that — a platform, no roof. Five seconds in the kind of rain that the rainy season brings would have soaked us completely. We sank gratefully into our seats, happy to have missed the really heavy rainfall that started as soon as we were aboard.

The little-engine-that-could pulled us into the mountains where the scenery was very beautiful. At first we could see the ocean; then the mountains surrounded us and we could see little homesteads, open meadows, and many, many cattle. These weren't Texas longhorns or Holsteins but the scrawny, humpbacked Brahman cattle that looked as though they had never been properly fed. In fact, that's the main advantage of this breed — they don't develop any fat. Much of this super-lean meat is sold to the United States, and the scuttlebutt around here is that the biggest buyer is McDonald's.

The large, open savannas and flat-topped trees reminded me of pictures I have seen taken in Africa. I almost expected to see a giraffe chewing on the leaves. As we chugged along to ever higher altitudes, we saw a patch-work of farmlands reaching almost to the mountaintops. Many of the things growing here would not have survived six months of drought; the dry season must be more or less limited to the coastal plains.

⚓

Acting on advice from our boating friends, we sought out the Canada Hotel, where the rooms were tiny, clean, and moderately priced.

San Jose, according to their Chamber of Commerce tourist literature, is a very conservative town. Ladies were warned that it is not considered good taste to wear shorts on the street. That was okay, Pattie and I didn't bring any, but we were not prepared for the sensation Rand and Jim created in their Levi cut-offs. Randy promptly went back to the hotel and changed into long pants, but Jim refused to do so.

He would have been wise to follow Randy's example. Wherever we went, men would stop what they were doing and watch him, talking with great animation; often they left their work and followed him down the sidewalk. Even though I couldn't understand what they were saying, I knew it wasn't flattering. Jim, who did understand the words, completely ignored all this attention, but his father and I were gravely concerned. He was attracting a large crowd of fairly rough characters, so we didn't let him out of our sight. We thought parents might be some protection to him.

Evenings were cool, and however stubborn Jim might be about his attire, he wasn't going to go around with his teeth chattering just to prove he was a free spirit. He changed into long pants, and the rest of us breathed a sigh of relief.

The following day Pattie and her two brothers went sightseeing by themselves. Neither Eldon nor I realized at the moment that thereby we lost all our Spanish-speaking helpers. We rode a city bus, thinking it might take us on a city tour as the one had in Acapulco, but it doubled right back to our starting point after about ten blocks. Well, maybe walking wouldn't be too bad after all; we did have a street map of the city.

As we paused before one of the government buildings, undecided, street map in our hands, one of the ministers from the Department of Justice, seeing our helplessness, elected himself to be our guide. Introducing himself as Martin Renaldo Haiienda, he asked if he could help us — and he most certainly could, especially because he spoke fluent English.

Eldon was overjoyed with this stroke of good fortune. He hadn't had an English-speaking Spaniard full of local knowledge since he'd left Juan Garcia behind. Mr. Haiienda took us through several government buildings, all the while giving us a lecture on Costa Rican law and government. He acknowledged that they had borrowed greatly from the United States, for whom he had great admiration.

Before leaving us, he marked on our map several more things we might like to see and suggested that we might enjoy going to the English cinema, not far from our hotel and much frequented by college students and the large colony of Americans who lived there.

When he mentioned that *Nicholas and Alexandra* was currently showing and that he considered it an excellent motion picture, we were hooked. We decided to go that night. But it was a very sad movie, and we almost wished we hadn't.

Every morning, Eldon went over to the big produce market close to our hotel. He enjoyed going through all the produce markets with their beautiful fresh vegetables; he never has done any farming, but it does fascinate him, and he thinks he would be a great farmer, given the opportunity. I think he's too occupied with boats, though, ever to find out if he has this aptitude.

Most of the time the whole family ate together in one of the little restaurants, but on our last day the boys and Pattie went their own way as they had on the first. Before, we had eaten burritos from an open stand and some fresh fruit from one of the produce markets. This time, though, Eldon wanted a genuine hot lunch, which required going to a restaurant and trying to read the menu.

There is something to be said for picking up your food from the market; at least you know what you're getting. Here most of the menu was completely unintelligible to me. One thing I understood: sopa con pollo. Soup with chicken. I thought it would be a soup with a little chicken chopped up in it. What we got was far better — a cream soup with chicken and vegetables served separately. We lucked out, and wouldn't have done any better if we had known a lot more Spanish.

⚓

Because the bus trip would not have any large chunks of time wasted in making connections, we decided to go that way back to the Coconut Beach, and it was a better choice than we knew. We saw far more little villages and small farms than we had on the train ride, and the bus went right by several large coffee plantations. With their dark, shiny leaves and red berries, the bushes reminded us of holly. We did see more actual jungle on the train, but evidences of human habitation are interesting, too. After we crossed the divide, we had a breathtaking view of many miles of the sea coast.

The truck that serves as a bus from Liberia to Playa del Cocos is totally open-air — no protection from the wind except a windshield, and I assume that was mainly for the driver's sake. We had just gotten started back to the beach and *Trilogy* when I felt a tickling between my shoulders.

I nudged Eldon. "Hey, I think there's a fly down my back. Try to get it out, will you? It's bugging me."

We were so crowded on this truck/bus that it was hard for Eldon to turn far enough to do what I asked, but he turned as far as possible, pulled my collar back about an inch and looked down.

"I can't see anything," he reported.

Just at that moment the fly, as I thought it was, came crawling out the arm-hole of my sleeveless blouse. It was about an inch and a half long, shiny black, and as evil-looking a specimen as I ever encountered at close range. It was all I could do to keep from screaming. Eldon brushed it off, and it scuttled away unharmed.

As for me, I don't think I ever quite recovered.

⚓

When we landed in Cocos, James Lahane, a young cattle rancher, invited Eldon and me to come out in the country and see his ranch. I had had enough riding for one day. But to my surprise Eldon accepted, and they both took off in Mr. Lahane's Land Rover.

The ranch is thirty miles long and from five to ten miles wide, populated with the skinny Brahman cattle and sixty employees who care for them. Eldon and his host covered most of the ranch by evening and started back to Playa del Cocos, but young Lahane got a bit impetuous on the mountain road and stripped the gears of his Land Rover. He wasn't stranded, however; he took Eldon on his motorcycle over to an adjacent ranch and got him a lift home. Otherwise, it would have been a long ride for two on a motorcycle.

Good thing I wasn't along.

Trilogy

⚓

When I picked up our mail, there was a wire from Carole accepting our invitation. It shouldn't have come as a surprise, but it did because so much time had elapsed since we wrote to her. We thought if she'd been interested she would have replied immediately. Since she didn't, we had more or less assumed she wasn't coming.

Pattie was delighted. She and Carole could share a watch, go places together, and make it easier for everyone. Eldon was dismayed that she wasn't coming until the first of June. We had planned to move on to South America the middle of May, and he was really upset by the delay.

Randy was totally occupied making a wind vane steering mechanism. As far as he was concerned, the delay was all to the good. He didn't want to make the five-hundred-mile crossing of the Gulf of Panama until this device was finished.

His plans, first drawn in San Diego, underwent some revision after he met three young men who had sailed their trimaran, *Triton*, from their home in Australia. These men had some good ideas to offer about steering vanes, based on valuable experience. They let Rand use their power tools and work tables on the beach at Playa del Cocos, and he was sure we would bless his foresight when we started to make large ocean crossings. Ian, Don, and Tony, the Australians, were also very sure we would need the automatic steering device, and they gave Rand all the help they could. The cruising community is a sort of brotherhood the world over, always more than willing to help one another.

Rand did have to interrupt his work about twice a week to go to Liberia with Jim. On one of these trips, Rand felt that he was getting to be fluent enough in Spanish to do some of the bargaining, which had been Jim's sole province up until now. Previously, haggling over every purchase had seemed demeaning to Rand, but he was beginning to realize that people expected it, enjoyed it, and respected Jim for being good at it. So he approached a vendor's stand where there were four or five dozen limes in a pyramid on the table.

"How much for the whole pile?" Randy asked.

"Ten colones."

"Too much, too much," Rand began his bargaining. "I will give you only six." (A Costa Rican colone was worth about twelve cents.)

Without further comment, the vendor put the limes in a sack, and Rand handed him a ten colone note. The man returned six colones to him. Rand started to point out his error, but the vendor waved his protests away with, "No, señor, it is correct; only worth four."

So ended Rand's bargaining career. He didn't think he would ever get the hang of it.

In the middle of the next week Eldon went back to San Jose to wire our bank in Washington for another thousand dollars, not knowing what difficulties might await us with bank transfers to the Galapagos or the Marquesas Islands. While in San Jose, with Jim as his interpreter, he visited the Ecuadorian and French consulates to make arrangements for visas. The Ecuadorian consul told him to wait at least until we reached Colombia for visas to the Galapagos. The French consul said no visa was necessary for the first thirty days in the Marquesas Islands; after that, the local authorities could allow you to extend your visit, or they could tell you to move on.

I was still an avid shell collector and spent as much time as I could in that pursuit. I had a large number of shells that needed a good washing. To avoid having a big mess on the boat, I took them all ashore and started scrubbing them. Any good sailor would have consulted the tide tables and known what time the tide would be high, but I didn't. Suddenly the tide was moving in, and my shells were all in danger of going out to sea. As I was frantically moving shells farther up the beach, Duncan MacGregor came along.

"Well, y' just flunked the sandbox test," he said as he helped me get my shells out of danger.

We knew Mother's Day was sometime in May. When it got to be the twentieth, my kids planned a little dinner for me and asked one of the local ladies to prepare it. Jim was hoping it would be "very ethnic," and I suppose in a way it was — but not as he expected. Costa Rica is as much of a melting pot as the USA ever was, and most of the settlers are not too far removed from European ancestry. The dinner consisted of beef Stroganoff, creamed potatoes, Caesar salad, and (of course) rice and beans. It wasn't perhaps as exotic as Jim had hoped, but it was delicious, which was more important.

After the dinner, we moved over to the little restaurant in the same building. Jim and Rand had been asked to play and sing for a party given there by some international importers from San Jose. Dessert was to be served, so we hadn't had any with our dinner.

The music was a great success. The applause was loud and long, and when our host discovered that my champagne glass was upside down, he shouted across the table: "You don't like champagne? Coffee is better, huh?"

Knowing he was a coffee exporter, I thought it wise to agree.

"Great!' he boomed. "I gif you coffee! The best coffee in the world, I gif to you! For Mother's Day, I gif it."

I wasn't just sure what he had in mind, but I thanked him as though I did.

The next day a hundred-pound bag of coffee beans arrived at the boat, and Jim was told that it truly was the world's best coffee. Most of it was shipped to Europe. Because it was very expensive, it was used to blend with other kinds of coffee beans.

After finishing the steering vane, Rand started working on some whisker poles so we could do wing-and-wing sailing on our next long trip. Carole wasn't expected until the first of June, and we planned to go out to Culebra and get the boat hull cleaned and copper-painted over the weekend. However, on Friday, May twenty-sixth, we got a telegram from Carole telling us she would be arriving in San Jose on Sunday afternoon. We had to rearrange our plans; we could do the copper painting after she arrived.

Jim didn't like the idea of running around San Jose most of the weekend carrying the money Eldon had ordered. He asked if I could put together some kind of money-belt for him. I added a zipper compartment to a tee-shirt that he could wear under another shirt. Pattie thought it was important for her to meet Carole, also, because they would be roommates for some time. The two of them had to leave early in the morning Saturday and wouldn't be back until Monday afternoon.

⚓

The Carole who came aboard the boat Monday was so different from my memory of her that I was nonplused. She was wearing knee-high boots with four-inch heels, a mini skirt, heavy eyeliner, and an expression of acute boredom that seemed to extend to all the people and things in her immediate environment.

My first reaction was to think, *why did she come? If she has no interest in us or the trip we're making, why is she here at all? No one has coerced her.* I tried not to show how appalled I felt, but I couldn't help thinking about other teenagers of our acquaintance who would have been delighted to make this trip.

Carole is the middle child in a family of five girls that ranged in age from twelve to nineteen. Things had been going badly in her world. Under the best of conditions, it is no easy task to raise a family through the teen years. But to make matters infinitely worse, her parents were on the brink of divorce, and her father was having business problems of no small magnitude. Carole's defense against this toppling world was to be defiant, cynical, and bored, trying to convince herself and others that she was a cool kid who couldn't be hurt because nothing mattered anyway.

At first, nothing pleased her. She had had so many disillusioning experiences in her short life that she wanted to remain aloof from everyone and everything. She wasn't too sure of acceptance in our family, and she was determined not to care. Underneath it all, she hadn't really changed — but it took a while before we could get through the "nothing matters" facade she had made for herself.

Much to her credit, in a relatively short time she began trusting people once more. Bit by bit her defenses, built in another time and place, began to come down. Basically, she was the same bright, talkative, affectionate person she had always been, and we learned to love her, not as a relative entitled to some claim on us but as a unique, talented family member — daughter to Eldon and me, sister to Pattie, Rand, and Jim.

⚓

Now, Pattie had more freedom than before; she and Carole could go ashore almost at will. Before long, the two girls were spending most of their time on the beach, mostly at the little restaurant where we had been guests of the German coffee importers.

The little beachfront restaurant with its wide verandah was always at least half-filled with people from the cruising boats and local residents. The teenagers sat around sipping soda pop while their elders nursed tall drinks of other varieties and spent long hours exchanging reminiscences and confidences. During the afternoons' fierce rainstorms, this little social hub was filled to capacity because it was not as stifling as the inside of a boat, all closed up to keep the rain out.

Almost as soon as Carole was aboard, we headed *Trilogy* out to Culebra and beached her at high tide. Randy's new whisker poles were pressed into service to keep the side hulls from tipping as *Trilogy* rested solidly on her keel. Rand, Jim, and Eldon worked fast and efficiently, first scrubbing the hulls as the tide ebbed, and then applying new copper paint. Even the boot top got a new coat of paint.

Amazingly, for the two days the boat was beached, there was no rain. As soon as we got back to Playa del Cocos, though, the rain resumed its regular schedule. Sometimes it lasted longer than two hours, and then we felt really put upon as though it had betrayed some gentlemen's agreement.

One day I saw the black clouds approaching and made a quick decision to spend the next two hours ashore. I could have run the skiff in myself, but I hardly ever did because that would have left Eldon with no way to get ashore. So I had Eldon drop me off.

We always had to get out of the skiff fifty or sixty feet from the shore and wade in; I was used to that, but it seemed to me on this occasion that Eldon stopped farther out than necessary. Usually it was about knee-deep; here it was much deeper. I thought we should get into shallow water so I wouldn't have to get my shorts wet. We spent a few valuable seconds arguing about this, and when I gave up and started to get out of the skiff, a wave caught the dinghy, spun us around, and landed me neatly on my back in water at least waist deep. So I arrived on shore dripping wet with my handbag full of salt water.

Pattie and Carole were on the restaurant verandah — surrounded by boys, of course. They were quite astonished at my soggy appearance.

"Hi, Mom," Pattie called while I was still some distance away. "What did you do, swim over?"

"Well, no, I didn't really do any swimming, just got dunked in the surf."

This little mishap hadn't seemed to me highly amusing, but as I started to tell about it, the girls found it more and more hilarious. Amid much laughter, I started to sort out all the wet stuff from my purse and spread it out on a table to dry.

"Didn't you look to see when the next wave was coming?" Pattie asked.

"I thought I was keeping track of it; obviously I didn't do a very good job," I said. Then another thought occurred to me. "And if your father saw it coming and didn't warn me, I'll kill him!"

When he came over through the rain, tired of being bottled up on *Trilogy*, he apologized so sincerely that I'm sure it wasn't intentional on his part. It wasn't his fault any more than mine, but I accepted his apologies.

⚓

Raphael Hertados, called Roffa, was the one who had brought Eldon back from Jim Lahane's ranch. After he met Pattie and Carole, he spent most of his time at the Hertados' beach house or at the little restaurant. He was there with his brother Frederick on this day, which was supposed to be our last in Playa del Cocos. Both of the Hertados boys (young men, really — Roffa twenty-four and Frederick twenty-two) had gone to college in the US and spoke English very well. He wanted to talk to Eldon, but it took him a long time to make his request known.

After much hemming and hawing, he finally got to the point. "Mr. Coon, I understand you are planning on leaving tonight?"

"Yes," Eldon agreed. "We're trying to get to the Galapagos Islands sometime this month."

"Could you possibly postpone it until tomorrow? Frederick and I were hoping your whole family could come over to the beach house tonight for dinner. We made our plans before we knew you were leaving so soon."

Pattie added, "Surely we can wait one more day, can't we? Carole and I have been helping to get the dinner ready, and it's going to be extra special!"

Somehow, the message of our imminent departure hadn't gotten through to the girls — which wasn't altogether surprising, considering that they were hardly ever on the boat anymore except late at night. Eldon agreed with good grace. What's one more day compared to disappointing so many people?

Our dinner included filet mignon, hearts of palm salad, and a pastry dessert that Pattie and Carole dreamed up. Charlie, another boy of twenty-two from Canada who seemed to be a friend of the whole Hertados family, was definitely devoting his entire attention to Pattie this evening. I had met him at the restaurant several times and thought him extremely good-looking, but no serious threat to Pattie's future. Tonight, though, I wasn't so sure.

Anyway, tomorrow we would be on our way again.

⚓

All the way to Golfito, our last stop in Central America, we had light winds. We took forty-five hours to cover two hundred fifty-six nautical miles.

At last Golfito, one of the wettest places on earth but beautiful when it isn't raining, rose dripping and sun-sprinkled out of a cobalt sea. The beach was feather-edged with palms of purest emerald and backed by row on ascending row of iridescent tropical trees, receding into deep shades of blue and purple. I had never seen forests of mango trees before, and I marveled at their magnificent height and rounded symmetry as they merged into the blue-purple jungle.

The rainfall here is reported to be anywhere between four hundred and six hundred inches annually. One result of this excessive rainfall is a profusion of vines that seem to grow everywhere and cover everything. Just keeping the jungle at bay requires constant, valiant effort from those who are trying to grow something else on this land.

Trilogy

We anchored out in the harbor. On the shore possibly
two blocks away, a decaying ship was beached half in, half
out of the water, upright, starkly silhouetted against the
evening sky. In this war-surplus ship, Captain Tom, an
infamous figure in these parts, had sailed down the coast as
far as his money and fuel would carry him, then run
aground here and continued to live on his boat. He had
built a house nearby, hardly more than a shelter from the
rain, and turned it into a shelter for runaway children,
mostly from the United States. I don't see how he squares
it with his conscience, knowing their parents are probably
frantically looking for them, but Jim says if he contacted
even one set of parents he would no longer be considered
trustworthy.

As soon as the tropical darkness settled down, suddenly,
the way it does, the music started up from Captain Tom's
headquarters, and for sheer volume it exceeded anything I
had heard up to this time. The little bay really rocked and
rolled. Jim, Rand, Carole, and Pattie went over to visit with
Captain Tom, but Eldon and I had had a long day. We
agreed that we could wait until daylight. I thought they kept
up this aggressively loud music all night, but Jim told me
that they quit around three o'clock in the morning. Long
before that, my kids were back in their bunks on *Trilogy*.

Jim and I went over to visit Captain Tom the following
afternoon. Carole, Pattie, and Rand elected to stay on the
boat for reasons unspecified. Eldon had no hesitancy about
specifying his reason: he had heard all the noise the night
before, and he wasn't going to get into it at closer range.

I soon learned that any questions or comments about
the captain's runaways were off-limits, although he talked
freely enough about himself and his experiences. The
music we had heard the night before had a P.A. system
that must have required electricity, but the house was only
lighted by candles and very dimly. Captain Tom remains
an enigma to me; the work he did, giving shelter and some

kind of employment to these runaway children, is surely exemplary, but there was still something furtive and sinister about the whole set-up. And those kids so far from home still haunt me.

⚓

We had an early-morning visitor the next day who was introduced to me simply as Bernardo. He was a large man, tall and broad; part of one foot was missing, which didn't seem to slow him down much although it gave him a rolling, side-to-side motion when he walked. His English vocabulary wasn't large, but the words he knew he spoke plainly, with little Spanish accent.

"I am for you guide," he announced. "I show you where is supermercado, fruits, rice, whatever."

My first reaction was to wonder who elected him to this office and what, exactly, I was supposed to do with him, but Jim and Rand came to my rescue. A rapid exchange of Spanish followed.

"It's okay, Mom," Rand reassured me. "Just like he said, he'll show you the best markets and get good prices for you. Jim and I have a lot of other stuff to do; so does Dad. It'll help if you do the grocery shopping."

Carole, Pattie, and I trudged along in Bernardo's wake; he seldom looked around to see if we were following as he rolled along, very macho, very self-important — and, as it turned out, very competent. He took us to the different markets, and we picked out the produce we wanted; then he did the bargaining. (I'm even worse at that than Randy.) We would never have been able to carry all the things we bought without Bernardo's help.

Before he left us, after delivering all our packages to the boat, he mentioned that his daughter did laundry if we wished to have some done. I wished, whether anyone else did or not. *The Seven Seas Bulletins* had mentioned that laundry facilities were available in most of these towns, from which I

assumed that I would find bright, shining laundromats. I
didn't ever see a laundromat after we left La Paz. Sometimes
the "laundry facility" was a communal concrete tub, divided
into compartments, each with a built-in concrete washboard.
More often it was a flat rock in a stream.

I quickly went through all the places I could think of
where dirty laundry could be hidden. I may not have gotten
it all, but I came up with an enormous amount, including
twelve sheets, and Bernardo staggered away with it all.
Later in the afternoon, to our astonishment, we saw a vast
and colorful expanse of sheets spread out over the white
beach on the other side of the harbor, and all the nearby
bushes supported towels and colorful garments that I
couldn't help recognizing.

I cursed my stupidity for not checking around with the
local people before I turned the laundry over to someone. I
was sure the sheets would come back full of sand, and all
the other things full of bugs and leaves.

I was wrong.

When Bernardo returned them two days later, neatly
folded, they were immaculate. I checked them over carefully, and I still don't know how his daughter, Isobel, got all
the fine beach sand off the sheets. The final result was
beyond criticism. No laundry could have done better.

⚓

While I was grocery-shopping, Jim and Rand were planning to get diesel oil, gas for the propane tank, and several
other heavy things. It seemed like a good idea to run over
to the town's main dock for this purpose, and I had been
told that *Trilogy* would be tied there when I came back from
the shopping expedition. Pattie and Carole said they were
going to look around town for a while, which left Eldon
and me alone on the boat at a time when we were going to
need a Spanish-speaking assistant very badly.

There were no signs saying KEEP OFF THE DOCK,

nothing to indicate that the only usable dock in town was privately owned by United Fruit Company. We found it out before long, though. Our first inkling that our presence here was unwelcome came when a man — how were we to know he was the superintendent of Chiquita Banana, a subsidiary of United Fruit? — started yelling at us in Spanish. Along with the tirade, of which we understood not a word, came a demonstration of jumping up and down and waving the arms so energetically that I thought perhaps he was trying to fly. When he gestured to our tie-up lines, we began to suspect that *Trilogy*, tied to this dock, was the culprit.

Without Jim or Rand aboard, Eldon was not going to try moving *Trilogy*. A strong current was holding us against the dock, and *Trilogy*'s bow was directly under the bow of a three-hundred-fifty-foot banana boat. Eldon tried to explain that he needed some of his crew before we could leave. Even if Eldon could have spoken in Spanish, this man wouldn't have heard or understood because his own torrent of Spanish never ceased. Somehow, he didn't even have to stop now and then to breathe.

Jim arrived after a few minutes of this and tried to talk both sense and Spanish to this purple-faced, excitable man, but it was futile. Jim climbed down the ladder from the dock and said, "It's no use, Dad. He passed the point where anyone could reason with him long ago." Then with an impish grin he added, "I think he passed it at the age of two."

"I really don't know what ails him," Eldon replied cheerfully, "but I'm sure it will get better if we just get out of here."

"We're not leaving until we get our oil drum aboard, and some of the other heavy stuff," Jim said. "There's no other place to do it. By the way, the guy up there who's calling curses down on us says he's going to fine us for tying up here without permission."

"Great," Eldon said with resignation. "In that case, we'll be paying for our use of the dock. We might as well use it till we get all our heavy stuff aboard. We'll never get another chance."

"Right on," Jim agreed. "He's already cursed us, our ancestors, and all our descendants. Unless he pulls a gun on us, we're staying."

"Where's Rand?" Eldon asked. "We're going to need him 'cause I think our oil drum just arrived."

As soon as he said it, he realized that Rand was helping to wrestle the oil drum to the edge of the dock. The four-hundred-pound oil drum was first secured by ropes, then passed down to *Trilogy's* deck. The dock was high, built to accommodate oceangoing cargo boats; if they'd dropped this heavy drum, it would probably have gone right through deck and hull to the bottom.

After everything was loaded, we backed *Trilogy* off, with some difficulty, and anchored out in the bay. "When you mentioned the possibility of a gun," Eldon told Jim, "I felt a much bigger urge to get out of there in a hurry. I don't trust a madman with a gun."

"He was mad in the sense of being angry, but I don't think he was insane," Jim replied. "It's partly the culture; they're not used to suppressing their emotions. They just let it all out."

⚓

Later in the afternoon, Eldon and I returned by way of the shore and watched the endless belt that has been loading cases of bananas for shipping since 1934. The supervisor of the loading operation came over and gave us a tour of the boat, explaining that this belt loads 150,000 forty-pound cases of bananas every eight-hour shift. Bananas are very fussy. If they get too cold, their sugar changes into starch, and no one is going to like them. If they get too warm, they ripen while still at sea, and the boat crew may have several million bananas to dispose of.

Eldon really wanted to see a banana plantation. It could be arranged, we were told, by seeing none other than the superintendent who had cursed us with purple prose and visage.

"Forget it," was my response to this information. "I wouldn't ask that character for any favors if I had to walk back to where we started this trip!"

"Okay," Eldon replied, "maybe we can work it out with someone else. We can try. I'm not jazzed about seeing that fellow, either."

Eldon wouldn't tell me how he arranged it without having to see the superintendent himself, but at seven o'clock the next morning he and I were on our way to visit a banana plantation — in an air-conditioned cab, no less. First, we went several miles up the river where the bananas were growing in countless rows with plastic bags over the stalks of bananas, one huge bunch of bananas per banana plant. The plant dies after producing its stalk of fruit, but another banana plant is already springing up from the roots.

"Are they all green like this?" I asked our driver, who was also our guide.

"They'd better be," he responded. "If we miss any of them until they turn yellow, they're totally wasted."

There isn't much about the care and preparation of bananas that I haven't seen. I progressed from total ignorance to this pinnacle of erudition during a period of seven and a half hours. After the first two hours, I noticed in myself a detectable loss of enthusiasm as information piled up that I hadn't been desperately wishing to acquire. After we saw how they were grown, cut, disinfected, and packed into boxes, we were taken to the factory where huge rolls of brown paper were made into boxes.

We ate lunch with all the workers, at least in the same building, but we were given a separate table. Eldon was having a wonderful time — no dwindling of enthusiasm for him. It was as though he had always wanted to learn all about how bananas are grown and shipped. If they had offered him a two-hour tour of the bookkeeping department, I'm convinced that he wouldn't have refused.

After lunch, our guide took us out to a palm oil plantation. Growing and processing palm oil is a relatively new industry here and promises to be very profitable. The plant manager, a tall, good-looking black man recently imported from the US, gave us the guided tour. First he handed us ear muffs. The noise inside the plant was unendurable for human ears. As he adjusted his ear pieces, he said, "The noise level is somewhere between a boiler factory and all-out war. I'm really excited about this business; it's going to have a great future. But I don't want to be deaf ten years from now."

I had a strong hunch that it wouldn't take ten years. Even with the ear muffs clamped on tight, it sounded as though all the kids in the world were banging on enormous, resonant kettles.

The palms, imported from Africa, are doing well in Costa Rica. They have a life expectancy of something like fifty years, and they produce a reddish-yellow cluster of fruits that look like dates and contain a lot of oil. So far soap, margarine, cosmetics, and shortening are being made from this oil, but the possibilities are almost endless.

After visiting the palm oil plantation, we were escorted back to the main office in Golfito where, as a parting gift, we were offered two forty-pound boxes of green bananas to take with us on the next leg of our journey. "On your boat," the young man who was helping us load them on *Trilogy* said, "they'll probably start ripening in four days. At the proper temperature on a banana boat, they would keep for two weeks before they start to ripen." Four days sounded fine; by that time we expected to be nearly across the Gulf of Panama.

Eldon had bought some ice cream in honor of my birthday. By the time we got out to the boat and got the bananas loaded, it was three o'clock, and the ice cream was melting. Our freezer compartment hadn't been able to keep anything frozen since the beginning of the trip.

The In-Between Countries

Carole and Pattie had last been seen in the company of three caballeros who had acquired their English in Alabama. The southern drawl superimposed on the Spanish accent was certainly different. The girls thought it was hilarious, and the boys didn't mind their laughing as long as they seemed to be having a good time. But it was time for the girls to be back at the boat. They had been told to be back at three for a five o'clock departure.

Jim and Rand finished up the ice cream that was rapidly turning into milkshakes. It wasn't any chore, but ice cream was seldom available on our journey. We knew the girls would be disappointed.

"Sorry, girls," Rand said as he scooped up the last of it. "Next time, get back on time."

I wasn't worried about the girls, being perfectly sure they were eating indigestible things and being entertained by Dixie Spanglish. But there were lots of chores they could have helped with, and I was going into a slow burn.

⚓

Bernardo brought back our laundry and also brought his daughter Isobel, a stunningly beautiful girl. He said she was twenty-eight years old, though she looked ten years younger.

I noticed she was wearing a wedding ring and asked about her husband.

"He is away," she said with a shy smile, "working."

Bernardo snorted, "Working! How you know he is working? He is gone now two years — no letters, no money!"

I felt very sorry for Isobel. She didn't act as though she was accustomed to arguing with her father, but she stood her ground. "He will come back," she said, softly.

"Huh!" Bernardo scoffed. "He never come back. You wait for him till you old lady, he never come back!"

A glint of tears shone in Isobel's eyes, but she still spoke very quietly. "No. He come when he get some money. He come and take me away." There was a note of defiance in those last words and in her brilliant, dark eyes.

Abruptly, Bernardo turned his attention to other things: the laundry, of course, but he had also made a little dish garden for me. Much care and artistry had made the miniature landscape. I was touched, even though I was angry with him for the way he treated Isobel. Her situation seemed tragic enough without him publicly humiliating her. I thought to myself, if that fellow doesn't come back for Isobel, he's crazy.

I thanked him and said, "That is a very lovely gift, and it happens to be my birthday, so it's a birthday gift as well. I really appreciate it."

In the middle of the garden, Bernardo had placed a small lizard that was as green as the foliage. "Good thing to have on a boat," Bernardo said. "He eat flies, bug, mosquito, all bad pest. You like him, I think."

That was optimistic, considering that I have never had much rapport with any kind of reptile. But he was a cute little dragon. We called him Puff.

⚓

By this time we were all getting worried about Pattie and Carole. We had passed our deadline for departure over an hour ago, and still no sign of them. In a strange place, getting dark, it gave us all a feeling of helplessness.

"I saw them over on the beach about one o'clock," Jim volunteered. "I told them not to forget we were leaving at five."

He went out on deck and took another look toward the shore, where nothing much was visible. Coming back inside, he said, "If they don't get here pretty soon, I'll go ashore and find them. Don't look so worried, Mom. They probably forgot all about the time."

At 6:45, just as Bernardo and Isobel were getting into their skiff on one side of the boat, a smart little power launch from one of the banana boats drew up on the other side of *Trilogy*. Pattie and Carole quickly alighted. The farewells were brief and, it seemed to me, rather cool. In my relief I paid little attention. In fifteen minutes we were on our way to South America, and as we traveled, the girls' story emerged.

For a couple of hours after Jim saw them, they walked around buying snack food and drinking soda pop. By three o'clock they were getting bored with that, and one of the boys suggested that they visit a beautiful Swedish banana boat that was anchored in the harbor. There was only a skeleton crew aboard, but two officers on deck welcomed them aboard and began a tour of the ship. Through some kind of hocus-pocus — and perhaps they were adept at this — they separated the girls from their escorts and began a poorly disguised campaign to get them into a convenient stateroom.

Pattie was frightened; these were not teenage boys. They were men in their late twenties or early thirties. Carole, the more worldly-wise of the two, was thoroughly angry.

Five o'clock came and went. Pattie told the officers that they were scheduled to leave at five, and they had to get back to their boat.

The most handsome and overbearing officer just laughed.

"You can't keep us here against our will!" Pattie told him as forcefully as she could, even though she was quaking in her sandals.

"Can't we now?" the big officer teased, but there was something not really good-natured about the teasing. "Your friends are going ashore," he said. "Now what are you going to do?"

The girls rushed over to the ship's rail. Sure enough, Jose, Michael, and Carlos were pulling away in their skiff.

"Hey! Don't leave us here!" Carole shouted at them. "These fellows are crazy!"

"I know," Carlos shouted back. "We're going to get the police. Don't worry; we'll get you off that boat!"

Even with the threat of police intervention, no effort was made to get the girls over to *Trilogy*. Time dragged on; the girls refused to leave the top deck where they could be plainly seen from the shore. At least there was no violence, although big-blonde-and-husky was plainly angry. His attempts at subtlety had been ignored, and his more obvious advances had been repulsed. His fellow officer had given up and left some time before.

"I can get plenty of girl friends," he finally sputtered. "I don't have to ask kids like you for favors!"

This the girls ignored. In the dusk, over on the shore, they could see that Carlos and his friends had rounded up some policemen. The rescuers hadn't launched a boat yet, but they were watching the group on deck with binoculars. Even to someone as boorish and persistent as this officer, it must have been obvious that the game was up. With poor grace, he ordered a shore boat and brought the girls over to *Trilogy*, trying to show his displeasure by a frosty silence. They couldn't have cared less about his displeasure.

So my impression that their farewells were none too cordial was well-founded.

"Oh, Mom!" Pattie exclaimed a half dozen times during their disjointed recital of the day's happenings, "he was a terrible man! I never want to see one like that again!" Carole was quieter, scornful, and just as decisive. "I've seen people like him before; I try to stay away from them."

Eldon and I, Jim and Rand all hoped that this experience might have taught the girls some of the hazards of going ashore by themselves in all these strange places. But in less than a month we were again not only having to caution them about similar dangers, but even having to restrain them physically in towns where rape and murder were common.

The In-Between Countries

CAROLE'S COMMENT:
A REBEL'S REWARD

It wasn't just the countries that were "in-between"; surely my life had arrived at some crossroads as well. Many people's early teen years are shaky, but mine had been particularly so. I'd run away from home several times, and there was less and less to return to each time. So, when I was offered the chance to participate in a grand adventure, I was ready! Yes, I could finish high school on time if I took a full course-load my senior year. No, life in Spokane would not grind to a halt if I left. I thought that I must have been a truly special person for something so extraordinary to happen to me, but (as I've since learned) I was, rather, the most troublesome of the five Saxton daughters. I was the most natural choice to send away; however, I can vouch for the fact that being a rebel paid off in spades!

Once I boarded the plane, the ride south became an experience of a very different order. The first leg to Los Angeles was not particularly remarkable, but it became more so on the long journey to Costa Rica. As the mileage mounted, the clamoring in my mind subsided, and at some point I quit thinking. There was no model upon which to build speculation about what I was racing toward. I didn't plan, I didn't conjecture, and I didn't worry. It was purely experiential — as if at any second I would fall off a cliff, or open a door and confront some mystery, perhaps meet someone I had always known but had never seen before. My psyche was supercharged with portent. I believe that was an ecstatic experience — an extended "moment" of exquisite anticipation that lasted about sixteen hours. Adventurers the world over know that feeling: it's the primer for the joy of discovery.

After the plane landed and I'd disembarked, even in the hustle and excitement of new sights, smells, and greetings by cousins Jim and Pattie, something remained suspended. Even though the adventure had begun, I didn't mentally exhale for a long time.

Maybe I never did.

CHAPTER TEN:

VILLAINS AND HEROES

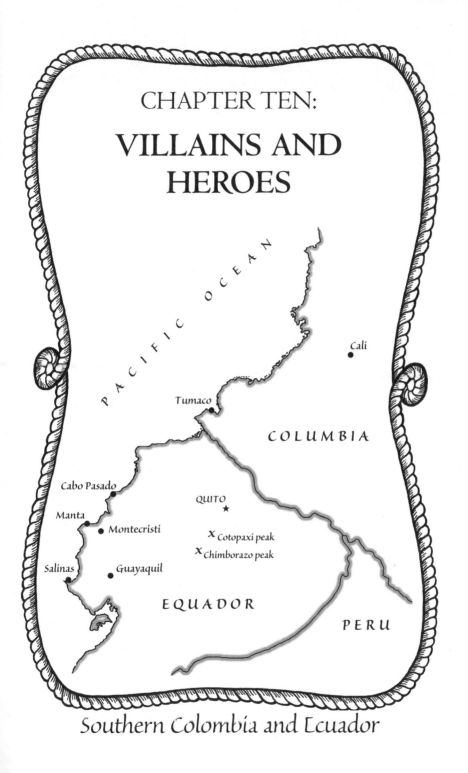

Southern Colombia and Ecuador

fter the intense demands of boat building —
those long days that extended far into the night — we were
only now beginning to realize that the pressure was off.

All of us had needed a slow period, time without inter-
ruptions and deadlines, time away from the frenetic haste
that had been so much a part of our lives. Although these
feelings had been coming on for a long time, it seemed
sudden, now, that we all felt some serenity and inner
peace. We had time to get to know each other. We were
thinking long thoughts and trying them out on each other.
Eldon and I were conversing with our grown children as
adults in a way we had never found time to do before.

And it seemed as though it would last forever. Our
wonderful illusion was that somehow we had dropped into
a sea of timelessness, without haste, without problems,
without end.

"Aren't we lucky?" we often said to each other. "Think
how many people would love to do exactly what we are
doing — but so few ever can."

We sang for the sheer joy of singing. It was a happy
time, and we knew it. Sometimes happiness is so nebulous
and fleeting that if you start to scrutinize it, it is gone.
This was a durable kind of happiness.

⚓

The day we arrived in Tumaco, Colombia, was the nine-
teenth of June, Randy's birthday. To me, Tumaco will always
seem just a little creepy and subtly dangerous, although this

opinion was not shared by everyone. In his diary Eldon wrote, "This is the best place yet, for my money."

Certainly it was different from any other place we had visited. I could never get away from a strange, back-of-the-neck feeling that unknown perils lurked not too far below its mysterious surface — even before Jim almost died there.

An estuary several miles long separates Tumaco from the sea. We first anchored in the estuary, where several other boats were tied up, while Jim went ashore to report to the port captain. When he returned, he advised moving up close to the oil dock, which was well lighted at night. On the following day, the manager of the oil dock urged us to tie up to his dock right under the floodlights.

"It is not safe out there in the harbor," he warned. "Too many pangas gliding around all night." (A panga is a sturdy, locally-made canoe that's been hollowed out of a single log.) His pessimism, he assured us, was founded on experience. "All these guys think you're rich because you have this fancy boat, and some of them would just as soon kill you as not — maybe rather."

On the way up the estuary, we had seen throngs of people on the shore. They crowded the long dock, built alongside the estuary, that seemed to stretch to infinity. For the first time in a new port there were no friendly waves, no calls of welcome, no smiles. The faces were impassive and watchful.

On the first night in the river's mouth, even before our friend at the oil dock so specifically pointed out the dangers, we felt uneasy enough to put our skiff and outboard on the deck and keep a night watch. The coast of Colombia is noted for piracy, which is one reason we bypassed most of it. Tumaco is only a small distance from the border of Ecuador.

Several cruising friends of ours have had unhappy experiences in these waters. One couple who left Costa Rica shortly after our arrival disappeared without a trace.

Their boat was found a few miles off the Colombian coast, stripped of everything that could be carried away, and no one was aboard. Piracy and murder, most people believe.

All night, that first night, pangas glided around our boat; frequently a hand came through a porthole, sometimes just to pull the panga along, but often the hand did a quick search of the area under the porthole. Mostly, the shelves under the ports held books, and apparently that wasn't what the hands were searching for.

When my watch started shortly before midnight, I came out from the lighted cabin into the blackest night imaginable. The companionway from the ama, the side-hull where Eldon and I slept, was very close to the side of the boat. I realized in a blood-curdling instant that someone was there. I heard a quick intake of breath, then a panga darted off into the night. I jumped a good healthy distance into the air and screamed — a scream to wake the dead. My voice is in the high soprano range, and under such stress can easily go above high C.

That scream brought Jim and Rand on the run. "What happened, Mom?" they asked, almost in unison.

"Someone was there!" I pointed to the side of the boat. "Right there, not a foot from my face when I came on deck!"

I was feeling shaky after all that adrenaline, and a little bit foolish. Everyone knew that the pangas had been circling us all evening like a school of sharks.

"Was he trying to board the boat?" Jim asked, with a quick glance toward his 30-06 rifle down in the cabin.

"As far as I could tell, he was already aboard. He must have still been in his panga or he couldn't have gotten away so quickly. You must realize that I was totally blind, coming out into the dark."

"Of course," Rand agreed, "but he didn't realize you couldn't see him. I'll bet that rebel yell sent him back to town as though the devil was after him!"

The boys had a good laugh and went back to bed, but

Villains and Heroes

Pattie and Carole stayed with me through my watch, which I really appreciated. In time we could see enough to know that no panga approached closer than thirty feet during my watch.

Eldon was due on watch at two o'clock, but he came up at one-thirty and told us to get some sleep. He had slept very soundly, as evidenced by the fact that he hadn't heard me scream about eight feet from his pillow. Later, he wrote in his diary: "Slept through my entire watch. How could I? We could have been boarded a dozen times."

In blissful ignorance, all of the rest of us slept peacefully.

No one that we met in Tumaco had ever seen a trimaran before. In fact, this year only two yachts from the US had put in at this port. It was natural that they would be curious about our boat. After we got up near the oil dock, which was close to the town, a constant stream of visitors wanted to come aboard.

A well-dressed man came aboard and asked if he could bring some visiting nuns out to see the boat. Five white-clad nuns from a hospital in Cali and a young lay-teacher came aboard. They were interested in everything they saw, and they wanted to know all about the trip we were making with our family. Noticing all the musical instruments, they asked who played them and if we would make some music for them to record. Jim and Rand, never reluctant, complied.

When it was time for them to leave, it was as though we had been friends forever. They hugged and kissed all of us, and the senior nun asked if she could pray for a special blessing on us. (Obviously our way of life seemed to her very dangerous.) She offered a beautiful prayer, asking God's blessing on us as we traveled and especially praying for our safety. We never forgot her generous concern for those not of her particular denomination. She was a wonderful example to those of any faith.

Trilogy

⚓

Back in San Jose, Eldon had been advised to get our visas for Ecuador and the Galapagos Islands while we were in Tumaco. Leaving Rand, Carole, and Pattie on the boat, Jim, Eldon, and I went ashore to see the Ecuadorian consul.

Tramping through the dusty little village, we couldn't believe that this was the business district for more than five thousand people. However, coming into town, we'd seen more people than that just on the dock. We decided to ask the consul about the local population. To our utter amazement, he told us that the population is between sixty-five and ninety thousand — estimated, because it's a long time between official censuses.

The Ecuadorian consul was housed in a neat stucco structure, one of the best-looking buildings in town. His opinion of Colombia was dismal. "Good thing you're going to Ecuador," he said. "The sooner the better."

"Don't you like it here?" I asked. I had always assumed that those in the diplomatic service would at least make a pretense of loyalty to their host country.

He looked at me as though I had said something truly preposterous. "How can one like it here," he asked explosively, "among savages and barbarians? I work here; I do not have to like it."

Tumaco is obviously a backward city in an undeveloped part of the country; I thought that might be the problem. So I asked him if he would rather work in Cali or Bogota.

"More of the same," he answered brusquely. "Robbers and villains! They don't know how to enforce the law in this country."

Then he expanded glowingly on the advantages of Ecuador, where "they know how to live and respect one another." I doubted if one little political boundary could make that much difference. Still, he was right to a degree. Coastwise piracy is better controlled in Ecuador, and we

definitely felt safer on Ecuadorian streets than we did in
Tumaco.

One thing I will say about this consul; he spoke his
mind. He was very dubious about the scenic or cultural
prospects in the Galapagos Islands. We planned to spend at
least sixty days there; he was sure that would be far too
much. "You won't want to be there that long," he
promised. "What do they have there? Rocks, sand, and
turtles. Three days will be long enough."

We didn't argue. Eldon asked, "How about the people
there? What are they like?"

"Very fine people," the consul answered quickly. "Very
law-abiding. It's not a good place to make a living, but
you'll have no trouble with the people. Good people."
Then another thought occurred to him. "I don't know
about the scientists. They have scientists from all over the
world at the Darwin Station. I don't vouch for them, but
the local people are fine."

We thanked the consul, picked up our visas, and
departed not one whit less enthusiastic about the
Galapagos Islands than we had been before. " You can be
very sure he hasn't been there," Eldon said. "Almost
everyone who hasn't been to the Islands thinks the same
thing." In addition to his reading, he had talked with other
cruising people who had spent considerable time there, and
knew that the consul was wrong.

⚓

Walking back through the town, we were pained to see
men of all ages, and even young children, with only stumps
where their hands should have been. These maimings
resulted from the use of dynamite for fishing. Though the
practice had been outlawed ten or more years before, it
obviously still continued — or else children eight or ten
years old would not be showing the unmistakable signs of
this dangerous practice.

Trilogy

We met a young couple here who were able to share their local knowledge with us. He was head of the Planned Parenthood office, and she was the public health nurse. Ironically, they were working at cross purposes. His mission was to limit family sizes, because overpopulation was keeping this community on the verge of starvation. The public health nurse, though, was trying to show these people how to keep three-fourths of their babies from dying in the first year.

The Planned Parenthood man was having a hard time getting his message across. These parents wanted large families. Generally, so many babies and young children died that parents produced lots of offspring in hopes that some would survive to care for them in their old age. (Certainly the government wasn't going to do it!)

"It's so frustrating," Planned Parenthood explained. "My wife is having better success teaching these people to keep their babies alive than I am teaching them to limit their families. I can imagine some of these families winding up with twenty or more children and no way to feed them."

That evening we were invited to have dinner with our friends from the oil dock. His wife and children had been down to the boat several times already, and they had invited us the day before. Like everyone here who is at all prosperous, she had servants who do all the cooking, laundry, and housework. She came down about five o'clock to tell us that dinner would be served at five-thirty. "With servants," she said, laughing tolerantly, "you really don't know when a dinner will be ready; they aren't good at keeping track of time. I just watch and make a guess."

It was a lovely dinner; apparently they had been working on it all day. Several kinds of meat were served in sequence, and also an abundance of fruit and vegetables. There were at least three salads. For dessert we had little meringue shells with a fruit filling, accompanied by demi-tasse cups filled with coffee, chocolate, and whipped cream

— very rich and delicious.

After dinner our host took Jim with him to visit some of the town's night spots while the rest of us went back to the boat. All went well for the first two hours or more. Then Jim suddenly became deathly ill. His friend, who had been drinking the same anise-flavored liqueur, much beloved in South America, was sure Jim had been deliberately poisoned.

It was all Jim could do, with his friend half-carrying him, to get back to the boat. Jim's friend stayed until after midnight to be sure he was recovering. What he could not understand was how Jim's drink had been poisoned and his not, or why. He was well aware of the pitfalls in this weird place. The fact that he was a local businessman would not have been any particular safeguard.

"If I had gotten the same thing Jim did, it would have been because someone wanted us both dead, and we would never have made it back here," he told Eldon and me very seriously.

Jim was violently sick for about two hours after he got back to the boat, and quite miserable the rest of the night, but he recovered. The only lasting effect was a deep antipathy for that kind of drink. "I just never want to see any of that licorice-flavored stuff ever again," he said the next day. "I don't want to smell it, let alone drink it, ever!"

⚓

The next evening the Planned Parenthood/Public Health couple took us out to one of the little places where they have live music. Most of the people here were drinking soda pop, although sterner stuff was available. Jim's stomach was still queasy, and 7-Up suited him just fine. Between musical offerings, Eldon, freed temporarily from boat-sitting by our friend of the oil dock, told us about his big frustration of the day — well, of the last two days actually, although he hadn't known it was going to be a frustration until that morning.

Eldon very much admired the little pangas. From the time we arrived there, he had let it be known that he wanted to buy one. After looking over quite a few, Eldon picked the one he liked best and agreed to buy it for five dollars plus our beaten-up bicycle. Jim and Rand hoisted the panga aboard, and the owners (we presumed) left with the money and the bike. Eldon was so happy with his shining little panga that he was practically petting it — running his hand over its smooth surface, anyway.

The next morning, at the crack of dawn, the panga's real owner showed up. He was not involved in the swindle; the panga had been stolen from him some time before. We didn't give up easily, but when he showed us five identical pangas all with serial numbers, of which ours was one of the sequence, as well as his cannery trademark on all of them, we had to give in and let him reclaim his property.

Mr. Planned Parenthood could contain himself no longer. He interrupted Eldon's narrative with a question, all in italics, "Do you have any idea what that bicycle is worth in this market?"

Jim answered; technically, the bicycle belonged to him. "We paid eight bucks for it in San Diego, and it hasn't improved much traveling on the back deck; small loss."

"Yes," Eldon agreed, "I don't mind losing the bicycle nearly as much as the panga. That was a cute little fella."

"The price you paid for it back in the US is irrelevant," our host continued. "It's what it's worth here that you should be thinking about. Bicycles are hard to come by here, and very expensive; you could have gotten a lot more than a panga out of it."

"Actually, we didn't even get that," Rand interposed. "What we got was ripped off."

"Right!" our host exclaimed. "And that reminds me. This country is overflowing with rip-off artists. I hope you haven't been buying any so-called gemstones or pre-

Columbian artifacts. Most of them are swindles — and much more expensive swindles than the one you just had played on you."

"Not to worry," I told him. "Our budget doesn't run to expensive souvenirs."

We had little expectation of dealing in the emerald market, but Jim had quite an interest in antiquities. "There really are genuine pre-Columbian artifacts around here, aren't there?" he asked.

"True, there are. But unless you're truly an expert, it is usually a fast and painless way to get swindled."

"Why painless?" I asked.

"Because you would never know you had bought a fake," our hostess said. "You can't imagine how devilishly clever these people are at aging them and making them look authentic."

Jim went home and looked long and hard at the little pre-Columbian figures he had bought a day or two before. They looked ancient, primitive, authentic. "They look good to me," he decided. "If they're fakes they're sure good fakes. I'm satisfied."

That's what the man said. If they were indeed a swindle, it was a painless one.

⚓

Eldon still thinks this is his ideal of an exotic, tropical port, but when it was time to leave Tumaco, I had no regrets at all. The dark shore, the long, long rows of pilings, the deep mass of people lining the estuary made me feel that we were running some sort of gantlet. I always felt that any change of mood in this crowd would not find them acting benevolent.

Early as it was when we left Tumaco, the wife of the oil dock manager came down to tell us good-by and to bring a parting gift of coconut candy — large, flat cakes, each one about five inches across, made of caramel and toasted

coconut. It was so good that we had to remind ourselves
and each other that every piece of it probably contained
not less than three hundred calories! Her husband came
down also to wish us farewell. They had been very kind to
us, the sort of kindness you can never repay — only hope
you can pass it on to someone else.

⚓

Along the shore we had to battle a strong current for
hours. We made such poor time that we didn't reach the
place where we'd intended to stop for the night; we passed
it at midnight, at which time it seemed just as well to keep
on running all night.

The next night we were close to Cabo Pasado, and
Eldon thought we should anchor there for the night. Before
we could get into the bay, we were stopped by five pangas,
all full of fishermen, eleven of them altogether. Most of
them were dark and stocky; two were tall and aquiline in
features. None seemed to project much friendliness. They
motioned for us to anchor there, although it was at least a
half mile from where any other boats were anchored. This
seemed strange, but we put the anchor down and the fishermen came aboard. In answer to our questions, they
motioned to some small houses on the shore and said that
was where their families lived.

As it began to get dark, we began thinking it would be a
good idea if they went home to their families, but we didn't
actually say so. Finally, they began to move toward their
pangas, but before they disembarked they asked very point-
edly if we had some extra shirts we could give them. Randy
went below and sorted out eleven shirts, trying not to get
anyone's favorite. They accepted them with a few grunts
that would have been hard to interpret as appreciation, and
they got into their pangas. All this time Jim never moved
from the corner where his rifle reposed conspicuously.

Eldon is usually very friendly and unsuspicious, but

something about this visit didn't sit well with him. He didn't at all mind giving them some shirts, but he had a very strong hunch that they were planning to return later in the night. He mentioned this possibility to Jim.

"Did you get the feeling that those fellows might be planning another visit after we're supposedly asleep?"

"I certainly did, and I think we'd be very smart to get out of here pronto!"

The water was shallow here in the river mouth, and the anchor came up quickly. In a few moments we were on our way, and didn't stop until we were in the harbor in Manta, Ecuador.

⚓

Manta, with a population not much larger than Tumaco, had a business district many times larger with impressive stone buildings six or seven stories in height. There were several large buildings under construction, indications of a healthy economy. The most impressive feature of Manta was its immense breakwall made of huge, jagged stones that somehow fit together seamlessly. Inside the breakwall was a fine, totally protected harbor.

The contrast between Tumaco and Manta doesn't end with the appearance of the two towns; Manta is full of bustling, purposeful activity, not just standing throngs of unoccupied, apathetic people. In fact, we saw fewer people on the streets in Manta, and they all seemed to be going somewhere, not just hanging around.

For the first time, now, we were south of the equator, having crossed it on our way to Manta. We had to skip the traditional dunking ceremony because no one aboard had crossed it previously, so no one was qualified to dunk the rest of the party. Just as well. Because of the cold Humboldt Current coming up from Antarctica, it felt like winter. Where this current governs the weather, there is almost always a cool breeze, sometimes uncomfortably cool.

Trilogy

⚓

Carole was not yet as fluent in Spanish as Pattie and the boys, but she was getting there; she had studied Spanish in school, and her linguistic ability developed rapidly as she gained self-confidence. I could understand a little Spanish, and more all the time; Eldon was the one who felt totally isolated from the Spanish-speaking people. Because he is so gregarious, this was frustrating. Fortunately, in Manta he immediately found several people with whom he could converse in English.

Our first guests, the evening of our arrival, were Gunther and Gail Beuchs. He was the manager of Van Camp's big tuna cannery in Manta, probably one of the best positions available in this town. The cannery supplied them with a large modern home and servants galore. According to Gail, servants are not an unqualified blessing. In this country, though, one's standing in the community is determined by the number of servants.

Before they had been on the boat fifteen minutes, Gail was asking me if we didn't have some laundry that needed to be done.

"You must have known some boating people before," I said. "Getting laundry done is one of the more difficult things about cruising."

"Bring it up to the house," she directed. "The more, the better."

"You're kidding!" I gasped. "You don't know what you're asking for!"

"Oh yes, I do," she said decisively, "indeed I do. I have four servants to do my housework. I'm not supposed to touch any cooking, cleaning, laundry — anything like that. Those jobs properly belong to the servants."

"Great!" I said. "I'd like that kind of a set-up."

"You think you would," Gail replied, "because you haven't tried it. I could do all the housework in that place easily in the forenoon, and have some free time as well as some privacy. Instead, I have to keep all those girls busy, and it takes all my time, not to mention all my patience!" She sighed, as though even thinking about it was painful. "They are so slow, so inept — you absolutely wouldn't believe it!"

"Well, on the bright side," I was beginning to understand better why she had so generously offered to do this for me, "I have enough laundry to keep them busy for some time."

"Good. Let's load it into the car tonight. Then no one will have to pack it up to the house, and I can start the girls on it early in the morning." Gail was beginning to sound as though she might enjoy this. "Why don't you and the girls come up for lunch? All those decisions, white, colorfast, colored and all the rest, will probably keep them busy most of the day."

Gail and Gunther were Californians, although he could claim Ecuadorian ancestry. He was in his mid-thirties, average height with brown eyes and light brown hair. Gail was several years younger, pretty, with reddish-blonde hair and a very fair complexion — not the sort that takes kindly to very much sunshine.

Gail was having a harder time adjusting to Ecuadorian life than her husband. He realized that the cultural change had been greater for her.

"A cannery is a cannery, wherever it may be," he said. "This one isn't much different from the one I managed in California. But for Gail, it's a whole new way of life. Here she's supposed to be a great lady. Everyone expects her to act the part, and they're very quick to pick up on any lapses from this high station. It makes her feel as though she's play-acting all the time."

A rumble of footsteps on the deck let us know that Pattie and Carole were back from washing their hair on the dock — with cold, but fresh water.

"Gee, I wish I'd known you wanted to wash your hair," Gail said after introductions. "Why don't you come up to the house in the morning and take a good, warm shower and shampoo it right? I don't think shampoo works as well in cold water."

"Better than it does in salt water," Carol replied, adding quickly, "but we'll be oh so happy to come up to your house and try again."

"A hot shower sounds like heaven," Pattie sighed. "When was the last time we had a hot shower? Roffa's beach house?"

"Right, Costa Rica," Carole said. "How long ago was that, a month? Seems longer."

"They wash it every day," I explained to Gail, "in whatever conditions they find themselves. Cold salt water, cold fresh water — the hair must be washed every day. I didn't realize until I had a teenage daughter that hair was so launderable!"

Eldon, Jim, and Rand were also invited for lunch, but because Gunther had offered to loan them a good mechanic and a good refrigeration man, they felt they should stay on the boat and get these things done. Before Gunther and Gail left, it was arranged that Pattie and Carole would walk up to the house — about five blocks — in the morning, and I would come up for lunch. Then, if the men could get their work finished, we would all go for a ride to see some of the country around Manta.

I got there promptly at noon and saw stacks of dry, folded clothes, sheets, and towels all over the laundry room. "Wouldn't you know," Gail exclaimed. "The dryer went on the fritz, and I can't call the mechanic because he's on your boat!" It wasn't exactly a tragedy, though. Most of the things that weren't dry were jeans and other heavy stuff. We could dry them in the rigging, I told Gail. That was where they were used to being dried.

She seemed to feel guilty at not being able to do the job

as perfectly and completely as she had planned, but what she had done was such a boon that I could hardly thank her enough.

When you travel around from one strange port to another, you learn how many wonderful, generous people there are in the world.

⚓

In spite of Gail's fear that her servants would manage to spoil something she had carefully planned, our lunch was very good and nicely served. After, we went for a ride in Gail's car. It was luxurious to leave the dishes to her servants and go riding around the countryside.

Eldon and the boys weren't able to come; it was just too important to take advantage of good mechanical help for problems with the generator, refrigerator, and other equipment. Eldon could foresee a time, farther out in the Pacific, when he'd find no better mechanic than himself.

Jim felt the same practical concerns as Eldon, but our graphic description of the luncheon triggered his desire for steak. Early the next morning he set out to look through the various meat markets, but he came back empty-handed.

"You won't believe this," he said. "Everywhere the meat was just black with flies, totally covered! And I didn't want to buy that. Finally I found a shop where there were no flies... well, plenty of flies in the shop but none on the meat. That struck me as very odd. So I asked the proprietor, 'How come, no flies?' He smiled and winked at me as he said, 'Black Flag.' That's why we aren't having any steak today!"

⚓

While we were as close as we were going to get, we decided to see Quito. Jim, Rand, Carole, and Pattie went first. After three days, Jim and the girls came back; Rand stayed in Quito to be our Spanish-speaking guide.

Our eccentric alarm clock, already suffering from rust

problems as many things do on the water, failed to ring, and we had to dress and get to the bus in fifteen minutes. Our departure was reminiscent of the beginning of our trip to Guadalajara. When we reached the bus, the motor was running, the doors closed. When we waved our tickets at him, the driver opened the door and gestured us to our seats. With luck almost unbelievable after such an inauspicious start, we found that the two seats directly back of the driver had been saved for us.

We left the scrubby, semi-desert coastland very soon and started into the mountains. And what mountains! Here are the headwaters of the Amazon; two of the world's tallest peaks, Chimborazo and Cotopaxi, are in this chain within the borders of Ecuador. The road was narrow and winding, cut out of solid rock. The scenery was breathtaking — not only because of the sheer drops into deep canyons on one or both sides, but also because of the shiny, rain-splashed jungle all around us. The sky was the deepest, most intense blue I have ever seen, and the air so clear that distant mountaintops looked as sharp as flint arrowheads.

Even though he wasn't exactly a cautious type, our driver was such an improvement over Hairbreadth Harry that I felt quite relaxed, enjoying the ride. I'm sure Eldon had never ridden with a driver like H.H., and he thought this one was bad enough. He kept looking over the side of our rock ledge apprehensively. At one point, after a hairpin turn that brought us perilously close to the edge, he commented, "I think this fellow is a little bolder than such a highway warrants." But I had a very secure feeling that anyone who had survived the trip to Guadalajara had more going for him than just luck.

As we went higher up the mountains, we left the orchids, the vines, and all the other brilliant flowers behind. Our final mountain pass before reaching Quito was about twelve thousand feet high. Quito only lacks a few feet of being ten thousand feet high. Set against mountains sixteen or seventeen thousand feet high, with cultivated fields extending two-thirds of the way from the plain to the peaks, Quito is superbly and beautifully situated. It was well worth the climb. Quito has a medieval, Spanish look, like El Greco's Toledo. We coasted down to the city, well satisfied with our first glimpse of it. Back of it all, serenely mantled in snow, rose Cotopaxi.

It was a good thing that I'd taken a look at Quito coming in, because that was almost all of it I would see. The beautiful old hotel Rand had chosen in the older part of town proved to be my undoing. Such places tend to get musty through the years, and I am very allergic to all those molds. I spent the first night battling hay fever and asthma, and the next morning moved to the newest hotel in town — never mind the superior architecture of ancient buildings.

By the time I'd recovered enough to go anywhere, Rand and Eldon had decided to get me back to the boat as quickly as possible. We caught the early morning bus to Manta.

Although the shops were all closed when we left, the streets were not at all deserted; everywhere Indian people were hurrying and carrying heavy loads, sometimes on their heads, sometimes in a backpack secured by a headband. The native people may be small, but they are remarkably strong. Even the women, in their black derby hats and dark skirts down to their sturdy shoe tops, were almost running as they carried things I probably couldn't lift.

⚓

Back at the boat, we found Jim very sick with a high fever and chest congestion. If he didn't have pneumonia, he had something remarkably like it.

"Have you taken any medicine?" I asked. "Penicillin was invented for pneumonia, you know."

Jim stared back with fever bright eyes in a gaunt face. "Nope," he rasped. It was folly to ask. One reason Jim was the custodian of the medicine chest was because he never touched the stuff.

"With a fever of 103 degrees and all that chest congestion, don't you think it would be a good idea?"

Jim closed his eyes wearily, as though it was just too much trouble to answer. Finally, he croaked out, "You have to take it for ten days; that's forty tablets. We only have enough for two major illnesses."

"So?" I said. "I would say this is one of them. Really, Jim, we can't afford to fool around with pneumonia."

"No," he argued. "Something more serious might come along."

"This is serious enough to suit me," I said firmly. "We've been traveling for a year and no one has been this sick."

"Why don't we try some hot and cold packs first? I thought that was what you always did for chest congestion."

Hot and cold packs are not wildly popular with my kids; they're not all that popular with me, either, although the rest of the family would never believe it. Just as I used to imagine my teachers sitting at their desks all summer longing for the return of their pupils in the fall, my kids think I just live from one chest cold to the next so I can torture them with this home remedy. I couldn't remember Jim ever asking for it before.

"Okay," I said, "we'll do that and wait three hours; if your temperature isn't better by that time, I'm going to call Gail and ask her to recommend a doctor."

In addition to the packs, I gave him steam inhalation with Vicks and Ben-Gay in the water. By the time I finished, he was breathing more easily and sleeping soundly. The next morning his temperature was almost normal.

⚓

Eldon had an incredibly long list of things he wanted to get done before we headed for the Galapagos Islands, but somehow Jim prevailed on him to go with us out to

Villains and Heroes

Montecristi, a small, poverty-stricken town noted for its straw artisans — the original home of Panama hats. The name "Panama" was attached to the hats because they were shipped first to Panama and from there all over the world.

Very early in the morning two days after Jim had recovered, we boarded a truck, this time a flatbed with no sides and plank seats in the back — no backs on the seats, either.

The road to Montecristi was listed as unimproved, and I've seen plowed fields that were smoother. To make matters worse, the truck didn't seem to have any springs. Although the distance was only fifteen miles, it felt much longer.

Most of the houses of Montecristi were made of bamboo and thatch; some were made from adobe, and a very few from quarried stone. In the center of town we found quite a large church whose dazzling marble interior proved, upon close inspection, to be wood cleverly painted to resemble marble. It was ingeniously done and symbolic of both the artistry and the poverty here.

Not since we were in El Salvador had we seen such poverty. But this was a proud poverty, not abject. These people are creators of beauty, and if the world does not pay good wages for beauty, they create it anyway. Their straw mats, tablecloths, even dresses made of fine filament straw were exquisite. But the creators of these things were working for almost nothing. There should be some sort of endangered species program for this village, because the art will certainly die if it is not better rewarded. When it does, the world will be a poorer place.

We visited the hut of an old man who had been making Panama hats for over fifty years. The average hat takes somewhere between two and three weeks, and he was currently working on hat number seven hundred eighty. He earned less than ten dollars per hat.

In the middle of a hard-packed dirt floor, a large tree trunk stood upside down with the branches spreading out to serve as legs. The table, cut off close to the roots, was about thirty inches in diameter. On top of the table was a block of wood shaped like the inside of a hat. The hatmaker leaned over this block, holding it tight against his chest as he wove the straw filaments, fine as the finest thread, around this block. Poor man! His back was hunched; his chest was caved in as though crushed by a huge boulder. He worked almost upside down most of the time, face toward the floor. If anyone were forced to work under such conditions, it would be slavery of the most inhumane kind, but this man was proud of his art. He only deplored the young people who were leaving the community rather than learning the trade of their ancestors.

"It has been handed down from our grandparents," he told us — Pattie translating — "and from their grandparents before them. It should not be allowed to die! We are artisans like no other in this material, but only the old people are doing it. The young people go to other jobs."

He sighed. "It is not an easy living."

We watched sisal being made into rope in one of these dwellings. I can't call these cottage industries. These primitive huts are far removed from any concept of cottages. We watched little children learning to make placemats and straw trivets, hair ornaments, whatever could be made from the apparently abundant straw. And we wondered how many would choose this occupation in adulthood.

Few, I guessed.

Jim and Rand got Panama hats; Pattie, Carole, and I got less expensive ones, with a lacy pattern over the crown and on the brim. Pattie got a lace tablecloth and several other straw articles because they were beautiful and — we might as well admit it — because they were cheap. We had scattered out while we were shopping; time was short, and we couldn't afford to follow each other around. We reassembled at the bus stop. Eldon was carrying, of all things, a plain wooden barrel. It seemed like a strange purchase from the famous straw market of Ecuador.

"What on earth is that for?" I asked.

"Sauerkraut."

We had been making sauerkraut because our cabbage would only keep two or three days otherwise, and it was true that we didn't have any good containers for large quantities of it. But this didn't look like the answer to me.

"Won't it leak?" I asked.

"No," Eldon said, "it won't leak. If I put water in it right now it would. But as the sauerkraut gets wetter, it will swell together gradually."

"How did you learn all about barrels of sauerkraut?" I was a little skeptical about using sauerkraut to replace fresh vegetables. "I suspect that with all that salting the vitamin C curls up and dies."

"I learned about barrels of sauerkraut at home when I was a kid. We used to make it every winter," Eldon said. "As far as the vitamins are concerned, we'll have a lot of oranges, carrots, beets, and squash with us. That should take care of any deficiency. Don't worry; I never heard of anyone getting scurvy in four weeks."

⚓

It was time to leave Manta. When Jim returned from his bout with the port authority, it was past noon. We had hoped to get an earlier start, but que sera. We were only heading down to Salinas, a resort area near the border of Peru. Salinas wasn't on our original itinerary, but Eldon had decided to go to Guayaquil to get our generator repaired. It was acting up, as usual, and we knew that we might not find any way to have it repaired farther out on the Pacific. Guayaquil was up the river from Salinas about fifty miles, but Salinas was a better place to leave the boat. Also, he felt he should get some more money in case we headed west to New Zealand. As far as anyone knew there weren't any banks on most of the islands we would be visiting.

Soon after he took the generator to Guayaquil and

arranged for the bank draft, Eldon got acquainted with the engineer on a big fish-buying boat at Salinas. This man was a skilled mechanic. Having been forced by circumstances to be very resourceful, he felt that no first-class mechanic should allow himself to be beaten by poorly designed equipment. After looking over our heat exchanger, he decided it needed to be redesigned, and he proceeded to do so. He actually had to machine new parts that it had never had, and discard some that he said shouldn't have been there in the first place. The result was a new heat exchanger that worked better than it ever had before.

Eldon had a profound respect for this man.

When the boys went back for a progress report on the generator, there wasn't much progress to report. The generator had been dismantled and new parts ordered from the factory; it was going to be expensive. The air freight alone was estimated to be twenty-five percent of the total bill, but so far no parts had arrived. Neither had the bank draft, nor would it for some time. I tagged along with the boys just so I could have a look at Guayaquil — not perhaps as large as Guadalajara but in the same class, spreading out mile after mile all over the river valley.

While I was gone, Pattie and Carole found some new friends. They were zooming around the countryside in a high-powered sports car. Carole's date was an internationally known soccer player, and Pattie's was the son of a prominent banking family with residences in both Guayaquil and Quito. After exhausting most of the recreational possibilities around Salinas, which didn't take long, the girls were invited to spend the weekend in Guayaquil, at the estate of the banking family. Pattie, very conscious that she was now old enough to vote, did not ask my permission — but did ask for my approval. It sounded like a pretty well-chaperoned party, so I didn't object.

Before the weekend was over, the entire host family began trying to get Pattie to stay for another week, offering to fly her over to the Galapagos Islands in their private plane if we wanted to leave before that time. But Pattie has acrophobia. She can be paralyzed on a fire escape or plat-form one story up in the air. Flying in small planes is some-thing she does not do; so that idea didn't get off the ground.

Eldon worried when Pattie got offers like these, but he would have worried a lot less if he had known how resolutely she kept herself free of romantic entanglements.

⚓

After almost three weeks the generator was finished, the money had arrived from our bank in Seattle, and I suddenly realized that now we were really going to start sailing into the sunset — genuine deep sea travel. I felt myself tingle the way I used to on Christmas Eve when I was a child. We were going to leave the mainland, whose sheltering shores and harbors we had skirted for thousands of miles, and head for the true South Seas, the fabled islands of Eldon's dreams. We had put in a tremendous amount of work getting ready for this — not to mention, always, the ongoing work — and I hoped fervently that he wouldn't be disappointed in this biggest adventure in a life quite well filled with adventures.

Jim and Rand were happy, cheerful, and easy to get along with. Pattie seemed much more satisfied since she had Carole for a companion, and Eldon, of course, was living out his boyhood fantasy with exuberance. I was happy that modern medical science has taken care of my seasickness. When Eldon used to talk about making this kind of trip, I'd say, "You can sail to these romantic places and I'll fly down and meet you in port." I'm glad it didn't have to be that way.

Quite often, Eldon was afraid the rest of us weren't appreciating our good fortune to the same degree that he was. That may have been true; we hadn't dreamed about it for forty or fifty years before it became a reality. "What frac-tion of a fraction of one percent of people ever get to do the things they dreamed of when they were young?" he asked.

One time I answered, "When I was young, I didn't have that kind of dreams. Sailing around the world wasn't even down there in my subconscious, or whatever I drew my dreams out of."

He answered soothingly, trying to console me for what I'd missed: "Well, of course. You lived too far away from the water." According to Eldon, anyone who wasn't raised near the ocean had a deprived childhood.

"It wasn't all that bad, you know," I defended my own childhood memories. "We used to swim in the Boise River and go camping in the mountains. Ice skating in the wintertime. It was a pretty good life — good clay tennis courts and friends with horses to ride." But it really was futile. He considers all land-bound adventures very puny compared with adventures on the sea.

Pattie and the boys smiled behind his back and said he was like a kid who had inherited a candy store. But they added, "He deserves it; he waited a long time and worked awfully hard for this."

One thing was getting to be a problem — Eldon did like to have things done in exactly the same way he did them. Randy was twenty-two, however; Jim was twenty-six. They had skills and opinions of their own, and they wanted some latitude in how things got done.

To avoid open conflict, Eldon vented his frustrations to me. "I just don't understand why they buck me on every little thing!" he said one day, thoroughly exasperated. "I've spent a lot of years and a bit of thought learning to do some things efficiently. Why must they do it differently and waste time?"

Now it was my turn to soothe a little, so I said mildly, "It's their time, and they have lots of it right now. What difference does it make?" He didn't find this a very satisfactory answer. It only convinced him that I wasn't as sympathetic as he had hoped.

I thought this over. Eldon was being too inflexible on

this point. There was a possibility of open conflict, especially as everyone got a touch of cabin fever.

Eldon thought it over, too, and the next day he pursued the discussion with new ammunition. "Don't you believe," he began, "that there's a best way for doing each thing, a way that saves the most time and effort?"

"Yes," I said carefully, "and I suppose each generation thinks it has found it. Did you ever think what it must be like to be a mother-in-law?"

"No," he answered, surprised, "but I'm pretty darn sure I'm never going to be one."

"Think about this," I said in my best counseling manner, which he hates. "A mother-in-law has learned to cook and keep house, and she has had some experience in child-raising. She tries to pass on all these skills to her daughter-in-law and only succeeds in antagonizing her. Don't be a mother-in-law to Jim and Rand."

Eldon wasn't ready to give up yet. "Don't you think I should give my kids the benefit of my years of experience?"

"You already have, more than you realize. But remember that societies where everything is done in ways inherited from the elders don't make much progress."

"If that's the case," Eldon said, part bitterness, part resignation, "my kids are going to make great progress."

PATTIE'S COMMENT:
CAROLE'S ARRIVAL

I'll never forget the day the letter came from my uncle Walter asking us about Carole joining our family for a few months. Dad, Mom, Jim, and Randy agreed that the ultimate decision must be mine because I would be the one sharing my "space" the most. I had to think about it for a while.

I weighed the pros and cons. On the pro side, I'd always liked Carole. I'd been closer buddies with her next oldest sister Leslie, and consequently I didn't know Carole as well. But I figured it probably wouldn't take us long to become friends, even though I still thought of her as the eleven-year-old I'd seen four years before. On a more practical level, I knew that with Carole along my freedom to go exploring would open up dramatically. Not only would I have someone to do things with, but dad would have a far harder time keeping us both on such a short leash.

On the con side, however, I worried about having to share my side of the boat, my little space. This was my place of escape, the one place where I could be totally alone. Even though I knew it was selfish and petty, I liked my little bunk area. My quarters were just slightly wider than my bunk bed and exactly the length of the two bunks joined foot to foot. All of my books and things were arranged on the other bed, the one Carole would need. I wasn't sure if I wanted to give up that area.

To be completely honest — I probably had so much junk piled on the spare bed that I wasn't sure if I could ever get it cleared off!

A more serious concern to me was the thought that Carole and I might not like each other or get along. I'd always felt able to get along with most people, but I'd never had to live with someone I didn't like. (Well, I admit I didn't always like Jim and Randy that much, but they were my brothers and that was different.)

Villains and Heroes

Despite all that, it wasn't long before the pro side won out and I knew that I wanted Carole to come with us.

Carole stepped off the plane in San Jose looking like something out of a heavy metal rock band with her long black hair, white face, dramatic black eye make-up, and black coat and clothes. Not only did it take a few moments for Jim and me to recognize her, but I started feeling like Miss Innocence and Purity of 1972 by comparison. I didn't wear much make-up, if any, and on the boat we lived a very healthy, wholesome life. Carole looked neither healthy nor wholesome. There was no question, I was out of my league!

At first it felt very awkward with Carole. We didn't seem to have that much in common. Even though she was a year and a half younger, many of her life experiences far exceeded mine. But my adjustment was no more difficult than hers. Her trust in anyone had suffered some severe blows along the way, and the message she broadcast was clear — she wasn't going to let me or anyone else manipulate or use her in any way. I wasn't used to such wariness, and I wasn't quite sure how I should handle it.

Initially I stuck pretty close to Carole whenever we went somewhere. I didn't know if she might take off with someone who looked interesting or who gave her a better offer than traveling with the Coon family. I doubt that I could have done anything if she'd chosen to take off, but it probably made me feel in control or something. I felt that her commitment to staying with us was very fragile. After a week or two, though, I gradually felt more confident that Carole was starting to enjoy the trip a little and wasn't going to disappear somewhere along the way.

Trilogy

Once Carole arrived, I did find a much greater sense of freedom and fun. We were able to go horseback riding on the Hertados Ranch as well as Jeep riding with some of the young guys who lived close to Playa del Coco. One of those guys was Charlie from Canada, as Mom has previously mentioned. She said she didn't see him as a threat to my future. It's a good thing she didn't know at the time how close he came to being her future son-in-law. I fell madly in love with this funny, intelligent, and adventuresome Canadian. As fate would have it, though, it would be twenty years before we would see each other again.

For the first few weeks I felt that a lot of things I said to Carole were met with cynicism and distrust. As she told me later, she really didn't believe that I was generally trying to be nice to her. She thought I was being too sweety-sweet and that I was a big fake — a Pollyana type. Carole had encountered enough manipulative, exploitative, and evil people in the last couple of years that she felt certain I had some ulterior motive for trying to be her friend. She kept trying to figure out what my angle was.

Now that I look back on it, I did have an angle — I needed her to be my friend. She was my cousin. In my mind, the good kid that she had been just a few years ago was still there. Granted, that same good kid had always questioned authority, had always demanded to know why, and had always been a big pain in the butt to her older sister and me; in spite of that, I'd always like Carole a lot. She was incredibly smart, and I'd always admired her ability to argue her way out of just about any situation, especially with her dad.

More than anything else, though, I knew that the relationship between Carole and me had to work or else our family voyage was going to hit some troubled seas.

For the first time, my focus shifted away from worrying whether this trip was working out for me. Now I felt responsible that it work out for someone else, for the good of the family.

A quantum leap in my maturation process.

When you live with someone on a boat, you learn either to love 'em or to hate 'em. Fortunately for Carole and me, it was the former. Bit by bit, Carole became more comfortable with all of us, most importantly (at the time) with me. We started discovering things that we shared in common. We had a very similar sense of humor, as well as a love of books, music, and talk. We spent many nights lying in our bunks discussing childhood memories and talking about all sorts of things, from guys to our philosophies of life. I found out all sorts of things.

Carole told me that she and her sisters hated it when they would receive another box of my outgrown dresses and clothes. It wasn't that I had more dresses than they did; I was an only daughter and Carole's parents had five. If my outgrown dresses were almost new, it wasn't because I loved getting all gussied up. It's just that Mom would periodically pack my clothes up and send them to my cousins in Seattle. My aunt was thrilled with the hand-me-downs. But imagine how it felt to the third of five girls, who never got closer to new clothes than a box of discards from cousin Pattie. Just about the time they were due for a shopping trip, good ol' Cousin Pattie would send another box.

Carole also filled me in on the family gossip. Her family lived a lot closer to our grandparents than our family did. Carole had spent quite a bit of time with them and other relatives. She took an almost wicked delight in telling me her version of what all the relations said about my family and me behind our backs. (You can be sure that most of what they said about me wasn't very flattering, much to my amazement and distress.)

As time went on, Carole and I started to share experiences that bonded our friendship, and our "cousinship." It wasn't very long before none of us could remember life on the Trilogy before Carole. She brought a whole new dimension that truly completed our family.

It didn't take Carole long to make her own friends among the itinerant cruising community. She would often take the dinghy over to another boat to visit with someone, or bring them back to visit with us. Carole didn't share my shyness. I'd sit on the deck and wave at people putt-putting past in their little dinghies; Carole would call out and ask for a ride ashore. She never wasted time on people she didn't like, and she could let them know how she felt very quickly. But she found lots of extra time for people she found fascinating.

I wondered, initially, if I would feel jealous of Carole. What if she talked to my mom a lot and asked for her advice, or did something with Jim and Randy without me. I'd never had to share my family before.

When it started to happen, it all felt very natural and right. Carole became much more a sister than a cousin. She became part of our family.

CHAPTER ELEVEN:
DARWIN'S ISLANDS

MARCHENA
ISLAND

FERNANDINA
ISLAND

Tagus
Cove

SAN SALVADOR
ISLAND

GENOVESA
ISLAND

James
Bay

Sullivan Bay

China Hat
Cove

Rabida
Island

ISABELLA

SANTA
CRUZ

Plaza Island

Darwin
Station

Academy Bay

Barrington
Bay

SANTE FE
ISLAND

Post
Office
Bay

Kicker Rock

Black
Beach

Wreck
Bay

Progresso

SANTA MARIA
ISLAND

SAN CHRISTOBAL
ISLAND

PACIFIC

OCEAN

Galapagos Islands

On the charts of Ecuador and northern Chile, a strip that covers three hundred miles of coastline is labeled *Storms are unknown in this region.* I doubt that many places exist where such a thing can be said.

Because of this label, we didn't expect to find any good breezes as we left Salinas. Unexpectedly, though, we picked up a good sailing wind just a few miles offshore. A fifteen or twenty knot wind doesn't constitute a storm by any stretch of the imagination, but on a close reach it wasn't smooth sailing, either.

I scurried below to take some marezine. Sometimes I feel like a zombie for about twenty-four hours after taking it. Surprisingly, though, I felt fine the next morning.

I was beginning to think that the constant motion of traveling, which caused us to compensate unconsciously all the time, was making us lose weight. Everyone except Carole had lost at least twenty pounds, and she hadn't had time yet. It wasn't because we didn't eat enough. I was always baking, so we even had desserts, at least for one meal a day.

The unusually cool weather, courtesy of the Humboldt Current and reminiscent of Alaska in the summer, made life really comfortable in the galley, and I took advantage of the comfort to make bread, granola, and cookies. Finally I roasted about ten pounds of peanuts to make peanut butter. One of the constant gripes we hear from other cruising boats is that the stores from Mexico south don't stock peanut butter. But peanuts are available everywhere, and peanut butter has to be just about the easiest thing in the world to make. All you have to do is roast and grind the peanuts and add a little salt. Presto! As fine a peanut butter as you could ever buy.

Our speed had been averaging a little over two hundred miles every twenty-four hour period. Because we left Salinas in the evening, we were going to arrive at Wreck Bay after dark. Some of us would have liked to squeeze into strange harbors at night rather than lie ahull (nautical for drifting) several miles out. But Eldon always says, "Not many boats are wrecked in mid-ocean. The shore is much more dangerous. Trying to make a landfall in the dark in unfamiliar surroundings is asking for trouble."

⚓

A quick glance around Wreck Bay told us that none of our cruising friends had arrived yet. Eldon, wind-beaten and weary after being up all night, hit the sack for a while.

While it was still too early to transact any business with the port captain, several local young people came aboard to visit. They really weren't supposed to until we had officially entered, but we visited in pidgin English until it got late enough to go ashore.

Jim jumped in the skiff at eight o'clock. When I saw he was going alone, I called, "Just a cotton-pickin' minute! I want to go, too!"

"Me too, me too," came the chorus, like hounds picking up a fresh scent.

"Hurry up then," Jim urged. "I don't want to get in trouble for not checking in."

We all jumped in the skiff, and our visitors got in theirs. As we nosed the skiff up on the golden sand, the port captain came partway down the beach to meet us. He brought his six-year-old son with him, a most attractive curly-haired, brown-eyed child dressed in a uniform identical to his father's. He shook hands all around just the way his father did and obviously took his duties as assistant port captain very seriously.

Jim and the two port captains disappeared in the direction of the official office, and the rest of us started looking for a grocery store or anywhere we could buy a cold, cold soft drink. In the back of a very rustic little store, we found an ice chest full of almost quart-sized bottles of various sodas. Any other time, I would have thought that too large, but this time it was just right. The brand names were unfamiliar, but that made no difference. It was wet, it was cold, and for some strange reason we had all felt a great need for it.

The first evening, Randy and Jim organized a hootenanny on the verandah of the scrubby little unpainted store. The radio reception here must have been good, because any song popular in the US was well known here, English words and all. Around fifty young people turned out for the concert. Every time the music stopped, they shouted requests for new songs and sang right along. After two hours, Randy, the lead singer, told the crowd that he was running out of voice. Even then, they kept calling "Una mas! Una mas!" for another half hour before the concert really came to an end. We closed with "Amazing Grace," repeated three times and sung by the whole crowd with such fervor that it brought tears to my eyes. And not mine alone, I noticed.

We got to bed late and were up very early to catch a bus (another truck with planks for seats) going up into the highlands and the little town of Progresso. The road was very steep. With no backs on the seats, I felt as though I might at any time fall backward into the lap of the person behind me. I could imagine each one in turn falling back like a row of dominos.

⚓

If we expected to find some sort of business district in Progresso, we were disappointed. It was just a farming community with a church, a school, and possibly twenty houses — at least, that was all we saw along the main road.

While we were passing one house, we saw some small, very yellow bananas such as we had seen in Ecuador. They had caught our attention because they are very sweet bananas. We were speaking in English, and the man of the house did not. But he saw that we were interested in the bananas, so he whacked off a big stalk of them with his machete.

I gave him some small change I had with me, and he tried to refuse, saying, "No, it is a gift." Rand finally got him to accept it by saying, "Thank you, and this is our gift to you." It was only two dimes and a quarter, but it was the equivalent of more than half a day's wages in Ecuador.

We walked around eating bananas and wondering what on earth to do with the skins. This was a very tidy village, and we couldn't just toss them aside. At last we found a big square pit that looked as though it was used for compost; we buried the banana skins there, hoping we weren't desecrating someone's grave.

People came out of their houses, giving us avocados, limes, oranges, and papayas — as much as we could carry. Progresso and all of the highlands are wonderfully green, evidence of prodigious rainfall and fertile soil. Almost everything you could think of that thrives in a tropical climate is growing there.

We hadn't even checked the bus schedule's return trips because we knew it was all downhill and, therefore, easy walking — or so we thought. None of us had ever walked over four miles on a steep downhill slope. At first it was an easy grade, and we frisked along like a bunch of spring lambs. Then it got steeper, and our knees began to tire. After a while my knees got so shaky that I had to walk backward to give them a rest.

Through farms and jungle we had progressed about a mile when we reached the orange groves. We needed a good excuse for a rest, and this was a very good one. These oranges probably were planted originally as a commercial enterprise, but now they were common property. Anyone who wanted could pick oranges there. And what large, flavorful oranges they were! Eldon immediately decided he was going to build his retirement home here in the middle of an orange grove, a fancy the rest of us had some difficulty dislodging over the next few months.

⚓

Jim, the biologist, was spending his time studying plants, flowers, and butterflies that were new to him. Unlike most of the animals in these islands, the butterflies were very wary of human beings. Jim had been catching butterflies in his hands since he was a small child, but he couldn't get close enough to any of these. Even if the missing flight-or-fight instinct eventually causes the demise of most of the Islands' inhabitants, there will still be plenty of butterflies.

There will be plenty of goats, too. They were introduced here by the whaling and trading ships, and they've never been at all indifferent to the approach of *Homo sapiens.*

Carole and I, discovering that running was easier than walking, ran the rest of the way into Wreck Bay. We didn't arrive much ahead of the rest of the family, because they got a ride in a Jeep, but we felt more virtuous for having made the entire trip on foot.

⚓

During the after-dinner discussion that usually centers around "What do we do next?" it was decided to visit Kicker Rock, recommended by some of the local inhabitants. If not for their suggestion, we would hardly have noticed it. On our charts it looked like a speck of black pepper.

It was going to be another morning of rising at dawn so that we could spend some time there and get back before dark. But knowing there wouldn't be much to see for a couple of hours, I decided it would be a good morning to sleep later.

When I woke up, Kicker Rock was visible, looking like a baby's bootie on the horizon. It soon began to look more like a big hiking boot with a crack in it from top to bottom, straight as a plumb line and five hundred feet high.

"We can sail *Trilogy* through that," Jim said casually.

Shocked, Eldon said, "You're kidding; you could hardly get a rowboat through that crack."

"No, I'm not kidding." Jim was very positive. "I have it on good authority that the passageway through this rock is fifty feet wide. That'll give us ten feet on each side; boats go through there all the time."

"Boats as wide as this one?"

"Probably. Just wait and see. There's room."

Because the rock towered so far above us, the opening still looked awfully narrow, even at close range, but by this time Eldon was intrigued with the idea of taking the boat through.

"Take the movie camera and run the skiff through first," he directed Jim. "Then, if you have any doubts about *Trilogy* being able to get through, you can come on back. Otherwise stay on the other side and we'll run the boat through. You can get movies of us coming through."

Jim didn't come back, so we started through.

It was dark in there, with the sheer rock faces stretching up like a street of skyscrapers. I felt as though I could touch those lofty cliffs on either side as Eldon held an undeviating center course. The two sides matched perfectly where they had broken apart.

After Jim got his movies of *Trilogy* coming through, he wanted to take the skiff into another fissure that was almost invisible at the base of the rock. If it turned out to be a blind alley, we could always back out.

The opening was not a straight break like the one we

had just passed through; it was a triangle not much wider than our skiff, with the apex ten to twenty feet above us. The surge of three or four feet raised and lowered us dramatically as we went along.

On one side of this crevice was a ledge about two feet wide. The surge carried us above it, below it, and sometimes for a few moments on the same level. Every few feet, seals reclined on the ledge, but we didn't notice them at first because our eyes hadn't adjusted to the dim light. The first time I found myself face-to-face with a bright-eyed, curious seal, I was much more startled then he was. He acted as though loads of people came sloshing up to his slippery ledge all the time.

I was uneasily aware that this would be a very dangerous spot if a heavier sea were running. Just the small swell of a very calm sea was sending us more than a third of the way to the top in some places; the remaining triangle above us represented such a small part of the total volume that it wouldn't take much more to fill the whole thing with water.

Not a good place to be if that should happen.

When we got back aboard *Trilogy* and explained what we'd done, Eldon said, "I guess you know that even in this kind of sea you can get a swell twice as large as most of them. That wasn't a smart thing to do."

I definitely agreed.

⚓

We had plans for going to Barrington Island the next day, which required clearing customs. Jim went over as soon as the office opened, but it still took until noon, with Eldon not trying very hard to conceal his impatience.

Jim was getting a system worked out to thwart some of the time-wasting. Usually, copies in triplicate were required, but he had learned not to offer all three at once. If he did, more often than not they would ask for a fourth copy, and it was always a hassle making it out in the customs office. Now when they asked for a third or even fourth copy, he would produce it, and place it triumphantly on the official's desk. They gave him a certain grudging respect, recognizing that he had learned to play the game.

⚓

Barrington Island, twenty-eight miles due west of Wreck Bay on San Christobal, is a small, barren island with beaches as white as salt. We anchored there in twelve feet of water; the sun reflecting off the white, white sand sent pale golden scallops of light up to the top.

All over the little bay seals were playing. Just to see what they would do, I tossed an orange into the water. Immediately, a seal picked it up, balanced it on his nose, and tossed it to another seal. He (more probably she) twirled it around for a while before tossing it back to the one who had it first.

All the seals wanted to play this game, and to make it more fair and not just a game of keep-away, we tossed out several more oranges. Now that they knew what to expect, they caught them in mid-air. We had all seen seals do this in captivity and assumed that it was something they had been taught to do. These were wild seals — if indeed any of the animals here can be called wild. At least, they were untrained. This was natural, spontaneous behavior and fascinating to watch.

Carole couldn't stand not to be a part of this wonderful game. She dove off the front deck right into the middle of them. Immediately, a seal tossed an orange her way; she couldn't catch it on her nose, but she caught it with one hand and threw it back. The seal was delighted and did several spins with the orange before returning it. Pattie ripped off her tee-shirt, preparing to dive in.

"I wouldn't do that if I were you," Eldon said, putting a restraining hand on her shoulder.

"Why not?"

Nothing would appear to be less dangerous than what Carole was doing. But Eldon was watching the far shore, where a big male seal was making his way into the water.

"Because seals can be dangerous, that's why. I'm watching that big fellow over there. See how he's looking in all directions? If he heads this way, I want Carole out, on the double!"

While they were talking, Carole swam over to the boat to see what was delaying Pattie.

"Out of the water." Eldon said it quietly but firmly, at the same time giving Carole a hand up the ladder.

Carole glowered a little as she asked, "What's this all about?"

Eldon pointed to the big male seal, now making his way very rapidly to the center of the group of smaller seals. He was still glancing around, trying to locate the culprit who had disturbed his harem.

"I saw him come off the rocks over there, and he looked as though he meant trouble."

Later, the Angermeyer family in Academy Bay explained more about the danger of diving into a group of seals. "If the big fellow had been there in the group, you probably wouldn't have lived to get back on the boat," Gus Angermeyer told Carole. He rolled up his sleeve and showed us a scar from elbow to shoulder that you could have laid a three-quarter-inch halyard in, and still had room to spare. The first thing that popped into my mind was "shark," but it hadn't been ripped open by a shark.

"That was the work of a big male seal," Gus said, directing his remarks especially to Carole. "I was pulling in fish, and he just quickly slashed me; if I had been in the water instead of a boat, he'd have killed me very quickly."

"But, I thought the animals here were tame," Carole faltered.

"You're making the same mistake lots of people do," Gus said. "They are tame in the sense of having no fear of people. But to the male seal this is guarding the harem, and he will attack any creature that threatens it."

Ultimately, Carole was glad she did it anyway. "Okay it was dumb," she said after giving it due thought, "It was foolhardy. But it was still a wonderful experience, and no one can take it away from me."

Later, when Jim and Rand swam with two friendly seals called Lou-Seal and Sea-Seal through beautiful lava caves and undersea castles, we always kept a sharp watch for the big males that we called Big Daddies. Once I helped Jim out of the water just ahead of those lethal jaws!

By the time we ate some dinner, night was descending on this beautiful little harbor in Barrington Island. The moon, three-quarters full, shed a magical brilliance over the water. Little black heads, eyes sparkling in the moonlight, kept swimming around the boat. Every now and then one barked as if to say, "Why don't you come out and play some more?"

In the morning *Trilogy's* shadow, blue-violet against the sand, seemed to float just off the bottom of the lagoon. Here the sand is so fine that some of it is always in suspension, giving the water a milky-jade appearance.

⚓

Even though Barrington Island doesn't have much of anything growing on it, we still wanted to go ashore; the very barren terrain made us feel as though we might be the first ever to set foot on it — purely an illusion, of course. But this was genuine, uninhabited wilderness.

Setting foot on it proved to be more difficult than we had supposed. The jetty and all the surrounding area were covered with seals. A quick glance around showed no super-huge seals, ten times larger than the rest.

"Looks like Big Daddy has gone fishing," Carole observed.

Knowing we had nothing to fear from the smaller ones, we tied up the skiff and started stepping over and around the torpedo-shaped bodies that were stretched out everywhere. Eldon threw himself down on the sand between two seals, putting an arm around the neck of each one, and had Carole take a picture. Even this concerned them so little that they didn't even bother to open their eyes. With no natural enemies on the land, their sense of security was monumental.

Pattie and Carole started hiking along the shore. The boys were planning to cross the island, a walk of several miles. In the absence of any shade, the heat was intense. I wasn't sure I wanted to walk very far in any direction. As long as there was a breeze, these islands, surrounded by water not warmer than sixty degrees Fahrenheit, keep comfortably cool. But today no breath of wind off the Humboldt Current came to our rescue.

In lieu of anything to drink, we had brought along a bag of oranges. As soon as Eldon started throwing away orange peelings, we found ourselves surrounded by little iguanas about eighteen inches long with tails of similar length. They were the same color as the dust and rocks and resembled nothing so much as small dragons, even to the armor plates down the back. They scarfed down the peelings readily enough, but when Eldon threw them some orange sections, they went totally crazy. Such a troop of them gathered around him that he could hardly keep from tripping over them.

Food is scarce on this island. The big, fleshy leaves of a type of cactus seem to be what keep the iguanas from starving. People around here say these creatures are lazy, that they sit under the cactus plants and wait for the leaves to fall instead of stretching a bit and eating them off the trees. (These Opuntia cacti, similar to prickly pears, are twenty-five feet tall and have bark on the trunks, which as far as I'm concerned qualifies them as trees). These iguanas, though, certainly didn't show any signs of laziness — not while the oranges lasted.

Darwin's Islands

Barrington Island is not very colorful, but as Eldon and I turned to go back to the boat, we had a bird's-eye view of *Trilogy* riding at anchor. The bay was a real jewel, with colors ranging from cobalt to turquoise, fading to pale jade green near the shore.

As we rode back to *Trilogy* in the skiff, a friendly seal swam right up to the side of the boat. Eldon reached over and gently touched its nose; the seal didn't flinch. Even the most skeptical person would have to conclude that she wanted to be friends.

It was far cooler on the boat than on the island, and we were relieved when Carole and Pattie whistled from the shore. Carole hadn't had very long to adjust to the tropical climate, and she might well have had a heat stroke. When Jim and Rand got back from their trek, not until after dark, they were exhausted from the heat.

⚓

When we got back to Academy Bay, I knew I had laundry cowering in dark corners all over the boat. But *Molokai Girl* was in port. Phil, Fred, and Elsie came over to visit. Hand-laundering is something I never mind postponing.

When they left to take care of their own chores, it was already mid-afternoon. Reluctantly I set about getting our laundry over to the beach, where there were six large stationary tubs made from concrete, washboards and all.

Concrete washboards are guaranteed to peel the skin off your hands in three minutes or less, and I doubt if it took that long after the actual scrubbing began.

No one else was around, so I put the laundry in three different tubs, soaped them all with the salt-water soap we had bought in Academy Bay, and began scrubbing. I used the palms of my hands as much as possible; even so, my knuckles lost all their covering of skin almost instantly. The hardest part was wringing the clothes. Each piece had to be wrung at least three times as the water changed. I was barely well started when my wringing muscles went on vacation; they simply refused to cooperate anymore. I drained off the soapy water, sloshed the clothes up and down, and wondered what to do next.

At first, I didn't even recognize the answer to my dilemma.

A young Ecuadorian woman came down to give her baby a bath. As she soaped and rinsed her young son, she began taking stock of my situation. She must have seen at a glance that I was a novice in an occupation in which she was expert. She smiled a little at my feeble efforts and asked if I would like some help.

I understood the Spanish word for "help," and my "si, si!" was fervent. She turned her naked little son loose and bent to the task.

Even though she worked fast and efficiently, it took her nearly an hour to do all of the laundry. I knew that more than verbal thanks were in order. I started surreptitiously looking through my purse, hoping that Providence, which had sent help in my hour of need, had also made sure to supply me with a small amount of cash.

Sure enough, in a little compartment in my coin purse, and folded to about one inch across, was a dollar bill. She took it happily, gratefully, without any nonsense about doing the laundry as a favor.

The boys pointed out to me later that she probably made more money working for me in an hour than her husband did all day, because laboring men got the equivalent of seventy cents a day. I didn't care; to me the job was worth more than that, but the dollar was all I had.

⚓

While we stayed in Academy Bay, we were invited almost every evening to one of the Angermeyer homes.

The Angermeyers, disillusioned with Hitler's rise to power and distrustful of the direction his government seemed to be heading, had emigrated from Germany in the 1930s. Their worst fears were realized not too many years later. Meanwhile, with unremitting thrift, toil, energy, and a touch of genius, they built comfortable homes and rewarding lives for themselves in this remote spot.

They have one problem, however, that burrows away constantly at their substance and leaves them with a hollow victory.

Being people of education and refinement, not to mention considerable intelligence, they could not be satisfied with an eighth-grade-level education for their children. One by one, they sent their children to the mainland of Ecuador, or other countries, for higher education. They paid the steep costs on the income that can be derived from farming and fishing. Thus, the parents remained in genteel poverty while their educated offspring could only find suitable careers far away from home.

I remarked to Gus Angermeyer one day that it hardly seemed fair. After all their sacrifices, they didn't get to have their children and grandchildren around them.

He was surprised, possibly somewhat shocked, at this comment. "It's fair," he said. "We made our choice when we were young, and we chose to come here. I've never been sorry. Conditions are different for our children; they have to make different choices."

He gave me a quick, head-high, proud look. "Weak people think life isn't fair. Strong people *make* it be fair to them."

I had worked with a similar situation in Alaska, where Alaskan Native parents were reluctant to send high-ability children away for college because it meant the children would never come back to live. "I know you've worked tremendously hard," I conceded. "But it seems as though your losses are almost greater than your gains."

"Oh, no!" he said forcefully. "If we let our children sink to the level of barbarians because we were not willing to make the effort, if we refused them the chance to make the most of their talents — that would be unfair."

Gus's work alternated between fishing and running charters with the boat *Romance*, built originally for the motion picture *Hawaii*. As we left Academy Bay bound for the Plaza Islands the next day, we found *Romance* under full sail about three miles ahead of us. With all those sails lugging, she looked as though she should be making about twenty knots. In less than an hour, though, we had passed *Romance* and left her dwindling in the distance. We did get some good photographs of this authentic hermaphrodite brig, fully rigged and accurate in every detail.

⚓

During our time in Barrington Bay we hadn't been bothered by the seals' noise. Here on Plaza Island, however, seals lay all over the dock and every available landing place, and they were holding forth in full voice. Swimming around our boat or stretched out on the shore — whatever they did, they did noisily.

"Like a cross between a lambing pen and the stock-yards," Eldon said as he brought out the generator. Usually we hated to run the generator in the uncorrupted wilderness, but here we needed something to compete with the seals.

The Plaza Islands have an interesting groundcover that comes in two colors: red and yellow. They don't seem to mix although they are obviously the same kind of foliage. In between, patches of chartreuse green lichen and white sand set them off nicely. I asked Jim, "Do you suppose they may be like hydrangeas, changing color according to the acidity or alkalinity of the soil?"

"Not very likely," Jim said. "It looks as though they're all growing in the same kind of soil. Acid soil is usually wet with all the minerals leached out. This stuff looks just the opposite."

Darwin's Islands

On the far side of the island we found huge cliffs of black lava. That was a surprise, but our astonishment was far greater when the whole cliff under our feet started moving.

On the black lava they had been invisible. But when large black reptiles started diving off the cliff by the thousands, we realized that we had startled a huge colony of the famous marine iguanas that have puzzled scientists for several decades. Between dives they have to lie in the sun and get warm in order to digest their food. We probably disturbed them halfway through the process and caused all kinds of gastronomic problems.

Here on the weather side of the island, waves that surge all the way from Antarctica, unimpeded along the way by any land mass, crash against the cliffs. The steady beating has sculpted the rock into fantastic shapes. I wanted to sketch them, even though Eldon was taking photographs as we went along.

When we went out to the boat to get my sketchpad and charcoal, Eldon decided to stay. Jim and Rand were climbing a steep bluff on the other Plaza Island, and he wanted to be able to hear them when they came down to the beach. Carole volunteered to go back with me.

I offered her sketching materials, but she declined saying, "I think the artistic talent in this family fizzled out before it got to me. Maybe I'll do some shell-collecting."

So far, the shell-collecting had been disappointing in these islands; the shells were small and drab in color. Almost immediately, though, Carole found one that was brilliantly colored and totally different from anything we had seen so far. It was just over an inch long, bright red, and covered with raised dots in concentric rings.

Carole brought it over where I was sketching. "Is this any good?" she asked.

"Anything as pretty as that would be good even if there were lots of them around, but I've never seen another one like it. It isn't in my shell books, either."

"Wow! Maybe I've found something really good! Will we have to wait until we get back to civilization to find out what it is?"

"I don't think so," I said. "The Darwin Station in Academy Bay is a scientific center. I'm sure that one of the scientists can identify it for you. If not, they'll have reference books that can."

What I didn't know then was how incredibly busy those scientists are. They work and plan for years to get a six-month appointment to the station and then try to get three years' work done in half a year.

⚓

On the leeward side of the island we found Pattie floating around near the shore in her one-man life raft — possibly napping a little. Her raft had drifted over into the area where a flock of pelicans were fishing, and one of them did a power dive not two inches from the side of the raft, splashing her thoroughly. She did a quick sit-up, wet and startled.

"C'mon over here," Carole called. "They don't want you out there; that's their fishing ground."

"Right," I added, "that was just a warning. Next time he's going to deflate your raft. Anyway, why don't you take that thing back to the boat and get the skiff? We can't all fit in that."

Eldon had already seen us and brought the skiff over. With their usual precise sense of timing, Rand and Jim whistled to be picked up just as dinner was ready to serve.

"You should have seen all the pelicans," Pattie told her brothers, "and the boobies and the tropic birds...."

"You haven't seen anything yet," Jim interrupted. "If you're interested in bird watching, wait till we get to Tower Island. There are millions of them there!"

I thought the expression "millions" was just normal hyperbole, never imagining there could be birds in that quantity.

Darwin's Islands

⚓

In the morning the wind was right to move out from the anchorage without starting the motor. We were well on the way to Tower Island before Pattie, Carole, or I woke up.

Long before we could see the island, we could see a big, black cloud over it. As we drew nearer, the sky began to look as though it had been sprinkled liberally with black pepper; closer still, we could detect movement among all the little pepper dots. Birds, in such numbers as I had never seen before, wheeled and swirled in this black mass. I marveled that they could fly in such close proximity without bumping into each other.

Later, when I saw how many birds were sitting on the ground, I wondered if the rest of them were flying simply because there was no room for them to land. How the water here must teem with fish to support them all!

Tower Island is a volcanic crater with an opening on one side, through which we came with the boat. The gap comprises about one-eighth of this almost-perfect circle. On the other side lies a lovely semi-circular beach of pale, not quite white sand. The rest of the crater is sheer cliffs. We could approach them from the beach; from the water, not without great difficulty.

We hurried over to the beach, laden with various kinds of photographic equipment. In lieu of any cameras — my Insta-matic having rusted beyond any usefulness — I was carrying two sets of binoculars. The largest one, heavier than most of the cameras, proved totally worthless because we could walk within six inches of almost any of the nesting birds.

These ground-nesting birds are doubtless the condo-minium dwellers of the avian world. The gulls and the boobies were industriously hatching nests full of eggs. Some of the frigate birds had hatched, although they were still in down. The nests were so close together that we could hardly step between them. Nor were they segregated according to species. Side by side were gulls, boobies, and frigate birds — truly an integrated neighborhood.

Although the birds showed no alarm at our presence, it was still hard to believe that we could photograph them without causing some commotion. Carole kneeled by the nest of a blue-footed booby and leaned closer until the nest filled her view finder. Just as she clicked the shutter, the fuzzy head of a baby booby thrust itself out from under the mother's wing and looked at us with sharp, bright eyes.

Several nests over, a large silver-white gull was concentrating on turning over her eggs, which all birds do by instinct to insure proper development of the embryos. Had she been at all worried by our presence, she certainly wouldn't have chosen that precise moment to reveal everything in her nest.

Farther back in the brush, we found wrens — at least they looked more like wrens than anything else we could think of, almost as small as hummingbirds — and finches and other birds whose nests are built up off the ground. They seemed less at ease as we tramped by, but even they were not sufficiently disturbed to leave their nests.

Pattie and Carole walked a quarter of a mile through the scrubby brush looking for baby birds. They couldn't find any nests unattended by parents. If there were babies, they were well covered.

Before evening a fresh breeze came up. Eldon was up and down most of the night, checking anchor gear and making sure we weren't drifting. The crater was deep, and the holding ground for an anchor wasn't large. Fearing a mishap, he nearly decided to leave in the early morning. Then, unpredictably, the wind subsided, and he decided to stay for another day.

The boys assembled movie equipment and went ashore right after breakfast. Eldon had tramped through the bird nests taking photographs for several hours the previous day, so he elected to stay on the boat rebuilding a valve on the galley stove.

Darwin's Islands

It was late in the morning before the girls and I got our chores done and were ready to go. They took a big bottle of shampoo because they thought they could get their hair rinsed better ashore than on the boat. As soon as we got the skiff pulled up on the beach, Pattie ducked her head in the water and proceeded to work up a good lather. The water was crystal clear, turning to dark blue in the crater's depths. It certainly looked as pure as it could get. A curious little seal was watching with great interest; Pattie hadn't seen her yet, but when her head came up above water after the first rinse, the seal's head was right beside her. They were both startled — Pattie because she wasn't expecting company, and the seal because she had never before found herself surrounded by soap suds. The seal tried to shake the soap out of her eyes, and then dived down to rinse it away. Pattie bobbed up and down a few times rinsing, and the seal bobbed, too. Then they swam around together very companionably. I took the binoculars and searched the bay, but couldn't see any big seals out on the rocks.

When two more seals showed up wanting to play, Carole and I swam out to meet them. Even an Olympic swimmer would feel outclassed swimming with a seal, and they really did swim circles around us. Sometimes Carole and I had to float for a while to rest, and it was obvious that the seals thought this was senseless. They barked to show that we could be doing something more productive. I'm not a long-distance swimmer, and I finally had to head for the beach. Carole and Pattie were ready to come, too. Not so, our pet seals; they swam up and down in shallow water begging us to come back in the water.

The three of us walked farther inland than we had on the previous day, and now we were rewarded by finding many baby birds — cute, fuzzy-headed, alert youngsters. As we had surmised, at this stage of their development it takes both parents to feed them.

319

Trilogy

Beautiful white tropicbirds were sailing around overhead. Their nests were over on the cliffs where Jim and Rand had gone, but those cliffs were high and very perpendicular, the access over land rugged in the extreme. We confined our walking to reasonably level ground; the thong sandals we wore were hardly suitable for mountain climbing.

After two hours, not counting the time we spent swimming with the seals, we heard a piercing whistle from the other side of the crater. Jim and Rand were down from the cliffs and ready to be picked up with the skiff. Anyway, it was time to round up something to eat; no one had taken any lunch along, and it was long past lunchtime.

Eldon wasn't enthusiastic about spending another night on anchor watch. Even if someone else took over, he would still be uneasy and probably sleep poorly. So, we headed over to James Bay, where we anchored a few boat-lengths away from a fish-buying boat from Manta.

Everywhere we went, the fish-buying boats were good to us, but especially so in Ecuador. They would say, "Well, what are you out of? We'll see if we have some.... Raisins? Sure, we've got plenty of raisins. Powdered sugar? Yeah, we've got it — might be a bit lumpy. (It usually was; I spent many hours sifting it.) Chocolate? Sure, lots of chocolate. Come on over and get it."

In addition to the non-essentials that we had gradually run out of, they always had a good supply of fresh vegetables and usually some kind of fruit. Our staples — fish, rice, and sauerkraut — were good at sustaining life, but these other things lifted the spirits.

I didn't know for a long time that chocolate is one of Ecuador's most important exports. A Swiss lady living in Academy Bay told me about it. "The Swiss," she said, "pride themselves on making the world's finest chocolate, but I think the chocolate made here in Ecuador is even better."

In the morning we looked around and didn't see any good landing places near the spot where we had spent the night. We ran along the shore for some distance until we saw a place that had once been inhabited. Many years ago a salt mine had operated here. When it was closed down, somehow the last workers to be evacuated were forgotten and left here for five months. They survived by hunting wild goats. By the time someone finally remembered to pick them up, they had nearly starved to death.

Of course, Jim and Eldon decided this would be a good place to go goat hunting. The goats, however, having been placed here for no other purpose than to be hunted, have had no opportunity to develop the passivity toward man that the native-born animals possess. Rather, they are driven by an overpowering desire to get as far away from human beings as possible — which they did, with our hunters following in hopeless pursuit.

While Pattie, Carole, and I explored the old mine and the buildings on shore, Randy stayed on the boat on one of his search-and-destroy missions. When we came back, he had blitzed through the boat like a super Mr. Clean, leaving such order in his wake that the rest of us were temporarily disoriented, not to mention seized with anxiety over which of our prized pieces of rubble he had thrown overboard.

The rest of the family are congenital junk-collectors, but Randy can be ruthless in his quest for order. Eldon always said after one of these sessions, "Just don't tell me what you threw away; if I don't know I'll probably never miss it. If I know, I'll be forever thinking of ways I might have used it."

The rest of us might well have said the same thing. I had an uneasy feeling that some of my precious possessions had been summarily dispatched — but I could never be sure what they were.

The goat hunters came back tired and frustrated. They decided to channel their efforts the next day into getting some good movies of the local fauna. Rand and Jim carried the tripods and all the cumbersome sixteen-millimeter movie equipment up to a lake nearby, where they had seen a flock of flamingos. With great effort and even greater patience they got themselves positioned so the flamingos were swimming directly toward the camera.

And then — total catastrophe!

Crashing through the brush came sixty tourists from one of the charter boats. The flamingos took flight in panic and disarray; the close-up shots were never to be.

Jim and his dad went hunting once more, but the rifle sight had not been adjusted for a long time, and Jim overshot. The goats didn't stay around to see if he was going to get more accurate later on. Jim has always been a very good shot. He even won a sharpshooter's medal from the local rifle club when he was a kid. To make his frustration complete, a sleek little yawl came into the harbor, and the skipper shot a goat within an hour after his arrival.

Soon after the dispirited hunters returned, *Molokai Girl* came into the harbor, and the successful hunter from the yawl invited all of us over to the beach to enjoy a goat barbecue. Carole, Pattie, and I weren't too particular about who produced the goat just so we had a chance to participate. While we were busy making barbecue sauce and chocolate cake, Jim was over on the beach with a target, correcting the gun sight.

These equatorial islands get amazingly cold when the wind comes in off the water. They had a big bonfire blazing on the beach, and everyone stayed close to it all evening. The goat was a big — therefore, old — one, and not as tender as it might have been. But with a big green salad from *Molokai Girl*, fresh bread from *Trilogy*, and soft drinks supplied by the captain of the fish-buying boat, it was a real feast.

Before the fish boat left in the morning, they filled our water tanks with pure water from their water-maker. That was a real boon; without it we would have had to go back to Wreck Bay or Academy Bay for water fairly soon.

Darwin's Islands

⚓

Every day was like a holiday None of us had ever experienced so much discretionary time, not since we were children. We all had our chores to do, but still lots of time for
swimming, fishing, hiking, reading, painting (for me), and
writing. We all wrote letters, even though they were mailed
in an irregular manner. Eldon kept up his diary — every
day since he was sixteen years old he had written a few
lines about the high points of his day, but never with this
luxury of time to complete his thoughts.

It was on the way to the Galapagos Islands that I started
writing our story about building the *Trilogy* and making this
trip.

Also, for the first time in many years, Eldon had time to
read. He was almost overwhelmed by the reading material
he'd missed while working sixteen hours a day. Here in the
Galapagos he finished *Cry The Beloved Country* by Alan
Paton, and now he was reading the story of Dr. Semmelweicz,
who demonstrated that puerperal fever was controllable by
antiseptic techniques and whose life-saving findings were
ignored by the arrogant medical community. Eldon had read
only the first three chapters and already he was angry.

Jim, with the newly sighted rifle, experienced much
better success on his next hunting trip. With several boats
in the harbor and all their crews hunting goats, we had a
barbecue almost every night. Of course, after the barbecue
dinners we had a sing-along that went on into the night.

⚓

Early in the afternoon five days after we first anchored
on James Island, we ran over to Jervis Island. Though it was
after dark, a full moon gave almost daylight visibility — or
so it seemed.

Sometime before dawn I heard Rand shouting, "Dad!
Wake up! We're drifting!"

Eldon was on deck in two jumps, and I wasn't far

behind him. We had drifted out of the harbor and several miles beyond that. The anchor was hanging straight down, all its chain run out. Pulling all of that up, with a forty-five pound anchor on the end of it, was a back-breaking job. When he and Jim finally got it all on deck, Rand drew a few deep breaths and observed, "Nothing like getting an early start, I always say."

"If you mean 'start' as in 'startled,'" I retorted, "you're right; there's nothing quite like it. But if you don't mind, I'd rather begin my day some other way."

The wind was favorable for a run to Sullivan Bay, noted for unusual rock and lava formations and for garnet-colored olivine sand. We had wanted to go there before. With the wind hopelessly against us, though, we had settled for other ports. Now the time was right.

The part of the island that we approached was filled with cinder cones. If they were all erupting at one time — and they probably had been, once — this would have been the greatest fireworks display this side of the Inferno.

One thing about being on a boat practically all of the time — we never wasted a second getting ashore whenever there was an opportunity.

Eldon had his heart set on climbing the highest peak back of the harbor. Not finding anyone else with a similar ambition, he set off by himself. The rest of us walked along the shore, greeting the ever-present seals and looking for the fabled wine-colored sand. Most beaches were white, brown, tan, or yellow — ordinary sand, not the product of super-heating in a volcano. Near the dark-red volcanic pinnacles, the sand was a deep maroon color. The beach material was translucent like garnets and amethysts; in fact, it was a type of glass.

Jim and Rand, making it more of a hike than a stroll, soon outdistanced Pattie, Carole, and me. Pattie had been deliberately walking slowly because she didn't want Jim to hear what she was going to say. The unusual variety of sand, all within the same bay, had given her an idea. We were all aware that Jim's birthday was coming up in a couple of days, and it was going to strain our ingenuity to think of something to give him.

"Mom," she said, "if I get some of all these kinds of sand, will you draw me a picture of *Trilogy?*" She was planning her sand-painting as she went along. "I want to make the background out of this deep red; that way most of the area will be of the olivine sand, and it will have more sparkle and shine than the others. I want the pure white for the sails and hull. The tan color is almost identical to our decks and trim, and I'll use the other colors for the water, and variations in the water's color."

"Sounds good to me," I agreed. "Sure, I'll draw it for you. We have some little pieces of Masonite around that should be a good, strong support for it."

"What'll I use to stick it on with? I know how to make flour paste, but I don't think it would hold too well. I don't want the sand falling off."

"I have a big bottle of Elmer's glue in my painting stuff," I said.

At this point, a most beguiling distraction showed up. Not fifteen feet away, motionless in the shade of a big rock, lay a tiny seal puppy watching us intently with his big, brown eyes.

"Ohhhh! Isn't he cute!" Carole exclaimed, stopping about five feet from the little seal. "Do you suppose his mother has deserted him or been eaten by a shark?" She took another step toward him, but I put my hand on her shoulder and stopped her.

"Hey! Don't touch him!" I said, rather more sharply than I had intended.

"Why not? He won't bite, will he?"

"I don't think so; that isn't what I'm worried about. If you touch him, it might make his mother reject him when she comes back. It would be just the same as killing him."

"Gee." Carole was really subdued.

"Maybe he's already been deserted," Pattie argued. "If his mother is here on the beach, she should have come over by now."

"His mother is probably out fishing. They leave these little fellows for days at a time." I was glad at this moment that I had done some reading about the habits of seals. "When they do feed them, the milk is so rich that the baby seals can go for a long time between feedings."

Still, when the little seal began following us down the beach, it was hard to keep the girls from picking him up. "Let's walk slowly back to his rock," I said, "and then run away; I don't think it's a good idea for him to be very far from the spot where his mother left him."

He barked and cried for a minute. But we could go faster than he could, and he settled down again in the rock shadow.

All evening we worried about the baby seal. Sharks eat seals, and the mother might not be coming back. Early the next morning we went back to the big rock where we had found him. At first we thought he was gone, then we realized that the shadow was falling on the opposite side of the rock now. There he was, with his mother — certainly not hungry any more. His little sides were so distended that he looked as though he had swallowed a volleyball.

Though he didn't want to follow us down the beach anymore, we felt good all day because this potential tragedy had had a happy ending.

To keep it a surprise, Pattie had to work on the sand-painting in her stateroom. Meanwhile, Carole came up with a birthday present for Jim that surprised all of us. With a little piece of driftwood, a few shells, and more than a little ingenuity, she made an owl sitting on the branch of a tree; a solid piece of lava served as the base. It was cute and clever. For some time Randy had been working on a macramé belt; Jim had admired it prodigiously, but he had no idea that it was intended for him.

I knew that Jim would prefer a pie for his birthday rather than a cake, but I was nearly out of pie-making materials. Looking through my cookbooks, I ran across a recipe for cranberry-raisin pie using canned, whole cranberries. At least those were ingredients we had. It turned out to be very good.

Jim was the one who caught the fish for his birthday dinner. Without it, I would have had to open some goat meat that I had just finished canning two days before.

It was here on James Island that Jim and Rand met their swimming partners, Lou-Seal and Sea-Seal. We had discovered delightful, limpid tidepools along the shore and, farther out, deep lava caves that resembled a submerged city. For sheer beauty, it would be hard to find anything surpassing these glowing, blue waterways, shading from turquoise and pale green to deep blue-purple with their turrets, spires, and arches of countless submerged castles.

The seals loved to play follow-the-leader through these labyrinthine ways. Sometimes, exercising a commendable degree of common sense, the boys refused to follow, realizing that their guides were smaller, more agile, and much more streamlined than they. When this happened, the seals came back and barked at them, calling them spoil-sports and party poopers.

After the second day of swimming with the seals, it occurred to all of us that we should have some movies of this once-in-a-lifetime sport. So we carried ashore cameras, tripods, film, and lenses and set up beside one of the best pools. For twenty minutes the cameras rolled, getting some marvelous pictures.

Then, out of nowhere, came one of the Big Daddies. He was headed straight for Jim. I yelled at Jim and reached out my hand. The big bull made a powerful lunge as Jim was clambering up out of the pool. His feet left the water just six inches ahead of the seal's vicious jaws. I glanced around to see if Rand was in danger, but he had just gotten out on the other side of the pool — not because he realized a Big Daddy was attacking, but because Lou-Seal and Sea-Seal had vanished.

We vainly hoped that the big seal would bug off after the boys were out of the water, but he had no intention of doing so. He cruised around close by, keeping the female seals at a distance. Clearly, he planned to remain in control of the situation.

After waiting thirty or forty minutes for him to leave, we reluctantly picked up our photographic gear, took it back to the boat, and headed for China Hat Cove.

It was still early in the day. Those of us who hadn't hiked up one of the craters when we first landed decided that now was a good time to do it. "I think I hiked up the tallest one," Eldon said, declining our invitation. "From there I could see into most of the rest of them. It's hard going — worth it the first time, probably not again."

He wasn't kidding; it was hard going. I had read that hiking boots could be worn to shreds in a few days hiking these craters of the moon. A trail existed until we got to the steep sides of the crater, but the trail wasn't much use to us because it was covered with seals who absolutely refused to move to accommodate us. Like a coolie hat, for which it was named, the crater sloped very steeply toward the top, and sometimes we slid back one step for every step we advanced. At last we stood on the rim — and instinctively stepped back a few feet.

The sides of the crater were totally sheer, two hundred feet of rocky cliff, straight down. There was no possibility of hiking in, not without mountain-climbing equipment. If anything ever came out of that crater, it came straight up as though shot from a cannon.

In unspoken agreement, we started back down the slope — easier going on the way down. We hadn't exactly conquered the crater, but we had seen it and we were ready to move on. Eldon had the boat all ready when we got back; the evening was warm and pleasant as we tacked down the coast in the direction of Academy Bay.

With big surf pounding the shores, evidence possibly of a storm thousands of miles away, and a heavy current setting us relentlessly shoreward, we tacked constantly to get sea room. *Trilogy* rode the lumpy seas very well. I don't pretend to be as good a sailor as *Trilogy*, but at least I didn't get sick. Neither did I take any marezine; that is always a small triumph for me.

⚓

Carole was on pins and needles to find out what kind of shell the strange and beautiful red one was. So, almost as soon as we got ashore, we walked over to the Darwin Station. Since the time when Carole picked it up, we had asked several people here in the Islands about it, and so far we hadn't found anyone who had even seen one like it. That only increased Carole's suspense and her conviction that she had found something out of the ordinary.

It was no trouble at all getting into the Darwin Station, but after that we began to wonder if we had suddenly become invisible. The scientists kept on peering into their microscopes and making notes. Even when they left their desks for a few moments, they still couldn't see us. No one looked up long enough to say "Hi," not to mention "Could I help you?"

There was no point in staying, but we did think the shell might be rare enough to deserve some attention, especially since it had been discovered almost on the Station's doorstep. But we couldn't find a scientist to look at it — or us.

Convinced that this was the unfriendliest, the most indifferent bunch of people we had ever encountered, we were preparing to leave when Carole simply exploded. "What a bunch of creeps!"

A young man, probably a graduate assistant, was straightening up test tubes and arranging pickled specimens of sea life. He was only an arm's length away, and he jumped as though just then becoming aware of our presence.

"Is there something I can help you with?" he asked in genuine American English.

"There sure is," Carole said, delighted that her outburst had somehow broken through the academic hypnosis. She pulled the shell out of her jacket pocket. "We can't find this shell in the books we have, and we wondered if someone here could help us identify it."

"Shells aren't my specialty," he said. "But over in that corner are some books about the size of an unabridged dictionary. It should be in one of those."

"Thank you," I said, looking at the huge stack of books. Finding our little shell in them might take longer than we could stay. "If you could give us some idea where to start looking...."

I wanted him to know we appreciated the help he had offered, in this place where human beings became invisible, but his assistance was going to be much more valuable if he carried it a mite farther.

He walked over to the stack of books and selected one, at the same time telling us the scientific names we should look for, names we could neither pronounce or remember. Then, suddenly, there was our shell — a color photograph bigger than life and accurate in every detail.

"Here's your shell," he announced, "but I don't know how it got to these islands. It says here that it's only found in the Red Sea and the Gulf of Aden." He wanted to know exactly where we had found it. Nothing in this encyclopedia of shells gave us any clue about how it happened to be on the beach at Plaza Island.

"I wouldn't worry about it," he said. "It could have been lost from someone's shell collection, or — who knows? I'll give you a far-out theory. Maybe some dope is trying to start a colony of them over here."

He noticed our incredulous looks and added, "Hey! Stranger things have happened. People are always trying to introduce things into these islands for gosh knows what kind of reasons. That would be highly irresponsible, but we're trying to protect these islands from invasion by foreign plants and animals, and we know that it happens."

We thanked the young man, who had probably spent irreplaceable time on our problem.

⚓

On the way back to the boat Carole asked to be let off on one of the visiting yachts. In town, a few days before, she had met the lady owner of the boat and had been invited to visit.

Being unacquainted with all the fine points of nautical etiquette, Carole didn't first bang on the hull and request permission to board. Instead, she climbed onto the deck and knocked on the companionway doors.

Only the man was aboard. He was drunk and furious at having his nap disturbed. He stormed out onto the deck and demanded that Carole leave at once. Jim was just tying up the skiff on *Trilogy*, not more than sixty feet away, and he started back at once, but that wasn't quick enough for this ill-mannered fellow. He grabbed Carole and, after a short struggle, tossed her into the water when Jim and the skiff were only ten feet away. With great presence of mind, Carole grabbed her glasses before she hit the water; she didn't have an extra pair in reserve.

On the *Trilogy* we watched this little drama in disbelief. Such a thing had never happened to any of us during all our years on the water.

Jim helped Carole into the skiff and proceeded to tell this incredibly boorish man what he thought of him. Long before he was through, the jerk vanished into the boat and pulled the hatch shut.

Trilogy

Back on *Trilogy*, Carole kept saying, "But his wife invited me!"

At first she was crying in shock and frustration, but her sense of humor soon reasserted itself. She started laughing about the whole ridiculous situation. "I couldn't believe he intended to push me overboard," she said. "But, just in case, I kept twisting around, keeping him closer to the edge." That, of course, is why he had to pick her up and throw her in the water.

The local people started telling us about the strange people on this boat. They kept all their food under lock and key. Their three children were never fed — just turned loose ashore. The local ladies told us they didn't mind feeding the kids, but it bothered them that their parents always bought the most expensive brands of liquor. The fact that the parents bought very little food made the children's story credible.

I was horrified that no one seemed to be able to do anything except keep the children from starvation. "In our country, some government agency would have had those children in custody long ago," I said to one of the concerned ladies who lived near the harbor. "Can't someone do something?"

She shook her head sadly. "I've checked everything I know of to get some help for the kids. Unless the parents physically abuse the children ashore before witnesses, the government can't intervene."

Kind-hearted woman that she was, she didn't want us to worry about the children as we traveled. "The children will never starve as long as they stay here," she assured me. "But I worry about their future. The boy tells me they are beaten severely if they touch any food beyond the pittance their parents give them. He's thirteen years old; he needs food to grow on. Also, he's getting very angry. That will be something to reckon with in a few years. It's a tragedy already, but I'm afraid there is worse to come."

Darwin's Islands

⚓

We were all ashore taking care of various problems before we started on the next leg of our journey — over the longest unobstructed sea passage on this planet.

I had a little time, so I walked for about three-quarters of a mile along the beach. A small fishing boat not more than thirty-five feet long was resting on its keel, propped up haphazardly with planks and bamboo poles. Even out of the water it looked small for an ocean-going boat, and any boat that leaves the harbor here becomes an ocean-going boat.

Some repairs were in progress; the owner, quite well along in years, was giving directions in English, and his crew spoke only Spanish. "Now, this here board'll have to go in right there." He pointed to a place on the hull where the board was to be scarfed in.

A veritable torrent of Spanish answered him.

"Right," he replied. "The X goes up. Put it under that other X next to the porthole."

Just as though they were all speaking the same language, the board was set in place.

"Don't you have to tell them anything in Spanish?" I asked after introducing myself.

"If I did," he said, "it would never get done. I don't know a single word of that dang language, and I guess I'm just too old to start learning it now."

At first, I thought the boat's name was HI, because those were the only letters painted on the bow. But he pointed out that the two portholes served as Os, and the real name was *Ohio*. I wondered if he'd been cruising the islands in this boat and had to stop here for emergency repairs. The boat looked as though it had been out of the water for several months.

"Heck, no! I'm a Peace Corps worker," he said. When he saw that I was just as bewildered as ever, he explained. "I've been in the cattle business all my life, and when the government of Ecuador needed an expert in that line, the

Peace Corps sent me. I couldn't pass their language course, but that wasn't as important as my knowledge about cattle."

He sat down on an up-ended box and motioned for me to do likewise. "Y'see," he continued, "here in these islands they don't have any bovine tuberculosis nor undulant fever, and they sure don't want any, either. So for years 'n' years no new cattle could be brought in."

He paused to see if I was understanding what he was telling me, nodded his head as though I had passed some kind of test, and went on. "But there's problems with that, too. After a while you get too much inbreeding, 'n' that isn't good for the stock."

He paused again, this time to see how the boat repairmen were doing. "They know a lot more about boat-building than I do," he threw in parenthetically. "I go through this rigmarole of giving orders, 'n' then they do just what they'd have done anyway."

"Well, to get back to the cows," he said after a long pause. "I'm here to decide which breeds will improve their blood lines and to supervise the artificial insemination. It'll take a while, but I got nothing but time."

"No family?" I prompted.

"Yes and no," he answered. "I'm seventy-three years old; my wife is dead and my children all grown and moved away from the old home town. The only thing I really miss here is corn flakes."

"Corn flakes?" For a moment I thought he was kidding.

"Yep," he repeated. "Good old Kellogg's Corn Flakes. I get so hungry for them things, I just ordered a case by parcel post. Won't be here for weeks."

"That will be horrendously expensive, won't it?" I asked, knowing that freight was charged by bulk, not weight.

"Reckon so," he agreed complacently. "But it won't cost more'n a thousand dollars, I s'pose." He gave me a mischievous look, eyes twinkling. "An' right now I'm so hungry for some corn flakes, I don't care if it does."

He gave his attention back to the boat, and I asked, "What are you going to do with your boat when it's finished?"

"You've probably noticed," he said, "that there aren't many fishin' streams around here. I'm a stream fisherman, but I think I can learn to catch fish out there in the ocean. People tell me you don't have to get far offshore to get good fishin'."

"How long will it be before your boat is ready?" I asked.

"Who knows?" he shrugged. "I'm in no hurry; people give me fish all the time. I just want the fun of catchin' them."

⚓

Plans were underway to go up in the highlands the following day, starting early in the morning. John Spare, who owns a travel agency in New York, has a ranch about four miles up in the hills. He'd invited the whole family to come and stay overnight.

I was trying to finish my picture of James Bay to give Captain Lasso, the boat skipper who had given us so many supplies. He had seen the painting in progress and asked if I would paint one for him. We were scheduled to leave soon for the Marquesas Islands, and I knew if I didn't finish it before his next trip to the Galapagos, I wouldn't have an opportunity to give it to him. Obviously, I was going to be staying on the boat.

Eldon planned to hike up and back the same day so I wouldn't be alone there overnight.

They hiked up the mountain at daybreak, early enough to meet the donkey trains delivering milk to Academy Bay. After a steep climb the way leveled off, and they found themselves in citrus orchards and avocado groves. Eldon headed back downhill soon after noon. He was not quite halfway back to the harbor when he developed a severe pain in his hip; after that he made very poor time, limping in late in the afternoon. I put him to bed and gave him some aspirin, something he would have refused normally. Because he had hardly ever taken a pain killer of any kind, it was effective, and he promptly went to sleep.

The next morning we awoke to the patter of rain on the deck. Eldon's hip was better, and he was never able to understand why he had had so much trouble with it. We both felt bad that the kids would have to walk back in the rain, but it was a warm rain.

Shortly before noon, Pattie and Carole arrived, their faces glowing with something more than exertion. They had an aura of happiness.

"What happened?" I asked.

"Yes," Eldon added, "you two look as though you'd both won your dream hero on The Dating Game."

"Better than that," Carole declared with conviction.

"It was like this," Pattie began. "We'd left the ranch and were walking down the hill when it began raining very hard."

"Really hard rain," Carole took up the story, "and we ran over to one of the avocado groves that was still fairly dry underneath."

"And we stopped there under the trees," Pattie continued. "And suddenly we had this weird feeling we were meeting an appointment there that had been determined since the year one..."

"...Divinely appointed," Carole interrupted. "Or at least supernaturally. There was a power all around us that I didn't understand, and I was maybe a little afraid of it, and before I realized what I was saying, I said 'Let's pray' — just like that. I've never done that before. Never been much of a pray-er really."

"We didn't have any idea what we were going to pray

about," Pattie went on, "but if Carole hadn't said that, I would have. I would have just felt compelled to. What we really did pray about was to ask Jesus to take over our lives."

"Yes," Carol broke in, "to really be in control, because we're just spinning our wheels trying to run things ourselves."

"He answered our prayer right then — instantly!" Pattie continued. "I know He did because we were just covered and overwhelmed and filled with such a feeling of happiness. You can't even imagine how it felt!"

"I feel so secure," Carol added, "as though I could fly — or just float — and Jesus would be there holding me up."

"Praise the Lord!" Eldon exclaimed, hugging first Carole, then Pattie, then adding me and hugging all three of us. "I've hoped and prayed for this day!"

Carole went into the cabin and brought out the accordion. Turning to me, she said, "I know you thought it was practically a tragedy that you left all your music back in Washington, and all we had was hymn books, but when I was learning to play the accordion, every one of those hymns was preaching a sermon to me. Some people don't pay any attention to the words they sing, but I can't help noticing them, and they really found a place in my heart."

We sang for some time with Carole playing. Then Rand arrived and joined in singing and prayers. The girls told Randy their story, and then, when Jim came, they told it again for him. In spite of his professed agnosticism, Jim seemed really glad.

Eldon who doesn't at all understand Jim's religious doubts and antagonisms, only said, "Maybe he's nearer the Kingdom than he thinks."

⚓

From the day we had found ourselves surrounded by acres of oranges free for the taking, Eldon had always planned to come back and get as much of the fruit as we would need for our crossing to French Polynesia. So it was

337

back to Wreck Bay, not only for oranges but also to finish some dental work for Eldon.

The same truck/bus with plank seats took us as far as the orange groves. In addition to several big burlap sacks that we all helped fill with oranges, Eldon brought along a five-gallon plastic container and the juicer we had brought from Mexico. As the mound of orange skins mounted, Eldon thought about the little iguanas on Barrington and Plaza Islands — ugly little things, but somehow they had won a place in his affections.

"Too bad we're not going back there," he said. "These orange peelings would never be wasted. I'd give them a bunch of oranges, too. It would almost be worth the trip just to watch them."

When we had our quota of oranges picked, we began to think about the Progresso bus; no one had the foggiest notion when it was scheduled to return. With all these oranges, we couldn't just walk down the hill. "I'll stay here with the oranges, and the rest of you can walk back if you want to," Eldon said. "Either somebody will give me a ride, or the bus will come by. No use wasting everybody's time."

Carole, Pattie, and I decided to walk, but Jim and Rand elected to stay with Eldon. It wasn't a bad choice; we were only halfway to town when Eldon and all the rest with their oranges came by in a Jeep.

⚓

The next day Jim and I bought groceries for the big crossing. We went back to the same little store on whose verandah the boys had staged their first sing-along in these islands.

Our freshly ground wheat flour made wonderful bread, but there were still things that needed white flour. We were out of that. The only size this store had was one hundred pounds, and I hated to buy that much. The roly-poly proprietress, who thought that I was hesitating over the price (ten dollars) and not the size, kept assuring me that this was the finest flour obtainable. It was, too, the best pastry flour I ever had.

In the long run, I was even glad we had one hundred pounds of it.

I didn't know, either, that Ecuador produces some of the finest vanilla in the world. When she brought out a large bottle of the "buneeya," I was very skeptical because it seemed to be a syrup, and not what I was used to. It was far better than what I was used to; later, I often wished I had gotten more of it.

Jim had arranged with the little lady to save a flat of tomatoes for us when the next produce ship came from Guayaquil, and she had solemnly promised to do so. The afternoon of our departure, the ship had come in. Business was brisk. Rand and Jim had already taken most of our supplies out to the boat before the greens arrived, but Jim made a trip back to get our salad vegetables.

There was no dearth of lettuce, green onions, green peppers, cucumbers — everything but tomatoes. All the yachting people were asking for tomatoes, but this small lady kept saying, "no ay, no ay" (which sounds like "no eye" and means, as far as I could tell, "we don't have any"). Jim was really disappointed. As he paid for the other vegetables, he said, "Look, I thought you promised you were going to...."

She interrupted him with a finger to her lips, "Ssshh, wait!"

After everyone else left the store, she led him to a corner of the back room where one lonely crate of bright red, class-A tomatoes reposed on top of other boxes. "This is the only one that came," she whispered, though no one else was around to hear. "I couldn't give it to you in front of all those other people."

Jim covered the crate with his jacket before he carried

it out of the store and thanked the lady profusely. "I think I would have kissed her," he told us in all seriousness. "But for all I know that might constitute a proposal of marriage in this country!"

⚓

Learning the geography of these islands was made immeasurably more difficult by the fact that every island had two or even three names. The islands were under English supervision until they were turned over to Ecuador fairly recently.

At the time we were there, the navigational charts still had the islands labeled in English. Nevertheless, you had to know the Spanish names, too. San Christobal, which includes Wreck Bay, was listed on the charts as Chatham. Santa Cruz, site of Academy Bay and the Darwin Station, was called both Chavez and Indefatigable. Barrington Island was also Santa Fe; James Island was San Salvador and Santiago — take your choice. Santa Maria, where the famous barrel post office is located, also answered to the name Charles Island. Tower Island, the bird sanctuary, was named Genovesa.

When Ecuador gets around to printing its own charts, the English names will gradually disappear; in the meantime it is confusing.

⚓

Before we left Wreck Bay, Jim checked for mail that might have come on the supply boat. There was a large packet of mail, and most of the news was not good.

My sister's twelve-year-old grandson, a spirited and active youngster with big, shiny gray eyes that always held hints of laughter and mischief, had drowned in the Payette River. He had been on a camping trip with friends. My uncle, two years younger than my mother, had also died. Other letters told of automobile accidents and life-threatening illnesses. Nothing, it seemed, back in the old U-S-of-A was as safe and secure as we had believed.

Eldon, who loves to paraphrase famous poems, made up his own version of "From Greenland's Icy Mountains":

> What though the gentle breezes
> Blow soft o'er Darwin's Isle,
> What good all this that pleases
> If all the news is vile?

After a period of general moroseness, we tacitly agreed to sweep it under the rug for the time being — not really willing to confront our intimations of mortality here in our little cockle shell skimming over seas five miles deep.

⚓

Leaving Wreck Bay early in the morning, we arrived mid-afternoon at Post Office Bay, where the famous barrel still conveys messages to passing ships.

We left a few notes for cruising friends who were planning to come this way. We also looked for any messages that might have been left for us, and we carefully checked the permanent markers left here by whaling boats, freighters, and yachts over the last two centuries.

Now, as a surprise for all of us, Randy brought out a plaque that he had made in utmost secrecy. It had the name *Trilogy* and the home port *Sitka Alaska* burned into it. He had sanded the surface to a fine satin finish and varnished the plaque. It was about eight by ten inches in size.

"Not very big, is it?" Jim asked, tentatively.

Rand was quick to defend his hard work. "It has something better than 'big.' It has class; it has dignity."

Jim still looked disappointed, which brought Rand to a not-very-slow burn. Eldon intervened.

"Take a look at that post, Jim," he directed. "Anything bigger than this would look ostentatious. We don't want to dominate this historic marker. We just want to leave a little memento to show we've been here."

"Okay." Jim was subdued but not apologetic. "You're probably right; it's just that all the time Rand's been working on this in such secrecy, I imagined it as being much bigger."

Eldon tried to regain the festive air such ceremonies are supposed to have. "Tell you what, Jim," he said. "When we get to Tagus Cove, you can put up the biggest sign you want, and I'll help you do it!"

Certainly Tagus Cove would be a better place for something really flamboyant, but I still couldn't see Eldon doing it. He tends toward understatement. This, I told myself, I'll have to see.

The girls and I walked down the beach while *Trilogy's* name was being enrolled among the water-based nomads of two centuries. When we came back, there it was — not yet weathered, but still looking as though it belonged. As Rand had said, it had dignity. And class.

Post Office Bay isn't really a harbor, and it offers no protection from any wind except one from offshore — but that was the direction the wind was coming from, and it seemed like a good spot to get some chores done. We wrapped and packed oranges, cut up one hundred pounds of cabbage for sauerkraut, baked bread, roasted peanuts, and finished as many chores as we could for the long voyage ahead.

We were right on the equator. The weather was perfect, neither too hot nor too cold. Eldon, probably the best weather-appreciater anyone ever sailed with, begged, "Don't ever take this beautiful weather for granted. So few places in the world have clear, sunny weather that feels one hundred percent comfortable, just enough cooler at night to be perfect."

Remembering years when we'd only had three days of real summer weather, we most heartily agreed. Almost superstitiously, we vowed to appreciate weather at its best — lest we find ourselves, through some quirk of fate, spending the rest of our lives in the Sahara. Or Nome, Alaska.

Darwin's Islands

Even when we lived in Alaska, though, Eldon was more sensitive about the climate than the rest of us. When our big autumn storms set in, usually before the first of September, and the birds started on their migration south, he looked at them and said many times, "They're the smart ones; we should do the same thing."

Like the birds, he had a built-in migratory instinct. But he hadn't been able to do what it told him.

We sailed a short distance around the island to Black Beach anchorage, where the Wittmers live. I got the impression that the Wittmers are related to the Angermeyers, although they may only be part of the same emigration from Germany. The two ladies are widowed now, their children grown and gone except for one daughter who lives on a ranch a few miles away.

We spent a delightful evening with these little ladies. In their fifty-year scrapbook they had pictures of many famous yachts, and their guest register included royalty from England and Europe and untitled millionaires from the US. They had saved letters from guests who had remained in correspondence with them. Famous names appeared on autographed pictures displayed on a large bulletin board.

They told us harrowing stories about misfortunes that had befallen some of these sailors.

The next morning Eldon and Jim hiked up to the ranch where Mrs. Wittmer's daughter lived. Her husband had died about a year before, and she was running the ranch by herself. It was a hard and lonely life.

Eldon offered to pick, harvest, or deliver the produce they had ordered, but she refused help of any kind. There was little they could do but come back to the boat. At dusk she came down the hill with three burros carrying oranges, lemons, bananas, papayas, green peppers, cabbage, tomatoes, carrots, leeks, and lettuce — almost more than our skiff would hold. The price in US funds, approximately $7.50.

Trilogy

At the Wittmer house we picked up twenty-five dozen eggs. They were all beautiful pastel colors, turquoise, pink, blue and green, one color per egg. The chickens responsible for these colored eggs are native to South America, known as Easter egg chickens. Inside, the eggs look like any others that come out of white or brown shells.

Just before heading out across the Pacific, we stopped in Academy Bay once more to fill our propane tanks. Even with full tanks, we had a good chance of running out of propane before we sighted land again.

We filled the water and diesel tanks, too.

⚓

A little Ecuadorian girl, ten or eleven years old, had come out to the boat each time we were in port. She had spent quite a bit of time with Pattie and Carole, and they liked her very much.

This time, as soon as we were anchored, she came out and stayed for two hours or more. When she left, Pattie realized that a silver bracelet, a graduation gift from her best friend, was missing. Pattie knew the girl had taken it. She had removed it from her wrist shortly before the girl's arrival, and she remembered exactly where she had put it.

Carole started checking over her jewel box and found that five pieces were missing, possibly more — she had never made an actual inventory.

The girls knew where the child lived, and they set out promptly to see her parents. When they arrived, only the mother was home; the child had seen them coming and run out the back door when the girls knocked. The mother listened quietly to their story. Then she walked into the next room and brought out a box filled with jewelry, some of it obviously expensive.

The things Pattie and Carole had lost were not of great value, but they were gifts from friends and relatives and, for that reason, treasured possessions. The bracelet was there, and the things Carol had missed. In addition, they recognized several other pieces they hadn't realized were gone.

The girls were appalled at the extent of the thievery. The mother, who had been polite but impassive up to this point, began weeping and said, "I have been afraid. I feared she was stealing, but I cannot speak the English, and always she gets these things from the boats in the harbor whose language I do not speak. She tells me they give her these things, and I am not sure. I think I will take them back to the boats, but I cannot understand them and they cannot understand me."

"Don't cry," Pattie comforted her. "That's a tough spot to be in."

"Here."

The mother thrust the whole box of stolen jewelry toward the girls. "Take all of these things. I do not want stolen things in my house."

Pattie answered, "We can't take the other things she's stolen — just the things that belong to us."

This brought on a new torrent of tears. Finally, the mother recovered enough to say, "I am so glad you girls speak Spanish. I have wanted to talk to someone about this for a very long time. I cannot go to the police; maybe they will lock her up. She is only a little girl even if she has been very bad; I do not want her to be in jail."

She paused, then added, "I do not want everyone to know that my daughter is a thief. I cannot move away, and people never forget."

That was a hard one, and the girls hardly knew how to advise this distraught woman. "Most of the people she stole from," Pattie began, "are long gone. I don't think there is any way to contact them. On the other hand, I don't think she should be allowed to keep this jewelry; that would reward her for being dishonest."

"No, no! " the mother exclaimed. "I will not allow her to keep them. I have never let her wear any of these things, even when I wasn't sure they were stolen."

By this time, the erring daughter had sneaked back into the house and was listening in the next room. "Tell her to come out here," Pattie suggested.

The mother dragged her, protesting, into the room, and Pattie gave her a lecture on how wicked it is to take advantage of people who trust you and steal from them. The child maintained a sullen and stubborn silence. Gone forever was the airy friendliness that had drawn both girls to her.

So far, Carole had allowed Pattie to do the talking; her Spanish was still somewhat hesitant. But she had an idea about how to dispose of the stolen property. "Maybe your church has a welfare fund or something like that. The jewelry could be sold, and you would know at least that something good was done with the money."

Relieved, the mother answered, "To be sure; that would be best. I will give it to the priest. I don't care if he knows. She will have to confess it anyway. He can send it to be sold somewhere where they know its value; here, no one could pay much for it."

She turned to her daughter with a fierce expression. "Never," she said, slowly and with emphasis on each word, "never will you go out to visit the boats again, not while I live!"

Although she kept her head down and tried not to show any emotion, in some subtle way the little girl showed relief — the worst had happened, and now she was off the hook. Her mother sensed this instantly and turned on her with biting anger.

"As for you, who steal from those who befriend you," she said, holding the girl's head up so she was compelled to look in her mother's face, "we will talk about your punishment after these young ladies are gone!"

Pattie and Carole returned to the boat, happy to have their prized possessions back but sorry it ever happened. They were especially sorry for the girl's mother, who appeared to be a very conscientious person.

⚓

I had gone ashore when the girls did. We came back to find that Rand had been improving his time by making himself a pair of shorts from a discarded sail.

Most of the material called "sailcloth" would make very poor sails, but this was the real thing. He had ripped out the seams of a favorite pair of worn-out shorts and used the pieces for a pattern, stitching it on our temperamental twelve-volt electric sewing machine. Copying the original, he made flat fell seams — although I'm sure he hadn't known such a thing existed before. They looked great, even the zipper!

I've seen third-year sewing students who couldn't do a good job putting a zipper in a pants placket. The rest of the family, accustomed to seeing Rand do well many things he had never done before, viewed this demonstration of versatility with a fairly blasé attitude, but I, who knew the most about sewing, was amazed.

Speaking of versatility, some of the accolades will have to go to Eldon as well. In his constant battle with recalcitrant motors, he sometimes has to manufacture parts from originals that have disintegrated beyond usefulness, and even beyond recognition, as a pattern. He does it, and the machine works; no one gives it a second thought.

For two days in Academy Bay while Rand and Jim took care of water, oil, propane, and other such things, Eldon took three of our electric toilets apart. For the parts that had worn out, there were usually no spares. As usual, no sweat; he just made new ones.

Part of this complete overhaul was preventive. When one part disintegrated, he replaced the same parts in the others so that the work wouldn't have to be done under less favorable circumstances.

Our two-day stay in Academy Bay lengthened into four.

Delays at this stage, when we were all poised to start our longest island-to-island sail, were hard to endure with equanimity. Our oranges had been stowed in the holds for a week; our fresh vegetables were rapidly wilting. All the little things kept coming up, as though they were bent on keeping us here forever. But on September seventeenth we hoisted the anchor.

One more stop at Tagus Cove — to put *Trilogy*'s name up on the cliffs with dozens of others from this century and centuries past.

Then, Marquesas, here we come!

JIM'S COMMENT:
What Mom Gave Up

It was the fall of 1959. I had just turned fourteen and was a freshman at Auburn Academy boarding school in Washington state. I was homesick but making the best of it when, to my utter astonishment, I got a call from Mom telling me she was in Walla Walla, Washington, with Randy and Pattie. She was going back to college to finish up her last two years, and she wanted to do it in one year.

After a twenty-year hiatus raising a family in Alaska, this would be no easy task.

She not only met that goal and graduated cum laude, but in a few more years she also went back to the University of Florida and got her masters in psychology, maintaining a 4.0 average in all her graduate studies.

Mom was the guidance counselor at our local high school, just a block from our very fine Alaskan home. She had tenure, a pension plan, a job she really enjoyed with a predictable and fulfilling future. I was again surprised when, after Dad sank the Manana II, Mom suggested they sell the house, quit her job, and move down to Seattle to work — so we could all be together while we built the boat. What bold changes!

Her decision to sell the house, of course, gave us the financial means to build the boat. More than that, her choice to involve the whole family created an atmosphere of support and synergy. Without this atmosphere, how could we have maintained the eighty-hour weeks we would put in for nearly two years to complete this massive project?

During that time, I saw us move, as a family, from dependence through independence to interdependence. I gained a completely new insight into what a family can do if the members all pull together towards a common vision.

Whenever we talked about doing a world cruise as soon as the boat was finished, I realized how vital Mom's enthusiastic support would be. Nevertheless, I had serious doubts that she would give up yet another good job with the state (and yet another great future) for this crazy dream. Even though she was always optimistic and supportive in these discussions, I honestly couldn't see her giving up her security in order to cruise.

I also knew how prone she was to seasickness, which made that support even less likely.

When it came time to leave, Mom was able to negotiate a year's leave of absence. The best of both worlds. As our voyage progressed, though, we began to realize that it could last a lot longer than the nine months we had originally planned. I secretly dreaded the approaching deadline, the moment when Mom would have to make her choice. If she chose to go back, it would end the trip for the rest of us.

The moment came somewhere along the southern coast of Mexico, when we had to decide whether to continue down the coast or head across to Hawaii. That's when Mom threw her support to continuing down into Central and South America. She really never said much about the job, nor about what she was giving up, but when the deadline came and went as we were enjoying the Galapagos Islands, I realized that Mom had really burned her bridges. We would continue to travel till we ran out of money.

Later I saw the destiny in it all and realized that Mom had made the choices of the heart. She had sacrificed the most, but the entire family had benefited. For, collectively, all our dreams were coming true.

Truly, the sum was far greater than the parts.

CHAPTER TWELVE:
THE REAL SOUTH SEAS

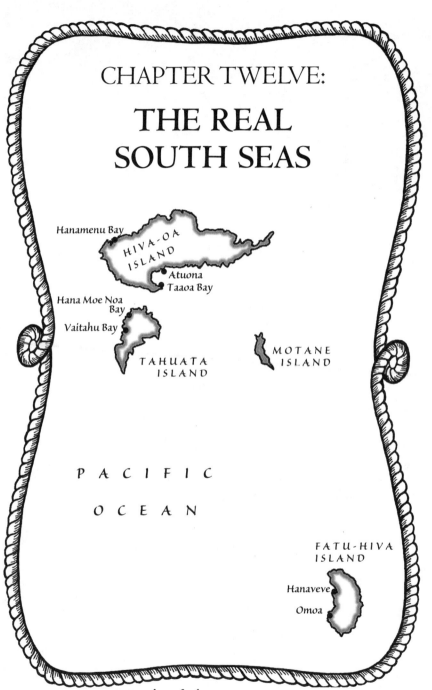

Hanamenu Bay

HIVA-OA
ISLAND

Atuona
Taaoa Bay

Hana Moe Noa
Bay

Vaitahu Bay

TAHUATA
ISLAND

MOTANE
ISLAND

P A C I F I C

O C E A N

FATU-HIVA
ISLAND

Hanaveve

Omoa

Detail of the Marquesas

s soon as we left the roadstead at Academy Bay, the wind was directly behind us, pushing us along at a strong eight knots. We had planned to stop for the night at Jervis Island, but with clear skies and a full moon, it seemed foolish to waste such a good sailing wind; we sailed on to Tagus Cove.

Tagus Cove was the most protected anchorage we had found in these islands. Fernandina guarded the entrance, and the south end of Isabela, curling around like a sea horse's tail, protected us from any southerly winds. Here we had to batten down for sea travel.

No more duffel left around on counters; nothing unbraced or unbolstered would be allowed to shift in heavy seas, impeding progress that might of necessity be rapid through the cabins.

And there was the matter of getting *Trilogy's* name emblazoned on the famous cliffs above Tagus Cove.

⚓

Back on Tower Island we had found a ship's transom about eight feet across and two feet deep, fiberglassed and in good condition. No one had known what to do with it; they'd stowed it in the bilge.

When the necessity for a sign presented itself, Eldon thought that carrying this piece of flotsam would be better than carrying paint up the cliff. The scrap was large enough to make a good sign and durable enough to last for the foreseeable future. Besides, it had a rather nice shape, different from a squared-off board.

Eldon had promised Jim the honor of placing this sign on the cliff, but Jim, by way of apology for disparaging the little sign at Post Office Bay, thought Rand should do it. Rand painted *Trilogy*'s name on the transom, and he and Eldon took it up the cliff.

When the sign was positioned and secured high above the cove, it was very visible but not overwhelming. "It looks good," I told them when they got back to the boat.

"Sure looks a lot smaller from here," Rand remarked. But he and Eldon viewed their handiwork with satisfaction. It looked good, and very permanent.

⚓

The next day, until noon, we were still putting things away and securing them for sea travel. It seemed like a good idea to eat lunch while we were still in the protection of the cove. In the very near future, we were going to eat a lot of meals without such protection.

At one-thirty, precisely two months after we'd left Ecuador heading for the Galapagos Islands, we sailed out of Tagus Cove on our way to the Marquesas Islands.

Everything on *Trilogy* was as shipshape as it was ever going to be; the sailors, too, were about as shipshape as they were ever going to be. From now on for the next three or four weeks there would be night watches — watches around the clock, in fact. But the night watches always seem worse.

Ahead of us was an unobstructed ocean a little more than the distance between New York and London.

⚓

Right out of the harbor we caught a nice, gentle southeast wind — not a wind for fast travel, but wonderful for comfortable travel. Then, suddenly, it veered around to northeast and came with greater force. By the time we were forty miles from land, Isabela's 5,500-foot peaks were pale blue bumps on the horizon, and we were running in big ocean swells a half mile apart.

A big ocean swell quartering on the stern is one of the most beautiful sights you will ever see. Each one looks as though it will easily overwhelm your little craft. It comes up behind you, mountain-high, dark blue at the base shading to turquoise, cerulean, and aqua close to the top, with feathery white crests. After towering at you menacingly, it slips under the keel and gently lowers you to the trough.

Eldon was at the wheel for the first few hours, which was proper; we were going to see the fabulous South Sea Isles of which he had dreamed so long.

He was happy that with the aid of marezine I had been able to make this trip, and he didn't want me to be sick. "Did you take your marezine?" he asked anxiously.

It was a real victory for me to be able to respond, "I don't think I'm going to need it; we've been going through some pretty good chop this last week, and I think my stomach's doing okay."

Some people never get over being seasick. I'm fine after I've become accustomed to the motion. But if we stay in harbor too long, I have to get used to it all over again. I wish my stomach had a better long-term memory.

⚓

Rand hooked up the steering vane, and the black equatorial darkness settled down suddenly. It soon was uncomfortably cold on deck. We all adjourned to the cabin; the one on watch only needed to look around every fifteen minutes. Nothing, absolutely nothing was going on out there!

By morning the wind had switched to southwest, and with each change of direction it gained velocity. We'd left Tagus Cove at a bare seven knots. We were now going more than ten, and the noise in the rigging doubled with each additional knot of speed. An overcast sky promised rain imminently, and before noon a light drizzle began —

surely not storm conditions, but a good day to spend in the cabin with the galley stove going full blast.

Carole curled up on the seat in the dining area and started polishing her fingernails and toenails. Pattie stretched out on her bunk with a book. Jim was at the helm; Rand and Eldon were checking our oranges — a job that had to be done every day. Each one had to be unwrapped, and every one with a sign of mold had to be thrown away. Right now, very few were spoiling. But that few could not be left to contaminate the others.

Reading is an honored pastime on lengthy sea voyages, and we all did our share of it. We had long since run through our original supply of books and replenished it from time to time by trading with other boats. In the last batch, acquired in the Galapagos Islands, Jim had found a Marquesan-English dictionary and studied it diligently, hoping to be able to converse in Marquesan by the time we reached those islands.

One of the borrowed books, which I wanted to keep but had since been traded off, was written by a man who lived in Atuona on Hiva-Oa around 1919. Atuona is the village where the French artist Gauguin lived during the last ten years of his life. He died there in 1903.

Because he was familiar with Gauguin's work and history, the author wanted to see where the artist was buried. Many people remembered Gauguin, but no one had any information about where he was buried. One old man said, "Sure, I remember him. He very sick. Not stay long. Soon he die; bury him, no one know where."

The author was able to find the house where Gauguin lived for the last few months of his life. Some of the artist's paintings had been incorporated into the building. They were in advanced stages of deterioration.

I passed the book around for the family to read because of the information about Atuona and the Marquesas, and also because some of the information didn't exactly tally against the present-day legends. Gauguin's grave has become quite a Mecca for art lovers. We wondered. If the grave couldn't be located during a year's residency sixteen years after the artist's death, why was it so easy to find now? We resolved to check it out when we reached Atuona.

We guessed the real story, but it probably won't have a wide acceptance.

⚓

Without either sun or stars in an overcast sky, it was impossible for our navigators to tell us precisely how far we had gone the first two days, but such a brisk wind allowed no doubt that we were making good time. Even though the steering vane did most of the helmsman's work, Eldon always stayed on deck during his watch, and I was trying to keep him company. It was night and cold, not much fun for a four-hour span.

Even though I was wearing ski pants and a warm jacket, my teeth were chattering.

"Are we still in the Humboldt current?" I asked. "If so, how long does it take to get away from it?" I had already forgotten how thankful we were for the sixty-degree water around us in the Galapagos Islands.

Eldon went down to the cabin and got out the wind and current charts. "We're at least four hundred miles west of the Galapagos now. No, we shouldn't still be in the Humboldt current — but we are. There's no other reason for such cold weather."

⚓

On the afternoon of the fourth day the skies began to clear. By evening it looked as though we might be able to see the sunset. So far, heading straight west, we hadn't seen one. I settled down on the starboard side of the boat to watch the sun go down.

The Real South Seas

Directly across from me on the port side I heard Jim say, "That's serious."

"Are you sure?" Rand asked, then: "Yeah, that's serious all right."

Instant alarm jangled all my little warning buzzers. What had happened? Did we have a fire aboard? A leak in one of the hulls?

I crossed the deck quickly and asked, "What's wrong? What's so serious?"

They both whirled around and looked at me in astonishment. Then a big grin spread over Rand's face. "It would be a lot of fun to string you along, Mom, but I won't do it this time. See that star over there, just above the horizon?" He pointed with the calipers. "That's Sirius, a star of 1.42 magnitude, and the first star we should see this evening. Jim and I are going to take some star sights."

Sirius was clearly visible for twenty minutes before sunset, and it only became brighter thereafter. Sunset, however, was a total fizzle. The clouds on the horizon turned very faintly pink at the top — no bright reds, no gold edges. I thought of Alaskan sunsets that lasted for hours with the whole sky glowing.

Oh well, you can't have everything at the same time or in the same place.

After ten o'clock Jim was on watch, and I went out on deck to keep him company for a while. These night vigils are always lonely, and this one was cold as well. Rand, Carole, and Pattie, who had the other night watches, were already asleep.

We talked about life — with a capital L — and about the immense changes each of us had made in order to go on this voyage. We talked about the changes that the voyage was inevitably making in us.

Whatever the future held, we thought of ourselves as meeting it together. As a family, we had always been fairly close. But traveling together, added to the boat-building experience, had brought a unity we hadn't had before. Jim and Rand, especially, had always assumed that if Eldon and I stayed in Alaska, they would probably live down in the "Lower 48." Skiing and golf were important to them, and Southeast Alaska isn't a good place for either one.

We talked about Carole, the change in her especially since she had become a Christian. Jim and Carole had been very close before her conversion experience. I wasn't sure how her new attitude had affected their relationship. I was also afraid that Jim might feel like an outsider — the only sane one in a bunch of Jesus freaks.

"Not at all," Jim replied to my question. "Carole is more at peace with herself and everyone else. She desperately needed something to tie to. To give stability to her life. Apparently this is it."

After a long period of silence, Jim went on. "I really do believe in God — although I have some trouble with a good many church creeds. I even think sometimes that God may have a plan for my life. So far, I don't know what it is. But if He ever lets me know, I'll do it."

I was taken completely by surprise. This was different from anything I had heard Jim say since he was fifteen years old.

"Be sure that He will, Jim," I said when I got back the power of speech. "He's working on it."

I knew that our wheel-watch conversations were confidential, but I knew Jim wouldn't mind if I told Eldon. When I did, Eldon was happy, but cautious.

"God has brought him this far," he said, "and He'll finish the job. No use in my bugging him. I've done that too much already."

⚓

On the fifth day after leaving the Galapagos Islands, we were almost a thousand miles from land in any direction. And yet, high above the mainmast circling around was a lone tropicbird. Rand, at the wheel, noticed it about the same time I did.

"What on earth is he doing up there?" I asked Rand. "Isn't he farther away from land than he's supposed to be?"

"He's probably wondering the same thing about us," Randy replied.

The next day, there he was again, high above us, keeping pace with the boat.

"I'll bet he roosts in the rigging at night," Rand said, "although I've never caught him at it. Maybe he eats flying fish off the deck."

That was a possibility. Even back in Costa Rica the flying fish had started landing on the deck at night. When Rand was on the early morning watch, he used to gather them up and fry them for his breakfast. Once at Playa del Cocos, when we were going out to the boat on a bright moonlit night, a flying fish hit Pattie on top of the head, having mistaken her blonde hair for moonlight on the water.

Every day for the next ten days the tropicbird appeared in the early morning, circled above us for thirty or forty minutes, and then disappeared until evening. We began to regard him as a good-luck omen.

⚓

We had such good winds that by day seven we had traveled almost fourteen hundred miles. We began to revise our estimates for arriving in Fatu-Hiva. Even with five hundred miles of doldrums, we still shouldn't take a full three weeks.

On this day, we had the strongest winds we'd seen since the storm off the Oregon coast. Jim thought we should drop the Genny and use less sail. Instead, Eldon turned south and ran with the wind for several hours. Fatu-Hiva is ten degrees south of the equator; at some time, we would have had to make a correction southward.

Trilogy

⚓

By the tenth day, our bananas were ripening faster than we could possibly use them. We would each have had to eat twenty bananas a day to keep up.

It was a good day for drying bananas, clear and warm, so we all helped cut them up and get them on drying racks. If we got any more rain squalls, such as we'd had every day so far, the bananas would doubtless spoil. Fortunately we didn't. In two days they were ready to be stored in gallon-sized mayonnaise jars.

Because we'd picked up three cases of canned albacore tuna from the cannery in Manta, mayonnaise consumption had escalated. So far, we had emptied three of the four jars that we'd bought in San Diego. Now, just after we finished storing the bananas in two of the empty jars, I started to open the fourth jar.

My hands were slippery and the seas were rough.

The jar squirted out of my hands and shattered on the galley floor — not just a nice clean break that left some of the contents salvageable. Staring back at me from the galley floor was a useless mound of glop, totally riddled with glass particles.

Pattie and Carole looked on in consternation. They were imagining the austerity program that lay ahead — no mayonnaise for salads and sandwiches. What they didn't know was that my mother, their mutual grandmother, had always made our mayonnaise at home. While I probably hadn't made it myself, I had watched it many times.

"All right now," I told the girls as soon as the mess was cleaned up. "If one of you will pour me a fine stream of oil, I'll make some mayonnaise."

"Can you do that?" they gasped in unison. "Really?"

"Really, I can. I've seen it done many times, may even have done it myself — though considering how I avoided housework in those days, that's more doubtful."

With Pattie pouring oil and me valiantly turning the

egg beater, we soon had a quart of mayonnaise, starting with an egg yolk, well beaten, and gradually adding oil. As I added vinegar and spices, the girls eyed me not so much with disbelief as with a great lack of comprehension.

"Is that the way all mayonnaise is made?" Pattie asked incredulously.

"Pretty much, I think. It can be made partially with a starch thickener. But Mama always thought that kind was inferior."

Carole asked, "What makes it get thick like that?"

"It's an emulsion," I told her. "You can actually combine water and oil in the same way, and it will thicken, but not this much."

Carole tasted the mayonnaise. "Tastes just like mayonnaise," she declared, marveling at the fact. "It even looks like mayonnaise!"

She turned around and looked at Pattie and me as a new thought struck her.

"Then we can make it whenever we want to, can't we?" she asked. "We don't have to be so darned careful for fear we'll run out."

"That's right; there's no shortage of oil," I agreed. "I didn't know you and Pattie were conserving our mayonnaise so carefully."

"Oh, we were, we were!" Carole exclaimed. "When we got down to that next-to-last jar, we were absolutely miserly with it!"

"That's right," Pattie seconded. "In a way, I'm glad that one broke. Carole and I will make the next batch, and it'll probably be soon."

Forgetting all about her dieting talk of the previous week, Pattie began covering the bread with a tuna-mayonnaise-relish mixture. The relish was also in a gallon jar.

Pattie looked at it intently and then said, "Mom, will you let me open the relish from now on? This is the only one we have."

Trilogy

Carole cut the sandwiches in half and began stacking them on a plate. As she did, she said, "I didn't know before that people could do so many things for themselves. I knew you could make bread, but I didn't know you could make flour. And peanut butter! That's the easiest thing in the world to make, but I never would have imagined it. And now mayonnaise! I feel as though I'm on a real back-to-nature kick!"

⚓

As the weather grew more balmy, the wind that had been pushing us so industriously vanished — not completely, but the present breeze wasn't even a close relative of the powerful gusts we had seen earlier in the trip. We were in the doldrums. We had enough fuel to motor our way out if we had to, but that would be a last resort.

On the fifteenth day, for the twenty-four hour period, we only logged one hundred forty knots

The tropicbird was still above our mainmast every day. He must have rested on the boat at night, some way, but not one of us ever surprised him at rest. There was no trouble now getting sun sights and star sights. Jim and Rand were still staunchly standing by their prediction that we would arrive on the seventeenth day, in spite of the gentleness of the wind.

In the late afternoon of day seventeen, Jim climbed up to the spreaders of the mainmast with a pair of binoculars around his neck. For a while, he thought he might be sighting land; some little bluish clouds on the western horizon looked as though they might be solid. After fifteen minutes he came down and laid the binoculars on the chart table.

"It's just a cloud," he said, discouraged. "For a while I thought it might be Fatu-Hiva."

I picked up the binoculars and trained them on the faint blue cloud in the distance. "Jim," I called. "Come over here. That isn't any cloud. See? It looks just like this drawing of Fatu-Hiva."

Jim studied the drawing, not nearly as excited as I was. Finally he said, "I'm afraid you're using quite a lot of imagination. It could be land, but I don't think so."

"No," I argued, "this is not imagination. The chances of a cloud duplicating that profile must be a zillion to one. Besides, clouds change shape all the time, and this hasn't changed in the last twenty minutes. It's Fatu-Hiva; you'll find out, but I'm sure right now!"

It was time for a star sight, which with other calculations placed us sixty-five miles due east of Fatu-Hiva. The little blue shadow maintained its shape and solidity as the evening descended.

"It's gotta be land," the boys at last conceded. "That is exactly where it would be." As navigators, they had acquired both expertise and confidence as we traveled. Now they proved to the rest of us that with sun and star sights they could determine our position within a square mile.

The island was too far away to reach before dark and too close to allow us to maintain full speed through the night. We ghosted along under shortened sail. In the morning Fatu-Hiva was dead ahead, rugged and colorful. All of us were on deck at dawn to see our first real tropical island.

What had looked, last evening, like pale blue blotting paper with its torn edge toward the sky emerged substantial and rainbow-hued. As the colors became differentiated in the early dawn, we could see pink, red, yellow, and pale green backed by enormously jagged purple mountains. Sheer cliffs, dripping with tropical vegetation, rose an astonishing two thousand feet out of the sea.

It was of these same islands Robert Louis Stevenson wrote, "The first experience can never be repeated. The first love, the first sunrise, the first South Sea island, are memories apart and touched a virginity of sense."

We looked at each other, thinking our own thoughts, but the look of satisfaction on each face said something that I interpreted as, "This is what it was all about. This is what we were working for, all those long days, building and planning." Eldon had tears in his eyes. This was his dream in living color. Unlike many things long anticipated, it did not seem less than we had imagined.

⚓

Coming into Omoa, we rounded a rugged headland reminiscent of Diamond Head in Honolulu but many times taller, greener, steeper. I still can't describe how I felt about this place. When one has been out of sight of land for two and a half weeks, even a section of dry, cheerless Baja would look good. But to come upon this sun-soaked, rain-sparkled jewel, one of the incomparable beauties of the world — the emotional impact is beyond description. I have never been so close to kneeling down and kissing the ground as in this place.

The kids put their feelings of amazement and awe into one heartfelt expression:

"Wow!"

Omoa is built along a river valley. The river meets the seashore to form a freshwater lagoon surrounded by coconut palms and flowering shrubs. The schoolhouse, red-roofed and spanking white, stands on a level, park-like space near the shore.

The whole town looks like a park, with well-mowed lawns everywhere. (The local goats make very efficient lawn mowers. They never need oiling, never run out of gas, and they don't leave the cut grass lying around except in the form of fertilizer.)

This little island, nine miles long and about a third as wide, has mountains rising abruptly over three thousand feet. Three tiers of mountains rise majestically back of the town. The first level is light yellow and blue-green — banana and sugar cane, remnants of attempted plantations, now untended. The next level is darker — mango and coconut trees and jungle growth. The top level is composed of blue and purple mountains, so tall for such a tiny island, wreathed in clouds and covered with jungle. Directly back of the school house is the church and, back of that, a wine-red volcanic spire that dwarfs the little church. Farther back is another volcanic formation, a rounded dome in shades of red, yellow, pink, and black. The profusion and intensity of color take one's breath away.

Omoa is not a land-locked harbor; the ocean swells, rolling unobstructed from Antarctica, break with a ground-shaking roar. The first time we went ashore some of the local boys brought Pattie, Carole, and me in with their outrigger. This task required a degree of skill none of our group would ever attain. There is a landing place, a big flat rock about eight or nine feet above the water level. By watching the wave action and catching it at precisely the right moment, they deposited us on the rock with dry feet and scarcely a hair out of place. Eldon and the boys came in on surfboards and got thoroughly dunked in that raging surf.

After my first trip ashore, I wrote in my diary: *I am absolutely stunned at the beauty of this place! Its sun and rain-drenched magical beauty, the incredible warmth and generosity of its people are beyond belief. This is what people are dreaming of when they dream about the South Seas. Until today, I didn't believe it actually existed.*

The little gullies and ravines were filled with fifty varieties of coleus plants in just about every color I can think of except blue. (In fact, there was no deficiency of color: you have to look sharp, but the tiny blossoms are forget-me-not blue.) Vying for space with the coleus plants were spider lilies three or four feet across, with clusters of flowers as big as my head. Some of the homes are built of concrete blocks; some are woven from palmetto or pandanus leaves and thatched. One man told us he could make one of these woven houses in five days if he already had the materials. Around every home is a profusion of flowers, and the interiors are squeaky clean.

This valley — with its tropical foliage, neat cottages, lawns and flowers, and its bizarre, gaudily colored volcanic formations — looked part coral isle, part English country-side, part Grand Canyon, and part the heaven of our dreams.

As we walked along the valley, people came out of their houses giving us fruit, flowers, and even little pastries. We paused for a moment to admire row upon row of red ginger around one house; before we could say, "Please don't cut down all your pretty flowers," the man of the house, armed with a wicked machete, had cut a huge bouquet of these lovely blossoms and handed them to me. The stems were three feet long, the blossoms ten to twelve inches.

Many of the people spoke a form of pidgin English, which they said was easier than French, the official language of the islands. Pidgin made communication possible.

Jim's study of Marquesan paid off right from the start. People were delighted that he was making the effort to speak their own language. One housewife was more profi-cient in English than he was in Marquesan, but she was so pleased at the effort he was making that she rushed into her house and brought him a dozen eggs. Eggs are scarce and very high-priced in these islands; this was a gift of some magnitude. All we could think on the way back to the boat was, "Oh, boy! Eggs for breakfast!"

It wasn't hard to tell which one of the *Trilogy* gang was the most popular with the Marquesans. Everywhere we went, the islanders dubbed Jim "Numera Tahi Mita'e" — number one, the best.

In the evening several young men from the village came out to the boat bringing gifts of fruit and ukuleles. Far into the night they played and sang. They all had their little transistor radios and knew dozens of Hawaiian songs, folk songs, and old classics.

Much as he loved the music, Eldon crashed early in the evening. He had slept very little the night before, and the day had been strenuous. By eleven o'clock, my boys were beginning to get sleepy, too; they'd each had a night watch and been up before dawn. This was the first time, but by no means the last, that they bade their guests good night and went to bed while the music continued. I hadn't heard such nice lullabies since I used to go to sleep while my dad played the violin.

While everyone else went ashore the next day, I stayed on the boat and painted Omoa as it looked from there. Although it had rained during the night, the village, with its weirdly beautiful volcanic outcroppings, was bathed in brilliant sunlight. The surf, wild, white, and high, contrasted with the shaded shore. An artist, like a word-smith, understands continually that her reach exceeds her grasp; even so, it's very satisfying to get such luxuriant wildness into a picture.

I wanted the light to stay just as it was in the early morning — and of course it kept changing. Working fever-ishly against time, I could empathize with Gauguin, who filled canvas after canvas while Death crouched at his elbow. Frustrated, working with acrylic paint that dried almost instantly in the tropical sun, I still had the satisfac-tion of getting the colors the way they are, riotous and unbelievable.

Plied with refreshments continually, Eldon and the kids walked the full length of the village. In the early afternoon, one man brought Rand out to the boat to get the banjo and guitars; it would be several days before the musical instru-ments got back on the boat. Eldon and the girls came back just at sunset, but the music was going full blast with a dozen musicians; Jim and Rand couldn't be pried loose.

Eldon and I had hoped the boys would stay overnight in the village rather than try to come out after dark. Visibility is poor at night, and the sharks are reputed to feed then. However, a few minutes after midnight, Jim and Rand came out on their surfboards; they'd had a tough time coming through the surf, and they were exhausted. Eldon was really put out with them for taking such a risk.

"Don't worry, Dad," Rand said contritely. "I'll never do that again. I really thought I wasn't going to make it!"

"You know you could have stayed in any house in the village, and they'd have been glad to have you," Eldon told them. "I was afraid all along you'd do this, and you could have lost your lives doing it. I want it understood from now on. You don't ever take this kind of chance."

"I know," Jim agreed, "it was dumb. You have our word we won't do it again."

"Good," their father said grumpily. "Now I can get some sleep, and so can your mother."

⚓

Over on the beach the next morning, I saw dozens of little tots of pre-school age playing in this massive surf. All the children swam like tadpoles, but it still looked awfully dangerous to me. One mother had two small children in tow, and it didn't seem to me that she was watching them carefully enough.

"Don't you worry about such small children playing here?" I asked, although it was obvious she didn't.

"No," she said looking puzzled, "I do not worry."

I decided to be even more blunt. "Do any of the children ever drown, playing here?" Where there is such a steep beach, the undertow is dangerous.

"Never," she answered as though giving a lesson to a not-very-bright child. "As you see, they learn to take care of themselves." They certainly did, although I could never understand how these little tots kept from being carried out to sea.

Carole and Pattie watched the kids playing in the surf and decided to give it a try. Having come in their bathing suits, it was quick work to shed their tee-shirts and shorts and deposit them above high tide level. It looked like fun all right, but I wanted to see some more of the village, so I hurried to catch up with Eldon and the boys.

I was surprised to see horses everywhere; they're not native to the country, but they are very useful in a place without automobiles. The horses, the goats, and most domesticated animals eat grass and coconuts and seem fairly healthy. Some of the older dogs have a semi-paralysis of the back legs that could be caused by a dietary deficiency — but that's only speculation on my part. When I asked some of the villagers about it, they only shrugged and said politely, "We do not know; it just happens."

⚓

Hanavave, another village on Fatu-Hiva about three and a half miles by water from Omoa, can also be reached on foot — a rugged sixteen-hour hike over the mountains. We had planned to go there fairly soon. But when our anchorage at Omoa became untenable, with really huge swells coming in from a tropical storm five hundred miles away, we set out for Hanavave's more-protected harbor.

It took us about thirty minutes to reach this safer anchorage. It was very rough going, in a beam sea. Pattie and Carole were fit only to stretch out on their bunks, having played in the surf all afternoon as the waves got larger and larger.

Pattie moaned, "I've got sore muscles that I didn't even know I had. I've never been so tired in my whole life!"

"We should have kept our tee-shirts on," Carole said regretfully. "I got sunburned and sand-scoured, and I can hardly tell which is which."

As far as we could tell, there was no way of communication between the two villages. Nevertheless, before we could get the anchor down, Polynesian boys were coming out on their outriggers, bringing their ukuleles and saying "himine, himine" (sing, sing).

Besides their musical instruments, they brought breadfruit, coconuts, and pompelmous. This last fruit, also known in other Polynesian islands as pomelo, is like a very large grapefruit but green inside and out, milder and sweeter than grapefruit. We became instant addicts, and although people brought some out to the boat almost every day, we could always have eaten more.

Guido and Lydia, a couple we had met in Mexico, were anchored here, and Eldon and I went over to see them. They had a harrowing story to tell, one that we could not begin to match. Coming from a more northerly direction than we, they had run into a tropical storm that was close to hurricane intensity. Even under bare poles they were going too fast, yawing in heavy seas and threatening to capsize. To slow and stabilize the boat they put out drogues (also known as sea anchors). Somehow, in the process, Lydia fell overboard. She managed to grab the sea anchor before she was swept away.

To save her life, Guido had to pull the entire sea anchor up to the stern of the boat. In gale-force winds and towering seas, it took him two hours. By the time he got a grip on Lydia, he no longer had the strength to pull her onto the boat. Lydia was too spent to help.

"I stood there for what seemed like hours," Guido said, "holding Lydia's wrists because she had no strength in her hands, tears of frustration running down my face."

Guido is a husky fellow and Lydia is small, but they were both so exhausted that she almost slipped away from him before he could summon one last burst of energy. "I cursed myself for a weakling, couldn't believe I wasn't strong enough for that one last pull, and when I finally heaved her up over the stern, I couldn't believe I had done it. We both cried."

You'd think that was enough in the trouble and terror department. But after they got to Hanavave, Guido fell fifteen feet headfirst out of a big mango tree. He was sure his neck was broken, but Lydia was equally sure she couldn't carry him. It took him some time to get on his feet, and Lydia propped him up as best she could until they got back to the boat. He eased himself into bed, still sure his neck must be fractured, and slept for three days. At the end of that time, he arose, like phoenix from the ashes, without even a stiff neck.

"Never had any more trouble from it," he told us, still amazed that he wasn't paralyzed for life.

⚓

Huge coal-black lava outcroppings guard the harbor at Hanavave; they are picturesque, no doubt, but hardly pretty. Even here, in a fairly well protected harbor, getting on terra firma with dry feet was not a certainty. The first time Eldon went ashore, he stepped on the breakwall and his feet immediately took off skyward while his head went in the other direction. Before he could get on his feet, a wave came along and dunked him thoroughly. I was afraid he might have a fractured skull, but he swore he didn't even have a headache. What he did have was some very wet clothing, but he refused to go back and change. He said he didn't want to repeat the performance.

One thing is certain in these islands: one doesn't need to make any plans for lunch ashore. As in Omoa, people brought us fruit, juice, and pastries to eat along the way, and other food to take home with us.

On the twelfth of October, which happened to be Carole's seventeenth birthday, we sailed back to Omoa to get the musical instruments Jim and Rand had left there on Saturday night. This was the first day the weather had been good enough to make the trip back. Cecelia Vaikau, who with her handsome Tahitian husband was visiting her family in Hanavave, went back to Omoa with us. Her four-month-old baby was running a fever, and there was no doctor in Hanavave. Two of her brothers went along for the ride, as well as two older ladies who wanted to visit relatives in Omoa.

Trilogy

Although it was a short ride and a smooth sea, the ladies promptly got seasick. This is traditional: women always get seasick; men, never. As soon as they were on land, they all recovered. Cecelia took her baby to the clinic, and the ladies made their calls. We were back in Hanavave soon after noon.

Pattie, Carole, and I had already asked about laundry facilities and been directed to the usual flat rock in a stream. The water was surprisingly cold, and we wasted no time getting the job done. As soon as we finished, we draped our laundered items over convenient bushes, the clotheslines of primitive communities, and went for a walk up the valley while they dried.

The road continued in a gentle slope for a short distance, after which it got steep and rugged. I began to appreciate the challenge of the sixteen-hour hike over the mountains to Omoa. The mountain trail is very narrow, passing between and under sheer rock faces several hundred feet high. We hadn't walked far when a large coconut hit the trail about twenty inches in front of me.

"Wow!" Carole exclaimed, "that was close!"

I looked up, and up. The coconut trees were there, all right, but at least three hundred feet above us.

"What would have happened if it had hit you?" Carole asked. We were all wondering the same thing. Were there more coconuts up there ready to fall?

"Probably it wouldn't have been very healthy." I was sincerely thankful that I hadn't been another step forward on the trail. "It wouldn't have killed me unless it hit my head, but an arm or shoulder would have been broken, I think."

As we walked along, we could see a waterfall across the narrow valley, high up on the blue-purple mountain. It looked as though it were falling right out of the sky.

⚓

Jim and Rand were supposed to be doing their laundry this afternoon, too, but when we came back to the creek, we found them standing on the bank laughing and talking with three of the local girls, who were diligently scrubbing their jeans and work shirts.

"No fair! No fair!" I protested. "Nobody helped us with our laundry!"

"Sorry," Rand replied. (He looked anything but sorry.) "We can't disregard local customs. Here, the girls tell us, it's not suitable for the men to do the washing."

"That's right," Jim said, also looking more smug than sorry. "We were starting to do it. But they were quite shocked, and they took it away from us."

"Sure," I agreed, "and I'll bet you hung onto it awfully hard."

"Well, not terribly hard," Jim admitted. "We didn't want to cause any problems."

The girls and I folded our laundry and took it back to the boat. Eldon had been taking some machinery apart, and he was tired and greasy. I told him about Jim and Rand, and how they had done their washing. "If you're lucky," I said, "maybe the local girls will feel as though it isn't suitable for the captain of this outfit to be doing his own laundry."

"No, sir," Eldon said emphatically. "They're not going to do my grimy old clothes! I'll go over and get it done in the morning before they know anything about it."

That is exactly what he did the following morning. I'm not sure that it improved his status as a seafaring patriarch, but he felt good about it.

Every night we had music until the wee small hours, and every day people brought us fruit, newly caught fish, bananas — anything, in fact, that they thought we might like. If we asked where we might get something (we had long since run out of oranges), they would say, "I get it for you; tomorrow I bring." And they did. We couldn't pay them for anything. "No money," they said. "It belongs everybody. No one sell it."

"Then let us pay you for your trouble," we said.

"No trouble; no work," they said. "It is for our friends."

We had been in the Islands for a month before we were able to buy anything, and then only because we were in a larger town with a grocery store.

One day Cecelia's younger sister brought me a fruit that looked like a medium- sized red pepper with a little, curved piece of driftwood on the side, like a handle. I had never seen anything quite like it.

"What is it?" I asked.

"Akachi," she said. That didn't help me much. I studied the little handle, and suddenly I knew what it looked like.

"It looks almost like a cashew nut," I said, sure that it wasn't.

She was so happy I had gotten it right that she practically glowed. "That right!" she exclaimed, "akachi. Not good now; have to be roasted before you can eat. Poison now."

I didn't know that before, although it's perfectly true. All the cashews I had eaten previously had been cooked in some way to make them edible.

"Can you show me the tree, bush, vine, or whatever it grows on?" I asked.

"Only two trees this island," she said. "Tomorrow I show you."

True to her word, she led me out into the valley where there wasn't even a visible trail, and she showed me the two trees. They were small, not more than ten feet high, and almost bare of both leaves and fruit. I tried to find out if they always molt this way, if they lose their leaves when the fruit is ripe, or if they had been recently imported and weren't doing too well, but this was all too complicated for her.

"Yes," she said, "leaves always fall; always fall."

The Real South Seas

Early in the morning Rand, Jim, and two local boys had
hiked up to the waterfall we had seen from the valley floor.
They came back to find us and half the village engaged in
himine, with Carole playing the accordion and Pattie as
lead singer. They had planned to go right out to the boat
and sleep after their arduous hike, but a large, enthusiastic
audience proved to be a better restorer than sleep. They
sang along for a while and then went out to get a guitar
and banjo off the boat. This time the music continued into
the night, but not on the boat.

Sophia, one of Cecelia's younger sisters, came out to
the boat the next morning with a gallon of freshly ground
coconut, and she gave all of us a lesson in making coconut
milk (which is delicious but deceptively rich, with almost
six hundred calories in an eight-ounce glass). First, Sophia
put some coconut out in a pan and barely covered it with
fresh water. She let it stand a few minutes, and then she
wrapped it in a tea towel and wrung it like a piece of
laundry. Three times she went through this process and
then handed me some of the coconut pulp; it had no more
flavor than sawdust. The flavor, like the calories, is in the
coconut milk.

Meanwhile, Jim was learning the men's version of the
tamare, a dance usually associated with Tahiti but popular
here as well. Cecelia's five-year-old sister can dance the
tamare like a professional. When she danced, she was all
feminine grace; the rest of the time she was a tomboy,
swimming, diving, and excelling at all the island sports.

⚓

We wanted to see other islands as well as Fatu-Hiva,
and, by law, we couldn't stay in the Marquesas longer than
thirty days. Otherwise we would have stayed on Fatu-Hiva
much longer.

Cecelia invited us to her mother's house for dinner the
night before we left. We were hoping to try the island

cuisine. But Cecelia had been living in Papeete since her marriage several years ago, and she was more sophisticated than the other people here. Considering that her dinner all came from a two-burner gas stove with an oven the size of a bread box, it was a sheer miracle. But it probably wasn't typical Fatu-Hiva fare. Her fish cooked in coconut milk and the little French pastries for dessert were truly gourmet items.

After dinner, which didn't end until after ten o'clock, Eldon waited for three hours for some sign of wind. Then he decided to motor out of the harbor and hope to catch some wind outside. He woke Rand and Jim out of a very sound sleep, and they managed to get the anchor up even though they were still half asleep. As soon as we got outside the harbor, we had enough wind for sailing, so the boys had to hoist sails instead of going back to bed. By the time they finished that chore, they were wide awake. It was one-thirty, a clear night with a bright half-moon shining across the water.

In the morning we anchored in Tahauku Bay on Hiva-Oa, the bay closest to Atuona. There are bays within the bay here. The largest, which includes all the others, is Taaoa Bay, or the Bay of the Traitors. There must be a story back of a name like that, but no one could tell me what it was.

Hiva-Oa is another wildly beautiful island, but we didn't have the warm reception we had grown to expect. The port officials regarded our entrance through Fatu-Hiva, where there is no port authority, as highly irregular. Yankees were not popular here, and the message came through loud and clear. When they found we were from Alaska, they warmed up about fifty degrees. Alaskans they equated with Canadians, New Zealanders, and other such frontiersmen, and, as such, we became pretty good fellows.

Jim and Rand were happy to establish some kind of friendly relations with them. We hoped to extend our stay beyond the thirty-day deadline, and if the authorities hadn't thawed out somewhat, our request wouldn't have stood a chance.

Atuona was the first town we had seen with graded roads and automobiles since we left the mainland of Ecuador. Before we actually went into the town, somewhat less then two miles, we decided to dress up a bit, maybe even press our clothes. On our first day, however, we just walked about a half mile. It was very hot. When we reached a place where we could see the next bay and some of the town, it seemed far enough. Next time, we would start out earlier.

We turned to go back to the boat, but suddenly we were all unbearably thirsty. Above our heads were hundreds of coconuts, just right for drinking but far out of our reach. Even if we could pick one, we had nothing to use for opening it.

Carole offered to shinny up one of the trees. "I'm the youngest," she said. "It should be easier for me to learn how they do it."

"Have you felt one of those tree trunks?" I asked her. "The skin would be worn off your legs before you got up ten feet!"

"They don't even touch them with their legs," Carole observed, "but I don't think I could just run up one of those on my tippy toes the way they do."

"Besides," I said as a new thought struck me, "have you seen any girls going up coconut trees?"

"Do you suppose it's like the washing being only for girls?" Carole asked.

Just then a boy twelve or thirteen years old came by, coming from Atuona. "Whatsa matta? You wanta coconut?" he asked with the typical Polynesian downward inflection at the end of each question.

"Oui, oui," I said quickly, "S'il vous plait." I knew all the kids here had to study French, so I'd been practicing a few phrases that were supposed to help in common social situations. (Until now, asking someone to climb a coconut tree had never qualified as a common social situation.)

Like a kitten, he was up the tree in a few bounds; unlike a kitten, he knew how to get down again. He tossed down a coconut for each of us and brought another one down himself. The boy didn't have a machete, but he had a knife with a wickedly sharp point. He made holes in all the coconuts with it so quickly that we were amazed.

That was the best drink I have ever had.

Earlier in our travels, I would have offered him some money, but I must confess that I had grown so accustomed to the Fatu-Hivans' royal disregard for the medium of exchange that I didn't even think about it. Neither did he, apparently. He drank the sparkling water from his coconut, accepted our thanks graciously, and went on his way.

Tahauku Bay, like most of the harbors in these islands, has a surge three or four feet high left over from the much bigger waves outside. Carole, Jim, and Pattie prepared to walk into Atuona early in the morning on the following day. Rand was running the outboard, planning to come back for Eldon and me an hour or so later. They coasted up to a big flat rock jutting out from the shore, and Carole and Pattie both jumped out of the skiff at the peak of the surge. Jim extended a hand to Carole while she got her balance on the rock.

Unfortunately, Carole didn't realize that Jim would have to wait for the next surge. She kept gripping his hand tightly while the boat went down four feet or so. Carole was pulled off the rock by the boat's descent, and Jim, standing in the skiff, was pulled into the water with her. Jim lost one of his shoes, and no amount of diving could locate it.

Everyone came back to the boat. Jim donned bathing

trunks and snorkel gear to look for his shoe, one of his only pair of good shoes, but it had vanished forever.

Jim's Leica, with a roll of almost entirely exposed film in it, had gotten dunked now for the second time. The first time had been Zihuatanejo, and we considered that film a probable loss. Eldon closed off all the light in the forward stateroom to remove the film, then took the camera apart, cleaned it with fresh water, and carefully dried it.

"Jim can put it back together when he gets back," he said. "If I do it now, we won't get over to town today."

"Do you think it's all ruined?" I asked. "I'd surely hate to lose all the pictures of Omoa and Hanavave."

"Your wishes aren't going to have much to do with it," Eldon observed wryly. "But the film was surprisingly dry. Some of it may be okay."

By the time Jim, Pattie, and Carole changed their clothes and grumped around for a while, it was after eleven. Rand decided to go on to Atuona with them. This time, they made the landing without mishap. When Eldon and I got ready to go, he thought it more prudent to land in a shallow place and wade ashore; that was better than getting wet all over. By now it was after one o'clock and the hottest part of the day, but we didn't mind after we got to Atuona. In the town, there was grass and shade everywhere, and it was much cooler.

Eldon was looking for a man named Lucian, whose son had a plantation on this island. We hoped to stop there, and Eldon thought it would be a good idea to ask ahead of time. Besides, he wanted the benefit of some local knowledge to guide us in our travels. Luckily, both Lucian and the son we planned to visit were in town, and Eldon found them in a little store/cafe combination right in the center of town.

Eldon hadn't brought a chart, but Lucian made a sketch of the island, and he and Ozane, his son, filled in everything they thought might interest us. Like Fatu-Hiva, this island has old abandoned plantations where one can get oranges, limes, and bananas. Mango season was just now starting, and we could get some of those, too. Ozane extended a cordial invitation to come and visit his plantation.

After about an hour, Rand came looking for us, and I went with him to the post office. Eldon was so delighted to find some English-speaking friends again that he hardly noticed our departure.

Rand thought we should get some postage now, while the post office was open, so that we could mail the letters all of us had been writing as we went along. While Jim was spending his time studying Marquesan, Rand had been just as industriously studying French. He had spent some time in France during the year he was in Europe, and he was sure he could make himself understood. He began by asking the postal clerk how much weight we were allowed for each stamp.

The clerk gave him a baffled look. Rand tried again, this time just asking the price of stamps. Again, there was no comprehension on the part of the clerk. Rand was nonplused. He had never had this much trouble making himself understood, not even in Paris.

"Why don't you write it down?" I suggested. "I've heard that the French spoken in places like this is much different from Parisian French."

The clerk really took umbrage at this and said in an icy tone, "I do speak English, you know." His accent was perfect BBC. Obviously, he had been having a little joke at our expense, but we didn't laugh very hard.

Since it was quite certain that Eldon was going to be occupied for a while, Rand and I decided to visit Gauguin's grave. On the way, we found Pattie and Carole, and we all went together. I was astonished to find the grave so massive, with several tons of stair-stepped rock slabs on top of it.

"If it was this big, and practically in the center of the

cemetery, why couldn't they find it fifty-some years ago?" I asked.

"I'll let Jim tell you about it," Rand said as we walked down the hill from the little fenced-in cemetery. "He's been checking up on it; it's an interesting story."

Jim was on the lawn in front of the government buildings, and we all asked him at once what he had found out.

"First," he began, "I learned that our speed of seventeen days, seventeen hours is the best they have recorded except for the *Brinestormer*, strictly a racing boat, which made it in fifteen days and some odd hours. For *Trilogy*, with no racing sails and heavily loaded, that isn't too bad."

"Good for *Trilogy*, but about Gauguin?" I prompted.

Jim began with his questioning of various officials. Only one fellow wanted to talk about it at all — most fortunate, because he had been here far longer than any of the others. "This was all before my time," the man had said. "Even before World War II, many people from France had visited the island. After the war, even more people came. They went back to France and complained, 'Why is it that one of our most famous artists is in an unmarked grave? Do something about it!' The pressure got worse; finally, the official word came from Paris, 'Find Gauguin's grave. No excuses. Find it!' What would you do?" he asked Jim.

"Hey, I'd find it," Jim answered. "I'd pick out a likely-looking grave and I'd say, 'This has to be it.'"

"So you have answered your own question," the French official said, not unkindly. "This official in charge of Atuona was no different from you. He did what he had to do, and now we have a fine-looking grave and marker to show our respect for a great artist. One thing you must realize. Gauguin was not famous, appreciated, or even especially well liked here at the time of his death. He quarreled continuously with his countrymen's administration of the islands and with the clergy; these were the only people who kept any burial records, and they couldn't have cared less. So that," he concluded with a sigh, "is how it all happened, and we have to live with the results."

Jim thanked him for his candor and his patience. It was very much as he had suspected. There was a small bit of satisfaction in having chased this little mystery down to its source, or as near it as possible.

Pattie and Carole, not being devoted Gauguin fans, had gone over to the little store where Eldon was still visiting with Lucian and Ozane. As Jim, Rand, and I walked over there, Jim mused, "I wonder, actually, how many graves of famous people are where they are buried."

⚓

Getting back to the boat in the late afternoon, we gathered up all our letters, stamped them with French stamps, and gave them to Jim to mail in the morning before we departed for Tahuata. When he returned, the port captain came with him. It seemed there was a pretty good friendship going — which was all to the good; we wanted to be able to stay in these islands at least sixty days.

On Tahuata, the port captain told us, a local policeman would come aboard and verify that we still had the same people aboard *Trilogy* that we had when we came, same passports and all those important things.

When we left the Bay of Traitors, we hoisted the mainsail and Genny and sailed downwind, wing and wing for about thirteen miles. The first place we stopped was Hana Moe Noa, totally uninhabited with a steep, white-sand beach, big surf, and towering, emerald-green mountains flanking the small bay.

I looked at the surf and then at Carole. She smiled back knowingly.

"Are you thinking what I'm thinking?" I asked. "What does that beach remind you of?"

"Omoa, and if you're thinking it would be fun to ride that surf up the beach for a while, I'm with you. Pattie, how about you?" Carole asked.

"Nu-uh, I don't think so this time."

"It'll be a lot of fun, you know," I urged. "You did it at Omoa."

"I know; I was never so exhausted in my life. Right now I have a letter started. You two run along and play," Pattie said. She must have gotten a letter from Jeff, her high school boy-friend, I surmised. Carole and I got into our swim wear. I pulled a tee-shirt on over my suit, because I didn't want my shoulders sunburned. Carole did the same.

Eldon and the boys had already taken the skiff and gone in search of oranges; Carole and I dove off the ship's side and swam over to the beach. The surf was perfect. We abandoned all sense of time and rode waves up onto the beach, let them pull us back, and then did it again. Heaven knows how long we would have kept it up, but eventually Eldon and the boys came back with twenty-five pounds of oranges and a good amount of tired. They had walked far and wide in their search for oranges that weren't sour. They were in no mood to run the skiff back for us later.

"That's okay," I said stoutly. "We swam out here; we can swim back."

"That's not necessary," Eldon said. "How long have you been here anyway?"

One endearing thing about Eldon is that, although he is a workaholic himself, he never likes to interfere with someone else having fun. If I had said, "Only fifteen minutes," he would undoubtedly have said, "Well, I'll rest a few minutes and then come to get you."

But when I said, "I don't have a watch on; I think we left about ten minutes after you did," he was shocked.

"That's over three hours ago!" he exclaimed. "If you don't know when you've had enough, I do. Get in the boat." So we did, quite meekly. I hadn't imagined we could have been there more than an hour.

I knew everyone was hungry, and I was feeling guilty

about that. Rand asked, "Was Pattie going to start dinner?"

"I didn't even think about dinner," I told him. "When Carole and I came over, we didn't plan to stay very long."

Pattie not only had started dinner, she had it ready to serve. So my lapse from duty didn't have any bad repercussions — except for one thing. When I was drying myself after a shower (what good a salt water shower does when you've already been in salt water for three hours, I do not know), I felt a warm glow and saw that I had a rosy sort of rash on the fronts of my legs and my tummy and chest. By the next day, this sand-scoured area was so sore that wearing any kind of clothing was torture. Carole had the same problem, but to a lesser degree because her tee-shirt was tight enough to give some protection. Mine was loose, and it had acted like a sand scoop, keeping the sand against my skin as I plowed happily up and down the beach.

The next day the patrol boat came by, as predicted. The officer looked over our passports and ship's papers; we didn't know exactly what this was all about, but apparently it takes the place of having to check in at every little harbor, as we had done so many times before.

The oranges Eldon and sons had brought back the previous day were bright green on the outside, bright orange inside, and more sour than any lemon in the world. With sugar added, they made wonderful lemonade, and most of us were quite happy with them. Eldon, however, thought all the raw sugar we were drinking was unhealthy. As soon as the patrol boat left, he announced that he was going in search of better oranges and asked for volunteers. Carole and I knew we wouldn't be doing any more body-surfing in the near future, so we signed on. Pattie was through with her correspondence and wanted to go. Jim and Rand said they had always planned to go — who else would carry the oranges we were going to find?

We tasted a good many oranges before we found any sweet ones. They were a mile from the beach, up in a small valley in the opposite direction from the one yesterday's scouting party had taken, and they were worth all the effort. Besides being sweet, they were twice as large as the sour ones.

I couldn't bear to waste all of the sour oranges; they did have a good flavor. So I made a syrup according to specifications Mrs. Wittmer had given me, combined it with the sour orange juice, and presto! We had lemonade concentrate in the refrigerator. Eldon still took a dim view of it, but I told him the sugar wasn't raw anymore. Besides, I was trying hard to believe the concentrate was chuck-full of vitamins.

⚓

We spent one more day in Hana Moe Noa, swimming, hiking, and just being lazy. Then we moved three miles to Vaitahu, another spot of breathtaking beauty. Sheer verdurous cliffs rose perpendicular just in back of the town; in the center of town, a volcanic cone several hundred feet high dwarfed everything else in the vicinity. Vegetation covered the bottom half of the cone, leaving the top fully exposed, an astonishing coral color.

Places of supreme beauty simply cannot be compared; each one is queen in her own right — Alaskan fjords and glaciers, Olympic rain forest, Swiss mountains, Banff and Lake Louise in Alberta, Jackson Lake in the Tetons. One cannot say that these Marquesan valleys are more beautiful, but neither are they less so.

On their first trip ashore, Jim and Eldon were immediately treated to more Marquesan hospitality. Several young men from the village accompanied them when they returned, bringing a stalk of bananas, mangos, avocados, oranges, and a dozen eggs. They also brought their guitars and ukuleles, distributed themselves over the deck, and played and sang all afternoon.

When the party broke up, we went ashore for volleyball until it got too dark to play. For the first time since we'd left South America, we had a truly gorgeous sunset. The sun, red and glowing as it should be in any good sunset, descended in splendor, surrounded by pink and purple clouds with incandescent copper linings and long scarlet streamers. As Eldon's mother used to say, it was "a glimpse of the Glory Land."

Randy had been coming down with something. He always runs a fever high enough to make anyone believe he's reached his last day on earth. Vaitahu has a resident doctor, and we were fairly sure he didn't make home calls; so, sick as he was, Rand went to his office.

At first the doctor wasn't particularly interested in doing anything for someone from the USA. Like the other French officials, though, he got much friendlier when he learned we were from Alaska. Rand wasn't absolutely sure if the doctor thought Alaska was another country, but he definitely preferred getting his pills from a friendly physician.

When Rand got back to the boat, Eldon was doing his best to converse with a delegation of grade-school children. The kids spoke pidgin English well enough to make themselves understood, but they were having some trouble with Eldon's speedy delivery. Rand was aware that his dad could use some help, but he simply had to get to bed. He took one dose of the medicine and crashed.

After the boat tour, Eldon took the children ashore and didn't get back to the boat for about two hours. When he did, he found Randy up and getting ready to join the rest of the family at the local policeman's house, where the group had some music going.

"You can't do that," Eldon said flatly. "You're sick."

"Not any more," Rand stated. "I've been cured."

"No medicine can work that fast," his dad told him. "Be sensible; get back to bed."

"Listen, Dad," Rand said, trying to be patient, "no one knows how I feel better than I do. I feel fine."

The Real South Seas

Reluctantly Eldon took him ashore, muttering, "That's got to be the most miraculous medicine in the world. There's something fishy here. Maybe you weren't sick in the first place!"

Eldon hadn't sat up with Rand as many nights as I had. I was used to these sudden high fevers and quick recovery, but Eldon was sure Rand would have a relapse. Nothing like that happened; the kids stayed until after midnight.

⚓

It took less than four hours the next morning to run back to Hiva-Oa and Ozane's ranch in Hanamenu Bay on the northwest shore. The usual cliffs and mountain peaks were there, but farther away. Here, the valley floor was level and extended back for several miles. The harbor was good; only a wind straight out of the north could have caused any problems.

Ozane and Marie, his wife, had planted some Hayden mango trees. With characteristic generosity, they shared the fruit with us, but the trees were small and not producing very many mangos yet. Back in the valley were huge, old mango trees loaded with fruit. Broken mango mush lay ankle-deep on the ground. Pattie and Carole scampered up the first big mango tree we found.

"These are great climbing trees," Pattie called from a height of twenty feet. "I don't see how Guido fell out of one of these."

Before they started climbing, I had cautioned the girls about brittle limbs on these old trees. Carole was already five or more feet above Pattie, and I called to her: "Carole, did you hear what I said? These limbs might break with you. Just because they're big doesn't mean they're safe."

"I'm testing every limb as I go," she called down cheerfully. "Here, catch." She tossed down a beautiful red-and-yellow mango, almost as large as the Haydens.

The girls were both tossing mangos down, and I asked,

"I don't suppose either of you remembered to bring a knife?"

"No," Pattie answered, "but you don't need a knife. The skins peel right off." That was true, but they dribbled down our fronts. It wasn't very tidy.

Pattie was reaching for a mango just in front of her and a few inches too high. She stood on tip-toe. Just as she got her fingers on it, her foot slipped. She dove forward — much the same as Guido had, I imagine, but Pattie was more fortunate. She landed tightly wedged in a crotch of the tree. She could only wave her arms and legs helplessly.

At first Carole and I thought it was very funny, expecting her to free herself at once; when we realized she really couldn't move, Carole started climbing down to help her. First, though, she unstrapped the camera from her belt and took a very candid picture of Pattie's up-ended southern exposure.

"Hey, cut that out!" Pattie yelled in protest. "Here I am being devoured by a people-eating tree, and you take pictures!"

"Very important to science," Carole replied, unperturbed. "No one has ever studied a people-eating tree in action before." She returned the camera to her belt and gave a big tug on Pattie's legs. Nothing happened. She pulled again; Pattie remained as tightly wedged as before.

"Do you need some help?" I called. "I can climb up there if you need me."

"No," Carole said, "I've got to get farther up; I'm pulling down too much." So far Pattie hadn't done much complaining about her situation, but when Carole asked, "Are you resting comfortably?" that was too much.

"I am not resting," Pattie declared vehemently. "I am being forcibly detained, and my skin is coming off in six places!"

Carole climbed up on a higher limb, took a good grip on Pattie's hips and pulled with all the strength she could muster. Pattie came loose, but then she nearly fell out of the tree when Carole let go. She had fallen in a head-downward position, and it was hard to get her upright again.

"Wow!" Carole puffed, sitting back on her branch and breathing heavily. "That's the first time I've ever lifted weights when all the weights were fastened down!"

"Yes, well, this was a new maneuver for me, too," Pattie said. "If you'd like to try it, I'll be happy to take your picture."

"Thanks, but no," Carole answered graciously. "I have to get on with my mango-picking."

I tied my shirt so I could wear it and use it to carry fruit at the same time. Even so, I could only manage about fifteen mangos. We bemoaned our lack of foresight in not bringing a proper container and left, carrying as many mangos as we could hold in our hands.

⚓

Eldon was up before daylight the next morning. He was going to make copra for Ozane — actually, more for Marie than Ozane, because she had been trying to do the work while Ozane was incapacitated.

Copra is dried coconut meat, from which oil can be extracted. The main work involves an ax, a strong back, and a small mountain of ripe coconuts.

Two weeks before our arrival, Ozane, carrying some goats out of the mountains, had developed a hernia. The doctor in Atuona was still deciding whether to repair the rupture here or send Ozane to a more skilled surgeon in Papeete. At present, Ozane was forbidden to do any kind of physical activity that might aggravate the rupture.

After Eldon left, I tried to get back to sleep but couldn't. I decided to go ashore if the skiff was available, and went out to look.

The *Sanborn* was also in the harbor. We had met Connie and Wade previously in our travels. Connie saw me and called, "Hi! Were you going ashore?"

"Thinking about it," I called back. "Eldon has the skiff."

"I'll take you over. I have to go ashore anyway."

Trilogy

While I wrote a quick note for the kids, Connie brought their skiff alongside. I could hear the sharp crack of an ax breaking coconuts a hundred yards away. Ozane was directing the operation, but he worried because of Eldon's white hair. He didn't think Eldon should be doing such strenuous work. Eldon thought that was very funny; after all, Marie had been doing it, and she was about half his size. In fact, he was having a fine time, glistening with sweat and proud of his progress. The sun was just coming up. Soon it would be much hotter.

Connie had some washing with her, and I helped — flat-rock-in-the-stream technique. It wasn't difficult because she didn't have any oversized beach towels. (If I ever go cruising again, I won't have them, either.) Marie brought us a clothesline to run between coconut trees, but I was accustomed to using bushes. Bushes don't require any clothespins, and most garments dry much faster when they're spread out flat than when hung perpendicular. I could tell Marie disapproved; probably only very slovenly people on Hiva-Oa used bushes.

After breakfast, Marie went upstream to gather some leaves that were growing profusely along the river's edge. They looked much like the house plant one of my neighbors had in Alaska, called an Elephant Ear. I asked Marie what she was going to do with them.

"Some goat meat," she said, "very tough. Cook these with it, it get softer, easier to eat." When she took the leaves into the building that served as a kitchen, I had an idea.

"Connie," I said, "why don't we pick some of the crisp little leaves in the center of these plants? I'll bet they'd be a good substitute for lettuce. My grandmother used to pick pigweed, dandelion leaves, and all kinds of stuff for salads."

"Okay," Connie replied, "sounds good to me."

Knowing there was an endless supply of these plants, we gathered just enough for lunch. Before we got back in the skiff, I started chewing on two or three of the little leaves. Suddenly, I felt as though I had a mouthful of ants, all biting. I spat out the leaves I had been chewing and looked at the remaining leaves to see if there might be some very tiny insects I hadn't noticed. Nothing. They couldn't have been cleaner. Connie was spitting hers out at the same time. My mouth and throat hurt so badly I could hardly talk, and when I tried, my voice was thick and fuzzy.

"Let's go back and talk to Marie," I gasped. "These things must be poison!"

We hurried back to Marie's house and showed her the leaves that were giving us such trouble. "We ate some of these — well, we didn't swallow them —" I explained, my throat so constricted that it was hard to say anything. "Are they poison?"

"Not poison," she reassured me. "It just hurt. Go away soon." She could hardly believe we didn't know the bad habits of these plants, but she explained patiently. "No one ever eat them raw. Never eat them at all. Only cook with meat, then throw leaves away. Only eat the meat."

She looked at us sympathetically and said, "Only last thirty minutes; you be all right after that."

That was good to know, although we still had some suffering to do.

"I must have swallowed some," Connie said in a muffled voice. "My throat hurts like the dickens!"

"So does mine," I replied, my voice sounding thin and far away. "And I know I didn't swallow any. It must get into the saliva, and you can't keep that from going down your throat."

About this time, I realized that it was getting easier to talk. Though my mouth and throat still hurt, the sharp, stabbing pains had stopped. Possibly ten minutes had passed since we'd tasted the makeshift lettuce.

"I think I'm feeling better already. How about you, Connie?"

Connie thought for a moment. "You sound better. Yes, I think it doesn't hurt as much as it did at first."

Marie nodded sagely. "Half hour," she said, "it be all gone."

On our way back to the boat, we stopped by the little knoll where Eldon stood surrounded by a sea of broken coconuts. It was now nine-thirty. He had been working continuously since six except for a short breakfast break.

"Hi," I called, not wanting to step on the broken coconuts, "don't you think it's time to knock off for a while?"

"One more hour," he called with a big grin that showed he was enjoying himself. "Then I'll knock off till three."

"But three is the hottest part of the day."

"I know." He spoke as one who has superior knowledge. "But then this will all be in shade. It won't be too hot."

When I got back on board *Trilogy*, Jim was getting ready to go hunting with Dale, another friend whose boat was anchored in the harbor. Dale called his tiny skiff *Huevo* because it wasn't much bigger than an eggshell. Hardly big enough for two, it capsized in the surf. Jim kept his gun dry, but the camera got wet again. Irritated at letting this happen for the third time, Jim refused to change his clothes, and he set off wet and soggy. As he passed Eldon, who had now leveled out the first big mound of coconuts, he handed him the camera.

"Here, Dad," he said in passing. "Will you take this back to the boat for me? It got wet again."

Eldon glanced briefly at the wet hunters and at the little *Huevo*, which had already overturned at least twice that he knew of, and all was clear. He nodded assent and hung the camera on a bush nearby.

At ten-thirty, Eldon came back and started taking the Leica apart.

"Someone ought to explain to that kid that this isn't an underwater camera," he muttered as he dismantled it once again. "Every other day he takes it swimming!"

At one-thirty Eldon started back to the beach with half

a pillowcase of laundry under his arm. I stopped him as he was getting into the skiff. "Look, you don't have to break coconuts all day and then do your own laundry. The girls and I will divide it up and do it with ours," I told him.

"Oh no," he said, clutching the pillowcase more firmly as though he thought I might take it by force. "I've got a perfect record so far on this trip; I'm not going to let anyone spoil it now." Before starting the outboard, he tossed an addendum over his shoulder: "Anyway, I'm just going to soap them today and finish up tomorrow. That'll take most of the work out of it."

He went off singing, "I've got a lovely bunch of coconuts."

At three o'clock the hunters returned with three goats, their clothing nicely dried, but their spirits dragging.

"Dangerous place to hunt," Jim informed us gloomily. "I came within a hair's breadth of falling off a two-thousand-foot cliff!" (Not many years after that, the twenty-two-year-old son of one of our cruising friends was killed falling in this same place.)

"I'm surprised that they told you to hunt in such a dangerous place," I said, alarmed. Jim is not one to overrate the danger of what he may be doing. Quite the contrary.

"That's where the goats are," Jim said wearily. "I'm going to bed; I'm pooped!"

Eldon came back just before dark, proud of maintaining the same ax-wielding schedule as men one-third his age. The next day he was back chopping copra with undiminished zest. The rest of us prepared for a big Polynesian luau — digging a pit in the sand and filling it with hot rocks, then goat meat, then leaves and a covering of canvas and sand. There was no smoke, no odor, but in three hours' time the meat was perfectly done.

After three and a half days of copra-making, during which Eldon never complained of stiffness or tiredness, the first coconuts he had cracked were coming apart from the shell. It was time to put them on the drying racks.

Trilogy

Ozane and Marie flipped the coconut meat out of the shells, filled gunny sacks with it, and carried the sacks down to the drying racks on the back of their only horse. On this fourth day of heroic labor, a storm was brewing. It was even difficult to bring the skiff back to the boat after the morning's work.

Jim had caught Randy's bug from the previous week. Jim's temperature was not as high, but 103.5 degrees was as high for him as 105-plus was for Randy.

It was an anchor-watch night for both Rand and Eldon. The winds moderated the next day, enough to make it feasible to go on to our next port of call.

CAROLE'S COMMENT:
NEVER DISAPPOINTED

Reaching Island Fatu-Hiva was a peak experience after our landless voyage, although I never tired of the exhilaration of sailing on the open ocean. I turned seventeen a few days later in Omoa and believe that scarcity made my birthday pumpkin pie the most delicious ever. Also on Island Fatu-Hiva is the most beautiful place I have ever been; and when I daydream and curl my toes in the sands of an exotic shore, it's to Hanavave that I return.

Even though the physical beauty of the islands was over-whelming, I don't think we would have enjoyed our stay nearly so heartily had it not been for the friendly, curious native people. The Marquesans distinguished themselves through their openness, unfailing generosity, and good humor. Reminiscent of Melville's Typee, there was certainly danger in the jungle, but we were by and large shielded from any wanton village members by the majority of good-hearted, helpful natives. This was certainly a different social climate from many of the countries we visited, especially Colombia, where an atmosphere of fear prevailed even in 1972.

Paradoxes serve as bookmarks in our memory, and recalling the often hard-drinking, chain-smoking habits of the Marquesans is far too easy. The tale of French traders exchanging alcohol and tobacco for island copra explains the how and why — but there is no rationalization that makes the sight of smiling, healthy natives staining the brilliant white of their smiles or drinking themselves into a stupor any less tragic. Alcohol featured prominently in the only really bad experience we had in the Marquesas, and I've often wondered if some of those villages might one day become less than picturesque. The serpent in paradise is as hideous as ever, I'll warrant.

In the Marquesas, I vigorously hunted mangoes, explored the secrets of a floating island crammed with nesting birds, and swam in a cave beneath a thousand-foot waterfall. I was also nearly stung by a foot-long centipede (one of the natives hissed a warning just in time), contracted typhoid, and gained twenty pounds! When I look back on those times, I realize how deeply important the people around me were. In the bosom of the Coon family, I felt very, very safe. No matter how rough the seas, however huge the obstacle or absurd the situation, I believed absolutely in the skill and integrity of the Coons "to overcome." I was never disappointed. And even though when I left Hawaii at the end of the trip I knew I'd left that security behind — I didn't yet know that I'd learned how to trust again. It takes time to appreciate gifts like that.

CHAPTER THIRTEEN:
THE SNAKE IN THE GARDEN

Detail of the Marquesas

hat night we all gathered around the dining table and began the discussion of where we would go after the Marquesas Islands. No one really wanted this conference at all; the majority of us were very happy with no plans.

Pattie and Carole got to speak first. Pattie told us what we already knew: that she wanted to get into college for the winter quarter. Carole only needed two credits to finish high school, and she didn't care too much whether she got them in New Zealand, Hawaii, or anyplace else that we might happen to be.

Jim and Rand really wanted to keep on going west around the world. However, they did see the need for getting a new business started before we ran out of money entirely. Eldon, always practical, thought the ideal place to start a new business was Hawaii.

I knew the boys considered Hawaii overpopulated and too touristy. But these very qualities made it more practical than New Zealand, which suffered from a depressed economy. I voted for Hawaii, a better place from which to send Pattie back to school.

Jim finally voted with Eldon and me — but only on the assurance that the stop in Hawaii was to be temporary. Give us a year, two at the most, we said. Then we'll go on around the world.

Rand was flexible. He said, "Just so the stop in Hawaii isn't too long. I want to go on around the world before we stop for good." Pattie voted for heading north to Hawaii. Carole wasn't sure she should have a vote on something so important; she said she'd just hang out with the rest of us.

Even though he had been the foremost expositor of Hawaii as our destination, Eldon was depressed by our decision to get back to work. He knew he was being inconsistent, but he was dealing with his emotions, and they don't have to be consistent.

"The trouble is," he said, more accurately than he knew, "if we don't make a success of the business in Hawaii, we won't be able to leave; if we do, it may be even harder."

Having discovered Tennyson's poem "Ulysses" for the first time, he felt that it fit his present situation exactly. He was veritably Ulysses at the end of his odyssey. He quoted, "How dull it is to pause, to rust unburnished, not to shine in use...."

"I can't imagine you rusting unburnished, exactly," I said. "You'll find plenty to do wherever you are."

That was no comfort to him. "What I want," he said is to 'sail beyond the sunset and the baths of all the western stars until I die.'"

After much discussion, we set November twenty-ninth as our date for leaving the Marquesas Islands and starting toward Hawaii. The crossing might not take three weeks, but it could; those things are unpredictable. In order to get the girls in school soon after the first of January, we needed to get to Hawaii by December twentieth.

After we reluctantly set our departure date, all of us — with the possible exception of Pattie — felt depressed and more pressured about the scant month remaining to see the rest of the Islands. (Jim had been assured in Atuona that we could stay for six months if we wanted.) It was going to be such a change to give up this nomadic existence and get back to monthly bills. The whole idea was monumentally unappealing.

⚓

The Snake in the Garden

Our next island was to be Ua-Pou. When we left the harbor, however, the wind was perfect to go in the direction of Ua-Huka. So, being nomads, we went to Ua-Huka.

We came eventually into a harbor called Vaipaee. The harbor was well-protected, with less surf than any of the others we had found. We anchored in fifteen feet of water close to the beach, where we could see several buildings and some outriggers. To our surprise, we also saw a small air strip near the water — not large enough for jet planes, but adequate for landing small aircraft. Near it was a pickup truck, and someone in the truck was beckoning to us.

Jim still wasn't feeling very good, so I stayed with him. Eldon, Rand, and the girls jumped in the skiff and went ashore. The beckoning driver turned out to be the head officer of this island under French colonial rule, a man named Chief John. He invited all of them to get in the truck, which he then drove at a furious pace over a road that was not built for speed.

We had been told that Ua-Huka was inhabited by only one family. It was quite a surprise to find over three hundred fifty people living here — almost all of them related to one another.

The chief ran the entire length of the road. Then he turned back and brought everyone to his house, where his wife served them tall glasses of fruit juice. He brought out a guitar and asked Rand to play. No one knew for sure if the very efficient "coconut wireless" reaches from island to island; possibly it does. It really looked as though the chief were expecting us, and possibly knew quite a lot about us. Rand never did figure out how the chief knew he was our principal musician, but he willingly complied, with Pattie and Carole singing along.

The concert was necessarily short; it was almost evening and our family needed to get back to the boat.

Trilogy

When they returned, Jim was up, pale and tousled but definitely on the mend. He wasn't going to be left on the boat another day. In fact, no one was going to be left on the boat; Eldon had long since given up any idea of keeping someone there constantly, including himself. Chief John came down with his truck again. I took a sketch pad with me; I might not have time to do oil paintings of all the spectacular scenery in this place, but I could at least have sketches. Every time the Leica got dunked in salt water, I had less expectation of having a good pictorial record of the trip.

Unexpectedly, Eldon asked to be let off at the foot of the mountain back of town. Unknown to any of us at that time, he was having some back problems and thought a good, vigorous hike would cure it.

It was hot. No one else really wanted to hike up that volcano in the hottest part of the day, so Eldon went by himself. He hiked up to the rim of the volcano, by that time realizing that his back was feeling worse. Then, on the way back down, all the little valleys in the lowlands began to look alike. Soon he was hopelessly lost.

He wandered around for two hours, looking for a stream that would lead him back to the ocean. Meanwhile, a tiny goat less than two weeks old insisted on following him. At first, Eldon tried to get it to go back wherever it came from, but the kid would have none of it. Eldon surmised that the little fellow had been abandoned, or perhaps his mother had been shot by some hunter. At that point, both he and the kid were in dense thickets; he picked the kid up. In time, he discovered a well-worn trail and followed it back to the village. When Eldon reached the chief's house, Chief John found a foster mother for the kid among his milk goats.

"I got him a stepmother, and he seemed happy with the arrangement," Eldon said when he got back to the boat. "It didn't help my back much carrying the extra weight, but he cried so pitifully when I tried to leave him that I couldn't do it." He still wasn't sure he had done the right thing. "Maybe I should have left him," he said. "Maybe his own mother will come back."

"If she didn't come when he was doing all that crying, she's not coming," Rand said. "Besides, you'd have had to go back tomorrow to see about it, and since you didn't know where you were, how would you ever find him? He would probably have died."

"He's happy and he'll live; I'm sure you did the best thing for him," Jim added. "Not the best thing for your back, though."

By this time Eldon's back was giving him real pain. He spent most of the next three days in bed, something he has hardly ever done in all the years we've been married.

However, when Chief John and his family invited us to a party at the community hall, Eldon heaved himself stiffly onto his feet and prepared to attend. He was thoroughly tired of staying in bed; besides, he wanted to find out what such a party would be like.

Chief John is Hawaiian rather than Marquesan, although farther back they all have the same Polynesian ancestry. His parents had emigrated to the Marquesas Islands when he was four years old. The Hawaiian influence is very strong on this island. The tamare has been combined with the hula; guests are greeted with a flower lei and an aloha kiss on each cheek. Later in the evening, we were also given necklaces of white cowry shells — headbands for Rand and Jim, which Rand said were about as comfortable as a crown of thorns. Nevertheless, they wore them all evening.

The chief was about sixty years old, a little over six feet tall, light-skinned for a Polynesian, with a kind and serious face. He seemed to be an excellent choice as patriarch and administrator of the island.

The chief's niece served us each a glass of fruit juice, and then the chief's wife came in to greet us. Like her husband, she was tall and very dignified with iron-gray hair and a tranquil expression. She wore a Hawaiian muu muu rather than the pareu favored by most of the ladies.

Eldon was interested in the original migration from Hawaii, and he asked the chief many questions. This brought on some nostalgia and reminiscences about his childhood and his parents' longing to see Hawaii again.

"Some day I go back there," he said. "Not to live — just to see. Beautiful islands, my father say. Tall mountains throwing fire in air."

"Was your father happy here?" I asked. "Did he wish he had stayed in Hawaii?"

The chief shook his head. "He not wish to go back and live, only visit. Much family there he miss." He laughed as he named off some of his father's brothers, sisters, and cousins. Then he added, "Much family here, too."

After half an hour of relaxed conversation, in which the chief's wife joined only occasionally, the royal couple rose ceremoniously and led the way to the community hall a short distance away. The building was about thirty feet wide by forty feet long. On one end was a raised platform, and around the edges were benches filled with local people. Many more were sitting on the floor in front of the benches. In the center of the room was a table set for ten people — the six of us, the chief and his wife, and the two schoolteachers. The teachers spoke French and German, but no English. They had been placed next to Jim and Rand so they could converse in German.

The table service was impressive, with many ornate silver dishes and glass dishes in silver holders. Between courses, all through the dinner, the chief's nieces sang and danced and the orchestra played. The girls knew that Jim had been learning the tamare, and invited him up on the platform. He did very well, considering the short time he had been learning, and he got the loudest applause of the whole evening.

The Snake in the Garden

After many courses, the piece de resistance appeared, carried on a spit between two husky villagers. It was a big goat that had roasted slowly over an open fire for forty-eight hours. I had long since passed the point of having any capacity left, and certainly had no appetite. Jim had been given the honor of selecting for each one of us our favorite part of the critter, and under the guise of asking me my preference, he whispered, "Don't worry, Mom, I'll make it small. Slip it to me if you can't finish it."

We had been so busy up to this time that I had forgotten about Eldon's back problem. I asked him how he felt. "Not great. But it's going to hurt wherever I am, and I'd a lot rather be here than anywhere else. It would have been a real shame to miss this evening."

Then the dessert arrived. It was an exquisite little pastry with a filling somewhat like pecan pie. The thought struck me forcibly — somewhere in that throng of villagers was the person who had prepared this delicacy. Capacity or no capacity, I had better make a heroic attempt to eat some of it. I managed one serving. Eldon and the boys took seconds, thirds, and even fourths as the dessert tray was passed again and again, so no one had any opportunity to feel that the dessert had been slighted.

With all the singing and dancing, the dinner lasted four hours. It was past eleven o'clock when we got back to the boat. As we were making our way out to the anchorage in the skiff, Jim summed it all up:

"Some day," he predicted, "in Honolulu or San Francisco or somewhere, we're going to be invited to see a Polynesian review. And it's going to seem a little bit fakey, and quite a bit disappointing, because tonight we've seen the real thing."

⚓

At the crack of dawn, here came the chief and six of his nephews to take Carole, Pattie, Jim, and Rand out to Teuaua, or Bird Island, to get some eggs. Hearing them board the boat, my first thought was *Good grief! Don't they ever sleep?* The kids dressed with unprecedented speed, and they were on their way in five minutes. After all, one does not keep a chief waiting.

Had Pattie known that she would have to climb a rope ladder thirty feet onto an overhanging rock promontory, she would never have gone on this trip. She hesitated in the boat until she and one Marquesan teenager were the only ones left. Then she grasped the ladder — just a knotted rope — and started up. As soon as she was a few feet above the water, the boy started climbing, too. Then Chief John gunned his speedboat and left her dangling, with twenty-foot manta rays swimming under her.

She froze right there.

Randy should have remembered her problems with acrophobia. She had tried several times to climb an observation tower when we were in Florida, and never could get above the first landing. But Rand was long gone with the other egg hunters.

With some encouragement from the kid beneath her, who couldn't pass her on the rope, she finally made it to the top. Some of the kids had come back, and they helped pull her up and over the top. The realization that she had it all to go through again was enough to make her feel uneasy all the time they were on Teuaua.

The Marquesan boys were very good at egg-collecting, never taking more than one or two eggs from each nest. They only looked for nests that didn't have a full setting of eggs in them; those, they said were the fresh ones. In some nests the gulls had hatched, looking like fuzzy little chicks; Jim took a picture of Pattie holding one of them. When they had a hundred eggs, they decided it was enough. We couldn't keep more than that refrigerated.

The descent for Pattie was much less traumatic than the climb. Her brothers and the Marquesans were now well aware of her problem, and they gave her no end of help getting back down. We never soft-boiled or scrambled the sea gull eggs; the flavor was a bit unusual. But I used them in cooking.

⚓

The chief had developed a real fondness for Jim and hated to see him planning for our ultimate departure. "You stay here, Jeem, Matai," he said one day. "Fine place here; you like. Here you can have three wives. I adopt you."

Jim didn't think that was a bad idea at all. In fact, he already had three candidates picked out — pretty girls with beautiful complexions and lovely big eyes. I began to think of Ulysses, who had his crew tie him to the mast and then stop their own ears as they rowed past the sirens. It was beginning to look as though we might have to do something like that.

In many ways our stay in Vaipaee was the zenith of our time in these supremely beautiful islands. The warm, hospitable people, living in surroundings more beautiful than Gauguin or any artist could paint, made us feel as though we could never completely leave this place — that some part of us would always linger here and call us back.

But if Vaipaee was the ultimate high of all our travels, it also succeeded in being the absolute low as well.

⚓

The last day before our departure, we took the chief and thirty members of his family out for a sail on *Trilogy*. When we returned, he invited all of us up to his house once again for an evening of music. Eldon and I both declined in order to make preparations for our departure; wind and tide conditions indicated that we should get an early start in the morning. We hated to miss this farewell party, but the majority of our group — and all of the musicians — would be there. When the kids didn't come home at a reasonable hour, we knew they would just spend the night at the chief's house.

But other things were happening that we didn't know about.

Early in the evening, Carole started feeling sick. Not wanting to spoil the fun for anyone else, she didn't say anything until she realized she was going to start vomiting. Then she told the chief's wife, who promptly put her to bed with an appropriate receptacle.

At this point, Jim and Rand wanted to take her out to the boat, but the chief and his wife insisted that she was too sick to be moved. Chief John's wife rubbed Carole's tummy with oil and aromatic herbs, which did make her feel better. The chief thought she should drink some 7-Up to settle her stomach. Pattie volunteered to go down to the little community store, and one of the chief's stalwart nephews was dispatched to accompany her. The nephew had a key to the store and a powerful flashlight.

"I'm sure the other fellows who saw us leave the chief's house thought we were going off into the bushes to make love," Pattie told us later.

Whatever their misconception, four of the young men from the village sneaked up behind Pattie and her escort, jerked the flashlight out of his hand, and hit him over the head with it — not a gentle tap. He was knocked almost unconscious, and while he was momentarily stunned, they started dragging Pattie off into the jungle.

When her escort recovered enough to get on his feet, he ran for help to the chief's house only about two blocks away. Pattie, however, thought he was deserting her. That frightened her more than anything.

She tried to pull away from the would-be rapists, alternately praying, telling them what a wicked thing they were doing, and promising them that God would punish them.

"If I never believed in the gift of tongues, I do now," she told Eldon and me. "I didn't know either French or Marquesan, but the words just came to me. I was talking as

fluently as if it were English. I told them the chief would
be ashamed of them because they were trying to dishonor
his guest. That really made them stop and think. It frightened them, too, when I told them God would punish them
for their wickedness. I repeated that about twenty times."

Apparently the young men hadn't anticipated any such
resistance; they stopped and conferred among themselves.
At the same time, they held onto her arms so tightly that
Pattie was black and blue and very swollen for the next
two weeks. While they were arguing among themselves,
they heard footsteps, many footsteps, thundering down the
trail from the chief's house. They let go of Pattie and
disappeared into the jungle.

Jim and Rand arrived first, then Pattie's escort who had
been hit on the head, then the other musicians, the school
teachers, and finally Chief John, straining every muscle to
get there as quickly as possible. No one had ever seen the
chief so angry. His eyes made even the innocent onlookers
quail in their rubber slippers.

A search party was sent out to bring the offenders to
the chief's house. A court session was going to take place,
and there would be swift punishment for the guilty ones.

Carole was still very sick; the chief's wife sat by the bed
massaging her, tears running down her face. That a guest in
her home, under the chief's protection, should be attacked
this way was a deep disgrace. What was immeasurably
worse — two of the attackers were her nephews.

The whole village assembled. By this time, it was past
midnight. Everyone was shocked at the sight of Pattie's
bruised arms, now turning dark blue. The chief made sure
she had no other injuries. Help had arrived in time, yet he
made it plain that he considered the offense no less serious
for that.

The gentle, fun-loving father figure now became the
stern judge. However small his constituency, there was a
kingly authority vested in this man. It was suddenly easy to

see why he was treated with such consideration and respect.

The teachers, who had left while the prisoners were being rounded up, were now summoned to act as interpreters. Pattie told her story in English; Jim and Rand translated into German for the teachers, who in turn translated it into French for the few who were most familiar with that language. Chief John translated into Marquesan for the benefit of the villagers. Next, Pattie's escort told his story in Marquesan, which Chief John translated into French; the teachers translated that into German, and Rand and Jim put it back into English. The two accounts, in spite of being warped and bent through so many languages, substantiated each other. In addition, Pattie's escort named the culprits involved, all of whom were well-known to him.

Then the chief spoke directly to the guilty ones. He withered them with his words. He told them graphically what shame they had brought upon him, upon their parents, and upon the whole village. He spoke to them in Marquesan, of course, and all of his words were translated into three languages, which somehow made them more impressive.

Three of the guilty ones were relatives of either the chief or his wife. He pronounced sentence on them first. They were to be imprisoned on the island and assigned, as prisoners have been for centuries, to hard labor at road-building. The boys shook when he pronounced their sentence, but no one argued or said it was unfair.

There was one, however, who was not a Marquesan; he was a Melanesian who had lived here for only two years. Pattie had felt from the start that this youth was the ringleader; others in addition to her escort confirmed this.

"You," the chief pronounced in cold, measured tones — his eyes boring right into this heartsick and unhappy youth — "you will go back to Papeete. There they can give you whatever punishment they are accustomed to impose for attempted rape. You will leave this island in police custody on the next boat. I will notify the police in Papeete in the morning. You will never return here; this is forever — as long as you live."

It was very quiet as the chief finished talking. He gestured to have the prisoners removed from his sight.

Pattie spoke up. "I don't want to be responsible for his being banished forever...."

Still speaking in Marquesan, which had to be interpreted, the chief interrupted. "He was a troublemaker, always a troublemaker. This is only the last and the worst. We don't want him here anymore."

Gently, as was her nature, the chief's wife now mentioned that Carole still hadn't gotten any 7-Up. Two trusted villagers were dispatched to get it. The trial had taken over two hours, and it was now very late. At the insistence of both the chief and his wife, Pattie and the boys decided to stay overnight. Carole was in no condition to be moved to the boat anyway.

Meanwhile, Eldon and I were sleeping soundly, knowing the kids were in good hands.

⚓

In the morning the chief sent Jim to bring Eldon and me ashore.

Jim was noncommittal about the chief's reason for wanting to see us; he only said there had been some trouble and the chief wanted to talk to us in person. What he wanted, we soon learned, was to apologize for taking such poor care of our daughter.

He and his wife were standing beside the truck, where we had met him so many times before. As soon as I got there, his wife put her arms around me and burst into tears.

Briefly, the chief explained what had happened. He wanted to be reassured that there were no hard feelings on our part. It was not difficult for us to give him this assurance. It was difficult, though, and almost impossible, to convince him and his wife that they had nothing to reproach themselves about. They were deeply humiliated; their honor had been tarnished. The chief felt that his ability to maintain a law-abiding citizenry had been placed in jeopardy, that somehow he had been negligent. Otherwise, how could this regrettable incident have happened? Hospitality was so important here — sacred really — that everything else was secondary to the flagrant breach of good manners.

I can never forget the sadness in the faces of this noble couple as we thanked them for all they had done to make our stay pleasant and memorable. We assured them that they had been the best of hosts. And yet, nothing would remove the gloom from their faces. The chief had total responsibility for his little island; in his mind the blame rested on him — and the shame as well.

Carole was feeling better. When Eldon and I returned to the boat, she and Pattie came along. The boys went back to the chief's house to get their musical instruments.

All Eldon's careful calculations about the proper time to leave the harbor were for nothing. It was now midmorning and the surf was high. Jim and Rand were lucky enough to get through it without any damage to their instruments. Some of the villagers were not so fortunate. One outrigger capsized in the surf; undeterred, its six passengers swam out to the boat. One lady, who was bringing three large pompelmous in a net bag, fastened the bag to her bra strap and swam out.

Only when we lifted the anchor — it was noon by then —did the last Marquesans leave the deck. Some got into their outriggers; some just dove overboard and swam ashore. The week we had spent here seemed much longer than that, yet all too short. We could only make our departure tolerable to ourselves by promising to return as soon as we possibly could.

⚓

The Snake in the Garden

Traveling in light winds, we realized by four in the afternoon that we could not reach Ua-Pou by nightfall. The safest thing to do was to lie ahull — that is, drift.

When we reached Hakahetau the following morning, conditions for anchoring were so poor that we ran down the coast and checked out two other harbors. They were worse — high surf, rocky beaches, and poor holding ground. Finally, we went back to Hakahetau and put down two anchors, the Danforth and the plow. Even so, it took three tries before we were sure they would hold.

Eldon went to sleep as soon as we were securely anchored, and the kids went ashore to explore the new town. I was still a bit skittish about this anchorage and the surf pounding on the shore, not as far away as I would like. It seemed like a good idea to put myself on anchor watch and paint a picture of this spectacular place at the same time.

Directly back of the town, a stone obelisk something like the Washington Monument rose over three thousand feet. There were six other jagged peaks flanking it on both sides, some over four thousand feet high. The peaks and pinnacles bore shades of purple, lavender, pink, green, and silver-white. In the foreground were hills of every conceivable shade of green and, on the shore, pink and tan sandstone cliffs were interspersed with dark brown and black. Add to that high, white surf and feathery coconut palms. It was exciting, and I wanted to paint it.

The hours sped by without my noticing until, suddenly, the light was gone.

The harbor at Hakahetau offers good protection from southerly or easterly weather. Unfortunately, that is not what we had. As evening came on, the surf was developing a full-throated roar, distinctly menacing. Eldon and I began to hope that the kids would stay ashore overnight. Around ten o'clock, though, here they came. They made their way through the surf apparently without mishap, only to find that a coral head had put a slit in the bottom of the skiff.

The boys pulled the skiff up on deck, and Eldon got up to assess the damage.

"Not too bad," he pronounced. "I'll fix it in the morning."

"I did it; I'll fix it," Jim said firmly.

"Okay," Eldon agreed. "We'll both fix it, but not tonight. I'm going back to bed."

No one was going ashore in the morning before the skiff was again watertight, and that took longer than I would have thought. Then, inspired by the picturesque view shoreward, Eldon and Jim decided that this would be the ideal place to take pictures for Christmas cards. It was mid-afternoon before we got over on the shore.

Rand and Jim had been invited to play some songs for the school children, and they went directly to the schoolhouse. To their surprise, half of the village had assembled there — nor were they going to be satisfied with the half-hour concert the boys had planned.

Carole, Pattie, and I were on the outskirts of the crowd that had gathered outside the building. When we realized the concert was going to last indefinitely, we sneaked off to explore the village. Eldon had a front-row-center seat, where it would have been very awkward to get up and leave. I knew he wouldn't anyway, being his sons' most appreciative audience.

The streets, of course, were almost deserted. In spite of the beautiful flowers and foliage, this village looked more tousled and raffish than any of the others we had visited. It was only too apparent that many of those who had not attended the concert had already had more to drink than was good for them. They were still friendly, however. I have never seen a mean drunk in these islands.

When our party reassembled, Jim and Rand announced that they had been asked to join the local musicians for an evening's entertainment. Eldon and I begged off; the surf

The Snake in the Garden

was still too high and boisterous and the holding ground too smooth for us to be really confident. It was an anchor watch night, as every night would be until the wind turned in a different direction. Since I am a night person and Eldon is always at his best in the early morning — why is it that these opposites always seem to get together? — I would stay up for the first few hours while he slept.

Around midnight, before my watch was over, the kids came back and reported on their evening. As we had suspected, there was more drinking than we had seen before, but none of the fights and ill will that often accompany drinking. The people were debauched in a passive, good-natured way. Pattie and Carole volunteered to stay up until two o'clock, and Rand was sure, if he could sleep for two hours, that he could manage the next watch. I knew that by four-thirty Eldon would be awake, but Rand said if he wasn't he would wake Jim. So the anchor watch was covered.

In an offhand manner, Jim mentioned before going to his stateroom that we were all invited to the chief's house for dinner the following evening. If the wind and high seas continued, we certainly wouldn't all be there, but I nodded confirmation.

⚓

In the morning, Eldon, who hadn't wakened until six and therefore felt guilty, announced that he would be the watchman this day and the rest of us could roam around if we chose. We climbed the first ridge in back of the town, which gave us a marvelous view in all directions. Then, cruising through the village, we picked up our lunch as people brought out all sorts of edibles from their homes — altogether a lovely custom, but not one that is likely to catch on in New York or even Hometown, USA.

After that, we walked up the valley where many huge mango trees stood, weighted down with fruit. Carole climbed up fifteen or twenty feet and started tossing

Trilogy

mangos to us. All went well until Jim and Rand both grabbed for the same mango, and Jim forgot that he had a knife in his hand. The blade stabbed through Randy's palm, right to the hilt, sharp steel sticking out three inches on the other side.

We were immobilized, staring at the gory sight and feeling just a little sick.

The knife had a slender blade. Rand pulled it out, saying he didn't think it was anything serious. I disagreed. Puncture wounds are very likely to get infected, especially when the weapon is not even a kitchen knife that gets washed once in a while. I wanted to go back to the boat at once to soak his hand in Epsom salts and bandage it with Neosporin, the ointment that had worked such magic on Eldon's infected arm in Acapulco. Rand thought all of this a great nuisance and quite unnecessary.

I was getting nowhere until I said, "Rand, an infection in that hand might put an end to your music-making for a long time."

We all went back to the boat and took care of the hand, which proceeded to heal up with no complications. Then we had to talk about who was going to the dinner and who was not.

Someone had to stay on the boat, and Eldon had elected himself. When Jim volunteered, Eldon said, "You and Rand will be expected to make music. I couldn't leave the girls here to cope with setting anchors. Don't argue; that's just the way it is."

He had a pretty unassailable argument there, but the boys had another idea: put down another anchor.

"Can't do it," Eldon said. "The other anchor needs a new eye spliced, and I was going to do that in case it was needed. The one on it is so frayed it would be worthless."

The five of us who didn't have self-imposed anchor watch went ashore and trudged on toward the chief's house. There was a lack of sprightliness in our tread,

414

brought on by the numerous miles we had already walked that day. We had been told to come at six, and we did. But it was awkward keeping out of everyone's way until the dinner was finally ready at seven forty-five.

In spite of not being nearly as well organized as Chief John's group had been, this chief's crew turned out a remarkably fine dinner. After dinner, the boys joined the orchestra, and Pattie and Carole accepted an invitation to dance with two of the local young men. If it had been the hula or tamare, they would have refused. But this was ball-room dancing, with which they were somewhat familiar.

In a short while, Pattie came over to see me. "Mom," she said, "I think I'm getting the same thing Carole had in Vaipaee. Do you think you could get one of the boys to take me out to the boat?" The boys were in the middle of the orchestra, on a platform and nearly inaccessible, but I told her I would try.

One of the Marquesan ladies, with quick perception, came over and felt Pattie's forehead and promptly put her to bed. Carole came along in a few minutes, and she was dispatched to get either Jim or Rand out of the orchestra. Before she got there, the boys noticed that all the ladies in their party had vanished, and they came looking for us. As soon as they realized that Pattie was ill, they made their apologies to the chief and helped Pattie down to the beach.

"Do you want to stay, Carole?" Rand asked. "I can take Pattie and Mom out to the boat and get you and Jim later."

"No, I'm ready to go," Carole replied. "They're drinking pretty heavily, and I think the evening is going to go downhill from here on." So we left. We may have been the reason for the festivities, but our absence didn't diminish them.

⚓

It was difficult to make any kind of repayment for all the lavish hospitality we received in the Marquesas Islands.

Trilogy

Before we left, I invited the chief and his wife and a half dozen family members to breakfast on the boat. They came, but hardly ate anything; they said that they didn't know food would be served and had already eaten.

I had given the invitation myself and made it very clear that food would be served. After they looked the boat over, however, they became convinced that we had no means of providing food on the *Trilogy*. They were sure that if we gave our food away, we would go hungry. Long ago, when these islands had three hundred thousand inhabitants, there were famines when the breadfruit crop was poor; individually, they may not have remembered these times, but their culture remembered.

The chief's family thanked us profusely for our attempt at hospitality, and we in turn thanked them. Jim took the chief's family ashore and we set sail for Nuka-Hiva.

⚓

The bay at Tai Oa is heart-shaped, with the best anchorage on the right-hand side — a land-locked harbor with very little surf. At one time three thousand people lived in the valley that feeds down into this bay; now the whole valley belonged to one family, and they wanted to sell it.

Early in the morning we walked over to the home of Daniel and Antoinette, the present owners of this beautiful valley. Their three sons, Alexi, Chevron, and Charles, took us on a sightseeing hike through hillsides full of bananas, coconuts, and dazzling flowers. The clear little stream that flowed through the valley formed a freshwater lagoon near Daniel and Antoinette's house. Looking out to sea, we gazed at rugged green cliffs that rose from one to two thousand feet at the harbor entrance. The view across the hibiscus and palm-edged lagoon was so beautiful that I doubt any human being could become blasé about it.

In the evening, Alexi, Chevron, Charles, and people from two other yachts in the harbor came over for an evening of music. I made a huge bowl of popcorn and several gallons of juice, which gradually disappeared during the evening.

Early on, Eldon, who had been up before dawn, realized he was too sleepy to play host any more. "Excuse me," he apologized, "I keep nodding off; I'll enjoy the music from my bunk." He told us afterward that it was very pleasant, but just kept getting farther and farther away.

Before all our guests left, we made plans to hike up to a waterfall that, according to our charts, is one of the highest in the world.

⚓

The barefoot Marquesans skittered around over the river rocks like mountain goats. The rest of us in sneakers or hiking boots proceeded more cautiously, following a rocky trail that crossed and recrossed the stream continually. I wore canvas shoes with thick soles like Belgian waffles. These were supposed to give me enough traction to climb the walls, were I so inclined. They slipped off the rocks anyway, frequently leaving my foot uncomfortably wedged in deep cracks. Occasionally we could see the waterfall, but it didn't seem to get any closer. Daniel's three sons spent most of their time sitting on large boulders, waiting for us to catch up.

It was only three miles, but it seemed like twenty-five. For the last half-hour before we got to the falls, we didn't see it at all. Then, suddenly, it was directly in front of us.

The thousand-foot fall began about a quarter-mile from where we stood. After a spectacular drop, the stream ran a short distance before it fell again, four hundred feet into a rock basin that it had carved through the centuries. There were two pools, with an underwater passage between them, and we all dove under the rock wall so we could experience the waterdrops falling like bullets on our heads and shoulders. The water was much colder than any of us had imagined, and no one stayed in the water for very many minutes.

Eldon spent most of his time taking pictures; he doesn't especially love swimming, and certainly not in water this cold. We climbed around and over the rocks that circled the pool, then, warmed by the heat and exertion, dove in again to cool off. Cooling off took less than five seconds.

We had hiked two and a half hours to get to the waterfall; Eldon thought we should start back by one o'clock, expecting that the return trip would take a similar amount of time. But we made better time on the way back — almost an hour better. About halfway, I fell and twisted my knee.

My battered, purple toes and toenails wouldn't have kept me from going to the luau at Daniel's place that night — in thong sandals, I hardly noticed them — but the knee was different. It swelled magnificently, giving notice that it wouldn't be participating in any active sports for some time.

For the first time on this whole trip, I was all by myself on the boat while everyone else was having fun. Eldon had been in this position many times, but this was the first time I really knew how it felt.

The next day, Daniel and his three sons joined Eldon and his two on a fruit-procuring trip. They returned shortly before dark with mangos, oranges, lemons, and a big stalk of bananas. We were going on to Taiohae the next day, and Daniel had warned us that Taiohae was the biggest town in the Islands. No unclaimed fruit groves would be available just for the picking.

We couldn't help thinking what a rude shock it was going to be when we had to start paying for this kind of merchandise.

⚓

The Snake in the Garden

On the way to Taiohae, only an hour's run down the coast, we had several passengers aboard: two young men from a Swedish ship who were hitchhiking around the world on a very limited budget, Charles and Chevron from Tai Oa, and a Marquesan friend who wanted to shop in Taiohae.

Poor little Charles, sixteen years old and as cute a kid brother as you could find in a day's walk, had fallen hopelessly in love with Pattie. She didn't realize he was so smitten until he started following her from shop to shop, buying anything she seemed to admire and bringing it back to the boat to present to her. With great tact, he always got something for Carole, too. Since Pattie was the one he watched, though, his gifts to Carole reflected Pattie's preferences rather than hers.

One day I mentioned that I would like to find some spider conchs, but all the ones in the stores were broken or damaged in some way. The next day Charles brought me two flawless spider conchs.

Surprised, I asked, "Where did you find such perfect shells?"

"That kind only by diving," he said. "They down twenty, twenty-five meters." I thought at the time he had done the diving, but Jim and Rand considered it unlikely. They said he probably knew some of the shell divers.

One day, when Charles brought Pattie an exquisitely carved ornamental walking stick and some pareu fabric she had admired, Eldon decided it was time to talk some sense into this young man. He took Charles aside and said, "Charles, I know how hard you have to work for the money you make. I've worked a little bit in copra myself. You shouldn't spend your money this way on Pattie. Don't buy her expensive things."

Charles replied with great dignity, "Mr. Coon, when we like someone, we enjoy giving them gifts. It is our pleasure."

419

Trilogy

Eldon, seldom at a loss for words, had a hard time thinking of a good reply.

⚓

Our days in Taiohae were busy ones for Eldon and the boys. They had repairs to make before our two-thousand-plus miles to Hawaii. Aside from our minimal housekeeping chores, Carole, Pattie, and I had more leisure time then usual.

I did an oil painting. If I had not already seen Omoa and Hakahetau, I'm sure Taiohae would head my list of beautiful places. It had the same tall backdrop of deep-ridged, velvet mountains fronted with low rolling hills of pale blue-green and bright yellow and a riot of tropical flowers, coconut palms, and flamboyant trees. The bay was crescent-shaped, its water clear and unpolluted, white and pale jade-green at the shoreline and shading to deep ultra-marine-blue on the horizon. If one were never to see another tropical port, this one is lovely enough.

Once or twice a day the girls and I checked in at Maurice McKettrick's store to see how the mechanical problems were coming along. One of them concerned the propane tanks; tanks of French manufacture had different valve sizes from ours, which were made in the USA. Maurice and Jim spent many hours on this critical problem — both our refrigerator and our little primus stove required propane.

⚓

Before leaving this place, we wanted to take a look at Taipi Valley, where Herman Melville lived for several months over a hundred years ago. The entrance to the valley was only about nine miles from Taiohae.

Controleur Bay is a three-pronged bay that is nearly as long as the distance to Taiohae outside the harbor. We chose to anchor in the middle estuary, called Hanga Haa, because it offered the best protection and because it led directly into Taipi Valley. Not since Omoa had we seen a place so well-groomed throughout. From the broad river on the valley floor through the banana, breadfruit, and mango groves to the neat little houses, the whole area looked like one big park.

It must be that most visitors here are looking for the stone tiki on a steep hill farther up the valley. Everyone we met said, "Stone tiki that way," pointing us in the right direction. We had come principally to look at Melville's valley, but we had no objection to seeing this tiki. At a fork in the road where we stood wondering which way to go, a lady on horseback loaned us her nine-year-old son, whose help proved to be very valuable. Without him, we would have ended our search when I found a black basalt tiki about three feet high with glittering blue eyes.

"Here's one!" I shouted.

"Not that one," the boy said disdainfully. "That small, small tiki."

When we finally reached the top, we came upon nine stone tikis, each one as tall as a man, standing in a clearing. We thought of Stonehenge and Easter Island, but no one here seemed to know the history of these monoliths, nor what their religious meaning or importance may have been. All they seemed to know was this: "They old, very old."

On Thanksgiving Day, we moved the boat into the right-hand estuary, called Hoomi Bay, and Eldon, Jim, Pattie, and I walked up the valley for about two miles. The pae-paes, stone foundations on which the Polynesians built their houses, were everywhere, dramatic proof of the huge population that once resided in these islands. The woven houses with thatched roofs have long since disappeared, but the foundations, level and skillfully made, will be there for a long time.

⚓

Trilogy

Anaho Bay was to be our last stop in the Marquesas Islands. The old coconut wireless was still working. As usual, outriggers met us with presents of fruit and requests to "himine." It is possible, we've been told, to cruise through these islands without a request for music and without native musicians bringing their ukuleles aboard.

It wouldn't have been half as much fun that way.

After the first evening of music, the men of Anaho — only three households where hundreds once lived — looked around *Trilogy* and, like others before them, couldn't imagine that we had enough food for our journey to Hawaii. They announced their intention of going goat-hunting the next day. Not if they could help it would we go hungry on our voyage.

I did show one of the ladies some of our dried vegetables — really quite good when rehydrated — but she shook her head in grave concern; this dried stuff didn't look at all appetizing to her. If anything, she was even more determined that we should have proper food for our voyage.

Besides the goat that the men brought in, they came with green bananas that could ripen on the trip, oranges, lemons, and melons. Pompelmous were out of season on this island, which seemed strange, but even the oranges have different seasons on different islands.

Eldon had been going for solitary walks since we came here; I knew he was trying to come to terms with what was essentially the end of our voyage. "I know I haven't any right to feel this way," he said sadly. "This trip has been so wonderful; back when I was dreaming and planning, I kept telling myself that my hopes were overblown, that it really wouldn't be so great."

He took a deep breath, and let it out in as much of a sigh as he would ever allow himself. "Well, it was better," he continued after a long pause. "Better than anyone could have imagined. And now it's hard to just end it, to put it away and close the door."

True, we could no longer delude ourselves that the seemingly timeless sea we had been sailing had no boundaries. Every day brought us closer to one of them. Gearing up for making a living was all part of the same adventure, and it was not unforeseen — but we all had a vaguely uncomfortable feeling that this wasn't going to be the most exciting part of the odyssey.

As I recall, Ulysses' travels had spoiled him somewhat for plowing with Telemachus. We, too, would be plowing before long.

For months we had been guests at large, treated like visiting royalty. It's amazing that one can get used to this, and how quickly one does. At first there is the sneaky feeling that it is all a mistake, that the pauper is being mistaken for the prince. In an embarrassingly short time, though, the royal clothes fit pretty well. The attentions begin to seem quite normal.

⚓

On our last night before setting out for Hawaii, we could tell that Eldon had made his transition and regained the cheerful, optimistic spirit we all relied on. All of the rest of us, in varying degrees, still had some thinking to do.

I tried to assess what this whole experience would mean to us in the future. All of us, of course, had accumulated glorious, Technicolor memories. But I could see that the greatest benefits would grow out of the changed relationships within the family. Few parents get the chance to experience a close family group once their children have passed into adulthood — especially a closeness such as we had known, with so few distractions. We had spent more quality time talking person-to-person than life had allowed us in the entire previous ten years.

I would be the last person to say that years of neglect can be remedied by taking one's family on an extended boat

trip. Some families have parted company at the first port
after a long sea passage and not wanted to see one another
for years. I can only say that it worked out well for us.

The voyage and the boat-building that preceded it had
welded us together, delightfully at times, distressingly at
others, but very solidly. We knew better than before what
each one was made of; with that had come a deep respect
for one another. Still today we have an esprit de corps not
unlike war buddies or victims of a common disaster.

From the time we began building *Trilogy*, and even
before that, we were never without self-appointed advisers
who worried about the risks we were taking. Jim, though
young, had left a promising career to help build *Trilogy*. I,
though not so young, had spent years of intensive study
and was well-established in my career. Eldon had reached
an age when it would be difficult to recover if the direction
we had taken proved to be in error. Rand, whose chosen
career was writing, would inevitably profit from his experiences. Aside from meeting a full-fledged hurricane or an
irascible whale, the risk to his future had never seemed
great. For Pattie, it had been an educational experience, all
on the credit side of the ledger as I saw it. Carole was
weathering her family's domestic upheaval with battened-
down hatches, thankful that she didn't have to look at the
storm. For her, too, I considered the voyage an asset.

The physical risks to life and limb had not been negligible; a thousand calamities always lurked in the realm of
possibility, but we had been fortunate. Life is uncertain,
anyway. Still, the one who plays it safe seldom plays it best.

Something weighed on each of us, though. It is a fine,
heady feeling to have the world before you at any age.
Eldon was yielding to practical considerations, but he
really wanted to sail "beyond the sunset and the baths of
all the western stars." We were all juggling, uneasily,
thoughts about the future.

The Snake in the Garden

Were we, perhaps, selling our dream short? Was it the greatest wisdom to stop now, just because it seemed prudent? Prudence hadn't exactly been our guiding influence in the past. Were we settling now for playing it safe when we should be thinking about playing it best?

⚓

For a few hours after leaving Anaho we anchored in Hakaenu Bay, where there was fresh water for laundry, shampooing, and all those things. Eldon was struggling to perfect our man-overboard gear. Jim made one last scouting trip and came back with twenty pounds of oranges and lemons.

We studied the plush, green mountains with their sharp ribs and purple gullies and tried to memorize them for all time. As we coasted slowly out of the bay, we saw one small, bright-yellow tree glowing resolutely on a bluff near the harbor entrance. Then the rugged peaks and shining sands faded into the distance.

We promised ourselves and each other that we would come back, not knowing whether we would ever be able to keep that promise.

PATTIE'S COMMENT:
Rapists

I learned a lot about myself that last night at Vaipaee.

We all wonder what we would do in life-or-death situations. Would we be weak or brave, cowardly or courageous, faithless or faithful?

I knew that part of my make-up tended to be timid. I had

tried to overcome this — what I viewed as a character weakness — but it always seemed to be lurking just under the surface waiting to embarrass me at inopportune times. I'd recently experienced it trying to climb up the bird rock. I'd literally felt that I could die from sheer terror. Courage didn't get me up that rope — a gut survival instinct kicked in.

After an episode like that, I never felt that I'd conquered the demon, that I'd triumphed over fear. I just felt relieved it was over, and I hoped to God I'd never have to go through anything like that again.

I wasn't a meek person; I could duke it out pretty good with my brothers. One time, when I was around eight, I accidentally knocked Randy out. Usually I lost our brother-sister fights, but when it came to verbal volleys, I held my own. My mother never could figure out how I could walk in all tomboy-disheveled after a big fight with Jim and Randy, then the next moment come in all dressed up in one of my frilly dresses and my mary-janes to play the demur little lady.

(I still struggle with that!)

At the party that last night, one of the village girls told me (between giggles) that Chief John's nephew liked me. I liked him, too, but only as a friend. I figured he was quite a bit younger. He was the cutest of all the guys there, and he had a sense of humor and a boyish charm that he conveyed in many ways, even though he didn't speak English and I didn't speak Marquesan or French.

I'd learned my lesson way back in Mexico. I made sure that he knew ours was merely a friendship. I knew enough French to say "Mi ami. No mi amour." (Or something like that.) French didn't come easily for me, not like Spanish. I

kept trying to speak French with a Spanish accent. Besides, I
only knew about five French words: ami (friend), Cristo
(Christ), mal (bad), bon jour (good day), and bon nuit (good
night).

When the two of us headed down the trail to get the 7-
Up, I never thought anyone would suppose we were leaving
for some other purpose. Looking back on the open sexuality
that existed in the islands, I understand the situation better
now. Anyone who hadn't heard the chief's conversation with
us would have assumed that we were going to have sex. This
was such a common practice that — if the truth be known
— most of the French teachers sent to the island could have
been arrested for statutory rape. Most of the young men and
women had been sexual with each other from a very early
age. In the Marquesas, sex came before relationships, not after.
It was the way they determined if they were going to be
boyfriend and girlfriend.

I didn't feel scared as we headed down the dark, winding
trail. I knew this was a path my friend had walked and run
on all his life. It didn't take us long to get there, even though
we walked about a mile. The soda pop was easy to find. We
were in a hurry to get back to the village so Carole would get
some relief from her pain.

But I remember feeling an ominous presence as we
started. I tried to disregard it; I often felt that way in the dark.

Suddenly I felt an arm slip around my neck. Someone was
behind me, but I couldn't see who. I could tell there were
more than one or two guys by the various voices I heard. I
knew that the chief's nephew was also being held. Foolishly, I
assumed it was all in fun, just a bunch of guys roughhousing

with each other. I figured they were trying to give me a little scare, just to tease me, and then they'd walk us back to the village.

How little I knew about the culture of these islands — and what thoughts lay behind the smiling eyes of some of those who watched us.

I couldn't understand the Marquesan that was being spoken rapidly between the guys. During the trip, though, I'd learned a lot about the way intent can break the language barrier just through tone of voice. In a laughing kind of voice, I said, "Okay, you scared us. Good joke." I tried to wriggle free from the arm that held me. The grasp only tightened, and suddenly it felt much more menacing.

Immediately I felt very frightened. The group was talking with the chief's nephew. I could tell he was trying to explain something, because he kept saying "no, no" as if they didn't understand. I had no clue what was going on. My eyes were adjusting to the dark, though. I looked over at the chief's nephew, hoping I could see his face well enough to get some idea what was going on.

The next thing I knew, he broke free and ran into the bushes, where he quickly disappeared. I was furious. I couldn't believe he would leave me there with these four huge guys. I could see them now. They were all between six-one and six-four, and they probably averaged about 210 pounds. Not much of a match for my five-six, 115 pounds.

They were young men, probably in their early twenties. I remembered them from the party, but they'd stayed out in the shadows or off to the sides. I didn't remember having spoken to any of them. All I could think about, though, was that cowardly little weasel who'd left me there, in a situation that was feeling increasingly dangerous, just to save his scrawny hide. I was already planning the words I'd have with him.

The guy whose grip had grown almost choking now took his arm from around my neck and grabbed both of my arms behind my back. I kept trying to wrench loose but to no avail. The four were arguing over something, but I could tell that the tone between them was changing. Two of them sounded kinder, as if they were trying to talk the other two into relenting. The first two (including the guy who held me) were adamant. The guy behind me sounded threatening — as though he was the leader. I knew they were negotiating about me.

As this arguing was going on, I was being pulled and yanked up the trail. Every time they would try to get me off the trail, I would throw my body the opposite direction. In fact, they had to work pretty hard to get me anywhere. Now two guys were holding me, one by the arms and the other trying to grab my legs, but I flailed and kicked so hard he couldn't get a good hold. I started to think that the nicer two weren't going to win the argument.

During the struggle I prayed constantly. "God, help me. Please help me get away. Show me what I should do. Please show me what to do."

Suddenly the arguing stopped. The aggressive two had let the others know that they were all in this together. I knew I was in grave danger.

My mind went into overdrive. I'd been terrified of being raped by these huge guys, then possibly beaten and abandoned in the jungle, but I'd been so busy praying and trying to tear myself loose that I hadn't gone into much detail in my head. Now the thought hit me. If they raped me, they'd have to kill me. We were on an island; everyone knew everyone. These guys could not leave a witness.

Abruptly I turned to the guys who held me the tightest. I didn't care that I was speaking English, because I knew they'd get my intent in any language. I was MAD.

"Do you want me to scream? I'm gonna scream as loud as I can!"

I mimicked a scream so they'd know what I meant. They all practically dove on me. "No! No!"

They didn't want loud noises. That was an important piece of information.

Because that communication had worked, I tried talking to them in English, hoping that some of them might understand it. Not a great idea. Everything I said was met with more grunts and more pulling and yanking.

At the moment that I was wishing I knew some French, the words I knew started coming into my head. Friend, Cristo, bad. Miraculously, I knew how to put them together, albeit in an elementary fashion. I yanked around so I could see my captors, and I knew I was speaking French when I said, "You are bad men."

They all looked startled.

I went on. "Christ is my friend!"

When I said this, their startled expressions turned to dark anger. The leader practically spat out the words, "No! Christ is bad!"

"Christ is good," I yelled. "He's my friend, and he'll save me from bad men like you!"

What I said triggered something in the leader. He barked an order to the other guys. Very roughly they started dragging me up the side of the trail. I knew at that moment I was going to die.

"Please, God, help me" was all I could pray.

Instantly I heard God say, "Go completely limp and pray out loud." I immediately made my body so flaccid that they had to drag me like a rag doll. I was being dragged on my stomach and legs like a dead person, but I prayed harder than I ever had in my life. I have no idea what I said, I couldn't understand it. Time stood still while the words poured out of my mouth.

I'll probably never know what those guys heard. All I know is that something or Someone changed their minds.

The next thing I remember is being jerked to my feet. A flashlight was shoved into my hand. Someone roughly pushed me forward. Words were spoken that sounded like "Go!" I didn't wait around for the correct interpretation. I've never run so fast in all my life.

I wasn't on the trail, but I found it quickly. I wanted to look over my shoulder, but I didn't dare. Running, running, running was all I could think of. Running for my life. The farther I ran, the safer I felt.

I heard a sharp whistle in the darkness. It was Jim. I don't know anyone who can whistle as loud as he does. I didn't want to yell out for fear the attackers were behind me and might have a change of heart. Soon I saw lanterns flickering in the distance and I knew help was on the way.

Suddenly I thought of Chief John's nephew. Anger welled up in me so strong that it gave me the extra strength to run the rest of the way. I didn't know if he'd set me up for the attack or just left me to my own defenses — either way, I could have torn him limb from limb.

As I got closer to the flickering lights, one lamp shone out brightly in front of all the rest. Soon I could see three people. Even though in silhouette, I could easily spot Jim and Randy just by the way they were running. As their images became clearer, I realized that the other guy was Chief John's nephew.

All at once I realized why he had "deserted" me. He'd gone for help, and the whole village had come to my rescue.

Jim immediately wanted to make sure I was okay. Most of the village surrounded me, too, holding my hands, patting my head, and generally letting me know they were glad I was not too badly harmed. A lot of the men ran on ahead, trying to track down the would-be rapists.

About that time I noticed that my arms were beginning to swell and turn color. One of the ladies had some coconut oil that she rubbed on them. The attention triggered a profound sense of relief, and I slumped into Jim's arms and cried for quite some time. All I wanted was to get back to the boat.

It was almost imperceptible, but as we walked back along the trail, I could feel Chief John's nephew slip his hand quietly over mine.

I honestly don't remember much after that. I know I wanted to go back on the boat for the night. I woke up the next morning with that sick feeling: "Something's wrong, but I don't know what." Then I remembered.

I had lots of questions.

Why had this happened in such a safe place? Would this completely destroy the relationship we'd built with these

The Snake in the Garden

wonderful people? Would Chief John's nephew feel awkward around me now? Had they caught the guys who attacked me?

Worst of all, my dad's ultimate fear had almost come true. He'd never let me out of his sight again. (Not that I wanted to be out of anyone's sight, not for a long time.)

Jim and Randy came back to the boat after the village meeting to tell me that there had never been a case of rape or attempted rape in the Marquesan Islands. They had no punishment for the crime except the same treatment they gave to murderers -- lifetime banishment to a French penal colony.

Even my protective brother Jim felt that was a little harsh. I agreed. But there was no alternative. If we pressed charges, that's what would happen.

Whether we did or not, Jim explained, these guys were already social outcasts. Everyone on this island was related, and the whole village was ashamed. They were already ostracized from their village and family, and that was a far worse sentence than any the government could impose. I felt that sentence would be adequate, and I agreed that we wouldn't press charges.

All I wanted to do was leave.

I had another feeling as well. I knew something about myself I'd never known before. I could be strong in the face of danger, even though I was terrified.

I knew that God had overwhelmingly protected me and was with me no matter what. I knew that whatever faced me in my lifetime was going to face a young woman with courage and strength.

The demon was finally conquered, and I finally felt a great sense of triumph.

CHAPTER FOURTEEN:
A DIFFERENT PARADISE

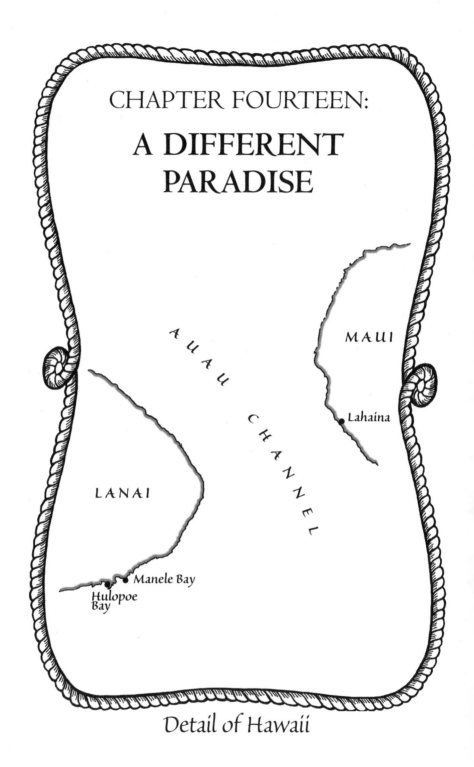

Detail of Hawaii

In my memory, the trip to Hawaii was all overcast skies, rain, and gray disheartening weather. The ship's log tells a different story. Two-thirds of the time we had sunny weather. Winds were light, but strong enough to get us to Hilo in less than twelve days. No one seemed eager to give our new life-saving equipment a mid-ocean test; consequently, the level of personal precaution and safety was at an all-time high.

After we crossed the equator, the temperature kept dropping. "Aren't the Hawaiian Islands supposed to be tropical — palm trees and all that?" I asked one teeth-chattering morning three days out of Hilo.

Eldon, at the wheel and bundled up as though it were winter in Alaska, replied, "Sure, but this is winter in the northern hemisphere. It hasn't been below 55 degrees so far, but the wind-chill factor brings it down."

"As far as I can tell, it brings it down below freezing!" I said. "It was the middle of the summer a few degrees south of here." When land was sighted on the eleventh day of our voyage, it didn't surprise anyone to find Mauna Kea and Mauna Loa covered with snow.

Not more than five minutes after we docked the boat in Hilo Harbor, several of Jim and Rand's college friends came aboard. Amid much back-slapping and discussion of college days as well as our sailing adventures, one of them asked if the boys would like to work construction for a while. Most of them were going back to the mainland for Christmas, and their building project would be slowed down if no new recruits showed up. Both Rand and Jim agreed that some jobs right now sounded like a good idea, so they piled into a car and went to see the construction foreman.

They were hired on the spot to begin work in two days.

While on shore, they picked up the mail. We had learned not to expect good news, and most of it was so-so. But Carole's was devastating. Her parents were getting a divorce; that was upsetting enough, but not entirely unexpected. Worse, and totally unexpected, was the news that Carole's younger sister, fourteen years old, had run away from home on the same day Carole left for Costa Rica. No one had heard from her, and all efforts to locate her had been in vain.

Carole telephoned her mother immediately and came back weeping quietly.

"How soon can I get home?" she asked. "I think Mom needs me. She seems...." Carole paused, trying to control her emotions. "She sounds distraught. As though she's about to fall apart. I don't know how much I can help...."

Again, we waited till Carole could say what she had to say. "I just have to be there; that's all."

I had planned to go with Pattie and get her started in college, but we weren't expecting to leave so soon. It was heartless, though, to send Carole off alone in her present state of mind. She wanted us to go with her, and we made up our minds to do that and spend Christmas with my parents.

⚓

By the time I got back to Hilo, our boat had been in the harbor for thirty days, and that was all the Coast Guard would allow for visiting yachts. After much negotiating on Eldon's part, they agreed to give us an extension until February first, but that was the last day before they would start assessing fines against *Trilogy*. The boys quit work on January thirty-first, and the next day we set sail for Hulopoe Bay on Lanai.

A Different Paradise

Kent Dawson, Jim and Rand's buddy since grade school days, and his wife flew down from Alaska to make the trip with us, and we got to Hulopoe Bay just in time to weather a five-day storm with winds up to fifty knots. It was two-anchor, around-the-clock watches for five days, and we had no way of telling whether this was normal weather at this time of year.

At last the storm let up, and we were able to sail over to Lahaina, still a sleepy little village in 1973 but beginning to wake up to an increasing number of tourists. Business-owners were happy to see the tourists, but many of the old-timers would rather they had stayed at home.

We didn't realize at that time how tight the housing situation was in Lahaina. We weren't actively looking for a place to rent yet, but one was more-or-less tossed in our laps the first weekend in Lahaina. Rand had been talking to the pastor after church, and the pastor mentioned that he would be leaving on May fifteenth. He knew how difficult it was to find a three-bedroom house close to the harbor, although at that time we didn't. He suggested that we talk to his landlord.

On such a small contingency our future depended.

We offered Mr. Wong a deposit, and he agreed to rent the house to us when the pastor's family left. When we returned from Honolulu three and a half months later, we began to realize that there was nothing else available.

⚓

After almost two years of travel, *Trilogy* needed repairs and cosmetic attention. Honolulu was undoubtedly the best place to have these things done; we spent the next three months in the Ala Wai Harbor, close to shipyards and ships' chandlers. While Rand and Jim painted, sanded, and varnished, Eldon sat for his captain's license for Hawaiian waters. He had been a licensed captain for forty years, but had never before taken an examination for captain of a sailing vessel. He had to learn a lot about all of the Hawaiian Islands, at least the most inhabited ones.

On June first, Jim sailed for the mainland on *Star Trek,* a yacht he was delivering to San Diego for the owners, and that brought in some income. A tax refund for 1970 and '71 also came along when we had nearly forgotten about it. Even so, the need to get to work was imperative.

On June third, we sailed back to Lahaina and moved everything ashore that we didn't want cluttering up our newly-designated "charter boat." Living ashore was strange. It had been nearly two years since the maiden voyage to Alaska.

Every day down at the harbor, Eldon talked to people about our proposed day-trip to Lanai. The response was overwhelmingly negative. "You'll lose your shirt," one fellow told him.

"Okay," Eldon replied. "I've never been anyplace where I could get along without a shirt as well as here."

Others said, "It's been tried before; nobody wants to go to Lanai." One dive-boat captain said, "You'll go belly-up. But go ahead and try it if you must. Don't say I didn't warn you."

A fainthearted man would have given up at this point, but Eldon was not easily discouraged. He had a vision of the kind of trip he wanted to make, a trip modeled on our experience for the past two years.

We made several excursions with local friends over to Manele Bay. We snorkeled, swam, toured the island by Jeep, and experimented with various barbecue menus. Randy caught the vision. "We'll just keep doing all the things we've been doing for the past two years and show everyone how much fun it is!" he declared enthusiastically.

Our first six-inch advertisement in the Lahaina paper brought no response. Not even a phone call.

Rand shrugged and, humorous as always, said, "Well, the family that sails together fails together." But he began an intensive campaign up and down the resort coastline, telling condominium managers and recreational directors about our trip. That, and an ad in the *Maui Beach Press*, brought a limited amount of response, and we began scheduling trips with some regularity. August was busier, and we began to feel more confident. What we didn't know was that business drops right over the edge of a cliff after Labor Day.

⚓

Late in July, Jim called from the mainland. He had been visiting an old college buddy, a dedicated, self-supporting evangelist. Eldon answered the phone.

"I've got some news for you, Dad," Jim began. "It's going to be a shocker, so maybe you'd better sit down."

"Good news or bad news?" Eldon asked, warily.

"Good, very good news."

"Okay, I've never seen any kind of good news I couldn't take standing up," Eldon assured him. "Let's have it."

"Dad, I've become a Christian. I was baptized this weekend."

"Well, praise the Lord!" Eldon exclaimed. Turning from the phone, he gave the rest of us a quick resume, then turning back to Jim he said, "I'm not as shocked as you think, Jim. I knew it was going to happen; I just didn't know when." After two or three minutes, during which he principally listened, Eldon turned the phone over to me and Rand.

"I'm a baby Christian right now, Mom," Jim confided, "and I have a lot to learn. But now I know for sure this is the way to go — the only way. And I'm really happy, deep down inside, in a way I've never been before. Well, I'll tell you all about it when I get home on the third of August."

⚓

It was good to have Jim home again; Pattie had come home from college early in June and wouldn't have to go back until the middle of September.

About the time Pattie went back to school, we began to realize that the end-of-summer season brought a big hiatus in the tourist business. From the first to the eleventh of October we had no trips scheduled. Eldon called a meeting to consider alternatives.

"You all remember the session we had down in the Marquesas Islands, when we decided to go to Hawaii?" He knew we did. "I'm sure each one of you prayed about that decision. I know I did. But we didn't pray about it as a group. It was a very practical decision as I recall, and I'm beginning to wonder if we've made a wrong turn. Maybe that decision wasn't God's decision."

I thought about that and said, "We don't have anything to complain about. We're still paying our bills on time. I'm not ready to say that we're doing something God disapproves of. He didn't ever promise instant success."

"True," Rand broke in. "And look how everything fell into place for us, getting a house and a car — not a thing of beauty, but good transportation. We have the only strip of interisland water that's reasonably smooth most of the time. The people who have gone out with us have been really jazzed about the trip; they take home stacks of brochures and give them to all their friends, and even to travel agencies. How can you believe that God isn't helping us?"

"I didn't really say that," Eldon went on. "What I said was that we didn't give God a chance to say yes or no about our plans. What I'm proposing now, if the rest of you agree, is to turn the whole operation over to Him, and turn ourselves over as well. Then, if this is what He wanted us to do, we'll know. It won't be a chancy thing; we'll really know by the success He gives us. If this isn't what He planned, we'll know that, too. I'll be a lot more comfortable doing what He has planned."

A Different Paradise

One by one, we gave our assent, and prayed.

That was our watershed experience, just as the test of having someone ask to buy our house had been the beginning. From that time on, business improved — slowly at first, but steadily. January and February were very busy months.

We had our answer, but Jim and Rand didn't want to get tied down permanently without going on around the world. In 1974 we set a deadline. May first, 1975, was the final date. After that, we would not take any more reservations.

It wasn't a difficult decision to make, but it proved to be a very difficult decision to keep.

⚓

"We've got a tiger by the tail," Jim said one night as we neared our deadline. A number of people who had made the *Trilogy* trip were coming back with friends and family, and it was Jim's job to turn them down. "It's just awfully hard to let go of it. These are friends of ours." He tapped the pile of letters for emphasis. "These people carried brochures home and gave them to everyone they could think of. Now they've persuaded others to come with them, and we say sorry. We can't do it. We're going sailing again."

"I'm not so sure that we ought to let go of it," Eldon replied thoughtfully. "I should have answered some of those letters myself, but I just couldn't do it. I like this place; it has the climate I've been looking for all my life. Besides, it's beautiful. There's a lot to be said just for living in the best spot I've found on this earth."

"You could add to that," Rand continued for him, "doing the thing you've found most enjoyable, the thing you would want to do even if you weren't getting paid for it."

"Definitely, you could add that," Eldon said decisively. "I vote for extending that deadline and reviewing all this in another year."

Trilogy

Before that year was over, both Jim and Rand had met the girls they would eventually marry. Almost immediately, dropping everything and sailing off into the sunset became much less important.

JIM'S COMMENT:
DESTINY

Way before he sank his boat, my dad had met these people with a nice yacht who had spent three years in Hawaii. They had talked to him about bringing his boat to Hawaii and actually coming to Maui — and actually coming to Lanai.

I remember my dad sitting at the kitchen table calculating how many barrels of diesel, figuring how he would carry the diesel in the main cabin of the boat in 55 gallon drums that he'd lash down, and imagining how he would fill his tanks when he needed them as he took his power boat from Alaska to Hawaii. Clear back in the '50s he had this idea in his brain.

We went on with our lives. Every time we'd run into a boat, though, he would always ask, "Have you been to Hawaii?" Every time he'd meet someone who'd been to Hawaii, he'd say "Tell me about Maui. Tell me about Lanai."

He had this vision in his brain, this concept of going from Maui to Lanai, back when none of us had ever been there, ever seen these places.

Of course it would have never worked in the '50s. But the idea was planted in the '50s.

We had a good opportunity to stay on the Big Island. I

remember the guy saying, "Jim, you know, you people don't have very much money. I don't understand why you'd walk away from a good job here."

He had an option on three acres of land near Hilo, and we were building a big commercial structure there. He was going to give us all the leftover materials, enough to build a home with, just give it to us.

But we still had to get to Maui, we had to get to Lanai. So we sailed over here.

When we got to Lanai, we dropped our sails in Hulopoe Bay. Suddenly it started to blow, and it blew seventy knots for about twenty-four hours. We put out three anchors and just held on for dear life. We just assumed that was the way the wind blew over there.

Then we snorkeled in Hulopoe. We ended up being there a month. We loved Lanai. The people there were such special people. And we still had the island feeling; we'd just come up from the Marquesas.

At the time, though, I never would have dreamed that I'd be spending my life here. I didn't feel that was my destiny. But we were so incredibly accepted, we never got the feeling that we didn't belong in this society here. We were strongly supported by the local population. And, eventually, both Randy I met local girls.

After three or four years, we started to realize that this was home. This is where we were going to be. And I love it here. This will always be my center.

We have these guided missiles in our minds. That's why it's so important to have some purpose in our lives. As the Cheshire Cat said, "Where do you want to go? It doesn't matter — you can take either road." If you have a concept, whatever it is, you'll just keep moving towards it.

You get this spark in your brain, and somehow the forces of the universe stack up behind you, moving you — with little course corrections — right to that point. Even if you don't know it's going on.

Only humans have the endowment of free choice. Between stimulus and response, whether we're conscious of it or not, we do have the ability, just during that millisecond, to choose. We choose according to decisions that we made back there, back when we first set up our goals and ideals. At that millisecond, we're just making a little course correction.

Destiny takes care of the rest.

CHAPTER FIFTEEN:
LEAVING THE SHIP

HAWAIIAN ISLANDS

NIIHAU

KAUAI

OAHU

Itonolulu

MOLOKAI

LANAI   Lahaina

KAHOOLAWE   MAUI

PACIFIC

OCEAN

HAWAII

Hawaii

ow comes the hard part. It was hard then; it isn't much easier now.

As business increased, and we had other people to take our places, Eldon and I took trips to places we had missed: Fiji, Samoa, Tahiti, New Zealand, Australia, and the Orient. Eldon would have preferred to go by boat, but it was faster to go by air. He couldn't stay away from the business very long without getting restive.

In the spring of 1982 we visited Singapore and Hong Kong with a short trip into China — a place Eldon had always wanted to visit — and then spent a few days in Japan. By the time we got to Japan, Eldon wasn't able to do much sightseeing because he was running a fever of over one hundred degrees. When we got back to Lahaina, Rand and Jim took him, protesting all the way, to Kaiser Clinic to see Dr. Strong.

The doctor discovered that Eldon was terribly anemic. Eldon didn't worry much about it. As soon as he had some blood transfusions, he felt wonderful.

We told Dr. Strong that Eldon's mother had pernicious anemia in her old age, and it seemed likely that there might be a hereditary tendency. But tests for pernicious anemia came back negative. Next, the doctor did a spinal tap. Eldon was impatient with all of this; he had lived for almost seventy-five years in well-nigh perfect health, and he was sure there could be nothing seriously the matter with him.

He was wrong.

Leaving the Ship

The results of these tests were as serious as they could get. Eldon was diagnosed with hypo-cellular leukemia, a disease in which the bone marrow stops manufacturing blood cells of any kind.

Pattie and her children were with me in Honolulu while Eldon was in the hospital. To this day, she thinks that he accepted his fate too easily. "He should have fought harder," she says.

She may not even know that he refused to have a bone marrow transplant. Pattie was the only one who had matching bone marrow, and Eldon refused to consider the operation — she had three small children, and she would have had to go to Seattle for an unspecified length of time.

Jim and Rand had a business to run, so Eldon only wanted them visiting on weekends. The rest of the time he preferred to have them attending to business.

He consented to have chemotherapy only because he knew his family thought he should.

Eldon knew that I was neither as philosophical nor as resigned as he. I knew God could heal him; every church in Lahaina — Methodist, Baptist, Catholic, Presbyterian, whatever — had prayed for him. I thought God should answer those prayers.

One day I was sitting by his bed trying not to look as sad as I felt, putting hot and cold packs on his arm where an I.V. had leaked under the skin. He took my hand in both of his and said, "Honey, I don't want everyone crying about this. I've lived longer than the threescore and ten already. I've had a wonderful life — done everything I wanted to do. Life doesn't owe me a thing. I never wanted to get old and feeble and possibly lose my marbles. Don't you think that, after I've trusted God with my life for eternity, I can trust Him to decide when the little bit lived on this earth should end?"

He died less than three weeks after he went to the hospital, just five days past his seventy-fifth birthday. His last wish was that his ashes should be scattered between Lahaina and Lanai, where he had sailed *Trilogy* so many times. The large tour boats advertised that anyone who wanted to go out in the roadstead for this ceremony would be given free transportation, and hundreds of people responded. Twenty-three boats from the harbor went out, a truly nautical funeral procession.

Eldon would have loved that.

⚓

One of Eldon's favorite maxims was this: *It is more blessed to give than to lend, and the cost is about the same.*

He helped many people during his lifetime, not waiting for them to ask; he ferreted them out. Many of them wrote or called when he was in the hospital, telling him how significant his help and influence had been. He was astounded at the enormous fund of good will out there for him.

I think the Lord was telling him, "Inasmuch as you did it unto one of the least of these, you did it unto Me."

⚓

And now? Life does go on. The wonderfully resilient human spirit adjusts to even the greatest losses, and a new generation is coming on. Each of my children has two girls and a boy. That's as fair a distribution as anyone could ask, and I make no pretense of being objective or impartial in my assessment of them. My nine grandchildren are the brightest, the most beautiful — the greatest! I claim the right of every grandparent to feel that way.

Pattie was the first one married, after two years of college. Her children, Jennifer, Jesse, and Jolene, were a continuing joy to Eldon while he lived and a great comfort to me in his absence. Now they are nearly grown, but they have managed to spend their summers in Lahaina most of the time since they moved to the mainland in 1985. Her husband, John Speer, is locally known as John-Boy in

Wichita, Kansas, where he is Director of Operations and Programming for a very large country music radio station.

Rand married an island girl, Pam Dodge, whom he met while she was vacationing among the scenes of her childhood. Her family had moved to Los Angeles when she was fifteen, but her heart always belonged in the Hawaiian Islands. Their children, Lily, Ginger, and Denver, have so much talent among the three of them that it almost frightens me, proud though I am.

Jim, after a five-year courtship, married Lynn Yee of Hawaiian-Chinese ancestry, born and raised in Honolulu. His brainy and affectionate bunch, MeiLi, LiAnne, and Riley, have helped tremendously to fill the empty places in my life.

Jim and Rand live next door to each other up in Kula and commute to Lahaina.

There are now *Trilogies I, II, III, IV,* and *V.* Jim is CEO; Rand handles advertising and day-to-day operations. Lynn and Pam share the task of making "Mom Coon's Famous Homemade Cinnamon Rolls," served every day on the boats. After many years, I was very happy to turn the job over to my daughters-in-law.

Carole found her path in academic pursuits. She earned her B.A. degree summa cum laude, then received her Master's with honors. For a while, she taught at Eastern Washington University, and now she runs her own environmental communications firm in Cheney, Washington.

Her sister returned home four years after she had run away.

I am the only one who still lives in Lahaina, in beautiful Puamana by the sea.

⚓

Trilogy began its faithful career as three long, unfinished hulls lying in a meadow near the shore of Lake Washington. Al Koban, the man who had begun the work and sold those hulls to Eldon, and who became a most valued friend, always kept track of what "his" boat was doing during the busy Lahaina years.

Not long ago, Al, too, died suddenly. His last wish was to have his ashes carried out to the Lahaina roadstead on the original *Trilogy* and scattered in the same place where, ten years before, Eldon's had been.

And some day, mine.

MOM'S LAST WORD

Having given each of my kids, including Carole, a chance to P.S. and second-guess this narrative, I'm going to give myself the same opportunity to summarize after the lapsed years.

Eldon and I both came from close-knit families, and we deeply and truly believed that the best place for optimum child development is within a loving family. To see the family unit so endangered in our frenetic civilization is profoundly disturbing to me. God knew what He was doing when he created the family; its importance simply cannot be over-stated.

Trilogy's voyage was a family journey. As Randy has so perceptively put it, it was undertaken as much to counteract the destruction of family values we saw all around us in the late '60s as it was to fulfill Eldon's dream. The bonds that were forged on this voyage — and the old ones that were strength-ened — are still in place, thanks be to God.

In thinking about God's master plan for us and about the way we followed along, blindly and sometimes hesitantly, a

Bible verse keeps coming to my mind. Eldon, like his parents before him, was fond of quoting Proverbs 3.6: In all thy ways acknowledge Him, and He shall direct thy paths. This principle was the lodestar of Eldon's life, a powerful promise and one that carries with it a strong obligation.

I doubt many people can truthfully say that in every act of their lives they have sought and obeyed God's leadership. Nor can we. But, however imperfectly we have followed, He has always met us more than halfway. We can only say in awe and gratitude: of all this world's promise-keepers, He is the best.

He kept promises we didn't even know He had made!

THE END